50 Hikes

Cayo Costa #3   *Clyde Butcher*

50 Hikes

In South Florida

Walks, Hikes, and Backpacking Trips in the Southern Florida Peninsula

First Edition

SANDRA FRIEND

Backcountry Guides

Woodstock, Vermont

AN INVITATION TO THE READER

Over time trails can be rerouted and signs and landmarks altered. If you find that changes have occurred on the routes described in this book, please let us know so that corrections may be made in future editions. The author and publisher also welcome other comments and suggestions. Address all correspondence to:

Editor, 50 Hikes™ Series
Backcountry Guides
P.O. Box 748
Woodstock, VT 05091

LIBRARY OF CONGRESS CATALOGING-IN-PUBLICATION DATA

Friend, Sandra
   50 hikes in south Florida : walks, hikes and backpacking trips in the southern Florida peninsula / Sandra Friend —1st ed.
      p. cm.
   Includes bibliographical references and index.
   ISBN 0-88150-531-5
   1. Hiking—Florida—Guidebooks.
2. Backpacking—Florida—Guidebooks. 3. Florida—Guidebooks. I. Title: Fifty hikes in south Florida. II. Title.
GV199.42.F6F76   2003
796.52'09759   2003049580
                            CIP

Cover and interior design by Glenn Suokko
Photos on pages 2, 33, 125, 159, 185, 251, and 313 © Clyde Butcher
Cover and interior photographs by the author unless credited otherwise
Maps by Mapping Specialists Ltd., Madison, WI

Copyright © 2003 by Sandra Friend

First Edition

Published by The Countryman Press
P.O. Box 748, Woodstock, Vermont 05091

Distributed by W. W. Norton & Company, Inc.
500 Fifth Avenue
New York, NY 10110

Printed in the United States of America

10 9 8 7 6 5 4 3 2 1

"The richest values of wilderness lie not in the days of Daniel Boone, nor even in the present, but rather in the future."

—Aldo Leopold

DEDICATION

To Jack and Gerry Horner, in honor of their many years of volunteer service to state and county parks, preserves, and hiking trails throughout southwestern Florida

CLYDE BUTCHER

Clyde Butcher's photographs explore his personal relationship with the environment. For more than 30 years, he has been preserving on film the untouched areas of the landscape. His images are captured with 8-by-10- and 11-by-14-inch-view cameras and are printed on fiber base paper, and then selenium toned for archival purposes. The photographic prints range in sizes of 11 by 14 inches to 5 by 8 feet. Clyde's photography can be seen in museums and major collections all over the world. A large selection of his work can be found at his two galleries and seen on his web site: www.clydebutcher.com.

Big Cypress Gallery
52388 Tamiami Trail
Ochopee, FL 34141
(941) 695-2428

Venice Gallery & Studio
237 Warfield Avenue
Venice, FL 34292
(941) 486-0811

50 Hikes in South Florida at a Glance

HIKE	LOCATION
1. Emerson Point Park	Snead Island
2. Oscar Scherer State Park	Osprey
3. Myakka River State Park	Sarasota
4. Caspersen Beach Park	Venice
5. Alligator Creek Preserve	Punta Gorda
6. Cayo Costa State Park	Bokeelia
7. Caloosahatchee Regional Park	Alva
8. Hickey's Creek Mitigation Park	North Fort Myers
9. Calusa Nature Center	Fort Myers
10. Six Mile Cypress Slough Preserve	Fort Myers
11. Estero Scrub Preserve	Estero
12. Lovers Key State Park	Fort Myers Beach
13. J. N. "Ding" Darling National Wildlife Refuge	Sanibel Island
14. Sanibel-Captiva Conservation Foundation	Sanibel Island
15. Corkscrew Swamp Sanctuary	Immokalee
16. Sabal Palm Hiking Trail	Naples
17. Collier-Seminole State Park	Royal Palm Hammock
18. Fakahatchee Strand Preserve State Park	Copeland
19. Fire Prairie Trail	Big Cypress Preserve
20. Paynes Creek Historic State Park	Bowling Green
21. Highlands Hammock State Park	Sebring
22. Lake June-in-Winter Scrub State Park	Lake Placid
23. Platt Branch Mitigation Park	Venus
24. Jack Island Preserve State Park	Fort Pierce
25. Hawks Bluff	Jensen Beach

DISTANCE (miles)	KEY	KIDS	CAMP	NOTES
2.7	H	★		Ancient temple mound
11.6	W	★	D	Important scrub jay habitat
20.1	W		B,D	South Florida's longest backpacking loop trail system
3.8	G	★		Search for fossilized shark's teeth
4.5	W	★		Varied habitats from pines to mangroves
5.9	H	★	D	Wild and windswept barrier island
3.4	W	★	D	Wet forests along the Caloosahatchee River
4.7	W	★		Watch for scrub-jays and gopher tortoises
2.1	H	★		Good family outing with varied trails
1.4	F	★		Boardwalk through lush cypress swamp
4.8	F			Adventuresome hiking along the Estero River floodplain
5	W	★		Plenty of views along canal system
6.2	W	★		Top birding site in South Florida
2.1	G	★		Explore the freshwater wetlands of Sanibel Island
2.3	W	★		Audubon perserve protects classic cypress swamps
2.2	F		B	Cypress sloughs that were once swampland real estate
7.5	F		B,D	Physically challenging but rewarding
6.4	F			A botanist's paradise in dark cypress swamps
5.2	F	★	D	Panoramic vistas along cypress-lined prairies
2.9	H	★		Frontier history and the peaceful Peace River
5.1	F	★	D	Ancient cathedral-like oak hammocks
3.6	F		B	Rare plants along the trail to a cypress-lined lake
2.7	W			Southernmost extent of Lake Wales Ridge habitats
4.2	W	★	D	Mangrove forests along the Indian River Lagoon
1.1	F	★		Rare coastal savannas just a mile from the Atlantic

50 Hikes in South Florida at a Glance

HIKE	LOCATION
26. Seabranch Preserve State Park	Stuart
27. Jonathan Dickinson State Park	Hobe Sound
28. Blowing Rocks Preserve	Jupiter Island
29. Jupiter Ridge Natural Area	Jupiter
30. John D. MacArthur Beach State Park	Palm Beach
31. Gumbo Limbo Nature Center	Boca Raton
32. Fern Forest Nature Center	Coconut Creek
33. Secret Woods Nature Center	Dania Beach
34. Greynolds Park	North Miami Beach
35. Corbett Wildlife Management Area	Palm Beach County
36. Royal Palm Beach Pines Natural Area	Royal Palm Beach
37. Arthur M. Loxahatchee National Wildlife Refuge	Boyton Beach
38. Tree Tops Park and Pine Island Ridge	Davie
39. Main Park Road Nature Trails	Everglades
40. Old Ingraham Highway	Royal Palm Hammock
41. Pinelands	Long Pine Key
42. Snake Bight/Rowdy Bend Loop	Flamingo
43. Bear Lake Trail	Flamingo
44. Bayshore Loop	Flamingo
45. Key Largo Hammocks Botanical State Park	Key Largo
46. Windley Key Fossil Reef Geological State Park	Windley Key
47. Lignumvitae Key Botanical State Park	Lignumvitae Key
48. Long Key State Park	Long Key
49. Bahia Honda State Park	Bahia Honda Key
50. National Key Deer Refuge	Big Pine Key

DISTANCE (miles)	KEY	KIDS	CAMP	NOTES
4.8	W			Coastal scrub preserve with scrub-jays
17.5	H		B,D	Excellent trail system for backpackers
2.5	G			Florida's only coastline with sea caves
2.3	G	★		Scrub sand dunes look like ski slopes.
3.5	G	★		Beach walk along outcropping of reef
1	F	★		Popular boardwalk in urban area
2.2	F	★		34 species of ferns along an ancient streambed
1	F	★		Dark swamps along South Fork of the New River
1.7	W	★		Iguanas and crocodiles on the Oleta River
5.2	H	★	B	Sounds of silence on Hungryland Slough
3.6	F			Pine lilies flourish along wet prairies
3.3	W	★		Excellent bird-watching along impoundments
3.1	H	★		Significant Seminole historic site
2.7	W	★	D	Popular nature trails in Everglades National Park
7.3	F		B	Walk along the edge of the river of grass
5.9	G		D	Examine solution holes up close
7.6	W			See flamingos in the wild
3.5	F	★		Easy walk through shady tropical hammock
1.3	H	★	D	Location of old fishing village of Flamingo
1.1	F			Largest tropical hammock in the continental U.S.
1.4	G	★		Coral reef rock exposed by quarries
1.3	H	★		Stone fences corral ancient trees
1.4	F	★	D	Diverse ecosystems on a short trail
1.1	G	★	D	Largest stand of silver palms in the United States
7.2	W	★		Diminutive Key deer and rare tree snails

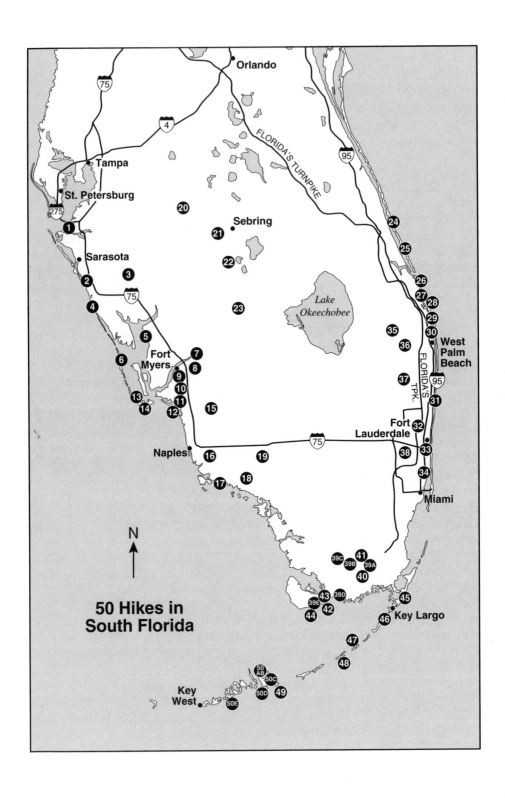

50 Hikes in South Florida

CONTENTS

Acknowledgments

Thanks to friends and family who joined me on my hiking expeditions, including Holly Ambrose, Rich Evans, Teresa French, Phil and Linda Friend, Jack and Gerry Horner, Beth Kelso, Carla Lewis, and Steve Meyers. I'll never forget the spunky ladies who showed up at Jonathan Dickinson State Park to tackle nearly 10 miles in summerlike heat: Elizabeth Cassen and Mary Miller, who took turns pushing the wheel; Val Johnson, Carla Lewis, and Kathy Wolf. Diane Raush also showed a lot of spunk by accompanying me on a cold and wet three-day backpacking trip through Myakka River State Park. Beth Kelso took on the challenge of Everglades National Park, where we had to don serious mosquito-protection gear to survey some of the hikes. Quicksandlike mud awaited on the wild and scenic Collier-Seminole Hiking Trail, where I was glad to have Chuck Wilson and Roger Rose along for the wade. Special thanks to David Black, Beth Burger, and Paul Cummings for enriching my knowledge of the fascinating flora at Corbett as we hiked.

Then there are the folks who took the time to assist me in learning more about the natural resources they protect and love. Thanks to Park Ranger Dave Garcia, who delighted me with his in-depth botanical knowledge and spider-catching abilities as we toured Lignumvitae Key Botanical State Park; Captain Jodi at Robbie's Marina, who came to work on her husband's birthday just to take me out to Lignumvitae Key; Park Ranger Joseph Nemec at Key Largo Hammocks Botanical State Park, who came in on his day off to teach me an incredible amount about Keys flora and fauna; and naturalist Ann McCullough, who led my parents and I out on the trail system at the Sanibel-Captiva Conservation Foundation.

Many people provided research assistance, background information, and access to various public lands. I'd like to thank Ann at Tree Tops Park; Park Ranger Brian Andrews, Cayo Costa State Park; Steve Bass, environmental education conservation manager for the city of Boca Raton; Park Ranger James Bell, Florida Keys National Wildlife Refuges; Monica Dorken, Charlotte Harbor Environmental Center; biologist Janice Duquesnel, Florida Park Service; Park Rangers Dylan Figueroa and Laura Ransom at Myakka River State Park; Pat Hennen, Manatee County government; Park Manager Eric Kiefer, Key Largo Hammocks Botanical State Park; Ms. Margolis at the Fern Forest Nature Center; Park Ranger Jack McCormick, Long Key State Park; Park Manager Gary McKee, Bahia Honda State Park; park biologist Mike Owen, Fakahatchee Strand Preserve State Park; Lori Piper, Education Department assistant, Corkscrew Swamp Sanctuary; Park Manager Paul Rice, Lovers Key State Park; Larry Richardson and Layne Hamilton, Florida Panther National Wildlife Refuge; Assistant Park Manager John Roche, Oscar Scherer State Park; Tyler Sievers, natural area steward for Royal Palm Beach Pines; Executive Director Michael Simonik at the Calusa Nature Center; Sandra Snell-Dobert, Big Cypress

National Preserve; Donna Sprunt, Windley Key Fossil Reef Geological State Park; John Staursky, president, Friends of the Florida Panther Refuge; Nature Center Manager Melissa Upton at the Sanibel-Captiva Conservation Foundation; volunteer Hal Wiedemann, Arthur M. Loxahatchee National Wildlife Refuge; Park Manager Pat Wells, Lignumvitae Key Botanical State Park; Ken Wiley, director, Blowing Rocks Preserve; and Park Ranger Roy Wood, Everglades National Park. Seminole War aficionado Chris Kimball helped dig up some facts on Pine Island Ridge, and Jack Hailman answered questions on the inhabitants of Seabranch Preserve State Park. Special thanks go to my good friend Warren Resen, for his hike suggestions and introductions to key people; Ranger Steve Robinson at Everglades National Park, who made excellent suggestions on the best hikes to tackle; and Ranger Patsy Hampton at Oscar Scherer State Park, who suggested that Caspersen Beach would make a wonderful free Gulf Coast beach hike.

Traveling through South Florida meant a lot of time on the road, and I couldn't have handled the logistics without the help of local experts. Thanks to Allon Fish of the Greater Sebring Chamber of Commerce for gathering information on hikes in his area; Nancy Hamilton and Jovina Huber, Lee Island Coast Visitor & Convention Bureau, for their assistance, suggestions, and research regarding hikes in the Fort Myers area; Maggie Pearson and Josie Gulliksen, Stuart Newman Associates, for providing park contacts and arranging accommodations in the Florida Keys; Shelly at the Kenilworth Lodge in Sebring; and April Sollars, sales and marketing manager, Xanterra Parks & Resorts, for arranging my stay at the classic Flamingo Lodge in Everglades National Park, which I used as a base camp while hiking the Everglades section of this book. During my exploration of the Florida Keys, I enjoyed the hospitality of several innkeepers. Thanks to General Manager Leo Gillespie at Ocean Pointe Suites, Tavernier; Jay Marzella and Sandy Sledge at quiet Parmer's Resort on Little Torch Key; General Manager Mike Weber at the very tropical Chesapeake Resort, Upper Matecumbe Key; and General Manager Greg Herman at the comfortable Marriott Key Largo Bay Beach Resort. I also relied on friends for accommodations. Thanks to Ted and Trudy Winsberg for a stay on the farm, Jack and Gerry Horner and the folks at Fakahatchee Preserve, Bill and Ginny Detzler, Carla Lewis, Doug and Pat McCoy, and Chuck and Betty Wilson.

One of the more special moments of my journey was my introduction to Niki Butcher at the Big Cypress Gallery (thank you, Warren!), which led to an offer for her husband, Clyde, to provide several of the photographs used in this book. Clyde Butcher is Florida's best-loved landscape photographer, and he and Niki work ceaselessly on conservation projects throughout the state. It is their hope, and mine, that your exploration of South Florida through its hiking trails leads you to understand how fragile and precious our ecosystems are, how imperiled they are by development, and how important it is to continue to set aside public lands for the protection of vanishing plant and animal species. When you hike in the Big Cypress (Hikes 17, 18, 19), stop in and visit Clyde and Niki at the Big Cypress Gallery, 1 mile east of the Oasis Ranger Station on US 41.

Introduction

It's a jungle out there!

My introduction to South Florida came in 1965, at a young and impressionable age. From Sarasota to Key West, I marveled at fantastic tropical plants with bizarre and scary names like *gumbo limbo, manchineel, lignum vitae,* and *poisonwood.* In the Everglades, I watched hundreds of roseate spoonbills crowd the trees around Eco Pond and stared in amazement at flamingos working their way across the mudflats along the edge of Snake Bight. Over the decades, continued trips to South Florida opened my eyes to the beauty and wonder of this incomparable tropical environment. As an adult, I returned to enjoy the thick tangled hammocks of the Upper Keys, the amazing sea caves along the Atlantic coastline north of Jupiter, and the quiet seashell-strewn beaches of the barrier islands along the Gulf of Mexico. Each visit unfolded new natural wonders unique to the region.

In the entire continental United States, only South Florida can lay claim to truly tropical habitats with native tropical plants. Rare ghost orchids grow in the humid depths of the Big Cypress, a region of vast prairies, haunting cypress strands, and deep sloughs filled with alligator flag. From its traditional start at Lake Okeechobee, the world's only Everglades sweep southward, a patchwork broken by agriculture and development. Punctuated by small tree islands, its sawgrass and cattail prairies lie under a slowly moving sheet of water only a few inches deep but more than 100 miles wide, immortalized by conservationist Marjorie Stoneman Douglas as the "river of grass." North of Lake Okeechobee lie the remnants of ancient sand dunes forming high and dry scrub habitats, while along the Gulf of Mexico and Atlantic coastlines the freshwater marshes of the interior meet the mangrove swamps of the barrier islands. In the Florida Keys, jungles of Caribbean plants top fossilized coral reefs surrounded by still, aquamarine waters.

South Florida, in a word, is different. Most of its habitats differ dramatically from those found elsewhere in the state, and these habitats contain a record number of endangered and endemic species, communities at risk from burgeoning population growth along both coastlines. The interior remains a vast and lightly populated mosaic of habitats turned to agricultural use—sugar cane fields carved out of the northern Everglades, scrub hills covered in citrus groves, pine flatwoods and prairies hosting massive cattle ranches. Because of agriculture, public lands in the interior are limited; with the exception of the Florida National Scenic Trail, most hiking trails are located along the coasts, not far from urban centers. Big Cypress and the Everglades, two distinctly different wet and wild wilderness regions, blanket the southern tip of the peninsula to the edge of the Florida Keys.

South Florida has two very distinct seasons: wet and dry. The wet season runs from May through October, the dry season from November through April. Most of the

Poisonwood bark

trails discussed in this book will be at least partially under water during the wet season. Standing water can range from several inches to several feet high during summer months, particularly in wilderness areas. Unless a trail runs along a boardwalk or along a beach, expect to get your feet wet when hiking in South Florida during the wet season. It's a different experience, and not entirely unpleasant as the water cools you down.

When winter snows fall from northern skies, it's the dry season in South Florida, and temperatures become comfortable. You can walk right out onto the solid bottom of a cypress slough, and the dreaded mosquitoes of the Everglades finally lose their resolve. Cypresses lose their needles, creating ghostly forests. Red maples and sumacs add splashes of autumn color. Seasonally out of sync with most of the rest of the nation, Florida provides a perfect winter playground for the active hiker.

HOW TO USE THIS BOOK

For purposes of this book, I've set my designation of South Florida as the counties south of FL 60. These include Broward, Charlotte, Collier, Dade, DeSoto, Glades, Hardee, Hendry, Highlands, Lee, Manatee, Martin, Monroe, Okeechobee, Palm Beach, Sarasota, and St. Lucie. Since the population of South Florida is clustered along the coasts, the Gulf Coast (I-75 corridor) and Atlantic Coast (I-95 corridor) sections contain the largest proportion of hikes in the book. The Big Cypress section contains hikes in the Big Cypress ecosystem, the sloughs and swamps surrounding Big Cypress National Preserve, while the Everglades section focuses on hikes in the Everglades ecosystem (rather than just in Everglades National Park) from its traditional

start on the eastern rim of Lake Okeechobee to the end of the peninsula at Flamingo. The Central section covers hikes north of Lake Okeechobee, well away from either coast.

There are more than 100 hiking trails in South Florida, although many of them are short strolls that expose the urban population to a touch of nature. Thanks to aggressive land-preservation programs, both Palm Beach County and Lee County offer an extraordinarily heavy density of hiking opportunities. The hikes presented in this guidebook are some of the best that South Florida has to offer. On the coasts, I actively sought out some wilder hikes on wilderness lands surrounded by urban areas. This book contains a mix of easy nature trails, beach walks, and short interpretive boardwalks, but also presents the adventuresome hiker with some challenging day hikes and backpacking trips. I have generally avoided paved trails, except where they lead to nonpaved trails. I have also excluded hikes along the Florida National Scenic Trail, as they will be covered in a separate book.

In many of the parks, forests, and wilderness areas I visited, there are multiple alternatives for hikes. I have shown all alternatives on the maps, but each discussion and all the mileage totals focus on a particular preferred route. Most of these hikes were measured using a Rolatape 415 surveyor's measuring wheel—yes, even in the swamps, where I discovered that it floats on mud and I don't. For beach walks and some remote island hikes, I relied on a Garmin Etrex GPS for measurement.

All attempts at habitat and plant identification are my own, using a variety of references. When there were multiple possibilities for a plant's name, I chose the one most commonly used in the local vernacular, such as *cabbage palm* for our state tree rather than the more regal *sabal palm* preferred by botanists.

KEY FEATURES

Each hike highlights a particular key feature—flora, geology, history, or wildlife.

Flora

Flora is perhaps what Florida is best known for—for both diversity and beauty. Of more than 4,000 types of plants, 3,600 are native to this state. Only California and Texas surpass Florida in botanical diversity. South Florida has a particularly rich proportion of rare, endangered, endemic habitats encroached upon by development, such as the pine rocklands of Dade and Monroe Counties, the coastal berms of the Keys, and the Everglades themselves, which once stretched south from the rim of Lake Okeechobee to the end of the peninsula. Cypress sloughs and strands provide bromeliads and orchids with the rain-forest-like humidity they need to flourish. Especially in the Keys and southeastern Florida, Caribbean species have naturalized to Florida's soils, creating lush tropical hammocks. Many trails are established to show off specific plant communities—boardwalks through cypress sloughs and mangrove forests, walks along sawgrass prairies and across the bright sands of the scrub.

Geology

Florida's karst geology provides an interesting look at an unusual landscape. *Karst* is the name for any type of terrain in which the bedrock dissolves easily. In Florida, limestone forms the "basement" of the state, often showing off fossils from millions of years ago. South Florida's most unusual and fragile habitats, the pine rocklands and the Everglades, show off karst features such as solution holes and epikarst—pits, holes, and grooves dissolved in bare limestone. Some trails focus on karst landforms, or lead you into reclaimed or historic mining operations, where bare rock is visible.

History

Many hikes focus on features of historic interest. South Florida's human habitation dates back thousands of years, with the ancestors of the Tequesta and Calusa peoples. Spanish explorers ranged across these shores in the 1500s. In the 1800s, the Seminole Wars brought the U.S. Army into the depths of the Everglades in hot pursuit of tribes who refused to be relocated out of state. South Florida remained a frontier until Henry Flagler's Atlantic Coast Railroad started shipping down tourists and settlers in the early 1900s; up until then, the swamps attracted only the hardiest of folks, people who lived off the fruits of the sea and scratched a living from pineapple, banana, and coconut plantations. Fortress sites, abandoned villages, and ancient temple mounds can all still be seen along South Florida's hiking trails.

Wildlife

Florida's diversity of wildlife can be enjoyed on many trails through lands set aside specifically for wildlife preservation, such as Ding Darling National Wildlife Refuge and the National Key Deer Refuge. Walk quietly and you'll be rewarded with wildlife sightings—barred owls and pileated woodpeckers in the trees, bald eagles and red-shouldered hawks circling overhead, and Key deer browsing in the mangroves.

HABITATS

Since Florida's topography doesn't easily lend clues as to where you are on a trail, hike descriptions focus on the changes in habitat that occur as a trail gains or loses elevation. South Florida's habitats show less variance than those of other sections of Florida, but include rare subtropical habitats not found anywhere else in North America. Different sources use different names for the same general habitat. The following summary explains the habitat designations used in this book.

Coastal Habitats

With more than 1,200 miles of coastline, Florida's habitats include many communities adapted to life along the sea, where wind and salt spray shape the environment. *Coastal dunes* are created by the wind and anchored by deep-rooted grasses such as sea oats. In the *maritime hammock,* windswept live oaks create a canopy above lush thickets of saw palmetto. Brittle grasses and succulent plants such as glasswort and sea purslane grow along the edges of *salt flats* and *salt marshes,* where herons, egrets, and ibises stride through the shallows. *Estuaries* and *coastal savannas* are extensive grassy salt marshes punctuated by islands of cabbage palms, typically found between barrier islands and the mainland. Mangroves grow particularly tall in South Florida, where in addition to *mangrove swamps* you'll find dense *mangrove forests* along many coastlines. In the Keys, a *coastal berm* environment develops between the mangroves and the shallow waters surrounding the islands, a sandy strand of low dunes and salt-tolerant vegetation. The unusual *transition zone* of the Keys is a salt-rich desert between the coastal berm and mangrove forest, supporting scrubby shrubs such as the bay cedar. The *coastal prairie* is shaped by the shallow seas around the Everglades and Keys, creating stark salty wetlands

supporting buttonwood and pickleweed on a base of sticky limestone marl.

Forests

Hardwood hammock is a catchall term for a forest of mixed hardwoods. In South Florida, you commonly encounter the *tropical hardwood hammock,* which starts out with a subtropical base of strangler fig and cabbage palm and, depending on the environment, adds on Caribbean trees such as gumbo limbo, mahogany, paradise tree, and satinleaf. The *oak hammock,* frequently dominated by live oak, is Florida's climax forest. *Pine flatwoods* are the state's largest natural community, covering nearly half of the land. With acidic, poorly drained soils supporting ferns, gallberry, saw palmetto, and a high canopy of tall pine trees, pine flatwoods feel very open. A clay layer beneath the soil holds in rainfall, causing flatwoods to stay flooded for a few days after a rainstorm. *Cabbage palm flatwoods* are the most common flatwoods of South Florida. They intersperse cabbage palms through a canopy of pond or slash pines, and occur in floodplain areas. *Scrubby flatwoods* have better drainage than most pine flatwoods, but the pines have more space between them, forming breaks in the canopy. *Pine rocklands* are Florida's most endangered habitat, where scrawny slash pines form the high canopy, poisonwood thrives in the understory, and limestone-loving ferns grow from the exposed karst.

Prairies

Treeless and open, prairies are extensive dry grasslands that can be seasonally inundated with water. Wildflower enthusiasts seek out prairies for their unusual and colorful flowers, such as the pine lily, pale meadow beauty, and elephant's root. Prairies may contain islands of oak

Alligators abound along Main Park Road's Anhinga Trail (Hike 39).

hammocks or cabbage palm flatwoods and are host to bayheads, cypress domes, and freshwater marshes. Less than 20 percent of Florida's prairies are under state protection; most have been converted to cattle ranches, sod farms, and citrus groves. The Everglades contains the world's only freshwater marl prairies, or *sawgrass prairies,* where vast expanses of razor-sharp sawgrass grow out of a base of exposed limestone covered with just a few inches of slowly flowing water, the "river of grass" that moves toward the sea.

Scrub

Scrubs form on well-drained, loose "sugar sand," deposited along ancient shorelines. They are thought to be Florida's oldest plant communities, in existence for more than 20 million years. A limited number of plants tolerate the extreme dryness of the scrub environment. In a *sand pine scrub,* tall sand pines dominate the forest, with an understory of oak scrub, rosemary scrub, and saw or scrub palmetto. A *rosemary scrub* is an unusual place where rosemary bushes up to 8 feet tall grow out of a white sand base; the ground may be covered in lichens. *Oak scrub* is dominated by sand live oak, wax myrtle, Chapman oak, and myrtle oak, with the highest diversity of scrub plant and animal life.

Swamp Forests

Red maple, sweetgum, red bay, bay magnolia, loblolly bay, and water oak are common residents of the *floodplain forest,* created by rivers that seasonally overflow their banks, scouring adjoining channels higher than the normal river level. Thick with bald cypress, pond cypress, and cabbage palms, the low-lying *hydric hammock* occurs along river and lake floodplains, experiencing flooding whenever water levels are slightly above normal. *Palm hammocks* provide slight elevation over the surrounding marshes. *Bayheads* receive their watery base from seepage, encouraging dahoon holly, bay magnolia, and loblolly bay to grow. Looking like a dome from a distance, the *cypress dome* forms in a low depression in a prairie, fed by seeping water. In South Florida, cypresses also grow in *sloughs*—long linear depressions in the limestone bedrock into which surrounding water flows—and *strands,* shallow depressions that cover broad swaths of land. Unless a boardwalk is available, don't expect to stay dry when hiking through a swamp forest.

Wetlands

In addition to coastal marshes, mangrove swamps, and swamp forests, Florida's moist habitats include *freshwater marshes,* which form along lake and river drainages; *ephemeral ponds,* occurring in low spots during the rainy season; *flatwoods ponds,* created from the trickling runoff in the pine flatwoods; and *wetlands,* shallow grassy basins in pine flatwoods, scrub, and prairies. Look for *flag ponds* in the sloughs and strands of South Florida, where the presence of tall alligator flag delineates a particularly deep depression in the swamp.

ADVICE AND PRECAUTIONS

Alligators

Alligators are rarely a problem for a hiker, unless humans have fed them. An alligator habituated to human presence won't get out of your way. If one fearlessly blocks your trail, do not approach it or try to walk around it. Make noise, stomp your feet, and let *it* move before you continue. Never feed or touch an alligator.

Bears

Consider yourself fortunate if you see a Florida black bear. Mostly active in the early-morning hours, this elusive mammal teases you with scat and tracks left on hiking trails. A full-grown Florida black bear rarely weighs more than 350 pounds and will quickly move out of your way if it sees you. No one has ever been attacked by a Florida black bear.

Crocodiles

Crocodiles are differentiated from alligators by their pointed snouts, lighter color, and preference for salt water. The American crocodile is an endangered species endemic to South Florida, and may be encountered along waterways from the Upper Keys up through Miami on the east coast, and throughout the Everglades and Ten Thousand Islands north to Sanibel Island on the west coast. While crocodile sightings are rare, take the same precautions with crocodiles as you would with alligators.

Camping

Tent camping (backpacking or car camping) in South Florida is best enjoyed between November and March, when the muggy nights with high temperatures yield to cooler evenings. Always carry insect repellent: Even in the cool months, you will encounter mosquitoes at dusk and dawn. Wildfires spark easily in Florida, so please refrain from building a campfire unless a fire ring is available—use a camp stove for cooking. Be sure to pack out all waste materials from your campsite. Where privies are available, use them; otherwise, dig a hole at least 400 feet from any campsite or water source. When camping in a primitive campsite, particularly an undeveloped site, follow Leave No Trace ethics. Leave the site as pristine as when you entered it. Eliminate any signs of a campfire unless there is an established fire ring. To protect your food supply, use a bear bag in bear territory—not just to foil the bears but also to outwit the wily raccoons that congregate near established campsites. Don't camp on the banks of a stream, lake, or pond—alligators *do* roam at night.

Deforestation

Even in protected areas such as state parks, state forests, and wilderness areas, a hiker is bound to come across gaping gaps in the forest—hammocks charred by wildfires, pine forests felled by loggers, and trees fallen like scattered matchsticks, victims of insect infestation. State and national forests issue permits to logging companies for regular harvesting of timber, and care is not always taken to leave a corridor of trees around a hiking trail. Sandhill and scrub habitats require wildfire to regenerate new growth. Logging frequently occurs to help restore these fragile habitats with fresh growth.

If you come across a hike segment where blazes are missing, use your best judgment in crossing an open area. Look carefully for telltale blazes on the distant tree line. If the trail has been following jeep roads, look for alternate routes around the clear-cut. Make sure that you know where you entered the open area in case you need to backtrack.

Heat and Dehydration

When hiking in Florida, it is very easy to become dehydrated without realizing it. The warm temperatures and sunshine will sometimes prompt you to drink, but not often enough. Dehydration and long exposure to the sun can lead to heat exhaustion, which starts with nausea, chills, and dizziness, and can lead to deadly heatstroke. If you feel any of these symptoms, stop hiking. Drink as much fluid as possible. Rest a while before attempting any further exertion. Always carry enough water for your hike. I carry a minimum of 1 liter per 4 miles, and twice that when temperatures are over 80 degrees Fahrenheit.

Hunting

Florida's prime hiking season is also the state's prime hunting season, which can lead to conflicts on certain state lands, such as wildlife management areas, water management district lands, state preserves, and state forests. During deer season, wear a lightweight blaze-orange vest when hiking these lands. Hunting is *not* permitted in county parks or state parks. Backpackers should be aware that certain lands are closed to camping during general gun season; some trails are entirely closed to hiking during the gun season, due to the perceived risk to hikers. For full details on hunting dates and restrictions in specific state lands, check the Florida Fish and Wildlife Conservation Commission's web site at http://floridaconservation.org/.

Insects

Thanks to our warm weather, Florida's insects enjoy longer lives than in most states—especially in South Florida. South of Frostproof, it's a rare year indeed when a chill hits the region, although the worst of the mosquito season is over by mid-December. Decades of control efforts in South Florida have limited the mosquito population severely, so that only the Everglades, Big Cypress, and some of the Florida Keys suffer from extreme clouds of these pesky bugs, especially in the wet season. When visiting these particular areas at any time of year, it's a good idea to carry a mosquito head net in your pack. Wear a lightweight long-sleeved shirt and long pants to minimize insect bites.

Numerous Florida counties report outbreaks of West Nile virus in the bird population, with some spreading to horses and humans. Always be cautious. It never hurts to spray before you hike. Keep a long-lasting sportsman's insect repellent in your pack. To keep off ticks and chiggers (also known as red bugs), spray your hiking clothing beforehand with permethrin. To minimize bug problems when you take breaks, carry a plastic garbage bag to sit on. Longtime Florida hikers recommend wearing long pants to beat the mosquitoes, and dusting your socks with sulfur powder (available over the counter from a compounding pharmacist) to fend off chiggers. If your legs feel itchy after a hike, take a 15-minute plunge in a hot tub or a hot bath to ward off any further effects from chiggers—microscopic bugs that attach themselves to your skin to feed. Check yourself carefully for ticks.

Spiders can be problematic to Florida hikers between March and November, as they tend to build large webs across the trail. Most commonly, you'll see the large golden orb spider in its sticky yellow web, and the crab spider, smaller but obvious because of the shell on its back. Be proactive. Pick up a stick (the stalk of a saw palmetto frond works well) and hold it tilted in front of you to catch any human-height webs. Try to duck under webs that you can see, because a spider's web is a masterpiece of nature—and the spider is helping to rid the forest of other pesky bugs.

Marine Life

Enjoying a barefoot hike along Florida's beaches means keeping your eyes open for the marine life that washes ashore, particularly clear, glassy blobs of jellyfish. Stepping on a jellyfish entails hours of intense pain. If you decide to enjoy a dip in the sea, bear in mind that Florida leads the world in shark attacks on bathers. Most attacks occur along the Atlantic Coast. On the Gulf of Mexico, wading in the sea calls for the "stingray shuffle." Set each foot down on the ocean floor with a resounding *stomp,* which alerts the stingrays to stay clear. In the Florida Keys, avoid stepping on coral. You'll damage the living organisms, and they'll damage you with dangerous cuts that quickly become infected. Washed up on beaches or embedded in sandy soil, dead coral can cut bare feet as sharply as broken glass.

Mountain Bikes and Equestrians

On multiuse trails, mountain bikes and equestrians may share the treadway. Allow them the right-of-way so they don't tear up the edges of the footpath. Multiuse trails are indicated in the text.

Panthers

Considered one of the most endangered species in the nation, the Florida panther roams the vast remaining wilderness areas of the Big Cypress and Everglades. Shy and elusive, the Florida panther is a subspecies of the cougar. They feed on deer and feral hogs, ranging across a home territory of up to 200 square miles. Since there are less than 70 individuals in the wild, panther sightings are rare—but not unknown. Humans are at little risk from the panther population. If you encounter an injured or dead panther, however, do not approach it. Contact the U.S. Fish and Wildlife Service

(941-353-8442) as quickly as possible regarding the animal's location and situation. Most of the cats wear collars and are tracked with radio telemetry.

Plants

No matter how far south you travel in the United States, there's no escaping poison ivy. Be particularly alert to the poison ivy vine that grows up trees along some boardwalk trails. Tread softly, also known as stinging nettle, has a beautiful white flower atop a tall stem; its leaves are covered with tiny stinging nettles. Avoid brushing bare skin against it.

Many trails are not maintained between the months of April and November, since most hiking occurs in late fall and winter. An overgrown trail can be painful when burrs and nettles dig into your socks. Consider purchasing a pair of low gaiters to cover your socks and shoes, or do as the experienced hikers do—wear long lightweight pants when hiking, even in summer. If you are sensitive to poison ivy, trails overgrown with Brazilian pepper may also cause a mild skin irritation if sap touches your skin.

South Florida is home to many unique plants, among them the poisonwood. It's found in tropical hardwood hammocks and pine rocklands, and scattered along disturbed areas, creating dense groves in the Keys and in Everglades National Park. With toxicity 10 times that of poison ivy, these trees can cause severe allergic reactions—including respiratory problems—in anyone sensitive to poison ivy. The distinctive mottled-brown-and-orange bark of the poisonwood can be confused with that of the pigeon plum, but the trunk of the poisonwood also sports sticky black resinous patches of the toxic sap. The leaves often droop, and each leaf is outlined in yellow.

When hiking where you might have to push your way through brush (such as at National Key Deer Refuge, the backcountry of Key Largo Hammocks Botanical State Park, or the wilderness trails of the Everglades), wear a hat, long sleeves, and long pants to avoid getting poisonwood sap on your skin or scalp. The sticky sap cannot be washed off with water—you must use an oil-dissolving soap or similar substance (such as WD-40) to remove the sap from your skin.

The most poisonous tree in North America is the manchineel tree, found in the same habitats as the poisonwood. It displays small crab-apple-type fruits that turn golden with a pinkish hue when ripe, and has attractive alternating glossy leaves similar to members of the ficus family, with fine serrated edges. The entire tree is poisonous: The Carib Indians used its deadly sap to tip their poison arrows. If a branch or leaf is broken, the manchineel will drip a milky acidic sap that will burn exposed skin. You must wash the affected area *immediately* if exposed to this plant, and avoid all contact with your eyes. Learning how to recognize and avoid both poisonwood and manchineel is essential if you plan to hike on wilderness trails in the Everglades and the Keys.

Proper Clothing and Equipment

Always carry rain gear! Storm clouds come up suddenly and unexpectedly, and can easily put a damper on your hike if you're not prepared. Find a jacket that will fold down small enough to attach to a fanny pack or will fit inside your day pack. If you are hiking more than a couple of miles, carry some sort of small pack. At a minimum, your pack should contain water, a first-aid kit, a flashlight, a compass, and emergency food. To beat the heat, a sturdy fanny pack with water-bottle holsters is a good choice. A hat is essential to keep your head cool. For safety's sake, use a hiking stick to "test the waters" ahead when you go tromping through a swamp.

Because South Florida's terrain is frequently sandy or wet, avoid heavy leather boots and "waterproof" lined boots. To minimize blisters, you need your feet to breathe. Look for a lightweight hiking shoe, a trail running shoe, or even comfortable running shoes. Some Florida hikers use sports sandals with socks. When your shoes get waterlogged, you want them to be able to dry before the next outing.

One of the biggest mistakes hikers make in South Florida is to wear jeans when wading into swamps. Cotton soaks up water like a sponge, adding to the difficulty of moving your feet—a hard enough task already when pushing your way through water. Find yourself a good quick-drying polypropylene or nylon pair of pants. Wear pants, not shorts, when going into the swamps: You don't know what's under the water, so the extra protection doesn't hurt. A lightweight long-sleeved buttondown nylon shirt provides protection from mosquitoes and the sun.

If you are backpacking or walking long distances, wear two layers of socks—a good hiking sock on the outside, and a thin polypropylene or silk/nylon sock on the inside (nylon knee-highs make a good cheap liner sock). Instead of rubbing against your skin, the socks will rub against each other. Avoid cotton socks. When they get damp, they abrade your feet. If you do feel a hot spot or a blister coming on, treat it immediately. Cover it with a piece of moleskin (found in the foot-care section of most drugstores) and apply a small piece of duct tape over the moleskin to keep it water- and sweatproof.

Interested in backpacking? While South Florida has fewer backpacking opportunities than the rest of the state, both Jonathan Dickinson State Park (Hike 27) and Myakka River State Park (Hike 3) provide excellent multiday outings. Several other shorter trails feature backcountry campsites. The Florida Trail Association offers several beginners' backpacking workshops each year—a great way to try out gear (and the whole concept of backpacking) before you spend any money on the hobby. While a hands-on workshop is your best bet, you may not have the time—so read one of the many excellent books on backpacking, including *Backpacking* (Adrienne Hall), *Backpacking: One Step at a Time* (Harvey Manning), *The Complete Walker III* (Colin Fletcher), and *Hiking & Backpacking: A Complete Guide* (Karen Berger). For specifics on backpacking in Florida, contact the Florida Trail Association for its latest guidebook.

Respecting the Resource

South Florida has a long history of poaching, from the shooting of egrets and roseate spoonbills for their plumes and alligators for their hides, to the collecting of tree snails for the curiosity of aficionados. Modern-day rustlers are still caught removing thousands of irreplaceable bromeliads and orchids from Florida's swamps. In general, all flora and fauna on public lands are protected by state or federal law and cannot be removed without special permission. Respect the future of our land by leaving everything exactly as you saw it.

Snakes

Florida's poisonous snakes include the southern copperhead, the cottonmouth moccasin (sometimes called water moccasin), the eastern coral snake, and three types of rattlesnake—timber, eastern diamondback, and pygmy. In addition, there is a Florida Keys subspecies of coral snake that does not sport the usual yellow bands. Although nonpoisonous, the black racer can be aggressive. In areas where the trail is overgrown, be wary of where you set your feet. Never handle a snake.

Sun

When hiking under the bright Florida sun, use a high-strength sports sunblock lotion and wear a hat for the protection of your face. Depending on the habitats you'll be hiking through—especially scrub and prairie—you may want sunglasses as well.

Unattended Vehicles

Use common sense when leaving your vehicle at a trailhead. Don't leave valuables in plain sight, and lock the vehicle. If a permit was required to enter the land or to hike the trail, be sure that it's showing inside the front windshield.

Water

When it comes to water availability, Florida's trails run the gamut—either they have plenty of it, or they have none. Because of drainage from citrus groves and cattle pastures into rivers and creeks, you cannot trust surface water sources to be pristine, with the exception of free-flowing artesian wells and springs along the trail. Even these can have an unpleasant taste due to a high sulfur or salt content, and would require filtering. In South Florida, most coastal water sources are prone to saltwater intrusion.

Not all water sources can be easily reached—a flag pond, for instance, may require some slogging through muck before you reach water. I mention water sources for backpackers, but suggest you carry your own supply whenever day hiking. Always use a water filter or chemical treatment such as iodine before drinking "wild" water.

Weather

While the average hiker wouldn't stray outside in a hurricane, the frequency of afternoon thunderstorms in summertime doesn't always keep a person off the trail. But darkening skies are no laughing matter. Violent thunderstorms can spawn fierce wind gusts and, occasionally, tornadoes. If you are caught out in the open during a storm, attempt to reach cover as quickly as possible.

FLORIDA STATE PARKS

Most Florida State Parks require an entry fee, varying from location to location. Residents can save themselves some money by picking up an annual Florida State Parks entrance pass ($30 individual, $60 family), covering all entrance fees for a year. The family pass is good for up to eight people entering in a single vehicle. Visitors can also invest in a Florida State Parks vacation pass, available in increments of a week at a time for $10 per week. Even with a pass, you will be charged a Monroe County tax (now 50 cents) when visiting state parks in the Florida Keys.

Florida State Parks are generally open 8 am—sunset. Many provide camping facilities, which must be reserved through a new centralized clearinghouse, Reserve America. For more information on the award-winning Florida State Park system, visit http://www.floridastateparks.org, or call 850-488-9872 for a free Florida State Parks guide.

NATIONAL WILDLIFE REFUGES

Founded by President Theodore Roosevelt on March 21, 1903, with the dedication of Pelican Island National Wildlife Refuge in Florida's Indian River Lagoon, the National Wildlife Refuge system protects lands used by migratory birds and vanishing species. With 21 refuges in Florida, 9 of them in South Florida, the U.S. Fish and Wildlife Commission manages a significant chunk of the South Florida landscape. Some National Wildlife Refuges (such as Crocodile Lakes NWR in the Florida Keys) are entirely closed to public access. Others, like Ding Darling NWR, Loxahatchee NWR, and the National Key Deer Refuge, provide public access on a limited basis. When visiting a National Wildlife Refuge, keep in mind that all animals *and* plants are protected—visitors have been arrested and fined for removing tree snails, orchids, and bromeliads from preserves in South Florida.

FLORIDA TRAIL ASSOCIATION

The statewide Florida Trail Association (FTA) encourages hikers to build, maintain, and enjoy Florida's trails, including the 1,300-mile Florida Trail, which runs from Loop Road in the Big Cypress National Preserve to Fort Pickens in Pensacola. Volunteers from the FTA maintain many loop hikes across the state, including several covered in this book. Although all FTA-maintained loops are blazed orange, the FTA does not maintain all of the orange-blazed trails in the state. In 1998, the state Department of Environmental Protection adopted orange as the standard color for blazing *all* hiking trails. Look for the FT sign at the trailhead for trails built and maintained by the Florida Trail Association.

Local chapters hold monthly outdoors-focused meetings and sponsor frequent hiking, backpacking, and trail work activities to introduce Floridians and visitors alike to the great outdoors, Florida-style. For information on a chapter near you, contact the Florida Trail Association, 5415 Southwest 13th Street, Gainesville, FL 32608, call 877-HIKE-FLA, or visit the group's web site at http://www.florida-trail.org.

FLORIDA TRAILWALKER PROGRAM

The Florida Division of Forestry's Trailwalker Program encourages you to get out and hike designated trails in Florida's state forests. As you complete each hike, send in a postcard to the program. After 10 hikes, the state awards you a Trailwalker patch and certificate. There are few state forests in South Florida; this book includes one Trailwalker hike (Hike 16). For a Trailwalker application, visit any of the designated Trailwalker trailheads for a brochure, call 850-414-0871, or visit the web site at http://www.fl-dof.com/Recreation/Trailwalker/.

SUGGESTED READING AND FIELD GUIDES

Alden, Peter, Rich Cech, and Gil Nelson. *National Audubon Society Field Guide to Florida.* New York: Alfred A. Knopf, 1998.

Bell, C. Richie, and Bryan J. Taylor. *Florida Wild Flowers and Roadside Plants.* Chapel Hill, NC: Laurel Hill Press, 1982.

Benshoff, P. J. *Myakka.* Sarasota, FL: Pineapple Press, 2002.

Butcher, Clyde. *Florida Landscape.* Gainesville: University Press of Florida, 2002.

Dietz, Tim. *Call of the Siren: Manatees and Dugongs.* Golden, CO: Fulcrum Publishing, 1992.

Derr, Mark. *Some Kind of Paradise: A Chronicle of Man and the Land in Florida.* Gainesville: University Press of Florida, 1998.

Douglas, Marjorie Stoneman. *The Everglades: River of Grass.* Marietta, GA: Mockingbird Books, 1947.

Fergus, Charles. *Swamp Screamer: At Large with the Florida Panther.* Gainesville: University Press of Florida, 1998.

Friend, Sandra. *Sinkholes.* Sarasota, FL: Pineapple Press, 2002.

Matthiessen, Peter. *Killing Mister Watson.* New York: Random House, 1991.

Nelson, Gil. *The Ferns of Florida.* Sarasota, FL: Pineapple Press, 2000.

____. *The Shrubs and Woody Vines of Florida.* Sarasota, FL: Pineapple Press, 1996.

____. *The Trees of Florida.* Sarasota, FL: Pineapple Press, 1994.

Niedhauk, Charlotte Arpin. *Charlotte's Story: A Florida Keys Diary 1934 & 1935.* Sugarloaf Shores, FL: Laurel & Herbert, 1998.

Orlean, Susan. *The Orchid Thief.* New York: Ballantine Books, 1998.

Pratt, Theodore. *The Barefoot Mailman.* St. Simons Island, GA: Mockingbird Books, 1971.

Richardson, Larry, and Peggy Bransilver. *Florida's Unsung Wilderness: The Swamps.* Englewood, CO: Westcliffe Publishing, 2002.

Ripple, Jeff. *The Florida Keys: The Natural Wonders of an Island Preserve.* Stillwater, MN: Voyageur Press, 1995.

Ripple, Jeff, and Clyde Butcher. *Southwest Florida's Wetland Wilderness: Big Cypress Swamp and the Ten Thousand Islands.* Gainesville: University Press of Florida, 1996.

Smith, Patrick. *A Land Remembered.* Sarasota, FL: Pineapple Press, 2001.

____. *Forever Island & Allapattah: A Patrick Smith Reader.* Sarasota, FL: Pineapple Press, 1998.

Standiford, Les. *Last Train to Paradise.* New York: Crown Publishers, 2002.

Taylor, Walter Kingsley. *Florida Wildflowers in their Natural Communities.* Gainesville: University Press of Florida, 1998.

Tebeau, Charlton W. *Man in the Everglades: 2000 Years of Human History in the Everglades National Park.* Miami: University of Miami Press, 1968.

Tekiela, Stan. *Birds of Florida Field Guide.* Cambridge, MN: Adventure Publications, 2001.

ADDRESSES

Hike 1

Manatee County Parks & Recreation
5502 33rd Avenue Drive West
Bradenton, FL 32409
941-748-4501, extension 6823

Hike 2

Oscar Scherer State Park
1843 South Tamiami Trail
Osprey, FL 34429
941-483-5956

Hike 3

Myakka River State Park
13207 SR 72
Sarasota, FL 34241
941-361-6511

Hike 4

Sarasota County Parks & Recreation
6700 Clark Road
Sarasota, FL 34241
941-316-1172

Hike 5
Charlotte Harbor Environmental Center
10941 Burnt Store Road
Punta Gorda, FL 33955
941-575-5435

Hike 6
Cayo Costa State Park
P.O. Box 1150
Boca Grande, FL 33921
941-964-0375

Hike 7
Caloosahatchee Regional Park
18500 North River Road
Alva, FL 33920
941-693-2690

Hike 8
Hickey's Creek Mitigation Park
17980 Palm Beach Boulevard
Fort Myers, FL 33920
941-728-6240

Hike 9
Calusa Nature Center
3450 Ortiz Avenue
Fort Myers, FL 33905
941-275-3435

Hike 10
Six Mile Cypress Slough
7751 Penzance Crossing
Fort Myers, FL 33905
941-432-2042

Hike 11
Estero Bay Aquatic and State Buffer
Preserves
700–1 Fisherman's Wharf
Fort Myers Beach, FL 33931

Hike 12
Lovers Key State Park
8700 Estero Boulevard
Fort Myers Beach, FL 33931
941-463-4588

Hike 13
J. N. "Ding" Darling National Wildlife
Refuge
1 Wildlife Drive
Sanibel, FL 33957
941-472-1100

Hike 14
Sanibel-Captiva Conservation Foundation
3333 Sanibel-Captiva Road
Sanibel, FL 33957
941-472-2329

Hike 15
Corkscrew Swamp Sanctuary
375 Sanctuary Road West
Naples, FL 34120
239-348-9151

Hike 16
Florida Division of Forestry
Picayune Strand State Forest
2121 52nd Avenue Southeast
Naples, FL 34114
941-348-7557

Hike 17
Collier-Seminole State Park
20200 East Tamiami Trail
Naples, FL 34114
941-394-3397

Hike 18
Fakahatchee Strand Preserve State Park
P.O. Box 548
Copeland, FL 33926
941-695-4593

Hike 19
Big Cypress National Preserve
HCR 61, Box 11
Ochopee, FL 34141
941-695-2000

Hike 20
Paynes Creek Historic State Park
888 Lake Branch Road
Bowling Green, FL 33834
941-375-4717

Hikes 21, 22
Highlands Hammock State Park
5931 Hammock Road
Sebring, FL 33872
863-386-6094

Hike 23
Florida Fish and Wildlife Conservation
Commission
Southwest Region
3900 Drane Field Road
Lakeland, FL 33811-1299
863-648-3203

Hike 24
Fort Pierce Inlet State Park
905 Shorewinds Drive
Fort Pierce, FL 34949
772-468-3985

Hike 25
Savannas Preserve State Park
9551 Gumbo Limbo Lane
Jensen Beach, FL 34957
772-398-2779

Hike 26
St. Lucie Inlet Preserve State Park
16450 Southeast Federal Highway
Hobe Sound, FL 33455
561-744-7603

Hike 27
Jonathan Dickinson State Park
16450 Southeast Federal Highway
Hobe Sound, FL 33455
561-546-2771

Hike 28
Blowing Rocks Preserve
574 South Beach Road
Hobe Sound, FL 33455
772-744-6668

Hikes 29, 36
Palm Beach County Department of Environmental Resources Management
3323 Belvedere Road, Building 502
West Palm Beach, FL 33406-1548
561-233-2400

Hike 30
John D. MacArthur Beach State Park
10900 SR 703
North Palm Beach, FL 33408
561-624-6950

Hike 31
Gumbo Limbo Nature Center
1801 North Ocean Boulevard
Boca Raton, FL 33432
561-338-1473

Hike 32
Fern Forest Nature Center
201 Lyons Road South
Coconut Creek, FL 33063
954-970-0150

Hike 33
Secret Woods Nature Center
2701 West SR 84
Dania Beach, FL 33312
954-791-1030

Hike 34
Greynolds Park
17530 West Dixie Highway
North Miami Beach, FL 33160
305-945-3425

Hike 35
Florida Fish and Wildlife Conservation
Commission
South Region
8535 Northlake Boulevard
West Palm Beach, FL 33412
561-625-5122

Hike 36
See Hike 29.

Hike 37
Arthur M. Loxahatchee National Wildlife
Refuge
10216 Lee Road
Boynton Beach, FL 33437-4796
561-734-8303

Hike 38
Tree Tops Park
3900 Southwest 100th Avenue
Davie, FL 33328
954-370-3750

Hikes 39, 40, 41, 42, 43, 44
Everglades National Park
40001 SR 9336
Homestead, FL 33034-6733
305-242-7700

Hike 45
Dagny Johnson Key Largo Hammock
Botanical State Park
P.O. Box 487
Key Largo, FL 33037
305-451-1202

Hike 46
Windley Key Fossil Reef Geological State
Park
P.O. Box 1052
Islamorada, FL 33036
305-664-2540

Hike 47
Lignumvitae Key Botanical State Park
P.O. Box 1052
Islamorada, FL 33036
305-664-2540

Hike 48
Long Key State Park
P.O. Box 776
Long Key, FL 33001
305-664-4815

Hike 49
Bahia Honda State Park
36850 Overseas Highway
Big Pine Key, FL 33043
305-872-2353

Hike 50
National Key Deer Refuge
P.O. Box 430510
Big Pine Key, FL 33043-0510
305-872-0774

I

Gulf Coast

Myakka Canopy Walk

Clyde Butcher

1

Emerson Point Park

Total distance (circuit): 2.7 miles

Hiking time: 1 hour, 15 minutes

*Habitats: Estuary, freshwater marsh,
hardwood hammock, mangrove forest,
palm hammock*

Maps: USGS 7½' Anna Maria

Where the Manatee River flows into Tampa Bay, Snead Island sits at a supremely strategic position. Settlers in the 1800s thought so, building a plantation on a tall hill looking over the bay. But this part of Florida isn't known for its hills. Hidden beneath the leaf litter and sword ferns, in the shade of the ancient live oaks, the hill is made up of millions of discarded oyster shells—one of the oldest known temple mounds in Florida. Known as the Portavant Temple Mound, it has a flat top 150 feet long and 80 feet wide, once commanding a spectacular view. More than 1,000 years ago, a village of the ancestors of the Timucua sat on this very site. In addition to the Portavant Mound, a smaller rounded subsidiary mound and several middens are scattered throughout the forest.

Encompassing 360 acres, Emerson Point Park protects this unique historic site as well as an interesting mix of habitats, including a rare look at the Tampa Bay estuary from its southern shore. Both a limestone path and a paved biking trail run around the park, and anglers can gain access to Tampa Bay down at the point. Snaking around the island, several hiking-only trails can be strung together with the limestone path for an easy and interesting 2.7-mile walk. The park is open 8 AM–sunset daily.

From I-75 exit 224, Ellenton/Palmetto, follow US 301 south for 3.5 miles to its junction with US 41. Where US 301 turns to join US 41, stay on the road you're on, which becomes Southwest 10th Street into Palmetto. After 0.7 mile, you cross

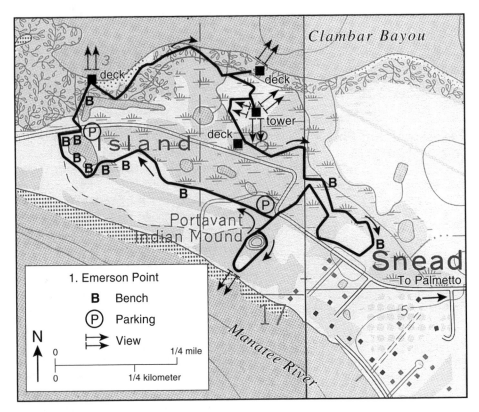

Clambar Bayou

1. Emerson Point

B Bench

(P) Parking

⊢► View

N

0 — 1/4 mile
0 — 1/4 kilometer

deck

deck

deck

tower

Island

Portavant
Indian Mound

Snead

To Palmetto

Manatee River

Business US 41. If you're coming from St. Petersburg, take I-275 exit 5. Drive south on US 19, staying to the right as it merges into business US 41. After 5.1 miles, you reach Southwest 10th Street. Turn right at the traffic light, which is Southwest 10th Street.

After 2.5 miles, you cross a small bridge onto Snead Island, where you'll see a sign for the preserve. Turn right onto Tarpon Road, then left at the stop sign. Follow the road as it narrows and enters the park after 0.8 mile. Once you're inside the park gates, watch for the parking area on the left for the Portavant Temple Mound. This is one of several small parking areas that provide access to the trail loop.

Start your hike from the Temple Mound parking area. Cross the limestone path

and head up past the interpretive sign to the PIONEER TRAIL sign. Walking through the junglelike understory of wild coffee, snake plant, and strangler fig, you feel like an explorer in an Indiana Jones movie. Fern-draped live oaks knit a dense canopy overhead. As you come up to the temple mound, a boardwalk provides an accessible path up the massive hill. Continue up the boardwalk to the top, and feel the passing of the ages beneath your feet. To protect the mound, the boardwalk extends across its surface, providing a few little nooks where you can sit and look out into the dense forest or down at the trails winding through the thicket of wild coffee. When the ancestors of the Timucua lived and worshiped here, they more than likely had a clear view of Tampa Bay, for their own protection. The massive mound of shells gleamed white in the sun, visible for miles across the sea, and was used as a stage for religious ceremonies. By the time Europeans arrived on these shores, the civilization had long since vanished. Early settlers farmed Snead Island starting in 1814. In 1866, Robert Griffith and his wife built their home atop the temple mound. Part of the foundation of that pioneer cabin sits off to the left.

Walk down the ramp to the front of the mound and continue along on a shell path along a row of tall royal palms—no doubt planted to beautify the view by one of the former occupants, as there was a house here until as recently as 1991, when the state of Florida bought the land. Remnants of an old flower garden, salmon-colored hydrangea and pink hibiscus bloom at the bases of the live oak and cabbage palm. Bloodred berries and white flowers drip from a Christmas berry. When you reach the interpretive sign by the river, walk to the water's edge, where the fingerlike pneumatophores of black mangroves reach out of the tannic water. Notice how heavily developed the far shore is; Emerson Point is a rare piece of public land on this coastline.

It's not readily apparent where the trail goes from this point, so turn around and walk along the left edge of the clearing to a live oak whose limbs stretch out over the grass. Just beyond the tree, look for a mowed and clipped path between the snake plants leading into the dark hammock. Still there from the days of the ancients, bleached conch shells lie strewn through the leaf litter. The trail twists and turns through the tall wild coffee and snake plants until it emerges at the far side of the mound at the bottom of boardwalk. Turn left and walk back toward the parking lot.

When you reach the limestone path, shared with bicycles, turn left to start the large loop around the park. Crossing a park road, you approach the RESTORATION TRAIL SOUTH sign. The trail curves to the left, immersing you in a wonderland of flowers and berries. Purple morning glory spills over the sea myrtle, while the dark purple berries of the American beautyberry gleam in the sun. Sporting spiky yellow flowers, gray nickerbean cascades over wax myrtle, competing with the giant blooms of moonflower for attention. This beauty is the result of an active restoration effort within the park's boundaries to eradicate the noxious non-native Brazilian pepper and Australian pine that once covered Emerson Point. Winding along the shell path in the shade of young live oaks, you pass a bench at 0.5 mile. Everywhere you look, there's something in bloom, from Christmas berry to cowpea, pokeberry to marlberry. Giant sword ferns and giant leather ferns grow along the edge of the restored freshwater wetland, where a little blue heron perches on a nesting box. The marsh creeps up to the edge of the trail, where it could flood the footpath after a heavy rain. An osprey calls out from the top of a pine snag while blue-winged teals drift across the open pond. The trail curves to the right to circle the marsh. Wispy pink muhlygrass looks like a soft fog on the water's edge. Looking across the wetland, you see a parking lot with a covered picnic bench. Stop at the next bench for an interesting view of the lake framed by a strangler fig caught in the act of engulfing a cabbage palm, as they are prone to do.

Passing more benches—there are no lack of benches along this walk—you come to a T intersection with the park entrance road and a paved bike path. Turn right and follow the bike path to the crosswalk.

The view of Tampa Bay from the observation tower

Cross over the park road and turn left to head over to the trailhead for the Terra Ceia Trail, a hiking-only footpath out along the bay. You've walked 1 mile. The trail narrows as it swings to the right and heads down a forested dike, a corridor defined by two canals lined with mangroves. Past the Spanish bayonets, turn left on the boardwalk to walk out through the mangrove forest for a sweeping view of Terra Ceia Bay and Tampa Bay. The Sunshine Skyway Bridge shimmers in the distance. Mangrove crabs scuttle across the observation deck. Look down into the clear water of the estuary and you'll see splashing schools of gar. White ibises roost in the tangle of mangroves around you. Moving silently, two kayakers paddle past, seeking the next cove.

Walk back up the boardwalk and turn left to continue on the main trail, which narrows tightly between the mangroves and the sea grapes. The ribbon of blue water tantalizes from behind the veil of mangroves. The trail drops off the dike, where shells spill out of its side—undoubtedly parts of ancient middens used by the builders of these mosquito control structures without a thought to their significance. Until as recently as the 1940s, prehistoric middens throughout Florida were torn up and used as road fill. Oyster shells spill out from between the roots of nearby mounds.

At 1.5 miles, you reach another boardwalk just before a long bridge. Turn left to follow it, and take a moment to enjoy the view from this observation deck on Terra Ceia Bay. An osprey rises from its perch, fussing as it struggles with a fish. Watch for white ibises picking their way through a maze of red mangrove roots. Return to the main trail and cross the bridge. Notice the slow movement of the water below, pulsing in and out with the tides. When you reach the next bridge, turn right to cross it. Ducking through the mangrove forest, it emerges in the shadow of a tall observation tower. When you reach the T intersection, turn right, then make a left at the fork to climb up the hill to the tower. At the top, take in the sweeping 360-degree view across Emerson Point, from Terra Ceia Bay to Tampa Bay and on to Anna Maria Sound where the Manatee River ends. Beyond Tampa Bay, you can see the distant skyscrapers of St. Petersburg—certainly a very different view than the ancients enjoyed from these hilltops.

When you come back down from the tower, take a left at the T intersection. The trail loops around to another T intersection. Turn right to follow a long boardwalk over a mangrove swamp. The smell of salt permeates the air. A kingfisher swoops low to scan for fish, while a young alligator noses into a small cove. Alligators aren't picky: You'll find them in brackish lagoons and estuaries as well as their usual freshwater habitats. The boardwalk ends at 1.8 miles at a T intersection with the limestone path. Turn left to walk the North Restoration Area Trail. This footpath twists and turns along the edge of the mangroves before turning right to enter a cabbage palm hammock dense with marsh ferns. As the trail swings out toward the road, you can see your car at the temple mound parking area. The trail then turns away from the road to wind its way past more wetlands. At the next T intersection, you have a decision. If you turn right, you can walk directly to your car and complete a 2.2-mile walk. If you turn left, you'll continue along the North Restoration Area loop.

Taking the left to extend your walk, you enter an oak hammock with a bench in the shade of a water oak. At the fork, keep left. Emerging into the open, the trail passes through a vast meadow along a mangrove-lined canal, where giant leather ferns grow in large clusters. Passing the other trailhead for the Terra Ceia Trail at 2.3 miles (which gives you an option to loop back around to the observation tower again by walking north along the bay), you come up to a bench flanked by ferns. The limestone path continues its curve to the right, doubling back on its route past the entrance gate to meet itself at a T intersection after 2.5 miles. Turn left to walk back through the oak hammock and past the incoming trail around the wetland. The trail curves past a strangler fig wrapped around a pipe encased in tabby (a concretelike mix of oyster shells and lime), part of the old pioneer homestead. Crossing the park road, the limestone path skirts one more duckweed-covered pond on the left before returning to the parking lot at the Portavant Temple Mound, completing the 2.7-mile circuit.

2

Oscar Scherer State Park

Total distance (two circuits, one round trip): 11.6 miles

Hiking time: 5 hours

Habitats: Scrubby flatwoods, pine flatwoods, oak scrub, freshwater marsh, hardwood hammock, oak hammock

Maps: USGS 7½' Laurel; park map

Flitting back and forth between the scrub oaks, they're a blur of blue until you get up close and they stop, curious as to your approach. It's a family of Florida scrub-jays, busy at work gathering acorns and nesting material, content in their scrubby flatwoods habitat not far from the hustle and bustle of Sarasota. With more than 1,300 acres of land, Oscar Scherer State Park preserves a crucial chunk of scrub and scrubby flatwoods in the midst of burgeoning Gulf Coast development. Opened in 1956, the original 462 acres were a gift bequeathed by Elsa Scherer Burrows as a park in memory of her father, Oscar. In 1872, inventor Oscar Scherer devised a process to dye shoe leather, sending ripples through the fashion world of that day. Today, the Scherer family gift makes a big difference in the preservation of the threatened Florida scrub-jay on this coast, as scrub lands continue to turn into housing developments. The scrub-jay population at Oscar Scherer State Park is one of the largest concentrations in South Florida, with 27 family units counted in 2002, with two to six members per family.

From I-75 heading northbound, take exit 195, Nokomis/Laurel, and follow Laurel Road west 3.2 miles to US 41. Turn right and head north 2.5 miles into Osprey. The park entrance is on the right just after you cross South Creek. If you're driving south on I-75, take exit 200, Venice/Osprey. Continue 3.8 miles west on FL 681 to US 41. Drive north on US 41 for 1.7 miles; the park entrance is on the right.

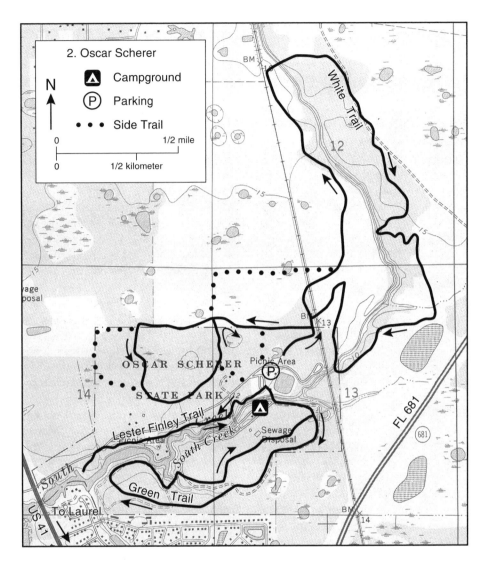

Two separate trail systems run through the park: one on the north side of the entrance road, through prime scrub-jay habitat, and the other on the south side, along South Creek. Because long segments of each trail system run through scrubby flatwoods with limited shade, you may want to break up your hiking into two separate days with early-morning starts, when the scrub-jays are most active. Take advantage of the park's campground and facilities for swimming, picnicking, and canoe or kayak rentals for lazy afternoons after each hike. This is a dog-friendly park: Leashed pets are permitted on the trail system.

DAY ONE: NORTH TRAIL SYSTEM (6.9 MILES)

As you continue down the park entrance road past the South Creek Picnic Area, the road passes the campground entrance at 0.9 mile and then splits in two at the Osprey Lake parking area. Off to the right lies parking for the nature center and picnic area; the hiking trails and swimming area are accessed from the left. Drive down the left side and park at the end to access the White Loop trailhead. Several interconnected color-coded loops make up the trails on the north end of the park, all of which are open to bikers as well as hikers. This hike route follows the most popular loop, the 5-mile White Trail, with a side trip into the pine flatwoods along the Blue and Red Trails.

Start your hike at the trail kiosk across the parking lot from the rest rooms. Interpretive information at the kiosk fills you in on the Florida scrub-jay, one of Florida's most threatened species. Living only in scrub habitats in the Florida peninsula, the Florida scrub-jay is found nowhere else on earth. The trail begins by traversing the scrub-jay's favored environment, an oak scrub with trees rising less than 10 feet tall, many decked out in vines dripping with the bright pink blooms of butterfly pea. Bright white sand characterizes the forest floor, where scrub-jays dig holes to create caches of acorns, a behavior much like that of squirrels. Each bird will use a leaf or twig marker as a clue to where the cache is buried. As you walk along, listen for the chatter of the scrub-jays in the trees. Look up to catch a glimpse of a bright blue sentinel in the high branches of a slash pine, waiting to sound an alarm if you draw too close to its food-gathering relations.

Gopher apple grows densely along the edges of the footpath, its fruits a favored food of the gopher tortoises that also inhabit this desertlike environment. As you wander through the maze of small myrtle oaks, Chapman oaks, and sand live oaks, follow the well-worn path and keep watch for small directional arrows at all questionable turns. For most of the length of the route, these arrows help keep you on the correct path. Emerging into an open area undergoing restoration to scrub habitat, you pass by clusters of golden aster, its long, slender silvery green stems topped with small yellow blossoms. When you reach the fence line, turn left and follow the footpath up to a fork, the intersection with the Blue Trail. You'll explore that route later. For now, keep to the right. At each subsequent fork, stay to the right and follow the fence line. The slim purple blooms of blazing star bob in the breeze.

At 0.4 mile, you come to a grade that runs perpendicular to the fence line. Turn right and walk around the gate to carefully cross the railroad tracks. Just beyond the gate on the left is a stone memorial declaring this area the MARY THAXTON MEMORIAL PRESERVE. Her efforts toward scrub-jay preservation led to additional acquisitions of land to expand the original park boundaries. This is the first of many benches along the trail. Take a closer look at the plaque on the seat, as it gives a bench number and the phone number of the ranger station in case you need assistance. You'll see this repeated throughout the park—they don't want anyone getting lost. Crossing a trail junction, continue straight, walking between the tall slash pines. The low oaks on the right are home to a family of Florida scrub-jays, squawking and fussing at your approach. Each family includes the breeding pair, mated for life, and several helper birds—offspring that delay their own breeding to help raise their parents' next generation of three or four hatchlings each year. Families defend a 25-acre territory, passing the land down from generation to generation.

Trail markers now include white-tipped posts as well as the small white arrow signs. Reaching the next fork, turn left. The bright purple berries of American beautyberry lend a splash of color against the backdrop of saw palmetto. Given the dense grass covering the forest floor, these scrubby flatwoods provided rangeland for cattle in the not-too-distant past. After 1 mile, the trail reaches scattered clumps of oaks and makes a sharp turn to the left. Follow the narrow track through the grass. Passing Bench 2, the trail continues from oak hammock to oak hammock. Watch for directional arrows and white blazes on the trees through this parklike setting. Turning right, you walk through a patch of casearweed and into a shady hammock with Christmas berry growing under live oaks and water oaks. Just past Bench 3, a firebreak takes off to the right. Continue on the narrower track to the left. After winding through several more oak hammocks, the trail emerges at Bench 4, where a six-lined racerunner dashes across a bridge that spans a small blackwater creek choked with water hyacinths. You've hiked 1.6 miles. After crossing the bridge, the trail curves to the right and enters pine flatwoods. Pine needles carpet the footpath, and the understory of saw palmetto stretches off into the distance. Reaching a T intersection at Bench 4A, make a right onto the jeep road. An extraordinarily stinky columned stinkhorn mushroom pokes like a finger out of the earth.

At 2.2 miles, you reach a fork. Keep to the left. Broad slash pines tower around you, sunlight illuminating every needle. Long streamers of Spanish moss dangle from high limbs. At the next fork, stay right. Blueberry bushes crowd around the bases of the pines, along with narrow-leaved sabatia and golden aster. Passing Bench 5, the trail leaves the jeep track and turns to the right into denser forest, with sand live oaks interspersed amid the pines yielding to a dense hammock of cabbage palms, many bedecked with goldfoot and shoelace fern. Watch out for deep ruts created by feral hogs rooting through the forest. Zigzagging through the palms, the trail plays hide-and-seek with a small creek, eventually turning away from it and back into the pines. Coming to a T with a jeep road at 3 miles, turn right and pass Bench 5A. Notice the deep gouges in the trunks of some of the oldest trees—catfaces, created when the pines were tapped for turpentine.

As you pass Bench 6, continue straight through the pine flatwoods until you reach a directional arrow where the trail turns right. Crossing a narrow bridge over a seasonally dry creek, you reach Bench 7. Follow the faint track through the grass toward a large cattail-ringed pond at 3.4 miles. An osprey cries as it wheels overhead, scanning the dark waters for bass. At the T intersection, turn right. The trail continues through the slash pines and past a moss-draped snag where redheaded woodpeckers have taken up residence. Sandhill wireweed pokes out from the grassy understory. You enter another shadeless scrub restoration area, where the trail keeps to the edge of the regenerating forest. When you reach the next T intersection at 3.8 miles, turn right, following the footpath back up the other side of the restoration area before it ducks left into the cool shade of an oak hammock to cross a footbridge over a broad tannic stream. Passing the next bench, you continue across a broad open "meadow" dominated by slash pines. Scrub plants attempt to retake their rightful place in the

Pine flatwoods

habitat. Turning right off the well-trammeled path at the T intersection, make an immediate left just beyond the back side of a RESTORATION IN PROGRESS sign, completing the loop portion of the White Trail after 4.2 miles. Stay to the left at the junction to exit the loop. You're back in the busy flyway of a Florida scrub-jay family. When one finally lands within sight, you're amazed at its size and bright coloration. Larger than an American robin, the mature scrub-jay is decked out in bright blue feathers and cocks its head in a parrotlike manner. Young scrub-jays start out with brownish white plumage that turns to grayish blue and finally the bright blue of the adults. There is no easy way to tell males from females, since their size and coloration are the same.

After you cross the railroad tracks, turn left to follow the trail down the fence line to its intersection with the Blue Trail at 4.5 miles. Here's your decision point. You can explore more scrub-jay habitat and some very pretty pine flatwoods by taking the Blue Trail to the right, or can call it quits for this side of the park by continuing straight ahead to complete the White Trail. For further exploration, turn right. Five scrub-jays wheel overhead as you walk through another shadeless scrub restoration area. Reaching Bench 9, you come to a T intersection with the Black, Yellow, and Red Trails. Turn right, walking through the expansive flatwoods to the next junction at Bench 12. Here, the Blue Trail takes off to the right along the park boundary fence. Continue straight, walking down the broad path along the boundary fence until you reach Bench 12A and the turnoff for the Red Trail at 5.2 miles. Taking this interior loop gets you away from the view of development encroaching on the park and into the beauty of these high and dry pine flatwoods. Saw palmetto fills the understory beneath the towering slash pines. You pass a trail on the left. At the next junction, make a left to stay on the combined Red and Black Trails. Off to the right, a section of low scrub lies beyond the scrubby edge of the flatwoods. Prickly pear cactus grows near the trail. The trail turns left at a T intersection; a few house trailers hide in the woods to the right. Watch for a large gopher tortoise burrow on the left, and a trap hidden in the saw palmetto to catch feral hogs.

You return to Bench 12B after 6.1 miles. Turn right and retrace your path to Bench 9. Although you could turn right and emerge at the upper end of the Osprey Lake parking area, your most scenic route is to head back down the Blue Trail through the scrub. Continue straight. When you return to the junction with the White Trail, turn right. As you head down the fence line, keep alert for a side trail to the right where footprints and bicycle tracks lead you out into the scrub. No sign designates this last turnoff to the parking lot, so if you go too far along the fence line and end up at the Youth Group Camp area, turn around and look for the side trail. Returning to the kiosk at the parking area, you've hiked 6.9 miles.

DAY TWO: GREEN LOOP, SOUTH CREEK TRAIL, AND LESTER FINLEY TRAIL (4.7 MILES)

Two separate hikes make up the South Trail System, both accessed from the nature center parking area at Osprey Lake. Dedicated in January 2002, the nature center features exhibits on the scrubby flatwoods environment and its creatures, including the Florida scrub-jay and the gopher tortoise. Pop in today to take a look at the exhibits before you hit the trails.

Green Loop

The Green Trail runs nearly 3 miles through prime scrub-jay habitat. Start your hike either from within the campground (if you're camping) at site 17, or from the TRAILHEAD sign behind the nature center, crossing the bridge over South Creek. When you reach the campground road, turn left at the CAMPSITES 17–20 sign, passing the campground host site. Stay on the road as it leaves the campground and enters an open oak scrub. At the fork, keep right. A post with red and green lines confirms your choice. Yellow buttons and butterfly pea add splashes of color to the roadside. At the T intersection, turn right, walking around the gate to continue down the forest road. Passing a trail on the right, you see a confirmation marker as you walk through the scrub oaks, alert as a flash of blue zips over your head. Bikers share this loop, so keep watchful for them coming around the bends.

Keep to the right at the next fork as you pass Bench 13. Slash pines tower overhead, some showing catfaces from the turpentine days—the deep scars made by a woodman's ax as he exposed the inner bark of the tree so it would drip sticky sap into a turpentine-collecting cup. A quail darts out into the path and runs down it before diving into the little bluestem grass. When you reach a crossroads of trails at 0.5 mile, continue straight. A barred owl glides noiselessly from the top of a slash pine toward its distant aerie. Painted blazes confirm your route. Reaching the southern boundary of the park, you start to see the roofs of houses on the left as the trail curves right. At 0.8 mile, you reach a junction. The shorter Red Trail continues straight. Turn left to follow the Green Trail, passing by Bench 14. Dropping in and out of a small drainage, you rise up into a sea of young oaks where scrub-jays are busy on the ground, collecting acorns. A sentinel regards you from its high perch on a slash pine limb. Approaching the park boundary fence, the trail makes a sharp curve to the right, where inkberry and narrow leaved pawpaw grow in the thicket of saw palmetto. When you reach another crossroads of trails at 1.1 miles, continue straight. The pine woods become denser, providing snippets of shade. Aromatic pennyroyal grows in large rounded mounds covered in delicate pinkish purple flowers. At the fork, stay right. The trail curves sharply to the right through tall yellow goldenrod, wax myrtle, and young saw palmetto growing back after a controlled burn. A rabbit slips across the path.

When you come to the T intersection at Bench 16, you've hiked 1.4 miles. Turn right to start the return trip on the loop, wading through an overgrown area of tall daisies and rattleboxes. The trail dips in and out of the shade as it follows the edge of an oak hammock, the oaks likely planted to define the edge of a farmer's field. Throughout the woods are grand old slash pines with extremely thick trunks. Although they're missing many lower branches, their upper branches form broad canopies. At 1.7 miles, a trail joins in from the right. Continue to the left and down through a drainage area, where pools of tannic water sit under the shade of cabbage palms. Giant leather ferns rise from the water's depths. The trail reaches a T intersection, and you see what looks like a campground road off to the left. Turn right at the TRAILHEAD 0.9 MILES sign, following the green arrow. Emerging into the shadeless and open scrubby flatwoods, the trail meanders through patches of little bluestem and purple lovegrass.

After 2 miles, the trail forks again. Take the sharp left, which wanders on into a patch of bright white sand. As the trail curves around into the shade of tall slash pines, you get a great view off to the right of the pines rising from an unbroken sea of saw palmettos, the pine needles glistening in the morning sun. A cool breeze ruffles the palmetto fronds. Blazing star and sandhill wireweed poke out along the footpath. Continue straight through the crossroad at 2.3 miles, as the trail climbs up into a patch of blindingly bright white sand surrounded by young Chapman oaks. It's a beautiful spot, with the saw palmettos blanketing the understory, the oaks adding a middle story, and the slash pines towering above, reaching for the sky.

You complete the loop at 2.5 miles when you reach a T intersection with the incoming trail, in sight of the gate. Turn left and walk around the gate, then turn left again. Follow the road back into the campground. When you see the ONE WAY sign, turn to the right and walk across the bridge, back to the nature center, ending the 2.8-mile hike.

South Creek and Lester Finley Trails
These are the only trails in Oscar Scherer State Park designated FOOT TRAFFIC ONLY, and the only trails that stay almost completely in the shade. If your time at the park is limited, these are the trails you'll want to hike. From the parking lot, walk past Shelter 2 and down through the picnic area toward the creek to find the trailhead sign SOUTH CREEK NATURE TRAIL. Continue down the narrow footpath along South Creek, a sluggish blackwater stream well shaded by sand live oaks, slash pines, and cabbage palms. A carpet of pine needles underfoot puts a spring in your step. Coming up to a set of baffles, cross the campground road and continue into the woods on other side. Coontie peeks out from beneath saw palmetto leaves. The trail winds through a corridor of saw palmetto, with red blanket lichen and sphagnum moss carpeting the overhanging sand live oak limbs. Occasional interpretive signs add to your knowledge of the ecosystem.

American beautyberry crowds the trail as you emerge into scrubby flatwoods, with Chapman oaks sticking up out of saw palmetto and silk bay growing along the trail's edge. On the other side of the creek you can see the prime campsites, along the water. Walking past Spanish bayonet under an arbor of cabbage palms, you draw close to the edge of the creek. An island in the stream features giant leather ferns growing out of a sea of black needlerush, belying brackishness to the water. You can see a pier up ahead on this side of the creek. Watch for low overhanging limbs as you continue along the trail. After 0.4 mile, you reach an observation platform on the water's edge. In the warmer months, watch for manatees browsing through the shallows as they make their way upstream from the Gulf of Mexico, just a few miles west of here.

When the trail forks, keep right, staying on the broad path between the cabbage palms as you pass a tall coral bean. The trail follows a natural levee created by seasonal flooding of South Creek. Moss-draped sand live oaks shade the path as you cross a bridge into the South Creek Picnic Area. The trail ends after 0.5 mile at the picnic area. Continue past the rest rooms down toward the canoe launch and turn right. Make a left to walk through the picnic area along the creek to the start of the Lester Finley Trail; its trailhead kiosk is at the far end of the parking lot.

Designated a barrier-free trail, the Lester Finley Trail has a hard-packed shell-and-clay surface and is edged with landscape timbers.

Laminated trail guides in a box at the trailhead help with plant identification along the way, keyed to numbered posts. A stretch of landscape stone helps prevent erosion. The trail offers beautiful views of South Creek while staying in the shade. You start to see white mangroves along the shoreline, attesting to the increasing salinity of the creek. Pause and enjoy the view from the bench at 0.7 mile. Moments later, you come up to a fishing pier and observation deck fringed with white mangroves. Notice the "ranger-in-a-box"? Press a button on the little box and you'll get an interpretive talk about this particular spot on the trail, as if you were on a ranger-led walk. Marsh ferns cluster under the saw palmettos as you zigzag past marker 6. There is no lack of benches along this trail as you continue down over a short boardwalk crossing a wet area.

Passing a native plant garden, you continue along the creek and cross a bridge over a sluggish side channel with an imperceptible flow. The trail curves to the left to rejoin the creek's edge, coming up to a water fountain in front of a bench. At the next bench, defining a fork, take a left. A baby brown anole perches on marker 11. As you emerge from the shade of the cabbage palms, you glimpse sea oxeye growing in front of a stand of buttonwoods. South Creek sparkles in the sunshine, a stretch of blue water headed toward the sea. When you return to the forked bench,

you've hiked a mile. Continue straight. You'll now be retracing your path all the way along the creek to the nature center. As you come back up toward the bridge, notice the trail that goes to left at the FVA (Florida Volkswalkers Association) sign; stay to the right and cross the bridge. Thick growths of wild pine, Spanish moss, and ball moss coat the trees; look down and you can see giant bromeliads dangling scarcely inches above the water on low-hanging limbs.

When you return to the beginning of the Lester Finley Trail, turn right and walk down through the picnic area back toward the rest rooms. Don't miss the SOUTH CREEK NATURE TRAIL sign on the other side at 1.4 miles, as that's the trail you need to take back to your car. Cross the bridge and continue upstream along South Creek. At the T intersection at the pier, turn left to follow the trail. Cross the campground road at 1.8 miles, and a few moments later you emerge at the Osprey Lake Picnic Area. Walk across the picnic area to the parking lot, completing a 1.9-mile hike.

You can also access both of these linear trails from the South Creek Picnic Area parking lot, just 0.4 mile up the park entrance road from the ranger station. If you want to explore South Creek by water, the canoes and kayaks at the picnic area are available for rent through the ranger station.

3

Myakka River State Park

Total distance (circuit): 20.1 miles

Hiking time: 2 days, 2 hours

Habitats: Cabbage palm flatwoods, freshwater marsh, floodplain forest, oak hammock, palm hammock, pine flatwoods, prairie, scrubby flatwoods

Maps: USGS 7½' Old Myakka, Lower Myakka Lake, Myakka City, Murdock; park map; Florida Trail Association map SF-4

As one of Florida's oldest and largest state parks, Myakka River State Park provides hikers with the best backpacking experience in Southwest Florida. Established in 1934, Myakka hosted one of several Civilian Conservation Corps headquarters around the state; work crews fanned out from here to build bridges, cut trails, and plant trees. Encompassing more than 28,000 acres, the park protects a significant chunk of one of Florida's imperiled habitats—the prairie. Once stretching from sea to sea in a wide belt north of Lake Okeechobee, Florida's prairies didn't appeal to the first pioneers on the frontier: With thousands of saw palmettos impeding progress, these broad dry grasslands seemed useless, so much so that a land surveyor in the 1840s gave up on his task, complaining, "This land in its entirety is so valueless that I did not warrant putting the government to further expense." Yet this mix of sedges and grasses hosts a wealth of wildflowers and wildlife, from colorful pine lilies to the endangered Florida grasshopper sparrow. Value is in the eyes of the beholder. And as you hike at Myakka River State Park, you'll come to know the value of the prairie.

To reach Myakka River State Park, use I-75 exit 205. Follow FL 72 east for 9 miles to the park entrance on the left. Stop at the ranger station to pay your Florida State Parks entrance fee, and ask for a map of the hiking trails. For a sample of what the backpacking loop at Myakka has to offer to hikers, stop at the Canopy Walk, just after

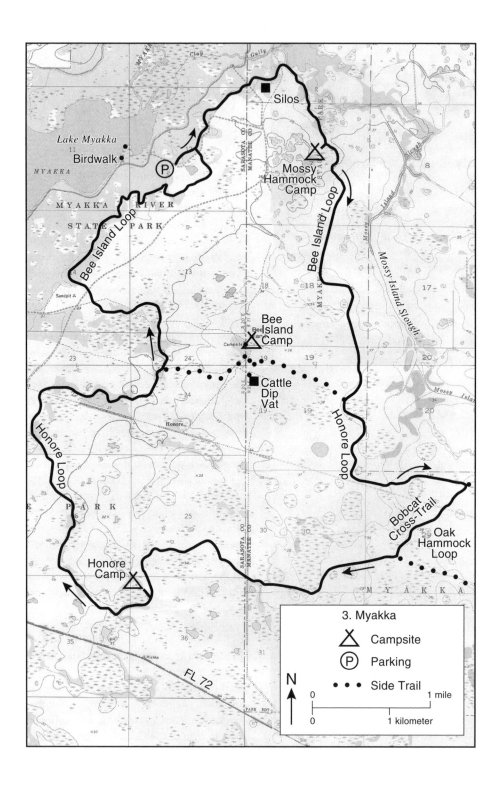

Lake Myakka
11
Birdwalk

MYAKKA
RIVER

MYAKKA
STATE PARK

Silos

Mossy
Hammock
Camp

Bee Island Loop

Bee Island Loop

Mossy Island Slough

Bee
Island
Camp

Cattle
Dip
Vat

Honore Loop

Honore Loop

Honore
Camp

Bobcat
Cross-Trail

Oak
Hammock
Loop

MYAKKA

SARASOTA CO
MANATEE CO

PARK

FL 72

3. Myakka

△ Campsite

Ⓟ Parking

••• Side Trail

N

0 — 1 mile

0 — 1 kilometer

the bridge over the Myakka River, on the right. This unique nature trail provides a 0.9-mile loop through a mosaic of prairies, wetlands, and oak hammocks, with a spur trail leading to the Canopy Walk itself—a swinging bridge suspended 40 feet in the air, enabling visitors to get an up-close look at the live oak hammock canopy. At the end of the bridge, climb the 72-foot-tall tower for a bird's-eye view of the Myakka River and its habitats. Along the loop portion of the trail, you'll enjoy bird-watching from the boardwalks that connect the hammocks together. Whenever the Myakka River floods, the trail vanishes beneath its dark waters.

After 2.9 miles from the park entrance, the park road reaches a fork. The left fork dead-ends at the Myakka Outpost, one of the most popular destinations in the park, where you can hop aboard a multipassenger modified airboat for a one-hour ecotour along the Myakka River. Tours run four times daily, with the last tour at 2:30 PM. Rent bikes, kayaks, and canoes here to explore the park, and stop in and browse the gift shop, with its array of field guides and historical books. The adjoining concession stand offers Florida "Cracker" specialties such as 'gator stew and orange sunshine cake.

Keep to the right at the fork to continue along the main park road, where you drive beneath the canopy of oaks along the shores of Little Myakka Lake, a broad expanse of the Myakka River. At 4.6 miles, watch for the sign for the Bird Walk, a pleasant boardwalk stretching 0.2 mile out into the waters of Little Myakka Lake. With two observation platforms, it offers bird-watchers great opportunities for spotting Louisiana herons, anhinga, and the many other wading birds that inhabit the marshes.

After 4.9 miles on the park road, you reach the gate for the Myakka Hiking Trail on the right. Use the combination given to you by the ranger to unlock the gate, and lock it behind you. Drive another 0.2 mile to the parking area, taking care to watch out for day hikers and bikers sharing the road.

MYAKKA HIKING TRAIL

Extensive and well maintained: That's the Myakka Hiking Trail. Designed and maintained by the Suncoast Chapter of the Florida Trail Association, the trail system contains nearly 39 miles of trail broken into four loops, enabling you to plan numerous route options, from a lengthy day hike on the Bee Island Loop to a four-day experience exploring all four loops. This narrative outlines a good weekend trip for backpackers who want to enjoy the park's various habitats. It jump-starts your trip with a short Friday-evening hike of 2.5 miles to the Mossy Hammock Campsite. Alternatively, you can start early Saturday morning (the park opens at 8 AM) and backpack the full 11.3 miles to the Honore Campsite. If you're more of a camper than a backpacker, you'll prefer taking the Bee Island Loop (a subset of this hike) to Bee Island, one of the most beautiful campsites in the park. Before starting out on any trip, check with the park rangers regarding conditions at the campsites, since both Mossy Hammock and Honore are prone to flooding during the wet season and after heavy rains.

Day One: Trailhead to Mossy Hammock (2.5 miles; 1.5 hours)

From the parking area, the trail system starts at the FT sign. Winding through a hammock of ancient live oaks, a blue-blazed trail leads you to the main loop. Live oak limbs draped in resurrection fern arch overhead, providing deep shade. You hear a shuffling sound emerging from the saw palmetto—one of the hundreds of resident armadillos rooting through the rich black soil for grubs. Skirting a floodplain forest, the blue-blazed trail ends at the main orange-blazed loop after 0.3 mile. A directional sign at the trail junction gives mileages to the various campsites. Turn left to hike to Mossy Hammock.

A corridor of saw palmetto defines the trail through the hammock. Around you, epiphytes thrive. Shoelace fern and goldfoot fern cascade out of the bootjacks of cabbage palms, while rampant growths of wild pine clamber up vines, sprout from tree trunks, and peer over oak limbs. Constant humidity makes the forest lush and green. As the habitat transitions into a palm hammock, the footpath gets mushy as it circles a willow marsh.

After 0.5 mile, you see a hard-packed limestone road paralleling the trail on the right. Around each corner, you encounter new habitats. From dense hardwood hammocks, you see marshlands. Scrubby flatwoods give way to hammocks of bluejack oaks. After 1.1 miles, you cross Fox's High Road, a popular bicycling route. Bicycles are permitted on all the old roads crisscrossing the park but are not allowed on the hiking trail. If you need to exit the trail system in a hurry, you can also use the roads as a high and dry route to get back out to the main park road—pick up a "Hiking and Biking" brochure at the ranger station for details on the road system.

Deep in an oak hammock, several round structures invite inspection—the foundations of silos from the former ranch that occupied this land. Remnants of that era are sprinkled throughout the prairies and hammocks, from the remains of the old ranch house to cattle dip vats used for removing ticks from cattle. Cows were led into the dip and immersed into a solution of pine tar, sodium carbonate, and arsenic trioxide to prevent tick fever. From 1906 to 1961, the federal government mandated treatments for all cattle shipped out of Florida. Arsenic contaminates the ground around the old vats.

Not far beyond the silos, you catch a whiff of sulfur in the air. Look under the marsh ferns and cinnamon ferns in the bog on the right and you'll see the white stringers of bacteria indicating the presence of a sulfur spring. After making a sharp turn to the right and climbing up a small rise, the trail swings right to follow Mossy Island Slough, a sluggish blackwater stream with high banks. In the wet season, it overflows across vast stretches of the trail. Rounding a bend in the creek, you walk beneath a junglelike canopy of ferns and air plants blanketing the live oak limbs.

After 2.4 miles, you catch your first glimpse of the vast prairies that Myakka River State Park preserves. Home to many unique creatures, including the burrowing owl and Bachman's sparrow, these dry expanses of grass and palmetto require frequent fires to rejuvenate the land. Myakka's grassy prairies, once used as cattle grazing land, nearly vanished under an onslaught of tall shrubs and palmettos. After years of carefully preventing forest fires, park managers realized that fire was necessary to maintain the habitat. Prairie restoration efforts began in the 1980s. As you will see from this and other vistas, the prairies rebounded.

Immediately after crossing a road that leads out into the prairie, you reach the sign for the Mossy Hammock Campsite. Turn right and step across a small stream. Follow the blue blazes down to the campsite,

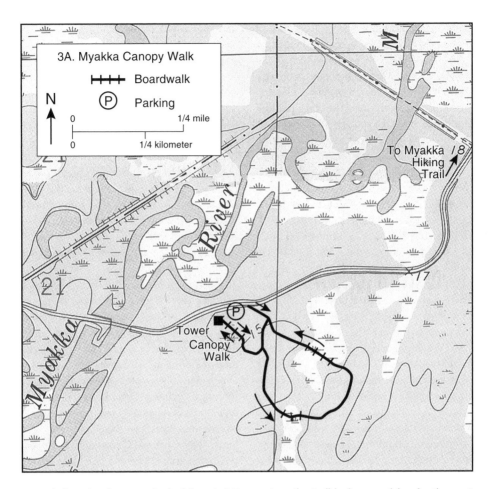

completing the first evening's hike at 2.5 miles. Tucked under the boughs of grand old live oaks on the edge of the prairie, Mossy Hammock provides a shady place to set up camp. Campers gather on the logs around the two fire rings and make use of the pitcher pump. Prime the pump by using one of the water jugs left at its base, and make sure you top it off after you use it. Because of the age of the pitcher pumps, the water may suffer from a rusty taste. Be absolutely certain to boil, filter, or chemically treat the water before drinking it. Use crumbled vitamin C or powdered drink mix to spruce up the taste. Enjoy a good first night

out on the trail before readying for the next morning's hike.

Day Two: Mossy Hammock to Honore (8.8 miles; 5 hours)

From your campsite, return along the blue-blazed side trail to the main orange-blazed loop and turn right, following the line of oak trees out into the open prairie. Spiky torpedo grass towers over your head, casting shadows on the orange-hued bushybeard bluestem grass. Frogs croak in a distant marsh. Off to the left, a vast sea of saw palmetto stretches into the distance—the palmetto prairie, once the most

---

common habitat blanketing this part of Florida. As difficult as the pioneers found it to traverse, you can be thankful that the trail builders at Myakka worked hard to remove the rugged stems of saw palmettos from the footpath. Wind rustles through the layers of grass, painting brushstrokes that reveal their unique textures. Walking out into the wide-open prairie, you follow the narrow trail between the orange-tipped fence posts. Keep alert for directional changes at the first few posts. Enveloped by the vast prairie, you experience a sense of awe. The arc of grasslands flows away in every direction; pine trees in the distance seem miles away. And they are.

At 0.8 mile, you cross a jeep road. Continue straight across to stay on the trail. Fluttering their yellow-tinged wings, palm warblers flit across the trail as you continue through the seemingly endless open expanse. After 1.2 miles, you reach the next jeep road. Continue straight. Pause every once in a while to look behind you and absorb the colorful spectacle of this immense prairie. In fall, you'll see a riot of wildflowers: bright orange pine lilies peeping up from damp spots, tall purple deer's tongues and blazing stars rising above the grasses, golden and white asters adding their spots of color. A lone tree stands along the trail at 1.9 miles, and on it, the first orange blaze you've seen in a while—a reassurance that you're still on the right trail. Winding its way toward the distant line of trees, the trail passes an indiscernible large white sign on the left as you cross over another jeep road at 2.3 miles. The tree line no longer seems so distant. Off to the right, power lines march across the far horizon.

After 2.5 miles, you cross another road and reach the far shore of the prairie. Look behind you for a rare Florida sight: You can see the last 2 miles of trail. Crossing a bridge over a small tannic drainage that cascades out to the prairie, you enter a thin sliver of oak hammock between two prairies. Cinnamon ferns thrive in the damp understory. From the grassy corridor under the oaks, you can look out across more of the prairie you just traversed. The junction with the Bee Island Cross Trail is at 2.8 miles. If you're opting for the shorter backpacking trip, turn right and follow the blue blazes for another 1.1 miles, turning right at the T junction to reach the campsite. Set on a high and dry hammock, the campsites at Bee Island command beautiful views of the prairie.

If you're hiking the full Honore Loop and camping at Honore Campsite, continue straight at the trail junction. Yellow canna and patches of lance-leaved arrowroot flank the trail as it winds through a wet area bounded by a ghostly forest of oak snags. Two black vultures look down from their appropriately dead perch. Emerging onto the prairie again, you cross a road, which then parallels the trail along the fence line on the left. Occasional blazes on posts and scattered trees define the route. As the trail rounds a large marsh at 3.6 miles, watch for the constant activity of birds. A swirling cloud of swifts rises from the willows like bees disturbed from their hive. Now paralleling a broad limestone road, the trail continues its eastward trek to a distant oak and palm hammock, where it crosses a bridge. Passing a sign that confirms your choice of direction (*toward the Bobcat Cross Trail*), you emerge into a scrubby prairie, where gallberry competes with saw palmetto for control of the understory.

At 4.8 miles, keep alert for the BOBCAT CROSS TRAIL sign. The orange-blazed trail in front of you continues along the outer

Open prairie

edge of the four loops, headed for the Oak Grove Campsite. The Bobcat Cross Trail forms the eastern edge of the Honore Loop. Turn right and head out across the prairie. Following the blue blazes, you reach two bridges flanking the central Old Railroad Grade, another popular biking route, at 5.1 miles. As you walk under the oaks and pines, the habitat yields to a swampy palm hammock lining a vast wetland. Its glossy skin shimmering in the sunlight, a six-lined racerunner scampers up a palm trunk.

After 5.7 miles, you reach a T intersection with the main trail. Turn right, following the trail through several wet palm hammocks. Rising up toward a stand of pines, the trail makes a beeline for the open prairie. When you cross the next jeep road, you've hiked 6 miles. Narrowing down to a slim corridor between the saw palmettos, the trail rises up into pine flatwoods, making a turn to the left to point at the power lines. Two red-bellied woodpeckers perch on the low branch of a slash pine. At 7.2 miles, you walk under the crackling high-tension wires to continue along the trail at the MYAKKA HIKING TRAIL sign. A marsh spills out over the trail, where hatpins and St.-John's-wort flourish in the dampness. Continue through the palmetto prairie, heading in the direction of another distant set of power lines. The line of pines you've been pointed toward for the past hour finally comes within reach at 7.7 miles. Take in the vastness of the palmetto prairie to the right as you walk into a hammock of oaks and cabbage palms. Stands of sand cordgrass ring a willow marsh as you emerge from the hammock and back into the prairie. After 8.7 miles, you come to the sign for the Honore Campsite. Turn right and walk down the edge of the marsh to the campsite, arriving at the water pump

after 8.8 miles. Carved into the underbrush of a palm hammock, the Honore Campsite features three separate patches of grass with fire rings, each tucked into its own niche along the trail. The one closest to the water pump has the most space for tents. Be cautious of ant nests around the logs by the fire rings, and keep alert for poison ivy when you slip off into the woods to "use the facilities."

Day Three: Honore to Trailhead (8.8 miles; 5 hours)

As you leave the Honore Campsite, make sure the priming bottles at the pump are topped off before you head down the blue-blazed corridor to the main trail. Turn right at the T intersection, following the orange blazes as the trail curves right into a series of palm hammocks edged by marshes. Flapping its broad wings, a Louisiana heron rises from the tall grass. You see hatpins, yellow star grass, and large wild bachelor's buttons growing in the damp areas. At 0.5 mile, you pass a double blaze. Soon after, the trail turns sharply right to cross an overflowing marsh, where tadpoles dart around your feet as you wade. A sea of saw palmetto sweeps around you as the trail rises to slightly higher ground. Crossing two jeep roads in quick succession, the trail enters a dense hammock of young oaks shaded by a canopy of slash pines, then continues into a swampy palm hammock, heavily rooted up by feral hogs. Raccoons use the trail as their superhighway; you see their tracks everywhere in the soft mud. Beyond a narrow slough, the trail reaches a tannic but clear sand-bottomed stream and turns left to parallel its course, following the ecotone between the cool hammock and the open palmetto prairie.

A red-shouldered hawk launches from

the top of a pine snag as you cross a jeep road at 1.1 miles. Off to the left is a strange-looking contraption: a hog trap, used to capture the feral hogs that decimate the natural landscape. Rounding a large marsh, the trail keeps to the line of oaks and pines along the prairie's edge. Squawking, a little blue heron rises up from the dark water. At 1.6 miles, the trail makes a sharp right away from the prairie into a shady palm hammock. Keep alert, as it's easy to lose the trail in the interplay of light and shadow, where drooping palm fronds hide the blazes and there is no distinct footpath. Emerging into the light, the trail turns left to head out into the scrubby prairie, where low bush blueberries crowd the edges of the trail. Draining pollywogs across your path, a marsh spills out over the trail at 2.1 miles. As you enter the cabbage palm flatwoods, golden aster raises its nodding heads to the sun. Deer's tongue and blazing star add splashes of purple to the fall extravaganza of color. Crossing a broad bridge and a fading jeep trail, you're back in the palmetto prairie. A bald eagle perches on the highest branch of a lone slash pine, surveying its territory as it grapples with its meal, a black racer. You enter another shady oak hammock, the oak branches thick with growths of wild pine and red blanket lichen. A broad bridge spans a swiftly moving tannic stream at 2.6 miles; beyond the bridge, look for the sign on the far right to find the trail. Keep alert for an abrupt right where the trail heads down a corridor of saw palmetto.

You reach the Old Railroad Grade, the park's most popular biking trail, after 3 miles. Passing under the power lines, the trail continues past a stand of saw palmetto with unusually long trunks lifting off the ground, starting into another corridor of oak hammocks bounded by the prairies. Making a sharp turn to the right, the trail parallels the power line. Thick growths of white lichen coat the trees along the marsh. Around 3.6 miles, the trail curves along the edge of an immense wetland where herons and egrets pick their way between the tufts of sand cordgrass. Turning left, the trail rises into a stand of tall pines and moss-draped oaks. Watch for the double blaze as the trail makes an abrupt left into the pine forest, following a stream. Enveloped in tufts of cardinal wild pine, a snag on the water's edge mimics a young longleaf pine. Continuing left, the trail emerges back onto the prairie and turns left to parallel the power line. Lovegrass forms a yellow mist between the saw palmettos. Dropping its lacy white blooms in the sticky mud, sea myrtle crowds the footpath. Walking past an orange blaze shimmering against the textures of a heavily worn snag, you come up to a slough draining into a large marsh on the left. Proceed through the shallows. Two white-tailed deer leap across the saw palmettos, their tails a blur of white as they retreat into the thickets.

At 4.6 miles, you reach the junction with the Bee Island Cross Trail, blazed in blue. If you've camped at Bee Island, this is where you join the main loop to return to the trailhead. Continue straight along the edge of the prairie, where you hear the mournful cries of sandhill cranes in the distance. Splashing across a drainage, you enter a thicket of saw palmetto under a canopy of sand live oak, then cross a large bridge over a blackwater stream before emerging back onto the prairie. When you cross the jeep trail, you've hiked 5 miles. Continuing down the corridor of saw palmetto, the trail enters an oak hammock and crosses another bridge. Keep to the left, as the footpath is indiscernible through the hammock, and the blazes pick up again as the trees close in. You emerge on the prairie edge into cabbage palm flatwoods. At 5.4 miles, a bridge spans a ditch, and the trail crosses over two small stone bridges flanking an old road. Leaving the hammock, you're surrounded by gallberry and sumac, sea myrtle and bushy bluestem grass, the trail a narrow swath through the tall brush. Beyond the next jeep trail, the trail crosses a bridge at 6 miles, meeting All Weather Road. Turn right and walk along the road, then left on the other side of the creek to continue along the orange blazes. Staying in the saw palmetto corridor, the trail twists and winds to follow the route of the creek, leading you into thickets of live oak draped in Spanish moss.

A barred owl glides silently overhead as you catch another glimpse of the prairie while walking through the parklike understory of this large oak hammock. Deer browse in the distance as you pass under the broad canopy of a grand old slash pine, its needles forming a soft carpet across the trail. Turning left, the trail noses out to the edge of the marshes. A draining swamp cascades down next to a natural archway of live oak. Double blazes lead you right and left through the hammock. For the next mile, the trail keeps to the shade of mature oak and palm hammocks while rounding numerous marshes; after a rain, the marshes will envelop the footpath. Tall alligator flag lends a clue as to the depth of the center of each marsh. After 7.4 miles, a double blaze leads to higher ground under the oaks. A giant wild pine perches in a low branch swathed in the fuzzy green of resurrection fern. You continue to circle a series of willow marshes, each adjoined by beautiful oak hammocks festooned with wild pine. After 7.9 miles, the trail turns left and emerges from the palm hammock onto the open prairie. Coming up to the edge of a pretty little tannic stream, the trail follows it upstream, crossing a bridge at 8.1 miles. Diverging from the stream, the trail turns left into a shady hammock. Beautiful bromeliads dangle overhead as you enter the next hammock just after crossing Fox's Low Road. Moments later, you reach the end of the loop at 8.5 miles. Turn left. Follow the blue blazes back out to the trailhead to complete today's 8.8-mile hike, ending your 20.1-mile circuit on the Myakka Hiking Trail.

4

Caspersen Beach Park

Total distance (round trip): 3.8 miles

Hiking time: 2 hours

Habitats: Coastal strand, mangrove forest, freshwater marsh, coastal hammock

Maps: USGS 7½' Venice; park map

Waterways and beaches are the lifeblood of Venice, a popular vacation destination south of Sarasota. Perched along the Gulf of Mexico, Venice features a long string of public beaches along the coast, ending at its southernmost tip with Caspersen Beach. In addition to more than a mile of unspoiled natural beachfront, Caspersen Beach Park provides an excellent spot for a moderate hike both on and off the beach. This is a popular weekend destination, but amazingly quiet on weekdays.

To find the park, take I-75 exit 193, Englewood/Venice, and follow Jacaranda Boulevard west for 0.7 mile to the stoplight with Venice Avenue. Turn right. After 3.7 miles, you cross US 41. Continue across the bridge and into downtown Venice, crossing Business US 41 as you enter the downtown shopping district. Stay in the left lane and turn left onto Harbor Drive North. Follow this road through the residential community and out past the airport. It passes several seaside parks before reaching a stretch just behind the dune line, ending after 3 miles at Caspersen Beach Park. Turn left into the first parking area and loop around past the rest rooms to park near the trailhead kiosk.

This hike consists of two parts: an easy stroll along the Caspersen Beach Nature Trail, followed by a walk down the beach. Take a look at the map and pick up an interpretive brochure. Starting off from the kiosk, you walk down a corridor shaded by tall cabbage palms draped with goldfoot ferns. In the shade, you'll see myrsine.

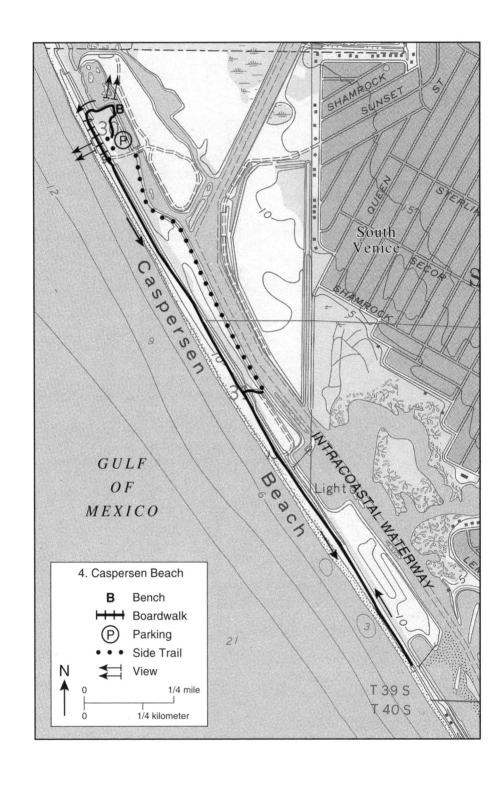

GULF
OF
MEXICO

South
Venice

SHAMROCK SUNSET ST

QUEEN

STERLIN

SECOR

SHAMROCK

INTRACOASTAL WATERWAY

Caspersen Beach

Light

4. Caspersen Beach

B   Bench
╪╪╪   Boardwalk
Ⓟ   Parking
• • •   Side Trail
⇄   View

N

0   1/4 mile

0   1/4 kilometer

T 39 S
T 40 S

Rounding a dense grove of cabbage palms, the trail parallels a freshwater marsh. A southern red cedar sprouts out of a tangle of sand live oak limbs. You smell the unmistakable skunklike odor of white stopper as you come up to a T intersection. Off to the left is a picnic area with barbecue grills. Turn right. Above you, woodpeckers have bored large holes in two cabbage palm trunks. Buttonwood shades a bridge over a mangrove-lined canal.

The trail makes a sharp left to follow an inlet. Painted leaf pokes up from a mat of thick grass, along with yellow fleabane. Mullet jump in the calm water. Mounds of lantana with yellow and pink blooms grow amid the mangroves next to young cabbage palms swaddled in Virginia creeper. As it comes up to a bench with a sweeping view of the waterway, the trail curves to the left, shaded by sea grapes. Take a moment to step out on the observation deck and survey the mangrove islands, where you might see an ibis or two poking between the tangles of roots. Watch for the pink flash of roseate spoonbills in the sky. The trail continues under a power line and over a bridge, climbing up into another grove of cabbage palms. When you reach the T intersection, turn right to emerge at the park entrance road. Cross the road over to the handicapped parking area and turn left.

A boardwalk runs south along the beachfront, protecting the fragile dune zone from trampling feet. It affords you a broad view of the busiest part of the beach, where swimmers frolic in the waves, sunbathers stretch out in the sand, and fossil collectors shuffle slowly through the blue-green water, tools in hand. If you noticed the symbol on the sign at the park entrance, you might know why—the beaches of Venice are a world-renowned collecting location for fossilized shark's teeth. Not only do tremendous quantities of fossilized teeth wash ashore, but the size of some specimens is astounding as well—up to 5 or 6 inches in length. These massive teeth come from the remains of *Carcharodon megalodon,* a prehistoric behemoth of a shark that outweighed *Tyrannosaurus rex.* At 52 feet long and with a dorsal fin more than 5 feet tall, this creature ruled the seas. The modern-day great white shark is puny by comparison, but the two share similar structure and shape of teeth.

Shark's teeth on Caspersen Beach run the gamut, however, from tiny black specks to the prized monster specimens. To find them, avid collectors poke around the scattered limestone boulders on the beach (brought in to help prevent further erosion) and scoop masses of shells from the tide line, sifting through them for their fossil prizes. Half scoop, half sifter, the metal netlike tool that hard-core collectors use can be picked up at most shops in downtown Venice. If you go collecting, it's not hard to spot the smaller shark's teeth just lying on the beach—most folks are after the big prizes. Remember to bring a bag to slip your finds into.

Walking along the fragile coastal strand, you enjoy a panorama of the sea. On the dunes, sea oats attempt to keep their tenuous foothold, and butterfly peas spill over the saw palmettos. Stand and watch for a while, and you'll see brown pelicans plunging into the water for their meals, plummeting from the sky like rocks with a tremendous splash into the waves. As the boardwalk turns and faces toward the parking area, turn right to stay on it. Crossing the main beach access, the boardwalk continues parallel to the sea,

Caspersen Beach

Railroad vine

the constant sound of the surf accompanying your footfalls. If you see a furry tail vanish over the side of the boardwalk, you've caught a glimpse of one of the resident raccoons that regularly raid the not-so-well-latched garbage cans.

After 0.4 mile, you reach a T where the boardwalk ends. To the left, it drops down to pavement; to the right, down to the beach. Here's where you'll start your beach walk. For the next 1.5 miles, this protected segment of beach remains unspoiled by development. Walk as far or as little as you want. Keeping to the tide line, you'll find the hard-packed wet sand easy to walk on, the constant strum of the waves a pleasant melody to accompany your thoughts. The sea grasses washing up on the shore look like wigs of auburn hair decorated with tiny shells, shot through with occasional pink or green

sprigs of seaweed. Small sandpipers and ring-necked gulls scatter across soft sand the color of ground white pepper. As you walk along, keep your eye on the many shell deposits above the tide line. The black specks are small shark's teeth or eroded portions of teeth, and you'll find your eyes drawn to them again and again. Take a moment to look into the ephemeral tidal pools, where the fragile tendrils of pink and white anemones float across the shallows. Walking along the beach, you'll pass scattered swimmers, a few anglers, and other folks enjoying a quiet walk. But the majority of people out on this part of the beach are the fossil collectors, carrying their long-handled scoops. Digging up scoops of the underwater shell banks, they sift them across the hard-packed sand, searching for the large prized teeth. How can you tell a tooth from a rock? Look for the distinctive pointed shape and feel the bone-marrow-type texture.

Up above you, on a natural shelf carved out by the action of waves during storms, a tropical hammock parallels the beach, a natural forest of sea grapes and cabbage palms, where bright purple railroad vine spills out over the sand cliff and onto the beach below. Snowy egrets wait patiently along the surf line for crabs to emerge. Markers above the high-tide line and inverted cagelike baskets buried in the soft sand note the location of a sea turtle nest while protecting the eggs from marauding raccoons. Loggerheads lay their eggs along this shoreline, following a call of nature that brings them back to the spot where they hatched. These threatened creatures are Florida's most common sea turtles, landing on these shores between April and September to deposit their clutches. Adults can reach 40 inches in shell length and up to 350 pounds.

Sun sparkles across the Gulf, where you see the shimmer of schools of menhaden offshore. The water is greenish but clear, and drifts of sea grasses float across the bottom. Dunlins and sanderlings scamper across the sand. After a mile, you see Australian pines in the distance, marking the end of the park—within Caspersen Beach Park, Sarasota County has done a fine job of removing exotic invasive species. You also start to see houses along adjoining Manasota Key. As you progress along the beach, the sand turns to more of a salt-and-pepper color, the black specks from the breakdown of fossilized shark's teeth. After 1.9 miles, you reach a flag-capped shelter posted PRIVATE PROPERTY. This marks the end of Caspersen Beach Park. Turn around and head back.

Walking back along the beach, you catch up with little flocks of sandpipers dashing in and out of the surf. After each wave, thousands of tiny coquina clams point themselves downward and struggle back into the safety of the sand, away from the prying beaks of the shorebirds. Five pelicans fly past in formation, skimming the waves. After 3.2 miles, watch for an access point on the right where you can climb up the dune to the old road that once stretched down this peninsula, an alternate route for hiking back to the parking lot. A sand road parallels it along the inner mangrove-lined waterway; both make good alternate hiking routes. But the beach has its own siren call. Continuing down to the boardwalk, you've hiked 3.6 miles. Turn left and retrace your steps along the waterfront boardwalk to the third access point. Turn right and cross the park entrance road to walk over to the parking lot. Coming back to the nature trail trailhead kiosk, you complete your hike of 3.8 miles.

5

Alligator Creek Preserve

Total distance (two circuits): 4.5 miles

Hiking time: 2 hours, 15 minutes

Habitats: Cabbage palm flatwoods, oak hammock, palm hammock, freshwater marsh, saltwater marsh, mangrove forest, scrubby flatwoods

Maps: USGS 7½' Punta Gorda; park maps

Covering 40,000 acres of land around Charlotte Harbor, where the Peace River flows into the Gulf of Mexico, the Charlotte Harbor Aquatic and State Buffer Preserve protects sensitive estuaries and freshwater marshes filtering water into the harbor. Encouraging hikers to explore the preserve, the Charlotte Harbor Environmental Center sits just off Burnt Store Road south of Punta Gorda. At the center, several hiking trails make up a trail system of 3 miles; just down the road next to the Department of Environmental Protection office is a separate trailhead for the Old Datsun Trail, a 1.7-mile hike. Taken together, these two trail systems offer pleasant family-friendly hiking through a variety of habitats.

From I-75 exit 161, Punta Gorda/Charlotte County Airport, head west for 1.3 miles on CR 768, which becomes CR 765 (Burnt Store Road) just before crossing US 41. Continue another 1.2 miles to the entrance to the Charlotte Harbor Environmental Center on the right. Hours for the grounds are 8 AM–3 PM Monday through Saturday, and 11 AM–3 PM on Sunday; closed holidays. After hours, you can access the Alligator Creek trail system via a walker's gate in the front fence, adding 0.4 mile to your hike.

ALLIGATOR CREEK SITE

The Alligator Creek Site encompasses the environmental center, several teaching facilities, and three interconnecting named trails: the Eagle Point Trail, the Flatwoods Trail, and the Three Lakes Trail. Pick up a

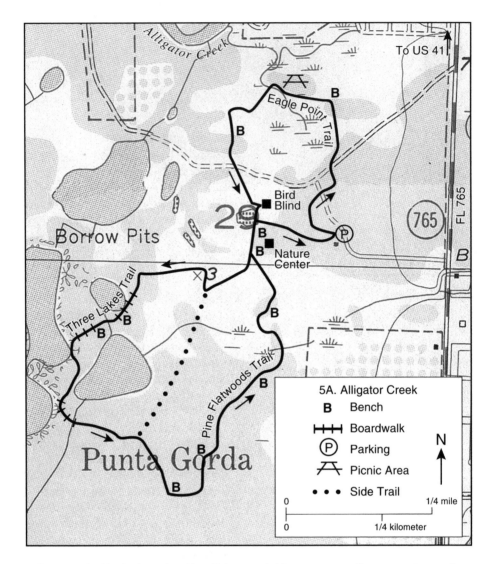

trail map at the kiosk along the drive. Drive around the loop to the right and park near the office and rest rooms.

The Eagle Point Trail starts to the right of the boardwalk by the rest rooms. Walk past the picnic benches to the blue-and-white TRAIL sign, then duck into the cabbage palm hammock. Sand cordgrass and star rush line the footpath. Crossing a wide mowed path, the trail continues onto a bridge over a small stream, where yellow blooms of tickseed add splashes of color to the grass. Be careful, as the sloped wooden surface may be slippery. On the other side of the bridge, you enter the cabbage palm flatwoods, one of the most common habitats of Southwest Florida. American beautyberry and winged sumac rise up out of the sea of saw palmetto surrounding you. Follow the arrows up to the

SOUTH FLORIDA FLATWOODS sign. Because this is an interpretive trail, you'll see plenty of identification signs and markers along the route. The arrow markers keep you on the correct path at each fork. Since side trails are not marked, be sure to follow the main trail. Notice the delicate purple blooms of deer's tongue and the bright streamers of blazing star in fall.

The habitat yields to scrubby flatwoods, with laurel oak, myrtle oak, and wax myrtle joining saw palmetto in the understory. At 0.3 mile, a spur trail leads to the left down to a canopied bench with a view of a salt marsh crowded with black needlerush. The preserve lies along Alligator Creek, a brackish tidal creek flowing into Charlotte Harbor, which feeds this marsh. Stop and take a moment to look out over the needlerush and espy a little blue heron poking through the marsh. When you return to the main trail, turn left. The walkway continues along the eastern edge of the marsh. Duck under the buttonwood as you come up to a T intersection. On the right are a few picnic benches on the edge of Alligator Creek, along with a canoe access point. Turn left and cross the high bridge over the creek, looking down at the white mangroves crowding the shores. On the far side, you come to a fork. Keep right.

Meandering through hammocks of live oaks and cabbage palms, the trail reaches a picnic bench at 0.7 mile, next to a dense stand of myrsine. Reaching a T intersection, the trail turns left directly in front of a dark pond reflecting the cabbage palms crowding around it. You hear a splash as an alligator slips into the water. At the next junction, keep right as the trail returns to cabbage palm flatwoods, skirting a large freshwater marsh. The Caniff Environmental Center looms in front of you. Off to the left is a small building that serves as a bird

blind. Duck inside and take advantage of the one-way glass to watch warblers, sparrows, and Baltimore orioles visiting the various feeders. Bird identification guides help you in your task.

As you approach the back of the environmental center, you've hiked 0.9 mile. You can walk through the center and back out to the parking lot, or continue your hike by turning right to follow the Flatwoods Trail. The trail crosses a bridge. At the fork, keep right to walk down to the observation deck along the pond. A little blue heron in its molting stage shows both yellow and white feathers as it struts along the railing.

Sit in the shade and watch for alligators cruising across the pond. When you return to the main trail, turn right, and right again at the next bench. The T intersection at 1 mile marks the beginning of the next trail loop. Turn right. The Flatwoods Trail winds through the cabbage palm flatwoods, carving a path through the thick jumble of saw palmetto and wax myrtle. At marker 18, the trail comes to another T intersection. The Flatwoods Trail goes to the left; turn right to follow the outer loop, the Three Lakes Trail.

Following the Three Lakes Trail, you walk through a series of palm hammocks along the edge of the estuary. Keep alert as to the twists and turns indicated by the directional arrows. At 1.3 miles, you reach the first of several boardwalks connecting the hammocks. It crosses a small waterway. A mangrove-ringed lake lies off to the right. The next boardwalk starts just beyond a bench. Sea myrtles and white mangroves crowd in closely as you cross. Surrounded by Spanish bayonets, a bench sits beneath a live oak covered in wild pine and resurrection fern. A red-tailed hawk lets out a piercing cry as you enter its territory. The trail continues on to another

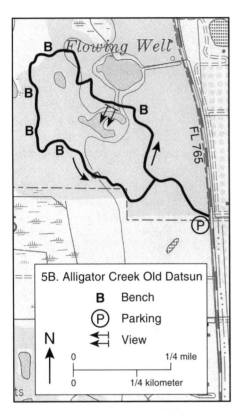

5B. Alligator Creek Old Datsun

B Bench

Ⓟ Parking

⇄ View

N

0   1/4 mile

0   1/4 kilometer

boardwalk, this one tunneling through the mangroves to reach the edge of a broad lake, where a strong salt and silt aroma fills the air. White ibises perch in the red mangroves. Sit on the bench and watch the water before following the boardwalk back to dry land, where sea myrtle towers over your head as you continue down the narrow path between palm hammocks. Mangrove rubber vines drape over the next boardwalk, which starts just beyond a picnic table. Crossing the final bridge, you return to the cabbage palm flatwoods.

After 1.8 miles, the trail reaches a T intersection with the Flatwoods Trail. Turn right to continue around the loop. Crossing a bridge over a dark canal lined with white mangrove, the trail drops down into an area lined with sawgrass—be careful of brushing against its sharp blades. At the next T intersection, turn left. When you reach 2 miles, a sign ahead of you says NOT A TRAIL. Turn left to follow the footpath, passing marker 24 before you emerge at a picnic bench. The trail crosses a bridge and reenters the flatwoods as a corridor through the saw palmetto. The crimson blossom of a phasey bean pokes out from under a palmetto frond. At 2.3 miles, you walk through a palm hammock with a picnic bench in front of a dense tangle of Brazilian pepper. The trail skirts the edge of this Brazilian pepper thicket until it crosses another bridge. After the bench at 2.5 miles, the trail curves to the left, emerging into an open area. You can see the environmental center in the distance. Within moments, you're back at the beginning of the loop, facing an END OF TRAIL sign. Turn right. At the T intersection, turn left.

When you return to the back of the environmental center, you've hiked 2.7 miles. Climb up the staircase to take a walk through the center, which showcases information on the various habitats found throughout the Charlotte Harbor Aquatic and State Buffer Preserve. Exiting from the front of the building, continue down the boardwalk and the paved path. Keep left at the fork. The boardwalk leads back to your starting point at the parking lot. You've completed a 2.8-mile hike.

OLD DATSUN TRAIL

Leaving the Charlotte Harbor Environmental Center, turn right onto Burnt Store Road and drive 1.5 miles south to the trailhead entrance, on the right. Pick up a trail map at the kiosk and follow the trail to the right, guided by arrow signs. You step over a gopher tortoise burrow as you walk along the mowed footpath, edged by casearweed. At the T intersection, turn right. The purple blooms of spiderwort and bright pink puffs of sensitive brier peep up from the tall grass as you enter the cabbage palm flatwoods. Slash pine makes up the high canopy, with cabbage palm and scattered live oak and laurel oak as the low canopy. After 0.2 mile, you reach the beginning of the loop portion of the trail. Turn right. As you walk, notice how the ground seems to be furrowed beneath the vegetation—signs of the vegetable farms that formerly occupied this land. Truck farming was once the lifeblood of this region, where settlers eked out a living planting hundreds of acres of tomatoes, potatoes, and beans. In 1905, Dr. Franklin Miles (of Miles Laboratory and Alka-Seltzer fame) set up the Miles School of Practical Agriculture and Free School for Truckers in Fort Myers. He taught farmers the proper use of pesticides, how to irrigate their land, and how to apply fertilizer for optimum effect. Massive farms still flourish to the east of the I-75 corridor, but they're mostly corporate affairs with migrant workers brought in to take care of the harvest. The small farmers of yesteryear are almost a footnote to history in this region.

You walk past a stand of bloodworts, their foliage looking much like lilies. The footpath can be a bit indistinct, but the arrow markers are well placed so you don't lose your way. At the T intersection with a jeep trail, turn right. As you skirt an oak hammock shrouded in deep shade, the trail curves to the right. Turning left past a thick slash pine, the trail passes a bench under the shade of the live oak hammock and continues into a dense palm hammock. Off to the left, beyond the trees, you can see a large freshwater marsh with yellow canna and marsh mallow clustered around the edges. Coots glide across the open water while a great blue heron takes

Masses of shoelace fern

wing. The footpath may be damp as you round a corner past the marsh.

Back in the shade of a palm hammock, the trail continues past beds of wood ferns growing beneath the cabbage palms. A false indigo vine cascades over a rotting tree. The trail carves a corridor through the thickening understory of saw palmetto. A Carolina wren flutters between the winged sumacs, crying *teakettle teakettle teakettle,* as a pileated woodpecker lands on the trunk of a tall slash pine. Coontie, also known as Florida arrowroot, grows wild along this section of the trail. A popular ornamental, it provided a food source for the Calusa and early settlers of this region, who dried and ground up its otherwise poisonous roots to create a starch from which they made bread.

The trail makes several sharp turns through the flatwoods before entering another palm hammock. Passing a bench at 0.8 mile, the trail turns to the left. A dark waterway lies off to the right as you catch a glimpse of the wetlands far to the left. You cross a bridge over a sluggish stream draining the wetlands, continuing past another bench in the shady palm hammock. Take care as to where the trail goes; some of the markers are missing. The path twists and curves between the cabbage palms, eventually turning sharply left. An American kestrel flies low above the fronds of the palms.

You reach a bench at 1 mile. The trail continues on through a string of cabbage palm hammocks, alternating stretches of open sun with deep shade. Shoelace fern hangs like a grassy hairdo down low on the trunk of one tall palm tree. Twisting and winding in and out of the hammocks, the trail passes another bench. At 1.4 miles, the jeep trail you're on continues straight, but the hiking trail turns to the left into an oak hammock. At the T intersection, turn left. Keep right at the fork, leaving the jeep trail for the mowed path. Stop and take a look at the kiosk, which describes the invasive plants that volunteers are attempting to eradicate from the preserve. A few moments later, you finish the loop. Continue straight to return to the parking area. Make sure to turn left along the mowed path when you see a paved road in front of you. When you reach the parking area, you've completed a 1.7-mile hike.

6

Cayo Costa State Park

Total distance (circuit): 5.9 miles

Hiking time: 2 hours, 30 minutes

Habitats: Cabbage palm flatwoods, coastal scrub, coastal strand, mangrove swamp, mudflats, tropical hardwood hammock

Maps: USGS 7½' Bokeelia; park map

Pirates, smugglers, fishermen . . . they've all made landfall here on a vast arc of beach south of Boca Grande Pass, approachable only by sea: La Costa. The ancient Calusa called these shores home, roaming the seas in their dugout canoes until European contact brought disease that ravaged their ranks. Spanish pirates, including the infamous Jose Gaspar, terrorized the Gulf Coast from their island hideouts in the 1700s and 1800s. As settlers moved into the new territory of Florida, fishing villages sprang up along the shallow inner channels of Pine Island Sound, pulling their bounty from the sea.

Lonely and windswept, Cayo Costa State Park covers parts of three Gulf barrier islands: North Captiva, Punta Blanca, and La Costa. You'll find precious solitude here along the hiking trails, where human presence has barely disturbed the island's commiseration with the sea. Because of its inaccessibility and beachfront views, the tent campground and cabins are one of the most popular in the state. But for that solitude, you'll pay. La Costa lies well offshore: Only experienced paddlers should attempt the crossing. Private boaters can take advantage of limited docking on the bayside. The majority of the park's visitors come over on the *Tropic Star,* the state concession ferryboat, which costs $20 per person for a day trip. It's a steep price to pay for a hike, but Cayo Costa is a special place. Treat yourself—and bring the camping gear.

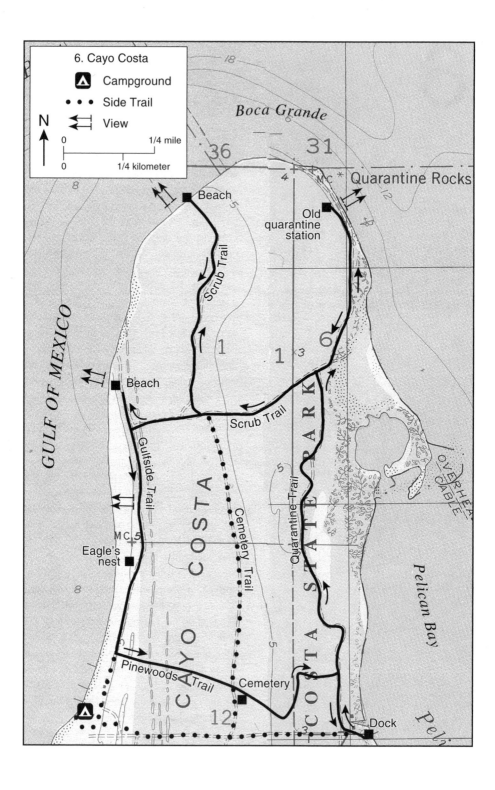

Campground

Side Trail

View

N

0   1/4 mile

0   1/4 kilometer

Boca Grande

18

36   31

4   MC *   Quarantine Rocks

Beach

Old
quarantine
station

12

Scrub Trail

1   1   3   6

GULF OF MEXICO

Beach

Scrub Trail

Gulfside Trail

Quarantine Trail

COSTA

5

5

OVERHEA CABLE

MC 5

Eagle's
nest

Pelican Bay

Cemetery Trail

8

CAYO

COSTA STATE PARK

5

Pinewoods Trail

Cemetery

12

3

Dock

Peli

Traveling southbound on I-75, take exit 161, Punta Gorda/Charlotte County Airport. Head west on CR 768 for 1.3 miles; this road becomes CR 765 (Burnt Store Road) just before crossing US 41. Drive 18.1 miles south to the traffic light at FL 78 (Pine Island Road) at Matlacha. From I-75 northbound, use exit 143. Follow FL 78 (Pine Island Road) 11.4 miles through Cape Coral to the intersection with CR 768 in Matlacha. Continue west on Pine Island Road for 5.5 miles, crossing over the bridges and out to the island. Turn right onto CR 767 (Stringfellow Road). Drive 6.2 miles to Barrancas Avenue in Bokeelia. Turn right at the sign that says CAYO COSTA FERRY. Drive past the post office to the second road on the left, Porto Bello Road. Turn left and follow the road until it ends in the parking lot of Bokeelia Marina, home of Tropic Star Cruises, the official ferry for Cayo Costa State Park. Round-trip fare runs $21.20 including tax (cash only). Call in advance (941-283-0015) to reserve a spot on the ferry, which leaves at 9:30 each morning. If you're camping, let Tropic Star Cruises know so you can be ensured a space on the appropriate return ferry. Day-trippers must be back at the park dock by 3 PM for the return trip.

Depending on the boat you board, the crossing can take from half an hour to an hour. Enjoy the scenic views of the Bokeelia waterfront. Fishing boats chug through the pass as brown pelicans dive in unison into schools of mullet shimmering beneath the waves. Out in the channel, watch for dolphins as they frolic in the waves created by your boat. When you arrive at Cayo Costa State Park, walk up the ferryboat dock to the kiosk and drop off your Florida State Parks entrance fee.

Most visitors wait at Cabin Road for the tram to cart them a mile out to the beach and campground. Hikers, however, should turn right and walk over to the visitors center. Open 8 AM–5 PM, it also serves as the ranger station and a concession stand, with interpretive exhibits on island habitats, T-shirts for sale, and an ice machine behind the building. Ask for a map of the hiking trails, and top off your water before hitting the trail.

Just behind the visitors center is a QUARANTINE TRAIL sign pointing to the right, toward a work area. Walk around the fence to get to the trail, which heads into the deep shade of a tropical hardwood hammock dominated by cabbage palms. Scarlet sage flaunts red blossoms in the shade of a mimosa-like women's tongue tree, while coral bean grows to the height of a small tree. The footpath is an old jeep trail under the sand live oaks. After 0.3 mile, you see the PINEWOODS TRAIL sign, your return route for this hiking loop. Continue straight, heading for the quarantine dock. When it gets wet, the footpath reveals itself to be slippery marl, so walk carefully on rainy days. Giant leather ferns rise out of standing water under the trees. Wild coffee and Spanish bayonet run rampant throughout the understory. A skunk-like odor draws your attention to the slender trunks of white stopper. Sporting unusually large leaves, poison ivy vines tangle through the forest.

You skirt a hammock of cabbage palms with a thick understory of giant leather ferns before the trail curves to the right under sand live oaks festooned in ball moss. Several furry black feral hogs scurry across the road and crash through the undergrowth. When the residents of La Costa gave up their homes in the late 1940s so the state could take over the island, they left their pigs behind—much to the detriment of the island's habitats, as

Shelling is superb along Cayo Costa's beaches.

the hogs have no predators here. While they keep the snake population low, the hogs constantly tear up the forest floor in search of grubs and roots to eat. The fingerlike roots of black mangroves rise from a murky water hole off on the right; the mangrove forest that covers the eastern shore of the island begins to press in on the trail. Notice the shells—oysters, clams, and large conchs—scattered across the trail and the forest floor. Bleached by age, these are the remains of one of the many Calusa middens on the island.

Sunlight gleams through the peeling bark of the gumbo limbo trees as you continue down the trail. The crimson trumpet blossoms of tropical sage stand out in sharp contrast to a backdrop of snake plants. At 1.2 miles, you reach the junction with the Scrub Trail. Turn right to continue walking down to the quarantine dock. Wild coffee grows tall under the gumbo limbo trees near a stand of century plants. More shells spill across the trail, indicating the location of another midden in the forest. Necklace pod trees show off their dangling yellow blooms and seed cases that look like strings of beads. This salt-tolerant species attracts ruby-throated hummingbirds on their annual migration, a last chance for nectar before the birds make the long flight across the Gulf of Mexico to the Yucatan Peninsula.

The trail narrows as it continues into the mangrove swamp, a mosquito-ridden place during the wet season. A jumble of red mangroves dangles impossibly long taproots from high branches down to the puddles below. You see a ribbon of white off to the right, through the trees—Pelican Bay. The sound of pounding surf increases as the trail draws close to the water's edge. A black racer vanishes into the tall grass as you emerge out into the open at

the site of the old quarantine station, at 1.7 miles. Look just below the osprey nest for the remains of the concrete pilings of the dock. In the early 1900s, foreign ships headed to Bokeelia would stop here first to be boarded by a doctor. Outbreaks of yellow fever and malaria killed thousands across Florida in those days, so the U.S. Health Department actively checked incoming vessels for signs of maladies among crew members. The resident doctor's home was not far from this clearing.

Turn around and follow this spur trail back to its junction with the Scrub Trail at 2.1 miles. Turn right to follow the Scrub Trail down toward the Gulf of Mexico. Coontie grows wild, scattered under the cabbage palm. Emerging into full sun, the trail winds through palm and oak hammocks, and up past an old slash pine. Looking like curled-up giant prawns, globs of orange jelly mold rise from the damp moldering debris of sea grape leaves. As the trail rises, the terrain becomes much drier. You've entered the coastal scrub. Watch for gopher tortoise burrows, the apartment houses of the scrub, which serve as protective dwellings for more than 360 different species of animals in addition to the lumbering tortoises that build them. The bright red fruits of prickly pear cacti provide food for the foraging tortoises.

After 2.5 miles, you reach the junction of the Scrub Trail and the Cemetery Trail. For a walk out to a quiet beach on Boca Grande Pass, turn right. The Cemetery Trail winds through the scrub, a place where scattered hammocks of sand live oak and cabbage palm punctuate large grayish sandy spots devoid of vegetation. The trail passes through an excavated area and zigzags through the sporadic shady hammocks. Tickseed blooms rise out of mats of bitter panicum. Unripe hog plums look like eggs nestled amid a spray of oval green leaves. After dropping down into a sweet-smelling corridor of yellow nicker-bean spilling over sea grapes, you emerge at the water's edge: Boca Grande Pass. Across the water are the condos of Gasparilla Island. Take a walk to the right and look up the beach—in sharp contrast, a beautiful scene of an unspoiled cabbage palm hammock along the shoreline.

After you've enjoyed some quiet time on this very private beach, turn around and follow the trail back to the last junction, reaching the Scrub Trail at 3.8 miles. Turn right. The Scrub Trail continues its slow descent through the coastal scrub, where ball moss grows thickly on spindly yaupon trees. Grass forms carpets across the bald spots in the scrub, and you spy the bright white berries of snowberry on the edges of the hammocks. As you begin to hear the roar of waves crashing against the shore, you reach the junction with the Gulf Trail at 4 miles. Take the right fork to the T intersection, then turn right to follow the Gulf Trail. Although you can hear the waves, you can't see them—a thick wall of vegetation separates you from the beach. But after a few moments, you emerge on a high spot that lets you look down the coastal strand to the rolling surf. Painted leaf clusters under the sea grape. Massive purple blossoms on the runners of railroad vine greet you as you step off the end of the Gulf Trail and onto the beach, facing Boca Grande Pass's meeting with the Gulf of Mexico. Off in the surf, a set of abandoned pilings create perches for pelicans and cormorants. It's a serene spot, where you're serenaded by the sounds of seagulls. Stretching off to the south, the slope of the beach is somewhat severe for walking, but take time at low tide to

browse the thick shell beds along the shore. Both here and on the beach south of the campground, you'll find many uncommon shells such as the glossy brown-spotted calico clam, the true tulip with its colorful bands, delicate bubble shells, tulip mussels with iridescent insides, and the spiny jewelbox, with its sharp pointed spikes.

Head back to the junction with the Scrub Trail. Continue straight along the Gulf Trail, passing a sign that says CABINS AND GULF BEACH, 1 MILE. Off to the left lie rolling relict dunes capped with cabbage palms and other plants of the coastal scrub. On the right, beyond a veil of necklace pods, you can see waving sea oats in the coastal strand, separating the scrub from the sea. Mourning doves pick their way across a spaghettilike tangle of love vine. Coming up to a high spot, you can see well across the wide coastal strand to the waves breaking offshore. Snags provide a place for ospreys to nest. Pelicans dive into the waves. You see a distant stand of Australian pine up ahead along this open and windy stretch. A massive eagles' nest towers above you in a tall snag.

At 4.8 miles, you reach a junction. Continue straight ahead past the GULFSIDE TRAIL sign to the cabins at the edge of the campground. The campground has 12 rustic cabins (each sleeping six) and 30 tent sites (eight people permitted per site) under the shade of the tall pines, with restroom facilities and outside showers. If you're pooped out or just want to spend some time on the beach, you can take the shuttle from here to get back to the dock. Trams leave the campground at 11:15, 1:30, and 2:45. If you go out to the beach, walk south to where thick shell beds form around the roots of plants along the lagoon—your chances of finding unique and unusual seashells increase the farther you get from the campground.

To continue your circuit hike, return to the junction and turn right to follow the Pinewoods Trail. Despite the name, you see no pines—you're walking through a very open coastal scrub with scattered cabbage palms. An explosion of shells and sand mark a gopher tortoise burrow. The scrub gives way to scattered hammocks dense with water oak and cabbage palm, myrsine and wax myrtle. Butterfly pea climbs up and over the low sea grape. When you reach the bench at 5.2 miles, you've come to the junction with the Cemetery Trail. Take a brief detour off to the right to see the pioneer settlement cemetery, where a split-rail fence surrounds graves outlined in conch shells. The fishing village of La Costa occupied this island until the 1940s, where fishermen were just as apt to join the lucrative rum-running trade as to chase after redfish and grouper. While the locals eked out a living, millionaires bought some of the adjacent islands, such as Useppa Key and Cabbage Key, as getaways for sportfishing. Boca Grande Pass is one of the top tarpon spots in the United States.

After you look at the cemetery, return to the Pinewoods Trail and turn right at the bench, walking into cabbage palm flatwoods: tall slash pines over a canopy of cabbage palms and sand live oaks. As the hammock becomes denser, it transitions to a tropical hammock. You catch a whiff of white stopper as the Pinewoods Trail meets the Quarantine Trail at a T intersection. After 5.6 miles, you've finished the loop. Turn right to continue back to the visitors center. When you reach the dock, you've completed your 5.9-mile hike.

7

Caloosahatchee Regional Park

Total distance (circuit): 3.4 miles

Hiking time: 1 hour, 45 minutes

Habitats: Hydric hammock, pine flatwoods, scrubby flatwoods, freshwater marsh, oak hammock, palm hammock

Maps: USGS 7½' Olga; park map

Before the first Spanish explorers reached this part of Florida in the 1500s, the Calusa ruled the land. Coastal dwellers, they built villages on great mounds of shells and dug canals up to their door-steps. Tall and slim, they were excellent sailors, paddling canoes of hollowed-out cypress. They lived off the fruits of the sea and fiercely protected their land from any incursions by other tribes. Although their warriors fought off Spanish attempts to move into their lands, they fell victim to smallpox and other European diseases for which they had no resistance. Like the other Native tribes of Florida, they van-ished from the face of the earth.

Little of the Caloosahatchee River still looks as it did in the days of the Calusa. This river was their superhighway into the heart of Florida, its broad ribbon flowing unfettered from Lake Mayami (now Lake Okeechobee) into the Gulf of Mexico, pro-viding them access to the Everglades and up the Kissimmee River into Central Florida. The centuries since the demise of their civilization brought dredges and locks to "tame" the river. Vast cattle ranches and vegetable fields take the place of the once extensive prairies, and expensive homes now line the waterfront around Fort Myers. Caloosahatchee Regional Park provides a rare look at unspoiled habitats along the Caloosahatchee River.

Originally intended to become a state park, these preserved lands are now man-aged by Lee County. The 768-acre tract in-cludes a rustic campground and separate

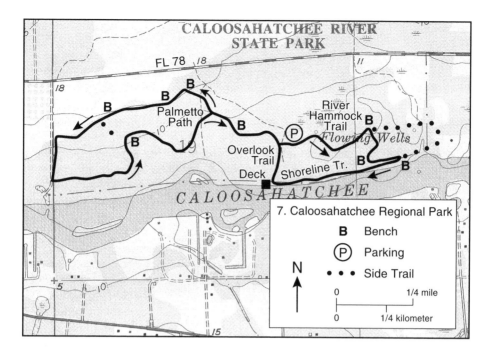

FL 78

River Hammock Trail

B   Palmetto Path

Flowing Wells

Overlook Trail

Deck   Shoreline Tr.

CALOOSAHATCHEE

7. Caloosahatchee Regional Park

B   Bench

(P)   Parking

N   • • •   Side Trail

0   1/4 mile

0   1/4 kilometer

trail systems for equestrians, mountain bikers, and hikers. To find the park if you're headed southbound on I-75, take exit 143, North Fort Myers/Cape Coral. Drive east on FL 78 (Bayshore Road) for 3.3 miles. The road ends at a T intersection. Turn left onto FL 31. From I-75 northbound, use exit 141, Ft. Myers/La Belle. Take FL 80 (Palm Beach Boulevard) east for 2.7 miles to a traffic light with FL 31. Turn left and cross the Caloosahatchee River Bridge, coming up to the intersection with FL 78. Driving north on FL 31, continue 1.2 miles to CR 78. Turn right onto CR 78. After 6.6 miles, you pass the Northside Trails entrance to Caloosahatchee Regional Park, used for access to the equestrian and biking trail portion of the park. Keep alert for the main entrance on the right at 7.2 miles. The park is open 8 AM–sunset. Like at most of Lee County's other parks, you'll pay a parking fee of 75 cents per hour or $3 per day. Get the ticket from the automated machine and display it inside your dashboard before starting your hike.

Four linked trails make up the hiking trail system on the park's south side. The Overlook Trail provides a short and direct wheelchair-accessible pathway down to an observation deck on the Caloosahatchee River. The River Hammock Trail winds through a dark hammock of cabbage palms and ferns, but the trail remains dry and well maintained—a good choice for families with children. Expect a more rugged hiking experience on the park's two other trails—the Shoreline Trail, which follows the edge of the river and splashes through a couple of wetlands, and the Palmetto Path, which loops from pine flatwoods into a wet portion of the hydric hammock. In the wet season, you'll wade down these trails. This hike links together the four trails to provide a broad overview of the habitats throughout the park. If you're hiking with small children, stick to the River Hammock Trail, the Overlook Trail, and, in the dry season, the short loop of the Palmetto Path. Trail markers with wooden icons act as confirmation blazes on each route.

Starting from the parking lot, follow the sidewalk down to the left to the trailhead sign for the River Hammock Trail. You immediately plunge into the darkness of a palm hammock, surrounded by tall cabbage palms draped with goldfoot ferns. Live oaks provide a dense canopy, with each oak limb swaddled in a thick growth of wild pine and resurrection fern. Shiny-leaved tropical plants dominate the understory, including marlberry, myrsine, and two types of wild coffee—tall *Psychotria nervosa,* with glossy green leaves, and *P. sulzneri,* with silvery blue-green leaves. Watch for their clusters of white blooms in summer, followed by crimson-, cinnamon-, and chestnut-colored coffee beans in fall. Growing tall and straight, coral beans show off their bright red blooms each spring. All year long, giant sword ferns and marsh ferns fill the spaces between the taller shrubs. The dark, rich soil squishes under your feet.

Passing a side trail to the campground at 0.2 mile, the trail continues past a bench to a fork—the beginning of the loop portion of the trail. Take the right fork. You walk down a corridor of tall cabbage palms as the trail curves to the right and the canopy of shrubs drops down low. Notice the deep diggings in the footpath, caused by feral hogs. When Spanish explorer Hernando de Soto came to Florida in 1539, he brought hogs to feed his men. Now a nuisance spread across all of Florida, today's feral hogs are descendants of that original Spanish stock.

The trail curves to the left past a bench as you duck under the pink roots of a grapevine, dangling like a beaded curtain from a swinging vine. Off to the right, you can see a bright open area beyond the forest—the Caloosahatchee River. After you cross a bridge over a sluggish stream, you come to a junction at 0.6 mile. If you're continuing back on the River Hammock Trail, continue straight. But if you're up for following the more adventuresome route— where you might get your feet wet—turn right. This short connector takes you down to the Shoreline Trail, meeting it at a T intersection. Off to the left is the park's kayak launch. Turn right to follow the Shoreline Trail down the river.

Trapped in a tunnel between tall grasses and casearweed, the footpath meanders along the river's edge but provides few direct views of the water. As it curves to the left, you get a brief glimpse of the Caloosahatchee before the trail drops back down into the grasses. A giant bromeliad dangles off the snapped-off trunk of a live oak. Climbing up and over spoil banks, the trail winds back out toward the water, still hidden from view by the tall grass. Wading across a swampy drainage, you continue into a long stretch of sawgrass. Take care to avoid brushing bare skin against it, as the sharp teeth on the grass blades can leave a nasty scratch. The trail turns back out toward the river, where the outflow from a freshwater marsh pours across the footpath. Skirting a marshy puddle filled with elephant ears, the trail continues along the river past small pond cypresses. Trumpet vine spills over a clump of sand cordgrass. After 1 mile, you reach the observation deck and the Overlook Trail. Take a moment to look out over the velvety blue waves, down the unspoiled shoreline on the northern bank. Houses with docks dot the southern shore.

Crossed palms along the Shoreline Trail

Turn around and follow the solid shell-and-clay footpath of the Overlook Trail past the picnic table and into a dark palm hammock, where stringers of shoelace fern spill over the bootjacks of the cabbage palms. Marlberry and wild coffee crowd the understory. You walk under dangling citrus fruit, sour wild grapefruits that provide both raccoons and insects a tasty treat. Like the hogs, grapefruit is another Spanish import from the early colonization of Florida. Spanish landowners in the 1500s were ordered to plant their land grants with citrus trees.

When you emerge from the forest behind the rest rooms, turn left and follow the sidewalk down through the picnic pavilion to the parking lot. Turn left again and walk down the sidewalk to the PALMETTO PATH trailhead sign. During the wet season, this portion of the hike may involve some stretches of shin-deep wading, and park personnel will post a warning at the trailhead. Don't let a little water get you down—it's a pleasant loop through the wildest portion of the park. As you walk down the trail, keep alert for the sounds of animal in the thickets of saw palmetto under the tall slash pines. You're entering a wet pine flatwoods, where a small herd of white-tailed deer lives and occasionally emerges to browse on the green grass islands in the parking area. Under the slash pine, greenbrier and grapevine smother the saw palmetto, and bracken fern pokes out of the pine straw. The path winds through pine and palm flatwoods with scattered sand live oaks—look up in the limbs of the oaks for giant bromeliads in bloom. Passing a bench, you continue down a corridor of winged sumac and sea myrtle. A gray squirrel scurries up a tall gray snag as a 4-foot-long black racer slithers to the base of the tree trunk.

At 1.5 miles, you reach the trail junction for the loop in the Palmetto Path. Stay to the right, following the broad path through the pine flatwoods, skirting an oak hammock. In a damp spot in the trail, a large crayfish stands guard, waving its claws with an attitude to try to scare off anyone coming down the trail. The trail curves left under a large oak furry in epiphytes and continues through a mix of cabbage palms and oaks, passing another bench. Turning to the left and away from an old trail, the footpath meanders up to a bench along a sluggish tannic stream piped under the path. As you emerge back into open flatwoods, notice the tall, gnarled slash pines on the right, their enormous canopies set against the blue sky. A fine carpet of frog's hair grass creates a dense, soft mat across the footpath. After the next bench, you reach a fork in the trail at 2 miles. If you turn left, this shortcut cuts off 0.6 mile from the hike and avoids the swampiest part of the trail. Turn right to continue on the outer loop.

Heading down a corridor of saw palmettos, you emerge into scrubby flatwoods, with Chapman oaks and gallberry rising up between the palmetto fronds. The slash pines overhead provide little shade. Passing the back side of a sign that says HORSES AND BICYCLES PROHIBITED, you come out to a T intersection at 2.1 miles. Turn left and follow this jeep trail along the swiftly flowing ditch. A mound of lantana flashes its scarlet-and-yellow blooms. You see a small farm on the opposite bank, with sugar cane and banana palm spilling down the embankment. Keep alert for the left turn at 2.3 miles, as there is no signpost. The trail enters a dark hydric hammock with standing water. Off to the left, you can see an open space between the trees, where the river lies. Depending on the time of year, this portion of the footpath may be under water. Ghostly white with variegated feathers, a barred owl swoops down low beneath the oak limbs, gliding off into the dark distance.

Rising up out of the swamp, you pass a palmetto icon sign, and the trail turns to the left under towering cabbage palms. Flanked by casearweed, you rise back up into the pine flatwoods to the junction with the shortcut trail at 2.6 miles. Keep right to stay on the outer loop, passing another bench. Turning back into the hydric hammock, the trail has a slight amount of elevation—just enough to keep it dry. Tannic waters flow beneath the palms, oaks, and Carolina willows in the forest. The perpetual humidity encourages thousands of air plants to flourish. Keep alert and you might notice a delicate butterfly orchid draped down from a live oak limb, or a giant bromeliad clinging to a Carolina willow. As you continue down the dark corridor through the hydric hammock, the trail becomes a narrow track bounded by tall grasses and casearweed. Rising back up into pine flatwoods, you meet the beginning of the loop at 3.1 miles. Turn right to head back to the parking area, completing your hike after 3.4 miles.

8

Hickey's Creek Mitigation Park

Total distance (circuit): 4.7 miles

Hiking time: 3 hours

Habitats: Pine flatwoods, bluffs and ravines, oak scrub, oak hammock, scrubby flatwoods, freshwater marsh

Maps: USGS 7½' Olga; park map

With suburban sprawl wrapping around the Fort Myers area, choking out prime habitat for gopher tortoises, burrowing owls, and Florida scrub-jays, developers must pay into a special fund to preserve lands to replace the habitats they've bulldozed and paved over. The 11,000-acre Hickey's Creek Mitigation Park provides habitat for these displaced species, limiting human recreational use to hiking, kayaking, and canoeing.

From I-75 exit 141, Ft. Myers/La Belle, take FL 80 (Palm Beach Boulevard) east. After 8.5 miles, the road narrows. Keep alert for a small sign on the right indicating the location of the park entrance. Park hours run 7 AM–6 PM and are enforced by an automatic gate. Plan carefully if you arrive late in the day so you aren't locked in! As at other Lee County parks, you'll pay a parking fee of 75 cents an hour or $3 for the day.

Start your hike by picking up a park map and wandering through the breezeway past the rest rooms out to the hard-packed shell-and-clay trail, a wheelchair-accessible segment that leads through the pine flatwoods to the edge of Hickey's Creek. Three loops comprise the trail system: the main Hickey's Creek Trail, the often wet North Marsh Trail, and the long Palmetto Pines Trail. While the Hickey's Creek Trail is suitable for families with young children, the other trails are best left to more adventuresome hikers with experience at route finding.

Slash pines tower around you as you meander through the sea of saw palmettos

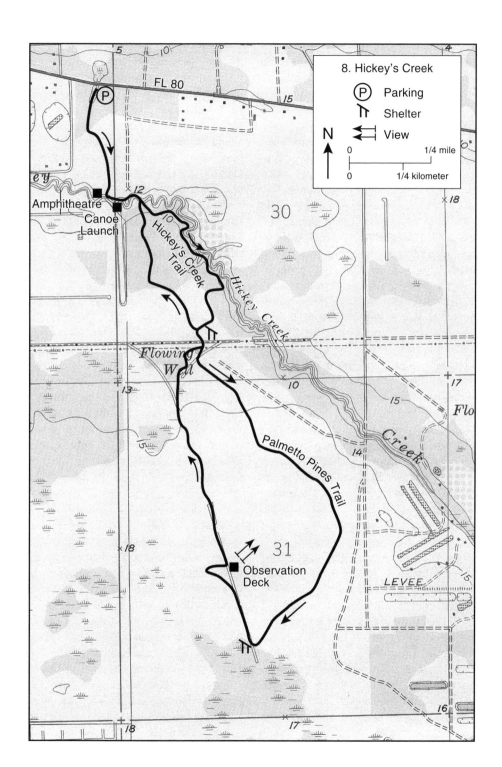

8. Hickey's Creek

Ⓟ Parking

⋔ Shelter

⇄ View

FL 80

Ⓟ

Amphitheatre

Canoe
Launch

Hickey's Creek
Trail

Hickey Creek

30

Flowing
Well

Palmetto Pines Trail

Observation
Deck

31

LEVEE

Creek

Flo

N

0   1/4 mile
0   1/4 kilometer

and approach a covered amphitheater used for outdoor programs. The sheltered benches look out over the stillness of Hickey's Creek, a blackwater stream sluggishly seeping through the pine flatwoods on its way toward the Caloosahatchee River. At the T intersection, turn left. When you see the FISHING PIER sign, turn right to wander down to this overlook along a bend in the river. Florida cooter turtles bob just below the surface; a string of bubbles indicates the presence of an alligator on the creek's bottom. *Tillisandia* cling to the gnarled branches of sand live oaks. Return to the trail intersection and continue straight, passing a side trail to the canoe launch. Goldfoot ferns cling to the nubby trunks of saw palmettos. After 0.5 mile, you reach the LIVE OAK BRIDGE sign. To the left is a fire ring and picnic area used by scouting groups. Turn right to stay on the main trail, crossing a long bridge over Hickey's Creek with a great view of the dark water and dense vegetation. Below, golden orb spiders bridge the creek, their silky webs glistening in the morning sun.

The Hickey's Creek Trail officially starts at the T intersection at the far end of the bridge. Turn left to follow the loop clockwise into a mixed forest of water oaks, laurel oaks, and cabbage palms, with purple American beautyberries brightening up the understory. Although the trail is not blazed as it zigzags along the creek, the footpath is obvious. Watch for a bench on the left, tucked away in the vegetation, giving a great view of the creek. Giant leather ferns wave from the far shore. Epiphytes crowd the limbs of the young oaks shading the trail. Keep alert for the many palmetto trunks poking out of the footpath, as a misplaced footfall could send you sprawling. The trail drops down into a small ravine and rises back up again. The still, dark waters

shimmer through the trees on the left. As the trail turns toward the flatwoods, you walk down a corridor flanked by tall saw palmettos before rising into an oak hammock. Shoelace ferns dangle from the trunks of cabbage palms. If you hear the sound of running water, you're not mistaken—when the pine flatwoods are draining, a steady flow pours down a small ravine and over a massive root, creating a small splashing waterfall. Step over the flow and continue along the footpath. At 1.1 miles, the trail climbs into and out of a small ravine before turning to the right. A side trail leads to the right to explore a peninsula bounded by the creek. Continue on the main trail and you quickly approach the BALD CYPRESS BRIDGE sign, reaching a T intersection on the boardwalk. Here's where the trail splits again. To the left is the 1-mile North Marsh Trail, a footpath frequently flooded in all but the driest months. This hike route sticks with the Hickey's Creek Trail, which turns to the right, leaving the creek and heading into the pine flatwoods. Once you enter the open, grassy area under the slash pines, keep alert to the directional changes of the trail by watching for orange-tipped poles that serve as trail markers.

After 1.3 miles, you come to the Hickey's Creek Trail Shelter, a bench topped with a solid roof serving as a shelter against rain and sun. Take a moment to rest before heading on, as it will be a while before your next opportunity to sit in the shade. Just beyond the shelter is the junction with the Palmetto Pines Trail, which follows a rugged and sometimes wet 2.5-mile loop through mostly open scrub. To cut your hike short (especially if you're out there with youngsters), follow the orange-tipped posts to the right to complete a 2.2-mile circuit. Otherwise, start down the trail marked by the white-tipped posts, passing under a set of high-voltage power lines. On the far side of the clearing, keep alert to the posts and arrows as the trail turns right, left, then left again and crosses a meadow. On the other side, turn right. The trail becomes a broadly cleared path into the scrubby flatwoods, reaching a T intersection at 1.7 miles. Turn right.

The footing along this section of the trail may be difficult and uneven—it all depends on how recently the trail has been maintained. But there are rewards for making this rugged trek. You're headed straight into the heart of Florida scrub-jay territory. Keep alert for their sharp calls and for the brightly blue birds themselves, perched on slender oak limbs and high up in the slash pines. Although they're reluctant to draw near, you're likely to see a few. Off to the left, in the distance, the palmettos meet a wall of scrub oaks, which is where the scrub-jays nest. As you draw closer to the oaks, the trail curves to the right, toward a group of cabbage palms. Watch the puddles for the frantic movement of thick pollywogs, destined to grow up to be the oak toads that roam the flatwoods. The white blooms of narrow-leaved sabatia cast reflections in the tannic puddles. As you cross an old jeep track at 2 miles, keep alert for the white-tipped posts leading you onward past the cabbage palms and into a stretch of young oak trees, perfect scrub-jay habitat. Listen closely and you may hear them hopping through the underbrush, gathering up acorns. Passing a faded trail to the left, you see low bush blueberry crowding along the edges of the trail, intermingled with young saw palmetto. Purple spiderwort peeks out of the tall grass. Curving to the right, the trail continues through the semishade of young sand live oaks before

Tarflower

it crosses a broad sand road at 2.4 miles. The habitat becomes more scrublike, and you see large gopher tortoise burrows in the bright white sand. Lantana grows at the base of a little hill along a pool of water off to the right—a naturally flowing artesian well, expanded and deepened long ago by a cattle rancher.

As the trail rises up into an oak hammock, it makes a sharp right and reaches the Palmetto Pines Trail Shelter at 2.7 miles. Take a moment to rest before continuing on to the next white-tipped post, climbing up onto an old tramway used by timber companies to remove the pines and cypresses that once made up this forest. Turn right. The elevation provided by the tramway affords sweeping views of the pine flatwoods, while the trail weaves between the shade of sand live oaks. A bald eagle soars overhead, scanning the palmettos for prey. You cross the broad sand road again at 2.9 miles. Shallow sloughs parallel the tramway, showing off mats of fanwort. Dipping in and out of open scrub, the trail continues under tall slash pines, which drop a soft carpet of needles on the footpath. Passing several young pond cypresses, the trail crosses a bridge at 3.1 miles. Turn right and walk out onto an observation deck with a great view of the pine flatwoods.

Continuing down the tramway, you must keep alert for gopher tortoise burrows creating deep holes in the footpath, and surface limestone sticking out of the ground. The trail continues to zigzag between the trees. Lilies drift across the dark water of a permanent pond. When you reach a T intersection at 3.7 miles, turn right. Watch for a white-tipped post on the left. You'll cross back under the power lines before coming up to the junction with the orange-tipped posts, completing your circuit of the Palmetto Pines Trail. Turn left. You're back on the Hickey's Creek Trail, completing the last of the loop. The orange-tipped posts lead you along a well-defined narrow footpath through the scrubby flatwoods. As you cross a jeep road at 4 miles, the sweet scent of tarflower fills the air. Watch for more gopher tortoise burrows hidden beneath tufts of wiregrass. Twisting and winding through saw palmettos and oak scrub, the path emerges at a boardwalk. After 4.3 miles, you've completed the loop. Make the left at the fork in the boardwalk to walk back toward the parking lot. Keep to the left as you cross the service road, and don't miss the trail as it turns to the right away from the fishing pier. Walking back along the shell path, you notice an oak toad hopping across the trail. After 4.7 miles, you return to the parking area, completing your hike.

9

Calusa Nature Center

Total distance (circuit): 2.1 miles

Hiking time: 1 hour, 30 minutes

Habitats: Pine flatwoods, cypress swamp

Maps: USGS 7½' Fort Myers; park map

Heaven and earth meet at the Calusa Nature Center, where a daily planetarium show—the only one in Southwest Florida—complements the center's main mission of introducing you to the natural history of the Fort Myers area. This is a great place to take the kids. Explore the reptile tanks to see the many species of turtles, snakes, lizards, and salamanders that inhabit the region, and learn the difference between the resident American alligator and American crocodile.

Two hiking trails range through the center's 105-acre tract. A gentle and dry 0.6-mile nature trail leads past an Audubon-maintained aviary of raptors and through a representative slough habitat, where volunteers battle to rid the swamp forest of invasive melaleuca. A more adventuresome swamp-tromping trail starts at a replica Calusa village and loops 1.5 miles around the edge of the property through the seasonal wetlands.

The Calusa Nature Center sits very close to I-75 on the eastern edge of Fort Myers. Coming from I-75 exit 136, drive west on Colonial Boulevard for 0.5 mile. Turn right onto Ortiz Boulevard. Continue 0.2 mile north; the entrance is on the left. The nature center is open Monday through Saturday 9 AM–5 PM, Sunday 11 AM–5 PM, with an admission of $5 adults, $3 children (which includes the planetarium show). Pick up a trail map and interpretive guide when you pay your admission.

To start your hike, exit the science center's back door and head down the

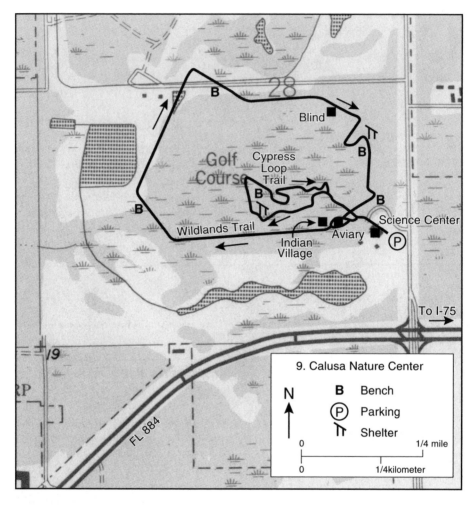

9. Calusa Nature Center

N

B   Bench

P   Parking

Ṫ   Shelter

0   1/4 mile

0   1/4kilometer

staircase, following the AVIARY sign. Turn right to walk through the small aviary, which showcases injured Florida birds of prey, such as the barred owl, the bald eagle, and the crested caracara. Continue around the central enclosure, past the bobcat, and make a left onto the Cypress Loop Trail, a wheelchair-accessible hiking trail. Part marl walkway, part boardwalk, it traverses a variety of habitats in the interior of the preserve. You pass a birdhouse for an American kestrel. Kestrels normally nest in abandoned woodpecker cavities, but this forest has few pine snags. Feathery pond pines nose up against slash pines occupying the slightly higher ground. Tall hatpins rise from the damp pine needles. After 0.1 mile, you reach the beginning of the loop at a shaded bench. Continue straight. Notice the many trees with peeling, papery bark—melaleuca, one of the most insidious invasive species in this part of South Florida. Spreading from landscape plantings in the early 1900s, melaleuca has taken over most of the cypress swamps along this coast. It creates

Alligator flag edges a flag pond.

a monoculture unsuitable for any native Florida wildlife.

The trail rises up onto a boardwalk to traverse a slough, where pond cypress and wax myrtles attempt to hold the forest against the invading melaleuca. Dahoon holly showers red berries onto the boards. You walk through a shaded observation platform with a bench, where an interpretive marker explains the important role of swamps in filtering groundwater. As the trail turns a corner to the right, the forest floor becomes a wonderland of ferns. Wood ferns and royal ferns emerge from the tannic waters of the swamp, clustering around the remains of ancient cypress stumps. The trail curves around to an observation deck along a flag pond, where alligator flag, also known as fire flag, grows tall along the pond's edges. Small purple flowers droop from the top of each flag in summer. Many taller, older bald cypresses ring the pond. Continuing through the fern-filled forest, you see scattered strap ferns, swamp ferns, and sword ferns. The tall, slender palms sprouting in the shade of cypresses are royal palms. A popular ornamental, the royal palm is native to the hammocks of Southeast Florida, with thousands of these graceful palms still thriving in the wilderness of the Big Cypress Swamp. In the late 1800s, frontiersmen would slosh through the swamps to dig out these palms and bring them to the cities, where they were used for landscaping. In Fort Myers, Thomas Edison oversaw the planting of hundreds of royal palms that still stand tall today along several miles of McGregor Boulevard.

Winding under the tall cypresses, the trail continues along the edge of the flag pond. As it turns away from the pond, it rises up into a hardwood hammock with a dense undergrowth of saw palmetto. After 0.6 mile, you reach a turnoff on the left for the Pine Loop Trail. During the wet season, this trail can be up to a foot under water. Continue straight, as you'll be using part of the Pine Loop Trail to complete your loop around the preserve. You end your walk on the Cypress Loop Trail back at the aviary.

To start the wilder part of this hike, turn right. Walk around the aviary's central enclosure and make a right at the screech owl exhibit. Follow the narrow marl path into the flatwoods. Keep right at the fork, continuing to an informative replica of a Seminole village, complete with extensive interpretive information on the original culture of this region, the Calusa. The Wildlands Trail starts here at the edge of the village. It can be rough and wet, but it's tame enough to bring the kids on if you don't mind muddying up their shoes. Follow the blue triangle blazes through the pine flatwoods. As you walk, be cautious of cypress knees in the footpath. There are some very interesting bases to the pond cypresses, some massively fluted, others with fat knees at the bottom. At 0.7 mile, you climb up a set of steps to a dike. Turn right, walking past a bench with distance markers. Surveying the forest from the berm, you can look down on wet flatwoods filled with young melaleuca trees. An intrusion of Brazilian pepper shades the trail on the left side, where a pair of cardinals wolf down the berries. Unfortunately, birds like the fruit of the Brazilian pepper, making this a tough exotic to eradicate—it is dispersed through bird droppings. The flatwoods are a dense thicket of pine and palmetto with interspersed melaleuca. You notice a canal on the left, filled with cattails and thick mats of *Hydrophilia,* an invasive aquatic plant choking the waterway. Originally brought to the United States from India as an aquarium plant, *Hydrophilia* now grows so thickly in South Florida's canals that it prevents fish from swimming freely.

On the right, notice the rocky solution holes created by erosion of the limestone bedrock. They create tannic water holes: You walk along a string of solution hole ponds with clusters of swamp fern along their edges. Look closely and you can see alligator trails through the aquatic plants on the left. At 1 mile, the trail turns right to continue following the dike. Here, the vegetation crowds in more closely as the trail curves along with the dike. As you pass a bench with distance markers, you hear the sound of a small waterfall caused by the outflow of the swamp forest over some debris into a canal. Canals parallel the trail on both sides now, and young slash pines attempt to gain a foothold on the dike.

At 1.4 miles, you emerge on the edge of a golf course, where a sign indicates that the trail turns to the right. Look for a blue blaze on a young slash pine and follow the worn path down the hill. An oak toad hops across the dry but narrow path, which winds between laurel oaks, melaleucas, and young slash pines. Grapevines cascade over the haymaking ferns. Pine straw carpets the footpath, while wiregrass thrives under the pines. Pink twinflowers peep out of the thick grass as the trail curves to the right through a dense grove of melaleucas. Look closely at the young trees, which are covered in reproductive spores. If you attempt to uproot, burn, or chop down the plant, it will release these thousands of spores to reseed the colony—and that's why it's so hard to get rid of.

Twisting and winding through the melaleuca, the trail comes to the edge of a swampy meadow, plunging into the water as a narrow flooded track to head into the forest of pond cypress and slash pine. Some of the misshapen cypress knees look like galls on galls. Wild pine thrives on the trunks and branches of the cypress. The trail makes a sharp right into the woods. Look down at your feet: You'll see mosquitofish swimming around. These tiny creatures do a great job of eating mosquito larvae. You pass a viewing blind on the right with benches and a roof on which palm fronds or dark plastic can be set to hide occupants from wildlife. The trail curves right to enter a corridor of saw palmetto in a dry stretch of pine flatwoods, then drops back down into the wet cypress forest.

At 1.9 miles, you reach the junction with the Pine Loop Trail. Turn left to avoid retracing your path along the Cypress Loop Trail, passing marker 28. A bench sits amid the cypress knees. The trail rises up a boardwalk to a covered rain shelter and then drops down into the swamp. You hear the screeching cry of a red-tailed hawk. Your blue blazes have yielded to green hiker markers bordered in white. After marker 32, the trail becomes a shell path on drier land. Near marker 34, there's an activity station where kids can match and rub animal tracks on a large sign. Passing the Keath Carsten Avian Garden, you can see the back of the planetarium as the trail curves around a picnic pavilion. Stay right at the fork. Grapevines and greenbriers creep up the trunks of the slash pines. A red admiral butterfly lands on a showy tickseed. You emerge at the PINE LOOP TRAIL sign on the Cypress Loop Trail. Turn left, passing the aviary on your way back to the science center. You've completed a 2.1-mile hike.

Take a peek under the building at the gaily painted picnic area for school groups. Alligators and turtles sun in their respective outdoor enclosures. Feel free to explore—especially inside the science center, if you haven't done so already. Children and adults alike will enjoy the many live exhibits in the nature center, particularly the extensive herpetological exhibit with little-seen creatures such as Florida's largest salamander, the greater siren, and Florida's only brackish-water turtle, the diamondback terrapin. Don't forget to catch the planetarium show before you leave.

10

Six Mile Cypress Slough Preserve

Total distance (circuit): 1.4 miles

Hiking time: 1 hour, 30 minutes

Habitats: Cypress slough, flag pond

Maps: USGS 7½' Fort Myers; park map

Water: the lifeblood of South Florida. As the rain falls during the wet season, it saturates the ground, flowing into the low spots, the sloughs. These modest depressions in the limestone bedrock of South Florida channel the steady fall of water toward the Everglades, toward the Big Cypress, toward the sea. Anchoring forests of grand old cypresses, each slough is a crucial link in the hydrology of South Florida. The 9-mile-long Six Mile Cypress Slough drains 57 square miles of wetlands, feeding Estero Bay. During the wet season, water levels rise several feet, forming a sluggish stream that drops its sediment in the swamps before the water reaches the mangrove forests of the bay.

Protecting more than 2,000 acres, Six Mile Cypress Slough Preserve is an important wilderness corridor on the eastern edge of Fort Myers. Its 1.4-mile boardwalk, accessible to wheelchairs and strollers, provides a quiet sanctuary for visitors to watch birds, cast for bass, or just immerse themselves in nature.

From I-75 exit 136, Ft. Myers, drive west on Colonial Boulevard. Turn left onto Six Mile Cypress Parkway. Continue 3.2 miles south to the park entrance on the left. The front gate closes automatically at 8 PM. As with all Lee County parks, there is a parking fee of 75 cents per hour or $3 per day, paid via a machine that dispenses parking permits. On Wednesday from July through October, arrive at 9:30 AM to enjoy a free guided walk of the preserve.

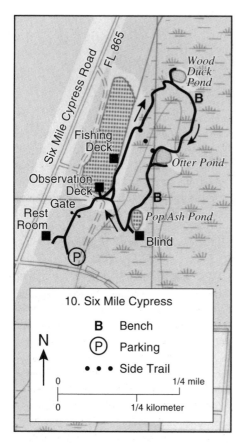

N ↑

0 _____ 1/4 mile

0 _____ 1/4 kilometer

Start your hike at the entry kiosk, following the boardwalk out into a blackwater swamp. The white blooms of duck potato wave from the tops of tall stalks; red maple and wax myrtle crowd the forest. A boardwalk to the rest rooms leads to the left. Continue straight, walking out into a cypress swamp. Loggers cleared the grand old cypresses of Lee County in the 1930s, so most of the trees you see along this hike are much younger. On the fringe of wet flatwoods, slash pines tower overhead. A leopard frog propels itself between the lotuses drifting across the open patches of dark water beneath the trees. Passing through a gate, you continue into the flooded forest. Be cautious walking

along the boardwalk in the shady sections or after a rain, as the boards can be slippery. Dense clumps of wild pine grow on the taller bald cypresses. Carolina willows cluster along a high spot paralleling the trail. A little blue heron bursts out of the underbrush, squawking as it settles on a branch of a slash pine. Rounding a corner, you see open water beyond the trees—Alligator Lake. Created by dredging to build Six Mile Cypress Parkway, this deep stretch of water provides a haven for little blue herons, white ibises, and alligators. As the trail rises up toward an interpretive kiosk, wood ferns cluster beneath the boardwalk. Turn left at the kiosk to walk out past an outdoor amphitheater to Alligator Lake. Purple pickerelweed grows along the edges. Several benches provide a place for you to sit and watch for wildlife.

Follow the boardwalk back along the left side of the amphitheater to return to the main trail, and turn left at the T intersection, where purple morning glories cascade over the underbrush. After 0.2 mile, you reach the beginning of the loop. Continue straight, picking up an interpretive guide from a container on the side of the trail. The boardwalk jogs to the left to follow the shore of Alligator Lake, where star rush grows along the shore. Watch for green boards in the boardwalk, as they correspond to stops in the interpretive guide. Pause at the fishing deck to look down. Although the water seems black from a distance, it's translucent when you peer into it. Tiny mosquitofish, *Gambusia,* dart through the shallows. Thanks to their diet of mosquito larvae, this swampy hike is surprisingly bug-free. As the trail continues on into the depths of the cypress swamp, the forest closes in around you. It's a dark and magical place. Look up and you'll be rewarded with glimpses of giant

Strap ferns

bromeliads and giant wild pine as well as several varieties of wild orchids. Wood ferns poke out of the slow-moving sheet of water, numerous species of *Tillisandia* creep up the mottled trunks of bald cypresses, and strap ferns cascade out of the rotting trunks of logged-out cypresses. With long, slender green leaves, these distinctive ferns are only found in the swamps of South Florida.

At 0.3 mile, you reach the cross-trail between the two boardwalk loops. Continue straight. Giant sword ferns drape down from the top of a cabbage palm. As the trail curves to the right, you see the tall forms of alligator flag outlining the edge of a pond. Sunlight filters through the cypress needles, lighting up each individual bromeliad, dappling shadows across the ferns on the forest floor. At the WOOD DUCK POND sign, turn left. A dozen bromeliads and more sprout near the base of an older bald cypress. The side trail ends at an observation platform with benches along the placid pond. This is the first of several flag ponds in the slough, named for the tall vegetation crowding around them during the wet season. Deeper than the rest of the flooded forest, these ponds provide a habitat for bluegill, gar, largemouth bass, and other species.

Returning to the main trail, turn left. At the next stretch of open water, take a moment to enjoy the oldest cypress in the slough, a gnarled pond cypress broader than it is tall. Its massive form reflects in the dark water of the swamp. In spring and early summer, look for swallow-tailed kites. Preferring to make their nests in ancient cypresses, these distinctive raptors migrate to Florida in February and March from South America. Mated for life, each pair works together to build a nest of Spanish moss and tiny twigs in the same neighborhood as their previous year's nest. The female sits on two eggs for nearly a month, accepting food brought from her mate. Both parents raise the chicks on a diet of frogs, snakes, lizards, bats, and small birds.

Turning away from its farthest point, the trail makes a sharp right and heads south. All around you, the forest pulses with life, cypresses and oaks covered in air plants and orchids. Goldfoot fern and shoelace fern decorate a tall cabbage palm. Resurrection fern marches across the roof of an observation deck, where you can sit and enjoy the silence of the swamp. Jogging to the right, the trail continues past a dahoon holly laden in bright red berries. A bench provides an overlook over a dark pool ringed with massive strap ferns, where water flows slowly toward a flag pond in the distance. You reach the other end of the cross-trail at 0.8 mile. Continue straight.

As the boardwalk curves around to the left, you pass an American elm swaddled in a thick growth of resurrection fern. Turn left at the sign OTTER POND to see the next flag pond. Off to the right, a giant bromeliad grows high above a giant strap fern. The spur trail ends at an observation platform with benches. Duckweed coats the near surface of the still water. Tall cypresses ring the pond, where the yellow-and-black form of an immature alligator ripples along the surface. A leopard frog clings to the base of an alligator flag, waving with the breeze. Walk back to the main trail and turn left. The boardwalk continues to zigzag through the swamp. You see the shimmer of water bugs against the dark water. After 1 mile, you reach another shaded observation deck with a view out into the swamp. Watch for the turnoff to Pop Ash Pond, the prettiest of the flag ponds. Turn right and follow the spur trail past more giant clumps of strap fern. Watch for the eggs of the apple snail, pearly white buttons deposited on tree trunks close to the water. The covered observation deck is built like a large blind—fabulous for watching and photographing the waterbirds that visit the pond. Watch for snowy egrets and white ibises, anhinga and Louisiana herons, and the occasional roseate spoonbill. Interpretive signs assist you in bird identification.

Continue back along the spur trail to the main trail and turn right. As you continue through the cypress forest, you see another boardwalk drawing near. After 1.2 miles, you complete the loop. Turn left to follow the boardwalk back to the parking lot.

11

Estero Scrub Preserve

Total distance (circuit): 4.8 miles

Hiking time: 3 hours

Habitats: Pine flatwoods, scrubby flatwoods, oak scrub, salt marsh, mangrove swamp

Maps: USGS 7½' Estero; park map

With more than 1,200 acres along the edge of Estero Bay, the Estero Scrub Preserve provides a unique look at South Florida's mosaic of habitats. Unlike most public lands in Florida, this preserve was acquired through eminent domain to prevent further encroachment on the Estero Bay estuary. Established in 1966, the 8,400-acre Estero Bay Aquatic Preserve was Florida's first aquatic preserve, a designation used for state lands protecting the wetlands around an estuary. Despite the surrounding suburban setting, this is an outing that will appeal only to the adventuresome hiker. Since much of the preserve encompasses wetlands, expect to wade through portions of the trail system year-round, especially after a heavy rain. Carry a map and keep careful track of the trail markers, which have arrows to point you in the correct direction. Most of the hike is in full sun, so bring plenty of water; a hiking stick will help you keep your balance in the wet spots and slippery mud.

To find the trailhead from the south, take I-75 exit 123, Estero. Drive west on CR 850 (Corkscrew Road) for 2.3 miles. Turn right onto US 41 and drive north 0.7 mile to Broadway. From the north, use I-75 exit 128, San Carlos Park. Drive 3.2 miles west on Allico Road to US 41. Turn left and drive 4.2 miles south to Broadway. Follow Broadway west for 1.4 miles to the NO OUTLET sign. Turn right (in front of the Florida Power & Light substation) and park in front of the trail entrance.

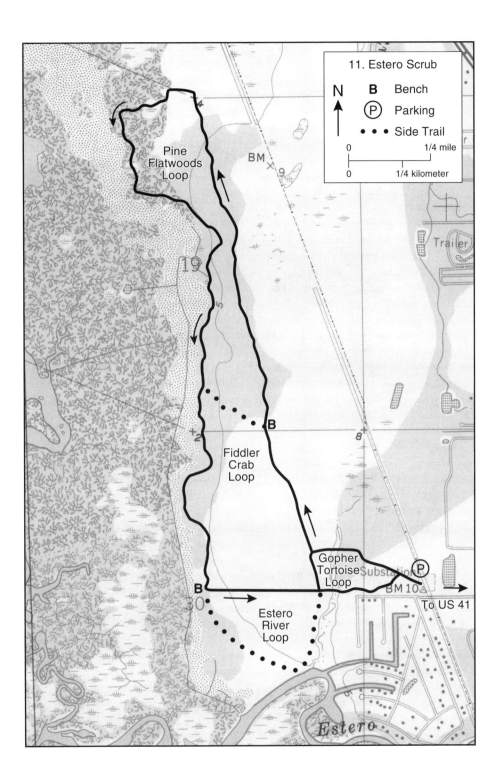

11. Estero Scrub

N

B Bench

Ⓟ Parking

• • • Side Trail

0		1/4 mile
0		1/4 kilometer

Pine
Flatwoods
Loop

BM ✕ 9

Trailer

BM

19

5

+2

8

Fiddler
Crab
Loop

B

Gopher
Tortoise
Loop

Substation Ⓟ

B

30

BM 10△

To US 41

Estero
River
Loop

Estero

Start your hike by walking over to the kiosk to pick up a trail map. Three stacked loop trails make up the trail system in the preserve, allowing you several options for hiking. This hike follows the outer Pine Flatwoods Loop, blazed with red markers. Turn left from the kiosk and follow the footpath along the fence line as it curves to the right, entering the pine flatwoods. Saw palmetto and gallberry blanket the forest floor under the tall slash pine. Keep left at the fork, where a jeep road comes in from the left. As the flatwoods become wetter, you will encounter stretches where the trail is fully under water.

Scattered throughout the flatwoods, you'll see spindly young melaleuca trees, natives of Australia and problematic invasive trees in this part of Florida. When wet, they give off a distinctly astringent odor. While Florida's pesky species is *Melaleuca quinquenervia,* a popular natural acne medication, tea tree oil, comes from the leaves of the closely related *M. alternifolia.* In this section of the preserve, melaleucas thrive in the shade of the slash pines, eager to soak up the dampness of the wet season. Although urban legend has it that developers dropped melaleuca seedlings in South Florida to sponge up the swampland, the species came to the region in 1906 as an ornamental landscaping tree.

You reach the upper end of the Pine Flatwoods Loop at 0.4 mile. Continue straight to walk the loop counterclockwise, rising up along the edge of an oak scrub. Tarflower stands tall with its sweetly scented, showy pinkish white blooms. Lichens emerge from the bright white sand, including *Cladonia prostrata,* dry and silvery green. You pass a firebreak that merges in from the left, and continue through the forest of slash pines and saw palmettos. Yellow-eyed grass rises from muddy puddles. As the land ascends a little, you reach a bench at the junction with the Fiddler Crab Loop at 0.8 mile. To shorten your hike, you can follow the yellow markers back around to the beginning of the loop for a 2.5-mile circuit. To keep hiking along the outer Pine Flatwoods Loop, continue straight. Although stands of melaleuca grow throughout the forest, an active eradication effort using herbicides has left many of the smaller trees dead or dying. Melaleuca is a tough tree to kill. At the slightest stress—such as a saw blade or fire—each tree disperses thousands of seedlings to ensure species survival.

After 1 mile, you pass a closed area with a road leading off to the right. Watch for the seemingly oversized acorns growing on the myrtle oaks and Chapman oaks in the scrub on the left. As the trail curves to the right, a trail marker indicates that it follows the right fork. Subtle blooms peep out of the scrubby flatwoods understory: white sabatia, yellow bachelor's button, and yellow star grass. A large grove of melaleuca grows off to the left, creating a monoculture mimicking a cypress dome. Unfortunately, unlike cypress, the melaleuca grove provides no useful food source for wildlife. A pileated woodpecker soars past, its broad wingspan and bright red comb making it easy to identify in flight. The trail rises into an area with many gnarled slash pines. Passing a cut going off to the left, continue straight. A thick understory of saw palmetto spreads out beneath the pines, unbroken until it meets a distant wall of melaleuca. The trail curves to the right, away from a firebreak and down a corridor leading to the northern edge of the preserve. Star rush grows along the trail's edge.

You see power lines on the right as the trail turns to the left to follow the fence line

A dense saw palmetto understory in the pine flatwoods

at the edge of the preserve. Unfortunately, the adjacent land has recently been cleared for development, both marring the view and resulting in storm-water runoff into this section of the trail. No matter the time of year, be prepared to wade up to knee deep through the next quarter mile until the trail is relocated away from the development. Turning left to follow the fence line, the trail makes a sharp left at 2 miles to return to the forest, and then turns to the right. Thanks to the disrupted drainage patterns, this next segment of trail—bordered by melaleuca—is the wettest in the preserve. If you're wading, take your time and step cautiously to avoid slipping. You'll breathe a sigh of relief when you rise up on the salt flats on the far side.

Buttonwood and white mangrove grow along the fringe of the estuary, where the waters rise and fall with the tides in Estero Bay. The trail turns left at 2.3 miles to follow the fringe of the tidal marsh. There is no defined footpath; it washes away with the tide. Watch for fiddler crabs and their mud balls—the debris left at the entrance to their home as they feed. Keep alert for each upcoming trail marker, and walk line-of-sight from marker to marker to make your way along the salt flats. A Louisiana heron scours the edge of the marsh, chasing after fiddler crabs. An immature little blue heron shows off its piebald molt. Glasswort and sea purslane thrive along the slightly higher ground. Providing footholds for young mangroves, large outcroppings of limestone along the vast open area belie the underlying bedrock of the region.

Look down into the water and you'll see the small shells of periwinkles as well as dozens of crab claws, left behind by wading birds after their meals. The trail curves to the right to follow a jeep track between the mangroves, emerging onto another salt flat, where a permanent drainage flows between the two flats. Disturbed, a flock of white ibises take to the sky, followed by a colorful roseate spoonbill. These bright pink birds sport a broad bill with a rounded tip, perfect for scooping and sifting through the soft tidal mud. Once hunted for their bright plumage almost to the point of extinction, the roseate spoonbill is one of the major beneficiaries of the Florida Aquatic Preserves program, as coastal lands continue to vanish under development.

At 2.8 miles, you pass a cut from the left that feeds water from the flatwoods down into the estuary, forming a small waterfall in times of high flow. Rising back out of the slippery mudflats, the trail works its way through a melaleuca grove. At a fork with a jeep road, keep right. Cabbage palms line the trail as it rises up to a grassy green corridor; raccoon tracks cross through a muddy patch. Swamp ferns grow under the melaleuca trees. The trail curves to the right. Emerging into another broad salt marsh, the trail makes a sharp left to follow the edge. After 3.4 miles, you reach the other end of the cross-trail portion of the Fiddler Crab Trail. Continue straight. As you follow the curve of the salt marsh, most fiddler crabs scuttle out of your way. But some stand defiantly in front of their holes, waving their large claw as a warning.

When you reach a cul-de-sac within the mangroves, keep alert for an exit trail to the right, a long corridor along the edge of the salt marsh. Bright dragonflies, golden-winged skimmers, flit above the mud as you walk across another broad open expanse, coming out to a bench on the left. At this junction, 4.1 miles into the hike, turn left to follow the yellow and red markers along the power line. A hog trap sits off to the left. Wax myrtle and cabbage palm grow along the edge of the trail, and star rush fringes the footpath. A patch of oak scrub sits high above the trail on the left.

At 4.4 miles, you reach the junction with the Blue Trail, which heads down to the Estero River. Of all of the trails in this trail system, the Blue Trail is most prone to flooding. If you've waded up to this point, you'll want to skip it; it loops out to the river and returns to the junction at the last bench you passed. To stay on the main route, continue straight. As the trail approaches a residential area, it makes a sharp turn to the left, away from the power line. Turning sharply right, it traverses the pine flatwoods. Emerging at a view of the substation, you've reached the end of the loop after 4.7 miles. Turn right to continue out to the parking lot, completing your hike of 4.8 miles.

12

Lovers Key State Park

Total distance (circuit): 5 miles

Hiking time: 2 hours, 15 minutes

Habitats: Maritime hammock, mangrove forest

Maps: USGS 7½' Estero; park map

At the mouth of Estero Bay, Lovers Key State Park protects more than 1,600 acres of maritime hammocks and mangrove forests covering four slender barrier islands. The largest, Black Island, provides habitat for red-tailed hawks and ospreys, woodpeckers and owls, its lush forests a counterpoint to the heavily developed coastline south of Fort Myers Beach. Enabling park visitors to immerse in the habitats, the 5-mile Black Island Trail winds along a series of peninsulas framed by canals and tidal lagoons, almost always in sight of the water.

From I-75, take exit 116, Bonita Springs/Gulf Beaches. Drive west on CR 865 (Bonita Beach Road), crossing US 41 after 3.7 miles. After driving through several beachfront communities, you'll cross a bridge to Lovers Key, distinctive with its lack of development. Watch for the park entrance signs 10.9 miles from I-75. Turn left. When you pay your Florida State Parks entrance fee, ask for a trail map for the Black Island Trail. Drive 0.8 mile down the entrance road to parking lot 2, and park at the trailhead on the left.

The trail system at Black Island consists of two separate trails linked by an unpaved service road and shared with bicycles. Start your hike at the Black Island Trail kiosk, where you can pick up an interpretive brochure and map. Benches flank the entrance. As you walk past a butterfly garden, the trail curves past marker 1 and into the woods on the right, a shell path under the shade of the tropical maritime hammock.

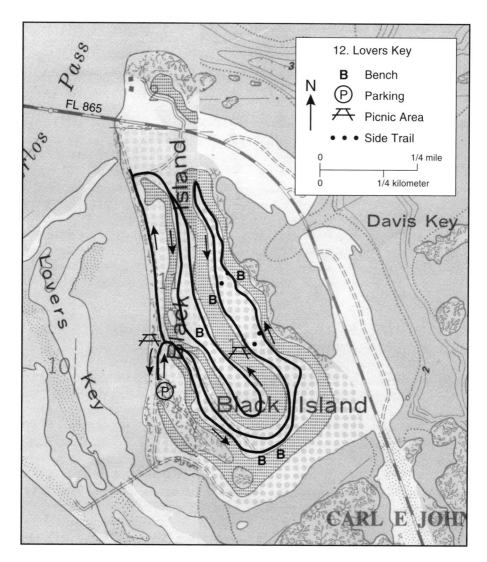

12. Lovers Key

B   Bench

Ⓟ   Parking

🎍   Picnic Area

• • •   Side Trail

A brackish mangrove-lined canal stretches off into the woods. Turning away from a picnic bench, the trail makes a sharp left to follow the waterway, following the slender finger of land between the canals—so slender that parts of the trail almost touch in places. Sweet acacia sprouts from the salt hay. A family of red-bellied woodpeckers picks its way through the buttonwoods on the shore. Cabbage palms crowd closely in to the trail. If water flows across this portion of the trail, you're in for a wet and buggy hike—after a rain, the many low-lying spots in the trail collect water, and the mosquitoes come out in droves.

Rounding a corner, the trail passes under a coconut palm. With blossoms glowing ultraviolet in the sun, morning glories spill across the understory. As the trail turns left, it parallels one of the many canals that break up Black Island, giving it a shape like a hand with fingers—the legacy of dredge and fill operations in the past, likely to create more waterfront property along Estero Bay. Across the canal, you see a picnic grove. Look behind you for a scenic view up the canal. An alligator slides into the water with a sudden splash. Although they prefer fresh water, alligators also roam brackish bays. A shortcut trail goes to the left, creating a 0.8-mile loop. Continue straight up the hill, which—at 30 feet—is one of the highest points in Lee County. As you drop back downhill, the trail curves sharply to the left. You see Australian pines rising beyond a wall of Brazilian pepper and saw palmetto. At 0.6 mile, the trail curves left past a covered bench, then drops down into a grassy area. As you come out to the canal, watch for ripples in the water. West Indian manatees drift through the channels in summer, enjoying a safe harbor away from motorboats. Past the bench, the trail curves left to follow the canal.

At 1 mile, a shortcut trail goes to the left, leading back to the other side of the trail for a 1.8-mile round trip. Continue straight, walking under the shade of the sea grapes. Beyond the bench, at 1.1 miles, turn left onto the spur trail to see a massive laurel fig. Tucked away in the forest, it looks much like a banyan tree, with giant prop roots descending from the tree limbs. Both are members of the ficus family, with dark, shiny green leaves. Return to the main trail and turn left. Continue down the broad mowed corridor along a stand of women's tongue, a mimosa-type tree decorated with white puffball blooms fringed in yellow. Australian pines tower above the trail, dropping their wispy needles to create a soft carpet. A high-rise peeks out over the vegetation on the far side of the

canal—marking the one and only developed spot on Lovers Key. As you approach a sign with an arrow, the trail turns sharply left up and over a hill delineating the end of this spit of land. Painted leaf grows profusely in the understory, where wild balsam apple dangles its orange seedpods. At 1.5 miles, take the side trail to the right. It leads into the shade of the hammock, ending at a laurel fig above the end of the peninsula, a high and dry spot below which the waters mingle. It's a nice quiet spot for reflection.

When you return to the main trail, turn right. Heading downhill, the trail curves left to follow the channel. White mangroves cluster along the shoreline. A yellow sulfur alights on a wild lime. Blackthorn grows in the shade of a peeling gumbo limbo. Lantana dangles its metallic blue berries like miniature Christmas ornaments. Just after you pass the bench at 1.8 miles, the shortcut trail comes in from the left. You enter an open area with a shaded bench on the canal and picnic tables all around. Continue straight, following the shoreline. At 2.2 miles, the trail turns off the broad jeep road and into the shade of the maritime hammock. A green anole scampers across the sea grape leaves. Spooked by your approach, a covey of mourning doves takes flight. As you walk under an archway of cabbage palms, the shortcut trail comes in from the left. White stopper fills the air with a skunky odor. The purple blooms of spiderwort peer out from behind wild coffee. A strangler fig shows off what it does best by encircling a cabbage palm trunk in its tight embrace. Looking like beached shrimp, bright orange jelly mold thrives in the decaying mass of sea grape leaves. Grapes litter the trail. You notice a change in the environment as pickleweed and sea oxeye intrude into the grass under the buttonwood.

Sea grapes along Black Island

At marker 10, you reach the picnic bench you first saw at the beginning of your hike. Here's your final decision point. If you turn left, you can walk back out to the parking lot, completing a 2.7-mile hike. To continue along the longer route, keep to the right. Head straight past the SERVICE VEHICLES ONLY sign and keep to the right as the roads forks. Walk down the road under the large clusters of necklace pods amid the white mangroves. Buttonwoods and sea grapes shade the trail. Watch for a turnoff on the right at the NATURE TRAIL sign, where you walk beneath a large sea grape with an umbrella tree growing up through it. Mangroves sprout from the stagnant water on the right. Mowed and marked by arrows, the trail parallels the canal. You pass the end of the loop coming in from the left. Continue straight, walking along the waterway past the tall Australian pines.

As the trail gradually sweeps to the left at 4 miles, you see the picnic area you've already walked through on the far side of the canal. Painted leaf grows in the shade of the sea grape, and sea oxeye fringes the shore. Rocks jut from the footpath, remnants of fill dredged from the bay. After it makes a sharp left, the trail completes the loop at a T intersection at 4.4 miles. Turn right, and keep to the left at the trail sign at the fork. When you reach the service road, turn left and follow it back to the fork, enjoying the deep shade along the way. Keep left to return to the picnic bench, and turn right at the picnic bench to exit, passing by the butterfly garden on the way out. When you emerge at the trailhead, you've completed your 5-mile hike.

Before you leave the park, take the opportunity for a swim on a unique Gulf beach. Backtrack to parking lot 1, where you'll find rest rooms and a concession stand. In addition to hiking and biking, Lovers Key State Park offers guided ecotours along the canal system, canoe rentals, and a free tram out to the beach (a quarter-mile walk across two bridges). The beach itself is rather unusual: Its narrow strand is little more than a thick deposit of seashells anchored by mangroves and buttonwoods. It's a great place for a picnic or a swim, and you can't beat the view of Sanibel Island surrounded by the placid Gulf waters.

13

J. N. "Ding" Darling National Wildlife Refuge

Total distance (two circuits, four round trips): 6.2 miles

Hiking time: 3 hours

Habitats: Freshwater marsh, mangrove swamp, mudflats, tropical hardwood hammock

Maps: USGS 7½' Sanibel, Wulfert; park map

Established in 1945, one of the most venerable and popular sites in the National Wildlife Refuge system, the J. N. "Ding" Darling National Wildlife Refuge sees more than 800,000 visitors a year. Most people come in winter, the dry season, when migratory birds pass through this crucial stop on the Atlantic Flyway. It's a place no bird-watcher should miss. Flocks of roseate spoonbills feed on the mudflats; reddish egrets pick through the mangroves. Rare mangrove cuckoos roost in the tangles of red mangroves along the salt flats. Protecting more than 6,000 acres—more than half of Sanibel Island—this preserve has its roots in early conservationism. A popular political cartoonist concerned with vanishing wildlife habitats, Jay Norwood "Ding" Darling served as the head of the U.S. Biological Survey under Franklin Roosevelt and is remembered for his efforts to expand the National Wildlife Refuge system. Darling also created and designed the first-ever duck stamp—the license sold for migratory bird hunting on U.S. lands. Funds from the stamp are earmarked for wetlands preservation.

Five trails afford hikers the opportunity to wander through various habitats in the refuge. Bring your binoculars and camera—you won't want to miss the birds, which are most active when the tide is out. To get to the refuge from I-75, take exit 131, Southwest Florida International Airport/Cape Coral. Head west on Daniels Parkway for 2.9 miles, getting into the left lane as you approach CR 865 (Six Mile

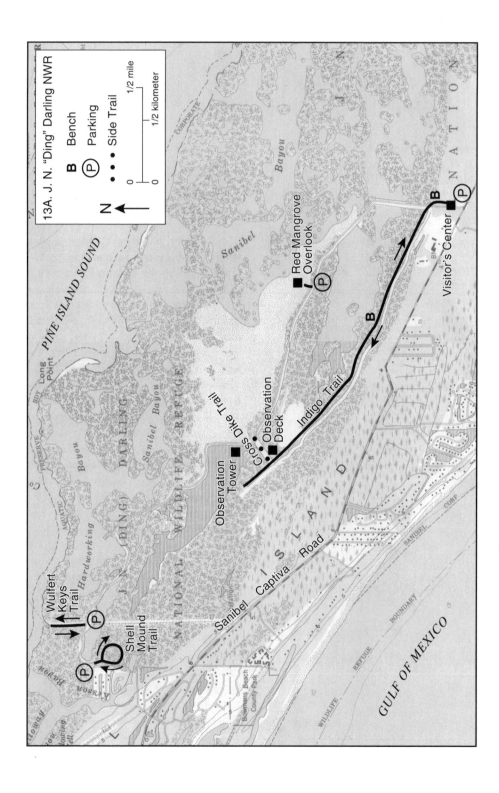

13A. J. N. "Ding" Darling NWR

B Bench

Ⓟ Parking

•••• Side Trail

N ←

0   1/2 kilometer
0   1/2 mile

PINE ISLAND SOUND

DARLING

J N DING NATIONAL WILDLIFE REFUGE

Sanibel

Sanibel Bayou

Bayou

BDY Long Point

PRESERVE

AQUATIC

Hardworking

Wulfert Keys Trail

Shell Mound Trail

Ⓟ

Ⓟ

Red Mangrove Overlook

Ⓟ

Observation Tower

Cross Dike Trail

Observation Deck

Indigo Trail

B

B

Visitor's Center

Ⓟ

SANIBEL CORP

CORPORATE

ISLAND

Sanibel Captiva Road

Bowmans Beach County Park

REFUGE BOUNDARY

WILDLIFE

GULF OF MEXICO

Cypress Parkway). Turn left and follow CR 865. When you cross Metro Parkway, the road becomes FL 865. After 2.8 miles, you cross US 41 and the road name changes to Gladiolus Drive. Continue another 1.5 miles and make a left onto Summerlin. Continue 11.8 miles down Summerlin and across the causeway to Sanibel Island ($3 toll). Turn right onto Periwinkle Road and follow the CAPTIVA signs through Sanibel to Sanibel-Captiva Road. You reach the refuge entrance after 5.1 miles, 1 mile past the entrance to the Sanibel-Captiva Conservation Foundation (Hike 14). Turn right and follow the entrance road into the parking lot.

Before you head out on the trail, stop in the educational center. It has extensive interpretive exhibits; a birding room with large windows, guidebooks, and binoculars; a movie theater; and a gift shop with field guides. Ask at the information desk for a map of the hiking trails in the refuge. The center has seasonal hours: It's open 9 AM–5 PM daily from November through April, and 9 AM–4 PM from May through October. The refuge is open sunrise to sunset daily except Friday.

Four of the trails start from Wildlife Drive, a 5-mile one-way scenic drive with interpretive signs. One of the trails is on the Bailey Tract on the Gulf side of the island. The longest trail, the Indigo Trail, starts here at the educational center, providing a 4-mile round trip through prime birding areas.

INDIGO TRAIL

Starting beneath the educational center, the Indigo Trail passes under the building alcove with the soda machines. Aiding in your understanding of the flora along the trail, interpretive markers are scattered throughout the forest. Bicycles are permitted on this trail but must be walked along the boardwalk, which takes you out over the tropical hammock and into the mangrove forest. In the deep shade of cabbage palms and sea grapes, saltbush attracts migrating monarch butterflies. Snowberry jangles its white droplets of berries. Orange jelly fungi protrude in glossy fingerlings from the leaf litter. Be careful as you walk, since the boardwalk can be slippery from moss. As the habitat transitions into the mangrove forest, the boardwalk acquires railings. Passing a bench, you walk among black mangroves, sea oxeye, and glasswort, smelling the sharp tang of the salt marsh. At 0.2 mile, the trail crosses Wildlife Drive. Continue on the shell path to the sign-in box, and drop in your $1 fee (free for children 15 and under, or for holders of this year's duck stamp) to hike the trail.

In the early-morning hours, the buttonwoods along the trail provide what little shade the mangrove forest has to offer; expect to walk in full sun all other times of day. Painted leaf shows off its poinsettia-type blooms under the shadows cast by tufts of bushybeard bluestem grass. Two snowy egrets sail overhead. Hatchling lizards, spooked by their shadows, dive for the cover of the thick grass. The Indigo Trail follows the top of a dike separating the mosquito control impoundments. Prior to control efforts, only the hardiest of settlers could tolerate life on Sanibel, where mosquitoes swarmed thicker than anywhere else in the United States—according to local lore, a record number of more than 365,000 was caught in a single trap on one night in the 1950s. Residents kept smudge pots burning to keep the mosquitoes away, and legend has it that the mailman wore a parka and a mosquito net in summer months to fend off the invasion. But with the ditching and dredging of the island's marshes into impoundments, the importation of mosquitofish to feed on mosquito larvae, and frequent aerial spraying of populated areas, this part of Florida no longer hosts quite such massive populations of mosquitoes. You'll mainly encounter them at dawn and dusk, and during the wet season.

At the 0.5-mile marker, you've hiked 0.7 mile–the mile marker corresponds to a starting point measured from where you crossed Wildlife Drive. You soon come up to a bench with some open water behind it, a good place to watch for alligators. Peeling gumbo limbo trees line the trail on the right as you approach the 1-mile marker. Along much of the hike, the vegetation hides the canals paralleling the trail. Stop and listen, and you'll hear the squawk and chatter of the birds hidden in the mangroves. In the early morning, expect to run into avid birders, binoculars at the ready, as they take their time moving down the trail. Watch for wading birds poking around the massive prop roots of the red mangroves, and keep an eye on the trees themselves for such elusive birds as the mangrove cuckoo–this is one of the few places in the United States where you can spot one.

As you approach the 1.5-mile marker, the waterway on the right opens up into a large impoundment where you can look off into the distance to watch for flocks of ibises browsing across the mudflats. Wild coffee grows at the base of a cabbage palm, while giant wild pine drapes from the tangled branches of the red mangroves. At 1.8 miles, you come to a junction with the Cross Dike Trail. This 0.2-mile paved connector leads past an observation deck with permanently mounted binoculars down to Wildlife Drive. If you're not planning to drive down Wildlife Drive today, you may want to hike down the Cross Dike

Trail to this roadway. Turn left to follow the pavement another 0.2 mile to the tall observation tower. This is one of the best places in the refuge from which to spot roseate spoonbills, their bright pink color standing out sharply against the green of the mangroves and the gray of the mudflats. Flocks of roseate spoonbills work their way across the mudflats of Sanibel Bayou at low tide, searching for a meal. If you take this side trip to the tower, add an extra 0.8 mile to your mileage for a total hike of 4.8 miles.

Beyond the Cross Dike Trail, the Indigo Trail narrows to a twisting track between the cabbage palms. Salt hay grows up to the edges of the footpath, bordered by sea oxeye. An alligator makes a massive splash as it jumps into the water–or was it a crocodile? J. N. "Ding" Darling National Wildlife Refuge is the northernmost known extent of the range of the American crocodile, distinguished from the alligator by its pointed snout and lighter-colored body, and a preference for salt water. Alligators also cruise the brackish lagoons around the refuge, however.

The trail ends abruptly where the dike ends, at the accurate 2 MILE sign, surrounded by a mangrove forest with small stretches of open water. Four glossy ibises fly in formation, skimming the tops of the trees. Turn around and retrace your path past the Cross Dike Trail. As the day wears on and the heat of the ground increases, keep watchful for yellow rat snakes and black racers sunning themselves on the dike. Alerted to your presence by your footfalls, they'll slink off into the grass. At 3.8 miles, you cross Wildlife Drive and head back onto the boardwalk, coming up to the soda machines at the visitors center with a desire for a cold drink. Your hike ends at the parking lot after 4 miles.

WILDLIFE DRIVE

Meandering 5 miles through the refuge, Wildlife Drive is the most popular destination for most visitors. This one-way road provides many spots where you can pull off the side of the road and watch birds from the comfort of your car, or get out and walk to the water's edge for a better look. Several short hiking trails provide an opportunity for you to stretch your legs and see some of the preserve's varied habitats. A drive on Wildlife Drive costs $5 per car (free to holders of the current year's duck stamp). If you're not here to hike, consider taking the guided tour that departs periodically from the educational center. It'll add to your understanding of the refuge and its inhabitants, and, since you're grouped together with other visitors on a bus, will help minimize emissions from cars using Wildlife Drive.

Red Mangrove Overlook

Just 1 mile along Wildlife Drive, a pulloff to the right enables you to walk out to the Red Mangrove Overlook. It's an interesting immersion into the mangrove forest, where brightly colored mangrove crabs scuttle around on their highways of mangrove roots and limbs. The air is infused with a murky, salty smell. As a critical part of the estuarine habitat, mangroves filter the water through their roots and provide a protected nursery for the young of many saltwater species. From the observation deck at the end of the boardwalk, you see hundreds of gar shimmering in the shallows. The clear water looks to be only a foot deep, but the soft nutrient-rich muck on the bottom might be more than 6 feet deep. Look closely at the mangroves around you for the stirring of birds, particularly ibises and egrets roosting in the shadows. Returning to your car, you've walked 0.1 mile.

Cross Dike Trail

Following a dike between impoundments of brackish water on the western side of refuge, this paved trail links Wildlife Drive with the Indigo Trail. If you haven't already wandered down it from the opposite direction, take the opportunity to walk out to the roofed observation platform. On the way, enjoy the vistas of the mangrove-lined waters, where green herons and snowy egrets pick through the shallows. Wild sweet peas climb up and over the massive sea grapes. Necklace pod trees dangle their showy yellow blossoms, attracting ruby-throated hummingbirds bound for Mexico in their fall migration. At 0.1 mile, you reach the observation platform. Use the mounted binoculars to scan the swamp for signs of alligators and turtles. One of Florida's most colorful turtles, the ornate diamondback terrapin, lives in these marshes. Diamondbacks are the only type of turtles that live in marshes, feeding on crustaceans.

The trail leads up beyond the observation platform to the Indigo Trail. Unless you plan to walk along the Indigo Trail from here (see the earlier narrative), turn around and follow the paved path back to Wildlife Drive for a 0.3-mile walk.

Wulfert Keys Trail

Beneath a set of power lines, stop at the parking area on the right for the Wulfert Keys Trail. This short round trip takes you out to the edge of Hardworking Bay, named for the difficult work of the fishermen there who set their crabbing traps by hand. Cross the bridge over a mangrove-lined canal, following the broad service road. Snowy egrets are everywhere: skimming low over the canal, flying high over the trees. You hear a plop as a large reptile drops into the water—perhaps the resident crocodile often seen along this trail. A silver-spotted skipper clings to the white blossoms of a mangrove rubber vine. A belted kingfisher swoops low over the tannic water. After 0.2 mile, the trail ends at the water with a sweeping view of the Wulfert Keys, an important set of islands serving as rookeries for herons, egrets, and roseate spoonbills in spring. A fishing boat putters past as a stiff breeze roars across Pine Island Sound. Look closely at the prop roots of the red mangroves nearest the sound—they're covered in clinging oysters. Despite the seeming challenge, snowy egrets have no problem navigating their flights in and out of the labyrinth of mangrove limbs. After enjoying the view, turn around and return to the parking area, completing the 0.5-mile walk.

Shell Mound Trail

After Wildlife Drive rounds a corner, the parking area for the Shell Mound Trail is on the left. A boardwalk leads into a tropical hardwood hammock. Use caution—it can be slippery when wet. Snake plants thrive under the gumbo limbo trees. Tall sea grapes shade the trail. At the trail junction, continue straight. Long, thin barbed-wire cactus clambers up and over the saw palmettos, displaying showy yellow blooms in late summer. A giant poinciana drips with huge bean pods like overgrown mimosa seeds, its lacy leaves creating a delicate green screen against the blue sky. Wild coffee sags under the weight of its dark red beans. The boardwalk continues up and over a shell mound covered in dense tropical vegetation. A citrus aroma pervades the air, coming from a grove of lime trees planted by an early settler. Dropping down off the shell mound, the trail loops into a mangrove forest with enormous trees—white mangroves towering more

than 30 feet. Sluggish tannic water glows with an orange hue, reflecting the tangled jungle of mangrove roots. Bromeliads flourish in the canopy. The boardwalk rises to complete the loop. Turn left at the T intersection, emerging at the parking area after 0.4 mile.

BAILEY TRACT

One of two outlying tracts of the J. N. "Ding" Darling National Wildlife Refuge, the Bailey Tract protects part of Sanibel's sensitive freshwater marshes. From the educational center, turn left onto Sanibel-Captiva Road and drive 2.2 miles to Tarpon Bay Road. Turn right and drive 0.7 mile. When you see the PEDESTRIAN CROSSWALK sign, slow down—the entrance to the Bailey Tract is on the right.

Take a look at the map on the kiosk before starting your exploration of the Bailey Tract, as there are several alternatives for hikes, ranging from 0.3 mile up to 1.1 miles. This hike follows the outer red loop. All trails are shared with bicycles as they outline the impoundments. Start your hike by crossing the boardwalk over to the dike. A little blue heron picks its way around a shallow tannic pond edged by tufts of cordgrass and ringed with cattails. Sand cordgrass and giant leather fern make up much of the landscape off to the right, where fresh water pools after summer rains. The trails are marked by a series of colored arrows. At the next kiosk, marking the junction, you'll find another trail map and interpretive information about the creatures that live in the freshwater marsh. Turn right to start a counterclockwise loop, following the narrow track along the dike.

This is a quiet place where the sea breeze rustles through the cattails. Off to the right are the freshwater marshes; on the left, the brackish impoundments with

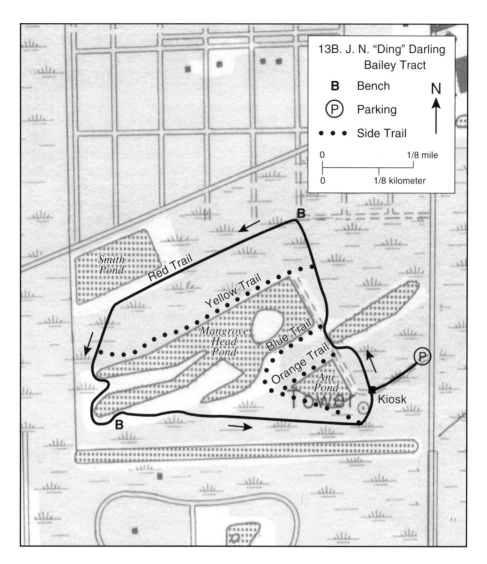

13B. J. N. "Ding" Darling
Bailey Tract

B Bench
ⓟ Parking
••• Side Trail

0   1/8 mile
0   1/8 kilometer

their mangrove islands. The orange-blazed trail takes off to the left, following a dike. Continue straight, along the buttonwoods. Thick crowds of giant leather ferns remind you of a tropical nursery as you come up to the blue-blazed trail at 0.2 mile. Continue straight, passing the trail junction with the blue and yellow arrows. A belted kingfisher flies up to the top of a mangrove. As you reach a bench on the left, the trail turns

sharply left to follow the outer edge of the impoundments. Off to the right, marsh ferns grow between scattered buttonwoods, and cattails ring deeper spots in the marsh. An osprey lets out a warning cry from the top of a buttonwood.

When you reach the T intersection, turn left; the gate on the right marks the eastern boundary of the Bailey Tract. Walking through the tropical hammock, you see

Web-like network of red mangrove roots

new construction encroaching on the canal defining the edge of the refuge. An alligator drops off the embankment with a mighty splash. At the next junction, the blue-blazed trail comes in from the left. Walk down it a little way to the bench, where you can sit and watch the osprey fishing in the impoundment. Feetfirst, it hits the water so quickly you can hardly believe it's caught something, and yet it flies away with a wriggling bass in its grasp.

Return to the outer loop and turn left. The trail turns a corner, making a sharp left to follow a canal lined with fancy homes. You walk past several tall shell mounds on which gumbo limbo and cabbage palms grow. An arrow sign indicates a left turn off the dike and across a wetland of sand cordgrass, bridged by a boardwalk. At the end of the boardwalk, turn left to pass by a tall birdhouse. You arrive at the large kiosk at the start of the loop. Continue straight past the kiosk to finish your hike at the parking area after 1.1 miles.

14

Sanibel-Captiva Conservation Foundation

Total distance (circuit): 2.1 miles

Hiking time: 1 hour, 30 minutes

Habitats: Coastal prairie, freshwater marsh, mangrove forest, palm hammock, tropical hardwood hammock

Maps: USGS 7½' Sanibel; park map

It's rare for a barrier island to have freshwater marshes. But on Sanibel Island, rainfall collects into sloughs between the ridges, channeling into the marshes and the brackish Sanibel River. Although it maintains a sluggish flow, it's not a true river—it was created for mosquito control by dredging out and connecting a string of alligator holes. Founded in the 1930s by concerned local residents, headed up by ardent conservationist J. N. "Ding" Darling, the Sanibel-Captiva Conservation Foundation worked to preserve these fragile lands and others throughout the barrier islands. Now managing more than 1,800 acres in several preserves, the Sanibel-Captiva Conservation Foundation maintains a nature center and a network of trails that introduce visitors to the freshwater marshes. The trails are open year-round on weekdays 8 AM–3 PM; during the dry season, November through April, the preserve is open on weekends as well. In addition to the center and trails, you'll find a native plant nursery and a small gift shop on the site.

From I-75, take exit 131, Southwest Florida International Airport/Cape Coral. Head west on Daniels Parkway for 2.9 miles, getting in the left lane as you approach CR 865 (Six Mile Cypress Parkway). Turn left to follow CR 865. When you cross Metro Parkway, the road becomes FL 865. After 2.8 miles, you cross US 41 and the road name changes to Gladiolus Drive. Drive another 1.5 miles and make a left onto Summerlin. Continue 11.8 miles down Summerlin and across

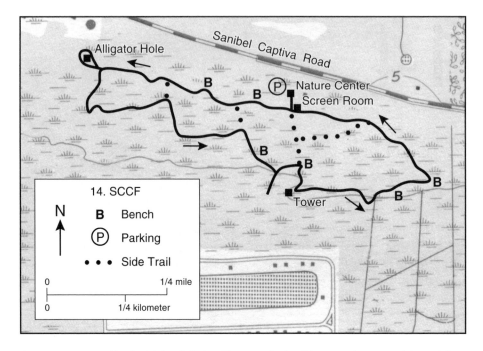

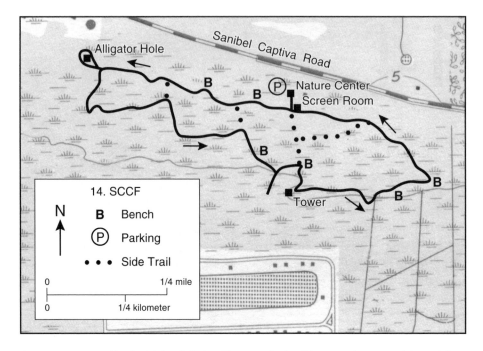

the causeway to Sanibel Island ($3 toll). Turn right onto Periwinkle Road and follow the CAPTIVA signs through Sanibel to Sanibel-Captiva Road. Keep alert for the small SANIBEL-CAPTIVA CONSERVATION FOUNDATION sign on the left, and turn left into the entrance after 4.1 miles.

Walk up to the nature center and pay your $3 entry fee (children under 17 and members free). Pick up a trail map from the desk before wandering through the center's exhibits, which provide an understanding of Sanibel Island's habitats. The hike starts behind the nature center, crossing a boardwalk over a broad swath of marshland. Giant leather ferns grow along the edges, on ridges made up of ancient Calusa shell mounds. You can see the shells at the entrances to gopher tortoise burrows, where the tortoises have kicked them out across the leaf litter. Coonties thrive under the sea grapes. Purple morning glories cascade under the marlberry.

At the T intersection, turn right to follow the Sabal Palm Trail, passing by a screen room designated the Matthiessen Teaching Shelter. The trail winds through the shade of a palm hammock, where goldfoot ferns drape from the cabbage palms *and* grow from the forest floor. Wild coffee crowds the understory. At the T intersection, the trail to the right returns to the parking lot. Turn left. Make a quick right to continue on the Sabal Palm Trail. Crimson blossoms top a tree-sized coral bean. Purple stringers of sea grapes dangle over a bench. The trail splits around islands of vegetation, where scattered interpretive markers help you identify the plants of this tropical hardwood hammock. Shiny-leafed myrsine grows throughout the forest. At the fork, you reach a signpost. Turn left, passing by a bench under a peeling gumbo limbo. Also known as the tourist tree because it's always red and peeling, gumbo limbo thrives on shell mounds, reaching heights of up to 60 feet. As an adaptation to hurricane-force winds, the gumbo limbo can sprout a new tree from a fallen branch. Farmers once used this quirk to their advantage, planting living fences of gumbo limbo limbs. An excellent hardwood, it's the material of choice for carving carousel horses.

A small opening in the forest enables you to look out over the freshwater marshes. Continue straight, ducking under the cabbage palms past an old hand pump from the farm that once occupied this high ground. In the late 1800s, Sanibel Island provided a new frontier for settlers to South Florida eager to start farming on their new land grants. Approachable only by boat until the 1960s, the island seemed an ideal place for growing fruits and vegetables, especially with a freshwater supply trapped between two ridges. Some settlers took advantage of the tropical weather, establishing pineapple and coconut plantations. Others planted citrus, tomatoes, and peppers. By 1920, the farmers of Sanibel were shipping out more than 150,000 crates of produce every year. But then the hurricanes struck, one after the other. When a 14-foot tidal surge enveloped the low-lying portions of the island in 1926, it dealt a death blow to farming on Sanibel. What the ancient Romans did to conquer their enemies, the sea did to Sanibel—salted the fields. Agriculture never rebounded.

Zigzagging past a cat's claw tree, the trail reaches a junction. Turn right to stay on the Sabal Palm Trail. Walking through the corridor of cabbage palms, you catch a whiff of skunk—the odor of a white stopper tree. These slender residents of the tropical hammock grow up to 25 feet tall, bearing juicy black plumlike fruit. Notice the whisk fern growing from the base of a cabbage palm. It's a primitive vascular plant, without fronds. A brown anole clings to the leaf of rabbit tobacco. The trunks of the cabbage palms show char marks from a recent burn. All around you, the forest understory twinkles with berries—bright purple American beautyberry, deep crimson wild coffee, and sea grapes in crimson and purple.

At 0.5 mile, you reach the junction with a side trail to Alligator Hole. Turn right, walking past more white stopper. Boardwalks create a loop around the old alligator hole. During the dry season, alligators dig hollows into the soft bottom of the marsh to keep water exposed, creating a cool environment for them and a precious source of water for other creatures. Go straight under the palms past the giant leather ferns to the boardwalk. Coontail fills the shallows. As you walk around the pond, look for leopard frogs in the grasses, and turtles in the dark water. Past the observation platform, continue straight. Make a left across the bridge. Turn right to start down the Upper Ridge Trail. As you walk down the mowed corridor through the sand cordgrass, the tops of giant leather ferns tower all around you. Sanibel's freshwater marshes are only 2 feet above sea level, and during the wet season, these low spots flood.

At the T intersection, turn left to walk through the open grasslands. Watch out for the burrs on the casearweed! At 0.9 mile, you reach a junction. Turn right to follow the Booth Courtney Trail. Cut directly through the tall cordgrass and giant leather ferns, the trail eventually rises onto a small shell ridge with an oak hammock crowded with myrsine, marlberry, and buckthorn. Dropping into a coastal prairie, the trail winds through an area where salt-loving plants such as sea purslane and

Pond apple

the T intersection, turn right to continue to the observation tower as the trail follows a boardwalk over a marshy area. White mangroves and buttonwoods shade the route. A pair of red-bellied woodpeckers flits between the trees. The boardwalk ends at the base of the tower. Climb up for a sweeping view of the river and the lowlands comprising the Sanibel's freshwater wetlands.

Continue along the river's edge on the West River Trail, where wild olive and buttonwood cling to the shell mound. Sawgrass intrudes into the trail in places—be wary of this sedge's sharp, serrated blades. As you emerge into a sunny area, clambering up and over a shell mound, you come down to a bench on the river at 1.5 miles. Giant leather ferns reflect in the slow-moving tannic water. The observation platform provides your last chance to sit and look out over the Sanibel River. A green heron picks along the bases of the mangroves. The trail turns to the left to follow an old mangrove-lined mosquito control canal shimmering with mosquitofish. Beyond the turn, tannic water laps close to the edges of the trail. Roots break up the grassy footpath. As the trail makes a sharp left, it crosses an old road before continuing down a broad open corridor of grasses. Star rush peeps out of the shadows, and purple morning glories emerge from the cordgrass. You pass a platform on a telephone pole, built to encourage ospreys to nest.

Turning to the right, the trail passes under a stretch of tall cabbage palms flanked by giant leather ferns and sea myrtle. After 2 miles, you reach the junction with the Elisha Camp Loop. Continue straight. Turn left at the WORK TRAILS sign, where the trail reenters the tropical hardwood hammock. Notice the tall stands of wild cotton, especially showy when they

pickleweed thrive. A corridor of buttonwood provides a brief respite from the sun. At the next junction, turn right to follow the West River Trail. As you pass a turnoff for the Booth Courtney Trail on the left, continue straight along the shell causeway above the marsh. A tannic swamp stretches out to the right.

After 1.2 miles, a bench provides your first overlook of the cattail-lined Sanibel River. Saltwater intrusion pushes up from the Gulf to meet the trickle of rainwater stored by the freshwater marshes, so you see plants from both environments represented here where the waters meet—wax myrtle and saltbush, mangroves and duckweed. The trail parallels the river, although it's hidden behind a screen of foliage. At sport creamy yellow flowers and fluffy cotton balls. Thanks to wrongheaded eradication efforts in the 1930s, wild cotton is now one of Florida's most endangered plant species. When you reach the screen room and junction with the Sabal Palm Trail, you've walked the entire outer loop of the trail system. Turn right to cross the boardwalk and return to the nature center, completing a 2.1-mile walk.

II

Big Cypress

Fakahatchee Strand #3   *Clyde Butcher*

15

Corkscrew Swamp Sanctuary

Total distance (circuit): 2.3 miles

Hiking time: 2 hours

Habitats: Cypress strand, flag ponds, freshwater marsh, pine flatwoods, wet prairie

Maps: USGS 7½' Corkscrew; park map

Fluffy white, dashing pink, stunning blue, and jet black: plumes, the fashion statement of the day in 1886, poking out of the tops of ladies' hats, when milliners paid $32 per ounce for egret plumes, twice the value of gold. To meet the public's rapacious demand for feathers, frontier hunters ventured deep into the Big Cypress Swamp, the Ten Thousand Islands, and the Everglades. In a day's work, a hunter could kill thousands of birds, wiping out entire nesting colonies of herons, egrets, and roseate spoonbills.

Formed out of public outrage against these deaths for the sake of fashion, the National Audubon Society came together in 1896 to boycott feathered hats and rally behind legislation to protect wading birds, particularly in Florida. By hiring game wardens to protect the roosting colonies during their nesting season, Audubon provided the policing needed to enforce these new laws. In 1912, a warden roamed Corkscrew Swamp, chasing away plume hunters who would arrive on horseback to take shots at the wood stork colony.

Corkscrew Swamp contains the largest stand of virgin bald cypress in the world, with trees up to 600 years old. More than 1,000 wood storks still nest here, arriving in winter and early spring. Named by pioneers for the twisting, turning path of the river that flows through it (renamed the Imperial River in more recent times), Corkscrew Swamp covers 315 square miles. It's an important part of Southwest Florida's drainage system as it feeds the

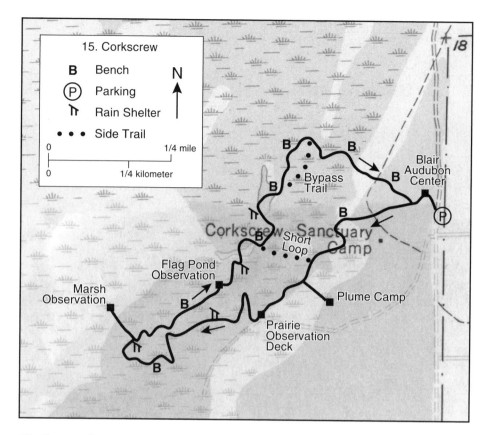

Big Cypress Swamp, channeling the summer rains southward. Owned by the National Audubon Society, Corkscrew Swamp Sanctuary covers more than 2,800 acres of this critical habitat.

To find Corkscrew Swamp Sanctuary, take I-75 exit 111, Immokalee Road/Naples Park. Drive east on CR 846. After 15.6 miles, turn left at the CORKSCREW MARSH SANCTUARY sign onto CR 849. Follow this road for 1.5 miles, which makes a sharp left, until you see the parking sign for the sanctuary. Turn right and park. Walk up to the front entrance. Rest rooms sit off to the left, and the boardwalk on the right leads to the nature center, with interpretive signs explaining the history of the Audubon Society's involvement in Corkscrew Swamp.

Open daily 7 AM–7:30 PM from April 11 through September 30, and 7 AM–5:30 PM from October 1 through April 10, the park charges an admission of $8 adults, $3.50 children, and $5 for Audubon members—well worth it considering the natural wonders protected by this preserve. Strollers and wheelchairs can traverse the entire boardwalk. To enhance your enjoyment of the sanctuary and its inhabitants, take the time to browse the exhibits and watch the film before heading out on the hike.

Your hike starts behind the Blair Audubon Center. Head straight past the RECENT WILDLIFE SIGHTINGS board and follow the boardwalk into the pine flatwoods. Some of the slash pines towering overhead are more than 200 years old, truly ancient for South Florida. Water lilies blanket a sluggish tannic stream that flows under the boardwalk. Built with a tropical hardwood from the Brazilian rain forest that requires no chemical treatment, this boardwalk is expected to last 50 years—unlike the boardwalks that preceded it, which would rot every few years and have to be replaced. The first effort to span the swamp started in 1955, just a year after the Corkscrew Cypress Rookery Association was founded to preserve this ancient swamp. Having logged the giant cypresses of Fakahatchee Strand (Hike 18) to the south, the Lee Tidewater Cypress Company and Collier Enterprises eyed these giants for timber. When the National Audubon Society assumed stewardship of the lands that the association had purchased, both companies donated additional acreage and cash to expand the preserve. The first 5,600-foot boardwalk through the swamp opened in 1956—a monumental effort that involved volunteers wading into waist-deep water to plunge postholes into the peat and muck while trying not to stir up alligators.

Crossing a paved area designated a wildlife crossing, you continue out along a wet prairie on the fringe of the cypress strand. Alligator trails lead through the sand cordgrass to a flag pond. As you approach the feathery pond cypresses, you pass an observation platform with a bench. Although these small cypresses look young, they've been stunted by the poor soils on the edge of the prairie. Most of the trees are more than a century old. Passing a side trail at 0.3 mile, continue to the right. The trail rounds the corner into the cypress forest, past large masses of alligator flag around another flag pond. Flag ponds are deep spots in the strand where water remains almost year-round, attract-

ing alligators. Also called fire flag, the tall plants signaled to hunters where to look for 'gators.

Thick with partially digested berries and the aroma of grapes, a mound of bear scat sits in the middle of the boardwalk. Along with the Florida panther, the Florida black bear roams this swamp forest, thinking nothing of clambering up and over the boardwalk on its nightly foraging trips. This preserve protects several other endangered species—the Everglades mink, the Everglades fox squirrel, and the Bachman's sparrow—in addition to the largest nesting colony of wood storks in the United States. As the trail zigzags through the epiphyte-clad cypresses, you hear the constant chatter of birds. Audubon Swamp Sanctuary is a world-renowned birding site, with nearly 200 species identified within the swamp. Few people come here to just zip down the trail. Bringing guidebooks, binoculars, and cameras, they spend hours walking the 2.3-mile loop in search of the small details that make this preserve so special.

As you walk through a grove of pond apple, notice the dangling fruits, similar in size, shape, and color to a Granny Smith apple. An important food for squirrels and raccoons, the pond apple is found only in the swamps south of Lake Okeechobee. On the right, a shortcut trail heads over to the Lettuce Lakes—providing a 0.7-mile loop back to the start for people with limited mobility. Continue straight. Emerging on the edge of a large prairie ringed by cypresses, you meet another side trail. Turn left and walk down to the Plume Camp rain shelter, once the site of a plume hunter's camp. Return to the main trail and turn left. The boardwalk follows the ecotone between the cypress swamp and the wet prairie, where zebra swallowtails flit among

Interpretive markers add to a hiker's understanding of the ecosystem.

the pickerelweeds. A mix of grasses, sedges, and wildflowers makes up the prairie. At 0.5 mile, a side trail leads to an observation platform on the prairie. Walk down and watch for alligators and wading birds. Least killifish shimmer in the dark water. You're wrapped in the sounds of nature: just the wind through the trees, the chirping of cicadas, and the calls of birds.

As you continue along the boardwalk, it curves into the shady bald cypress swamp. Giant strap ferns emerge from amid the sword ferns under stands of pond apple. With each footstep, you move deeper into the swamp. The cypresses increase in size, and you see patches of open water between trees. You reach a rain shelter with benches at 0.7 mile. Half submerged in the tannic water, the rotting logs become rafts for royal ferns, strap ferns, and swamp ferns. A greenish pig frog sits on a log, grunting. This is the species that frog hunters pursue for the frog legs found in restaurants.

Look up and marvel at the ancients. These are the grand giants of Corkscrew Swamp, bald cypresses rising up to 130 feet tall, with girths of up to 25 feet. Forests of resurrection fern and bromeliads carpet their thick branches. A red-tailed hawk swoops low, letting out a piercing cry. Watch for swallow-tailed kites: They roost and nest in the tops of bald cypresses. Look down at the squat fat cypress knees and the swamp lilies—ghostly white against the black water. A side trail leads over to an observation platform under the cypresses, where you can sit beneath these giants and marvel at their glory. Past the observation platform, the trail turns to the right, passing a flag pond ringed by massive cypresses. A red-bellied woodpecker calls to its mate. The trail curves to the right past another stand of pond apples to a spot where strangler figs clamber up over snags and onto the bald cypresses themselves, daring to ascend the heights of the giant cypresses.

At the T intersection, you've walked 1 mile. Turn left to visit the Marsh Observation Platform. Notice the intricate symmetry of each leaf of alligator flag grazing the railing. A flicker perches in a lower branch of a cypress. An eastern pondhawk dragonfly, resplendent in iridescent green and black, rests on a lily pad. As you turn to the left to climb up the observation platform, the showy reddish pink blooms of wild hibiscus catch your eye. At the top of a stem 5 feet tall, each flower can be up to 8 inches across. From the platform, you enjoy a sweeping view of the freshwater marsh, its waters hidden under a sea of Carolina willows and scattered red maples. Return along the spur trail to the main trail and continue straight, passing the Alligator Den rain shelter at 1.2 miles. A little farther along, a platform on the right overlooks a flag pond. A scruffy-looking young cardinal perches on an alligator flag and tears at the leaf, munching on it. This is yet another ideal bird-watching spot, as birds flit in and out of the understory plants surrounding the pond.

Walking past a set of benches along the boardwalk, you pass several huge clumps of giant leather fern. With 32 species of ferns to ponder, you'll be amazed at the jumble of species collected in this section of the swamp, including water spangles drifting across the open water. After 1.5 miles, the boardwalk begins its route across the Lettuce Lakes portion of the preserve. Water lettuce floats on the surface of the ponds—all flag ponds, and up to 5 feet deep. The Lettuce Lake rain shelter provides a spot for you to sit and look for alligators cruising through the water hyacinths. The shortcut trail joins in from the right at 1.6 miles. Continue straight, walking along the Lettuce Lakes. Pond apples reflect in the dark water. As it passes through the Barred Owl rain shelter, the trail turns right and crosses one of the deepest ponds. You emerge into the full sun along a broad pond. Near a water-level recorder, several benches encourage you to look out over the dark water. Coots fuss in the shadows. At 1.8 miles, you reach the Bypass Trail. During wood stork nesting season, the main trail will be closed so as not to disturb the colony; follow the route indicated when you arrive. Along the main trail, grand cypresses rise overhead, providing the critical habitat needed for the wood storks to breed and raise their young. The only stork that nests in the United States, the wood stork breeds each winter, with a month-long incubation of three or four eggs. The bonded pair spends four months raising their young.

Past another set of benches, the boardwalk curves to the right. An alligator rests in stillness of the black water, its head scarcely protruding. You reach the junction of boardwalks; continue straight, past the end of the Bypass Trail and the new boardwalk built for student groups. Stunted pond cypress decked out in bromeliads rise all around you as the trail zigzags back out to the wet prairie. After crossing the prairie, you can see the environmental center. A pair of benches in the pine flatwoods provides your last birding opportunity along the loop as you return to the WILDLIFE SIGHTINGS board. You've walked 2.3 miles. Jot down your observations before you head inside to browse the extensive array of natural science books at the gift shop.

16

Sabal Palm Hiking Trail

Total distance (circuit): 2.2 miles

Hiking time: 1 hour, 30 minutes

Habitats: Pine flatwoods, cypress strand

Maps: USGS 7½' Belle Meade; park map

Driving down US 41 into Naples in the 1960s, winter vacationers in Florida saw massive billboards advertising Golden Gate Estates, a brand-new subdivision that the developers intended to be the biggest in America. Encompassing more than 57,000 acres, it stretched to the south and east of the city of Naples.

What prospective buyers didn't realize, however, was that the land sat on the northeastern edge of the Big Cypress Swamp. Since the cypresses and pines that made up the deep forest had been logged, winter visitors simply saw a grid of roads and canals breaking up a vast open landscape. Using high-pressure sales tactics, the developer sold off hundreds of multiacre tracts to people who had no clue that from June through November, rainwater drained through the swamps and covered the land up to 2 feet deep on its way to the Gulf of Mexico. Of course, the land could never be developed into the dream subdivision they planned. In 1967, the developer pleaded guilty to using "false, misleading, deceptive, and unfair practices" to sell the land and went bankrupt. Thousands of buyers were stuck with their swampland lots. In the 1980s, the state of Florida put together a plan to buy up the land and create Picayune Strand State Forest. In order to do so, they had to track down and buy up acreage from more than 17,000 landowners—one of the most complex land acquisitions in Florida history.

On the South Golden Gate Estates tract of Picayune Strand State Forest,

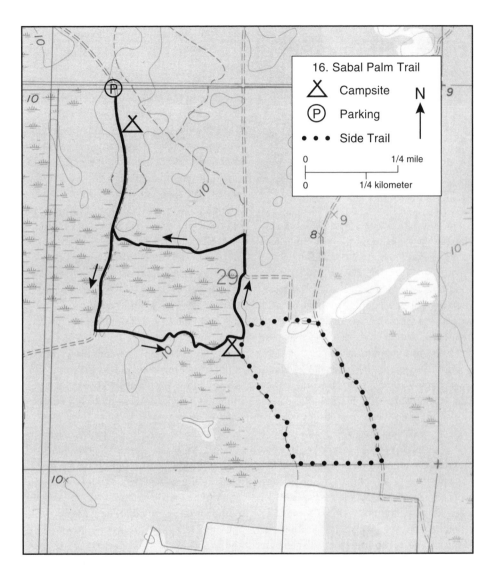

which adjoins both Fakahatchee Strand Preserve State Park and Collier-Seminole State Park, the Sabal Palm Hiking Trail showcases wet flatwoods and cypress slough habitats. Built by an Eagle Scout from Naples, the trail is now part of the Florida State Forest Trailwalker program. Two primitive campsites enable overnight stays. But this is *not* an easy hike. If you visit in the wet season, as you'll be wading in dark water up to your hips in many places. Even in the dry season, expect to find scattered deep spots you'll wade through. Use a hiking stick for balance, and bring a friend—this is a haunting, lonely place off the beaten path. Hunting is permitted in the forest during certain seasons; check www.floridaconservation.org for the exact dates. Wear blaze orange if you're here during hunting season.

Pine lily

To find the trailhead from I-75 exit 101, Naples/Marco Island, take CR 951 (Collier Boulevard) south 4.8 miles to Sabal Palm Road. Turn left. Follow the road beyond the pavement's end. After 3.4 miles, keep alert on the right for a driveway leading back to the trailhead parking and kiosk.

Pick up a map at the kiosk—you'll need it, as the return route is not clearly signposted. Orange metal hiker markers and silver arrow symbols point the way up the trail, which starts off in the pine flatwoods. This is a young slash pine forest, with an understory of wax myrtle and saw palmettos. Blooms of yellow-eyed grass sit upon their tall, slender stalks. In fall, look for the showy red pine lily, one of the most dazzling flowers of the pine flatwoods. At 0.1 mile, you pass the first campsite—simply a picnic bench set in a clearing. Although there appear to be attempts to eradicate them, melaleucas are scattered throughout the pines. As the trail meets faint side paths and firebreaks, large arrows point you down the correct path. Dropping down into the slough, you're surrounded by the young pond cypresses characteristic of the Big Cypress Swamp. When the trail is inundated with water in the wet season, bladderwort thrives throughout the slough, its telltale yellow blooms rising above their wispy floating vegetation. A carnivorous plant, the bladderwort has tiny white bladders that trap and digest small insects.

Passing the next firebreak going off to the right at 0.4 mile, you immediately come to another one coming in from the left. Take a look at your surroundings and remember them, as the firebreak from the left is the end of Loop A—and it's not marked. Up in the trees, epiphytes dangle from cypress limbs, along with purple morning glories spilling down a small cypress. The trail rises up into slash pines and melaleucas, nice open flatwoods with a grassy understory and scattered clumps of saw palmetto, with patches of marsh ferns at the bases of trees. A red-bellied woodpecker flits from snag to snag. At 0.7 mile, the trail reaches a T intersection with a jeep road. Turn left to continue along the loop. All along the trail, sabatia grows in small clusters. Wild pine, a colorful epiphyte with pinkish purple flowers, blooms from the trunk of a tall slash pine. Duck potato rises out of a marshy area. As you walk along the edge of another cypress slough, you see the pink blossoms of marsh mallow poking out of the tall grass. Despite the name *Sabal Palm Hiking Trail,* you don't see the first sabal palm—another name for cabbage palm—until nearly a mile into the hike. Pickerelweed grows along the edges of the trail, which may be particularly wet through this section as you walk down through a mix of cypresses and pines. Wheeling overhead, a red-shouldered hawk fusses over its territory.

The second campsite sits at the junction of Loop A and Loop B, at 1.1 miles. It includes a barbecue grill as well as a picnic table. This is your decision point. For a longer hike—not recommended if the trail has been flooded thus far—turn right to follow Loop B counterclockwise through the cypress strand, adding 1.3 miles to your hike. Keeping to the shorter hike, turn left. The trail enters a stand of towering slash pines, rising up into the forest, with underbrush crowding close on both sides. The narrow corridor is an old tram road used to access the cypress swamp for logging during the 1940s and 1950s, when cypresses towering more than 100 feet covered this land. It will take centuries for the young cypresses here to recapture the grandeur of their forebears.

At 1.3 miles, the trail reaches Wiggins Field Road, one of the many old subdivision roads built for the former South Golden Gate Estates. Continue straight along the hard-packed limestone until you reach a small green sign that says SABAL PALM HIKING TRAIL and an arrow to the left. Turn left and return to the footpath, which now follows a firebreak through the wet flatwoods. A yellow sulfur alights on orange butterfly weed. The broad leaves of star rush poke up through the dense mats of grass. Although the trail runs relatively straight, it goes through several brief but sharp sets of right and left turns to adjust its course, and it is in this section that the flatwoods drain into the trail at all times of year, especially after a rain. Wade carefully. As the trail enters a cypress stand, you see the bright red berries of dahoon holly, a splash of color against the otherwise green-and-brown forest. Morning glory vines dangle from the trees as you follow the arrows around another sharp turn, venturing deeper into the cypress swamp.

Although it's difficult to distinguish that you've completed the loop, at 1.8 miles you reach a rough T intersection with a hiker marker posted on a tree off to the left. Turn *right* to exit the trail. You pass a firebreak going off to the left. Continue down the trail. There are no markers facing you in this direction, but the footpath should be obvious. Rising back up into the pine flatwoods, you pass the picnic table at the first campsite. Within a few moments, you reach the end of the trail at the kiosk, completing your 2.2-mile hike.

17

Collier-Seminole State Park

Total distance (two circuits): 7.5 miles

Hiking time: 4 hours, 30 minutes

Habitats: Cabbage palm flatwoods, cypress slough, oak hammock, pine flatwoods, tropical hardwood hammock, mangrove forest, salt marsh, scrubby flatwoods

Maps: USGS 7½' Belle Meade, Royal Palm Hammock; park map; Florida Trail Association map SF-9

Barron Gift Collier was a busy man. At the age of 26, he'd made his first million. Flush with cash from his prosperous streetcar advertising business in New York City, he turned his attention to Florida after a vacation visit to Useppa Island in Pine Island Sound in 1911. Investing in the wild and rugged Lee County coastline, he bought up vast tracts of land from Useppa southward to the Ten Thousand Islands. Spurred by the dubious vision of Florida governor Napoleon Bonaparte Broward to drain the Everglades, he sank his business profits into turning swampland into real estate by digging drainage canals and building roads. In return for bailing out the state's financial problems with the construction of the Tamiami Trail (US 41) across the Everglades, he asked for a county to be named in his honor. And thus Collier County, home of Naples and Marco Island, bears his name today.

When Collier died in March 1939, he was Florida's largest landowner. To his credit, he'd left large tracts of land unsullied, in part because they were tangled swamps, and in part because he wanted the federal government to create a national park that encompassed what was then the largest natural grove of royal palms in the United States. When the U.S. government showed no interest, the state of Florida stepped in and created Collier-Seminole State Park, opening along the Tamiami Trail in 1947.

Two trails showcase this tropical environment where the Everglades and the Big

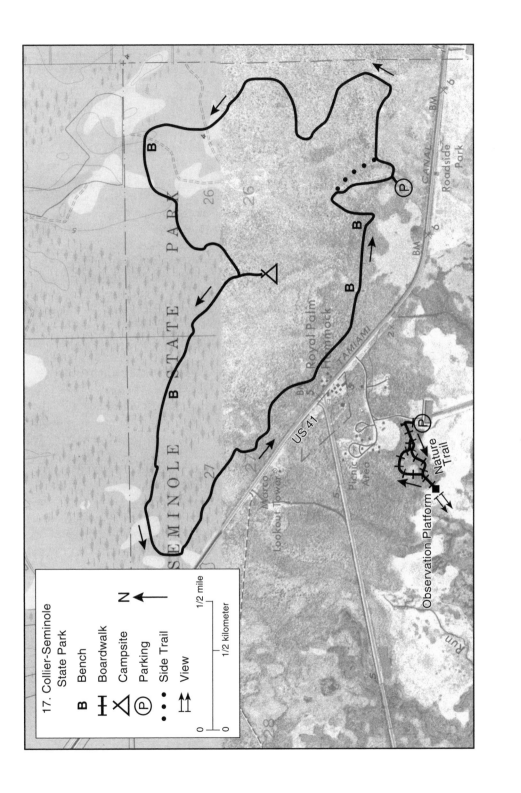

17. Collier-Seminole
State Park

B Bench

Boardwalk

Campsite

Parking

Side Trail

View

N

0   1/2 mile
0   1/2 kilometer

SEMINOLE STATE PARK

B

B

B

B

B

26

26

27

27

28

5

5

4

4

4

5

US 41

TAMIAMI

CANAL

BM ×6

BM ×6

BM ×6

Roadside
Park

Royal Palm
Hammock

Marco
Lookout Tower

Picnic
Area

Observation Platform

Nature
Trail

Run

5

Cypress meet. The Royal Palm Hammock Trail provides an easy 0.9-mile taste of the wild as you follow a boardwalk through a royal palm hammock and out along the fridge of the vast mangrove swamps of the Ten Thousand Islands. Intrepid explorers and backpackers can take on the rugged 6.6-mile Collier-Seminole Hiking Trail through pine flatwoods, hammocks, and cypress swamps north of US 41.

To get to Collier-Seminole State Park from I-75, take exit 101, Naples/Marco Island. Drive south on CR 951 for 7.1 miles to US 41. Turn left to continue east 8.5 miles to the park entrance on the right, which lies just beyond a small Miccosukee Indian village. From the east coast, enjoy the scenic Tamiami Trail (US 41) on your drive to the park. The Collier-Seminole State Park entrance sits 15.5 miles west of the FL 27/US 41 junction north of Everglades City. When you pay your Florida State Parks entrance fee, ask for maps for both trails. Continue in on the park entrance road. A pulloff on the right lets you get out and examine the walking dredge used to build the Tamiami Trail. This massive piece of machinery is now a national historical mechanical engineering landmark. Responsible for carving a swath through the swamps, it dug a canal that provided the rock needed to create the roadbed of US 41. Work crews followed close behind in portable bunkhouses. Each crew would move out into the rocky, holey surface of the swamp, blasting apart pine rocklands and cypress sloughs with dynamite to allow the dredge to pull up material small enough to use as a roadbed. After 13 years of problem-laden construction, the road officially opened on April 26, 1928, when a motorcade from Fort Myers reached Bayfront Park in Miami. Collier was in attendance at the formal event, giving a speech titled "The Development of the Last American Frontier." We can be thankful that the rigors of construction in Big Cypress and the Everglades helped stem that dream of development, and that the lands along the corridor have been preserved for posterity. Today, the Tamiami Trail from Naples to Miami is South Florida's premier scenic highway.

Stay to the left when you reach the fork in the road; the right fork goes into the campground. Off to the right is an unusual piece of pseudo-Greek architecture, a memorial to Barron Collier. The road ends in a parking area along a boat basin, with a picnic area overlooking the mangrove-lined canals. Several tour boats depart from the dock daily, offering ecotours into the Ten Thousand Islands. Check at the concession stand, where you can also rent canoes, for timetables and rates.

ROYAL PALM HAMMOCK TRAIL

Turn right and park in front of the Royal Palm Hammock Trail trailhead sign. This 0.9-mile interpretive trail is a wild but gentle introduction to the habitats protected by Collier-Seminole State Park: *Wild* because the boardwalks are old and slippery, and mosquitoes collect here by the millions; *gentle* because you probably won't get your feet wet, and you can go at an easy pace. As you enter the junglelike corridor, masses of turk's cap drip crimson from the surrounding shrubs. Wild coffee and myrsine flank the trail. Walking past tall, peeling gumbo limbos and primordial giant leather ferns, you pass under a Jamaican dogwood. Although it's not a true member of the dogwood family, it sports white and pink blossoms in spring. Its nickname is the "fishfuddle" tree, because the Seminoles would drop its crushed leaves in the water to stun fish.

Despite the bright sun overhead, the forest creates a tightly knit canopy, keeping

Hikers marvel at the native royal palms along the Royal Palm Hammock Trail

the trail dark. Strap ferns sprout from rotting logs and the bases of oaks. Young royal palms stretch their fronds in the shade. Although you often see royal palms planted in bare, open areas for landscaping, they naturally flourish in shady places until they mature, topping out the hammock canopy at more than 100 feet. Most of the older royal palms that once made Royal Palm Hammock a special place have died: victims of hurricane winds, lightning strikes, and old age.

After 0.2 mile, you reach a fork that signals the beginning of the loop. Keep left. The trail immediately becomes a boardwalk, which can be slippery in places from lichen growth. Don't try to rush along it. You smell the skunklike odor of the white stopper tree nearby. Trees crowd closely along the boardwalk, forcing you to duck under resurrection-fern-draped limbs. Sea oxeye signals the intrusion of brackish water into the hammock as you drop down off the boardwalk onto a marl footpath, walking under a live oak covered with epiphytes. Shoelace fern cascades down from cabbage palm. The trail becomes a boardwalk again, passing a shaded bench. As the sky opens up overhead, giant leather ferns press up against the boardwalk. You come to a T intersection at 0.4 mile. Turn left. This spur trail leads through a dense tunnel of white and red mangroves, where swamp lilies and giant leather ferns rise out of the black water. The boardwalk ends at an observation platform on the edge of a vast salt marsh dotted with white mangroves. Climb up and take in the panoramic view, the northern edge of the great mangrove forest of South Florida that stretches through the Ten Thousand Islands of the Everglades to Florida Bay. This watery wilderness beckons intrepid canoeists, who ply the maze of waterways from Chokoloskee to Flamingo. *This* is Florida's last unspoiled frontier, unreachable by road, untouchable by plane.

Turn around and head back down the spur trail, continuing straight past the bench when you reach the junction. Mangrove rubber vine cascades down over the white mangroves, showing off its massive trumpet-shaped blooms. Sea oxeye intermingles with glasswort, and the shiny, succulent leaves of sea purslane sparkle in the sun. Pond apples dangle their large fruits over the trail. Ducking under a propped-up cabbage palm trunk, the boardwalk turns left along a corridor of giant leather ferns crowding in upon the trail. You pass another bench at 0.6 mile. As the boardwalk continues around a corner, it tilts sharply to the left, making it difficult to walk on the slippery surface. Use caution. It ends soon after, and the trail leads you back into the tropical hardwood hammock.

Reaching a T intersection with the incoming trail, you've completed the loop. Turn left and head back toward the parking lot. As the trail winds through the tropical hammock, take the time to look for the many royal palms hidden amid the tangled understory. After 0.9 mile, you emerge at the parking lot.

COLLIER-SEMINOLE HIKING TRAIL

To walk the Collier-Seminole Hiking Trail, you must check in at the ranger station and get the combination for the locked gate leading to its parking area. Let the rangers know if you intend to stay overnight at the backpacker's campsite or are just day hiking the trail—if you're day hiking and don't check in before the park closes, they will come looking for you.

This is one of South Florida's most beautiful trails, but it's not for the inexperienced. Some wilderness savvy is in order. Do not take small children on this trail. Unless you visit on a chilly day in the dead of winter, the mosquitoes are fierce: Wear long pants, a long-sleeved shirt, and a hat; carry insect repellent; and bring a mosquito head net just in case. This can also be a very wet hike, where you'll slog through ankle- to knee-deep water through several stretches of cypress swamp. A permanent slough crosses the trail, and until it is bridged, you'll wade through several streams bounded by thick, sticky mud. Bring spare clothing and shoes to change into after the hike. Backpackers may want to carry a large trash compactor bag to put their packs into for water crossings. Because the water can become very deep in the slough, do not attempt this trail during the wet season or after a recent rain. Always consult with the park rangers as to trail conditions before walking.

From the Collier-Seminole State Park main entrance, drive 0.8 mile east on US 41. Stop at the gate on the north side of the road, and use the combination to unlock it. Lock it back up behind you. Driving a little way back along the dirt road, you come to a broad spot next to a human-made pond. Park here but do not block the gate. The trail starts at the FT sign, following the blue blazes across undulating terrain through stands of sand live oaks in the scrubby flatwoods. Wildflowers peek out from beneath the charred slash pines: the large radiating pink blooms of Sabatia grandiflora, the purple arcs of blazing star, and the yellow spikes of yellow star grass. Keep alert for sawgrass leaning out into the footpath, and walk gingerly to avoid its razor-sharp edges. After 0.1 mile, you reach a T intersection with the orange-blazed loop trail. Turn right and immediately begin to wade into a deep, dark

hammock; the trail, the low spot, tends to be wet where cypress knees as big as footstools poke out of the inky water. Emerging from the cypresses, the trail rises into cabbage palm flatwoods. Like bright purple bubbles, apple snail shells lie scattered across the footpath. Prairie grasses create a fog under the pines, colored by dashes of yarrow, bladderwort, and glades lobelia.

At 0.5 mile, the trail crosses an abandoned forest road and, at a double blaze, makes a sharp turn left into dense forest. Although narrow, the trail corridor remains distinct. Tall bamboo grows under the gnarled pines. The landscape opens up into a wet prairie with young slash pines and scattered cypresses. Corkwood rises from the dark puddles as the forest becomes a dense, low canopy of young bald cypresses under the high canopy of slash pines. Emerging from this wet section, you rise up into a drier prairie. Bright yellow tickseed stands out against the brownish green grasses. Cypresses close in around the footpath again at about 1.3 miles; keep alert for each blaze as you wind through the maze of trees. Mats of pickerelweed with their purple blooms remind you that this section of the trail remains under water most of the year. In the Big Cypress ecosystem, like the Everglades, summer rains fuel a constant shallow sheet of water that flows southward through the cypress forests. The water spreads across the landscape during the wet season; in the driest months (February and March), it flows down the sloughs, the slight depressions in the limestone bedrock.

Another forest road crosses at 1.5 miles. If you need to cut your hike short, this is your last chance to do so before heading into the heart of the swamp—turn left and walk 1.5 miles back along the road to the gate at the parking area. Otherwise, continue across the road past the FT sign and into the prairie beneath the pines. The footpath is indistinct through this section, so keep watching for the next blaze. The trail veers left into cabbage palm flatwoods. At 2 miles, you cross another road; continue past the FT sign. The first of several benches along this trail shows up soon after, giving you a chance to pause before walking into a pine flatwoods with a thick understory of saw palmetto. Many of the pines are spindly and misshapen, victims of vicious hurricane winds. As you turn at the next double blaze, watch for scattered beard's-tongue poking out of the wiregrass.

Leaving the flatwoods, the trail makes a right turn into a cypress swamp. Wood ferns poke out of the coffee-colored water as you slosh though. The brief interlude ends as you rise up under the pines into a tight corridor between the vegetation. After 2.8 miles, you reach the blue blaze to the backpacker's campsite. It's another 0.4 mile (each way) to the campsite, which provides no facilities save a dry clearing in the middle of this mosaic of swamps, prairies, and forests. If you choose to camp there, be sure to carry in adequate drinking water for your trip. Continuing along the orange blazes, you walk through a high and dry forest where pine needles dangle like tinsel from the branches of wax myrtles and sand live oaks before dropping down into a narrow corridor through a cypress slough. While slogging along, take care to avoid tripping over cypress knees hidden under the dark water. Rising up onto a small pine flatwoods hammock, you feel the comforting softness of thick pine needles carpeting the footpath, and find a bench at 3.4 miles. Notice the delicate Simpson's grass-pink—terrestrial orchids with pouting

magenta-and-white-striped mouths. Enjoy this dry moment, as the trail immediately plunges back into a wet forest of young cypresses.

Deep into the swamp, you notice thousands of bromeliads of every shape and size clinging to the limbs and trunks of the cypresses. A lacy fernlike growth emerges from the base of one large cypress: a whisk fern. This endangered plant has an odd appearance, its twiglike branching naked of fronds. It thrives in the same hot, humid environments as the bromeliads. Just beyond, another swamp oddity: a jug-handled cypress knee, caused by an abnormal growth of the knee back into itself. Rising straight and skyward like the pillars of a Greek temple, bald cypresses line both sides of the submerged footpath.

As older trees yield to younger ones, sunlight filtering through the needles diffuses to lay patterns across the murky water. Rising up onto a pine island at 3.6 miles, you pass a clump of cardinal wild pine above an orange blaze before entering a forest overtaken by an insidious growth of Brazilian pepper. But there are small wonders to behold. Watch for an orchid that appears to be speckled ladies' tresses, with tiny fringed-mouth blooms radiating out from a tall central tall stem. Two thickly buttressed cypresses form a portal into the next section of swamp, where you wade between primordial sprays of giant leather fern and the green lattices of swamp fern. Brazilian pepper takes over, crowding the trail corridor. Beware of tripping over cypress knees well hidden by ferns as you duck under the Brazilian pepper, emerging into an open cabbage palm flatwoods. Hatpin and bog button, tickseed and grass-pink peep from the grass as the trail turns to the right, winding through a stand of saw palmetto before it drops briefly back into the swamp. Brazilian pepper arches overhead, creating tunnels you must duck through as the trail rises back to higher ground. After 4 miles, you start to hear traffic on US 41.

A cypress branch dips low over the trail, displaying an astounding array of tiny bromeliads growing in neat rows as if part of a well-cared-for nursery. You then drop back down into another stretch of swamp at 4.5 miles. Displaying its purple blooms, a climbing aster twines around a loblolly bay. A confusion of tracks tears up the footpath as it dries out again: the destructive diggings of feral hogs. Crimson maple leaves drift across patches of still water beneath cypresses cloaked in their autumn glow of burnt-orange needles. Wild coffee lines the trail as it winds its way through a hammock of laurel oaks and slash pines. You hear a clamor in the underbrush as several large hogs run for cover. Despite the cypress knees, the footpath is covered with crunchy oak leaves. At the double blaze, make a sharp left. Thick shoelace fern cascades down the trunks of cabbage palms in the shady hammock. The trail winds past a swampy area thick with willows. At 5.2 miles, you see Miccosukee chickee huts hiding in the woods. This small village is part of the Miccosukee Reservation, so respect their privacy and do not approach the village from the trail. The Miccosukee is one of the tribes that fled into the Everglades during the Third Seminole War; members trace their lineage to Creek and Muskogee ancestors who moved south into Florida at the invitation of Spanish explorers in the 1500s. When the Seminoles sued the federal government for reparations in 1947, having lost most of their land to the new Everglades National Park, the Miccosukee requested separate political recognition. Each tribe now governs its

own people within and around the Everglades and the Big Cypress.

Keep alert soon after you see the chickees, as it looks like the trail goes right, toward the village, but the blazes lead you to the left. The footpath narrows, and you catch a whiff of a skunk smell—white stopper. Its bark was once used as a curative for diarrhea. The dense tropical understory of the hammock gives way to a mucky, mushy footpath surrounded by giant leather ferns and swamp ferns as you wade into the wettest part of the cypress swamp, approaching a series of sloughs that drain into the mangrove marshes on the south side of US 41. Plans are for a series of bridges and boardwalks to span these perpetual drainages, but for now hikers must wade. Be mindful of the deep, thick boot-sucking muck that lies just below the water's surface—use a hiking stick to probe each step as you wade. You reach the first slough at 5.6 miles, the footpath paralleled by a fallen log that looks tempting as a bridge but is too moss covered to be anything but treacherous. The next slough is a mud hole, and the one just past it, facing the bench, is even worse—watch out for the vast bank of deep mud along its near edge, a mud so viscous it resembles quicksand. Mangroves crowd the far shore upstream. Take a moment to rest on the bench after your wade.

Rising back up into a shady hammock, the trail snakes between laurel oaks and cabbage palms on its way to the centerpiece of this hike—a tiny remnant of the vast royal palm hammock that once covered the high ground between the swamps. En route, you'll encounter more slippery mud holes. Crossing a bridge, you notice the first royal palm off to the left. Many more royal palms tower overhead as the trail winds through the hammock, passing a bench at 5.9 miles, zigzagging between the bases of these regal trees. Several sloppy sloughs run through this section of trail. The next bridge doesn't quite bridge the gap across a pond, so you must slog through some more water before reaching shore. Keep alert for a sharp left turn at a double blaze at 6.1 miles, where the trail rises up into cabbage palm flatwoods. The wettest part of the hike is behind you. When you reach the forest road, turn right. It's the homestretch—a dry, easy walk back to the parking area. After 6.6 miles, you emerge at the gate and parking area, completing this tiring but beautiful hike.

18

Fakahatchee Strand Preserve State Park

Total distance (two round trips): 6.4 miles

Hiking time: 4 hours

Habitats: Cypress strand, flag pond, freshwater marsh, prairie, royal palm hammocks

Maps: USGS 7½' Weavers Station, Deep Lake West; park map

Diversity: the hallmark of nature left to its own devices. Within the humid depths of Fakahatchee Strand, nature is free to work its magic. From the ancient cypress trees of Big Cypress Bend to the delicate Fakahatchee ladies tresses dangling from branches deep within the swamp, natural diversity runs wild at Fakahatchee Strand Preserve State Park. Draining the Big Cypress toward the Ten Thousand Islands, the Fakahatchee ("forked river" in Seminole) Strand is a swampy wilderness filled with natural wonders. Forty-four species of orchids have been found in Fakahatchee Strand, giving the park the nickname Orchid Capital of the United States. Among these beauties are the clamshell orchid, with its tentacles of yellow-green dangling from a scalloped reddish purple bloom, and the rare and delicate ghost orchid with its haunting white blooms. Something's always in bloom in the dark depths of the Fakahatchee, from frosted flower orchids to *Tillandsia fasciculata*. There are 14 types of bromeliads and 36 varieties of ferns. Hammocks of royal palms grow along the edges of cypress-lined sloughs. It's a botanist's delight.

Fakahatchee Strand Preserve State Park is also an enormous place. Covering more than 85,000 acres, it's the biggest state preserve in Florida, its boundaries touching a patchwork of public lands protecting the Big Cypress. And it's a wild place. Both access and facilities are limited, since the purpose of this preserve is

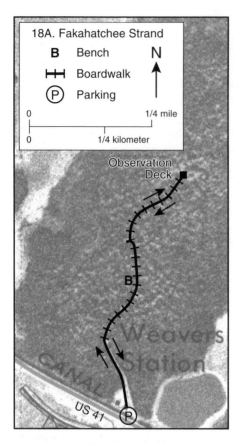

18A. Fakahatchee Strand

B   Bench   **N**

Boardwalk

(P)   Parking

0   1/4 mile

0   1/4 kilometer

Observation Deck

US 41

BIG CYPRESS BEND BOARDWALK

From I-75 southbound, take exit 101, Naples/Marco Island, and head south on CR 951 for 7.1 miles to US 41. Turn left and continue east. After 8.5 miles, you pass the entrance to Collier-Seminole State Park (Hike 17). Continue another 6 miles and you reach the western boundary of Fakahatchee Strand Preserve State Park. After another 2.6 miles of driving, you see the large sign for the BIG CYPRESS BEND BOARDWALK. Turn left just past the Miccosukee Indian Village (open during winter).

From the east, use I-75 exit 80, Everglades City/Immokalee. Drive south on FL 27 for 17 miles. When you reach US 41, turn right and continue west for 6.9 miles to the Big Cypress Bend Boardwalk parking area. Parking is extremely limited, so if the parking area is full, use the pulloff area on the south side of US 41.

Start your hike along the limestone path with its paralleling canal. A kiosk displays a map of the entire preserve and a list of its endangered species. You start to see the massive bald cypresses as you pass a picnic bench and come up to the beginning of the boardwalk. This particular section of the strand escaped the logger's blades of the Lee Tidewater Cypress Company. In 1966, Big Cypress Bend became a registered national natural landmark. Look up: Even the tallest of the cypresses are covered in bromeliads. Interpretive markers add to your enjoyment of the trail. Plants of the tropical hammock cover the dry spots. You see young royal palm, wild coffee, and myrsine. A bounty of ferns surrounds you: lacy royal ferns, tall red-tipped marsh ferns, and slender sword ferns. Cinnamon ferns grow out of tiny islands of decaying wood, while water spangles drift across dark pools. At 0.3 mile, you reach an

to protect the many rare and unusual species that live here.

One short boardwalk trail along the Tamiami Trail provides access to a classic Fakahatchee sight—a swampy cypress slough, where the ancient trees host thousands of epiphytes. Hikers are also welcome to explore the old tramways running throughout the park. A network of blazed trails with overnight camping is in the planning stages; with volunteer aid from the Florida Trail Association, watch for it to emerge over the next several years. This narrative follows two existing hikes: the popular Big Cypress Bend Boardwalk near Everglades City, and the much wilder East Main Trail in the center of the strand.

Ancient cypresses along the Big Cypress Bend Boardwalk

observation deck built around the base of two massive bald cypresses.

At the next sharp right turn in the boardwalk, scout the limbs of the tall cypresses overhead for signs of bald eagle activity. A mated pair nests nearby, their aerie hidden in the high limbs off to the left. Sword ferns peer out from crannies in the enormous bases of the cypresses. Above you, ferns, orchids, and bromeliads decorate the branches. A grand old giant of a bald cypress towers overhead; younger ones are taking root in the wet thickets along with pop ash, a member of the olive family that thrives in South Florida's strands. The bright red berries of dahoon holly stand out against the sea of dark green foliage. Walking past the base of another enormous cypress, you notice the strangler fig that wraps it in an emphatic embrace. Slender red maples drop their leaves into the slowly flowing water of the slough. Despite the attraction of the millions of small plants on the wet forest floor, from drifting water lilies to the purple blooms of pickerelweed, you constantly want to crane your neck skyward to look at the grand old epiphyte-draped cypresses.

The boardwalk makes a hard right and you walk down a shady corridor, where pond apples dangle like Christmas ornaments. Strap fern grows out of a mat of decaying vegetation and stumps. Giant sword ferns wave their 3-foot-long fronds. A healthy young royal palm flourishes in the deep shade. The boardwalk crosses over a flag pond, bounded by the tall alligator flag, ending after 0.6 mile at an observation deck. A set of benches overlooks a broad flag pond encircled by sentinels of cypress. A young alligator drifts past, yellow and black against the dark water. On the other side of the pond, its massive mother scans the pond from her quiet cove. Alligator flags ring the deep water, and air plants dangle from the low limbs of oak and cypress.

Turn around and follow the boardwalk back through the swamp, retracing your route. Keep alert for animal life. You hear the splashes of deer moving through the swamp and see the spreading leaves of lilies ruffling beneath the tannic water. Florida panthers are known to stretch out and sun themselves on the thick limbs of live oaks. A cluster of spider hatchlings pulse with life within their web as they work their way out into the world on tiny lines. An ugly invasive Cuban tree frog sits on the boardwalk rail. Two large green dragonflies chase each other like fighter pilots through the underbrush. Whisk fern drapes from a dying cypress, while several red-bellied woodpeckers work their way up the lower limbs of a Carolina willow, hopping along as they climb.

When you reach the end of the boardwalk, you've walked 1 mile. Continue along the gravelly limestone path. Cabbage palms stretch out over the tannic water, casting reflections in the canals. Emerging at the parking lot, you complete your 1.2-mile hike.

EAST MAIN TRAIL

Although the Big Cypress Bend Boardwalk is the only signposted trail in Fakahatchee Strand State Park, hikers are welcome to wander the park's many tram roads during daylight hours. For now, one of the more interesting and easy hikes you can take within the depths of the park is the East Main Trail, which starts at Gate 12 on Janes Scenic Drive. From I-75, exit 80, Everglades City/Immokalee, drive south on FL 29 for 14.6 miles to Janes Scenic Drive. If you're coming from Big Cypress Bend Boardwalk, drive east on

US 41 for 6.9 miles to its junction with FL 29, then north on FL 29 for 2.4 miles to Janes Scenic Drive (CR 837). After you turn onto Janes Scenic Drive, the road immediately turns sharply to the right. Heed the sign OPEN DUSK TO DAWN. Unless you make special arrangements with the park prior to your visit to stay in one of the remote camps scattered across the preserve, you should not leave your car on the road at night. While it's not a dead-end road, Janes Scenic Drive ends at the preserve's western boundary with Picayune Strand State Forest (Hike 16), which contains a dangerous maze of abandoned roads and should not be attempted after dark, even with a good map.

Just 0.9 mile up the road, the small visitors center sits on the left. Stop by for a brochure and use of the rest rooms, or to make arrangements (reservations necessary) to join one of the four-hour swamp tromps led by the park biologist Mike Owen on the third Saturday of each month, November through February, starting at 10 AM. You *will* get wet on these guided hikes—but you'll also see rare beauties like the ghost orchid up close. Consider it an immersion into another world.

As you continue north on Janes Scenic Drive, the pavement turns to limestone. The road narrows to a lane and a half. Drive slowly or you'll miss the panorama unfolding around you. Fakahatchee Strand is one of the world's largest strands, a shallow limestone valley channeling a constant flow of water southward from the Big Cypress Swamp into the salty mangrove forests of the northern Everglades. Measuring 20 miles long by 3 to 5 miles wide, it contains a dense cypress forest broken up by broad wet prairies. Like its neighbor to the southwest, Collier-Seminole State

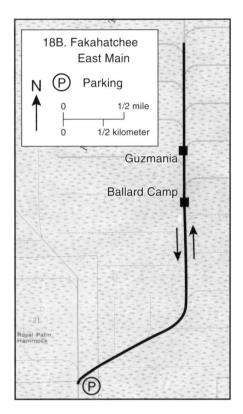

Park (Hike 17), Fakahatchee Strand is one of the rare places in the United States where royal palms grow naturally. Here, they grow by the thousands. More than 5,000 of these grand giants are dispersed throughout the hammocks of Fakahatchee Strand.

The road makes a sweeping curve to the left, where you look out over a haunting landscape of young cypresses rising along the edge of a massive prairie. Curving into the woods, the road is now bounded on both sides by cypress swamp, the dark water reflecting the thousands of epiphytes in the trees. After 7.3 miles of driving down Janes Scenic Drive, you reach Gate 12. Park in the broad parking area on the right, just before the gate, and start your hike by walking around the gate to access the tramway. More than 100 miles of tramways once crossed the strand, breaking up the natural flow of the swamp. Built in 1947 to allow access by the loggers from the Lee Tidewater Cypress Company, the tramways supported railroads that pulled the logged cypresses out of the strand. The building of the tramways created parallel canals that drained the swamps. Even with these "improvements," it was not an easy place to traverse: One worker described it as "a green hell." The small village of Copeland where the park office stands was the company town, but logging crews on duty lived in tent camps on the edges of the swamp. At one point, Sears Roebuck shipped mail-order cypress houses from an assembly plant just a little north on FL 29 from the park entrance. By 1952, Lee Tidewater had removed more than a million board-feet of cypress from the Fakahatchee. In 1966, it sold 75,000 acres to developers who attempted to market the most dried-out part of the swampland as part of Golden Gate Estates (Hike 16). In 1974, the state of Florida purchased the tracts along FL 29 to establish Fakahatchee Strand Preserve. Many of the tramways were intentionally destroyed to restore the natural water flow through the strand, but certain ones still stand. East Main remains in good shape and is regularly maintained up to the Ballard Camp, a distance of 1.5 miles. Beyond that point, you're welcome to keep hiking, but you may find yourself bushwhacking and slogging through wet spots. This hike follows East Main for a 5.2-mile round trip.

The forest crowds in closely along this one-lane jeep track, with Carolina willows providing shade. Royal palms tower above the edges of the tramway, decked out with wild pines. Wild coffee and marlberry dominate the understory. Dense giant sword ferns create a thick hedge along both sides of the road. All around you is the strand, cypresses rising tall from the dark water, where lotuses drift across the surface. Pickerelweed shows off both slender white and purple blooms from one deep pool. As you walk along, your visibility of the swamp varies according to the amount of underbrush along the sides of the road, but the swamp is always there. After 0.5 mile, cabbage palms line the tramway. You start to see more open swamp. Where you cross a culvert, water flows freely under the road. Be cautious of alligators that like to settle in the mud near the outflow to capture stunned fish. Sword ferns define the roadsides as if planted in perfect rows. Strap ferns dangle from their perches on the bases of cypresses. At 0.7 mile, you reach a dark, humid swamp where the trunks of pond cypresses are thickly covered in epiphytes. Look for massive numbers of butterfly orchids, the most common of Florida's orchids. Passing under several royal palms after 1 mile, you walk along a denser cypress forest with many more orchids. You come to a wide spot in the tramway. Look closely to the left of the cabbage palm for dark coco plums dangling from their shrubby trees. They're not only edible, but tasty, too. Their soft flesh has a very mild taste, but it takes a handful to satisfy—the plums are mostly pit.

As you walk by more clusters of butterfly orchids and bromeliads in the cypresses, the sky opens up, revealing more royal palms. You see a clearing ahead. After 1.5 miles, you reach Ballard Camp. This private camp includes a rustic cabin built in 1957—which managed to survive both Hurricane Donna and Hurricane Andrew—as well as an outhouse. A fishing pier leads out to a large pond, where alligators cluster en masse during winter, when water in the Fakahatchee is at a premium. This is one of many deep sinkholes found within the strand; some descend nearly 100 feet. Rainfall along the marshes of the Caloosahatchee River flows down through Corkscrew Marsh, draining nearly 60 miles south into the north end of the Fakahatchee Strand. When the rainfall stops, the swamps begin to dry up. By January, the swamps around this tramway can be bone dry.

Just beyond the cabin, the tramway forks, and you can see an outhouse down the left fork. Continue along the right fork, along the edge of the dark swamp. Look carefully at the pop ash and pond apple trees for some of the more unusual types of epiphytes that grow in this strand. Growing high in the trees, the powdery catopsis contains a "tank" of water at its center. A powder forming on the leaves above the tank creates a slick surface. Insects slip into the water and drown, providing the nutrients for this plant's survival. Perching on the sunny tops of pond apple trees, fuzzy-wuzzy air plants trap nutrient-rich rainfall on small hairs on their leaf surfaces.

At 1.8 miles, you reach another wide spot in the tramway at a swampy place– Guzmania, named for a specific genus of the bromeliad family. It's a popular destination for hikers who come here to wade into the swamp and peer at the amazing variety of bromeliads, including numerous *Tillandsia,* from *T. balbisiana* to *T. utriculata.* Guzmania contains an incredible number of Fuch's bromeliad *(Guzmania monostachia),* the only *Guzmania* native to the United States. Like powdery catopsis, it's another large air plant with a central water tank. Supported by the perpetual humidity created by the depths

of the strand, these grow in massive thickets well up in the trees.

Past Guzmania, the tramway may not be well maintained, depending on the time of year. You can turn around here and walk back through the Ballard Camp to complete a 3.6-mile round trip, or forge ahead as far as you feel comfortable walking. You're headed in a straight line, so you just need to leave enough time to walk back to your car before dark. Passing flag ponds and deep pools with water lettuce adrift across their surface, you walk under a particularly tall royal palm with bushy fronds and an extremely thick rounded trunk. Lichens and bromeliads climb up its concrete-colored surface. The trail ducks under a stand of invasive Brazilian pepper, emerging into an area with surface limestone underfoot, bounded by tall sword ferns. Royal palms line the tramway much as they do artificially on many boulevards in South Florida cities. As the tallest trees in the forest, they provide a perch for raptors, including the tropical short-tailed hawk and the more common red-shouldered hawk.

At 2.4 miles, you step across a stream of water flowing swiftly from one side of the swamp to the other, slicing the tramway in two. Royal palms and cabbage palms are intermingled in a broad area just beyond the water. The tall bush with red blossoms sporting yellow tips is firebush, one of the more colorful shrubs in the strand. Ripening from a crimson color, dark black berries dangle from a lower limb. Pond apples and coco plums compete for space along this strip of dry land as you reach the shade of a large water oak on the edge of a cypress swamp. You've walked 2.6 miles. The tramway narrows down considerably past this point and, in the wet season, becomes entirely inundated by overflowing swamps. Use this shady spot as a place to rest. Turn around and follow your route back through Guzmania to the Ballard Camp. You reach the Ballard Camp at 3.7 miles. Continue down the tramway to Gate 12. After 5.2 miles, you've completed your round-trip exploration of the East Main Trail.

19

Fire Prairie Trail

Total distance (round trip): 5.2 miles

Hiking time: 2 hours, 30 minutes

Habitats: Cypress strand, cabbage palm flatwoods, oak hammock, prairie

Maps: USGS 7½' Deep Lake; park map

There is nowhere else on earth like the Big Cypress Swamp—wild, rugged, and vast. Encompassing more than a million acres, this patchwork of cypress strands, deep sloughs, and prairies blankets the southwest tip of the Florida peninsula, where freshwater wetlands drain into coastal estuaries. Hydrologically, it behaves much like the Everglades on the southeastern coast: Rainfall trickles southward, moving toward the sea. But in the Big Cypress, rainfall collects in nooks and crannies in the limestone bedrock, flowing as sluggish surface streams down wide strands and narrow sloughs eroded into the spongy limestone. Cypresses thrive in the sloughs, where the perpetual warmth and dampness encourage epiphytes to flourish.

Protecting more than 700,000 acres of this fragile ecosystem, the Big Cypress National Preserve was established by the U.S. Congress in 1974 in response to public concerns regarding planned development along the northeastern edge of the swamp. But even though the National Park Service manages it, the Big Cypress doesn't rate the special protections afforded to national parks. Despite federal promises to end the practice in spring 2002, gas and oil exploration permits are still handed out, and more than 100,000 gallons of oil are extracted from beneath the swamp every day. Off-road vehicles (particularly the popular swamp buggies) are permitted, as is hunting. Many inholdings exist within the preserve, including traditional Seminole and Miccosukee villages. Several limestone

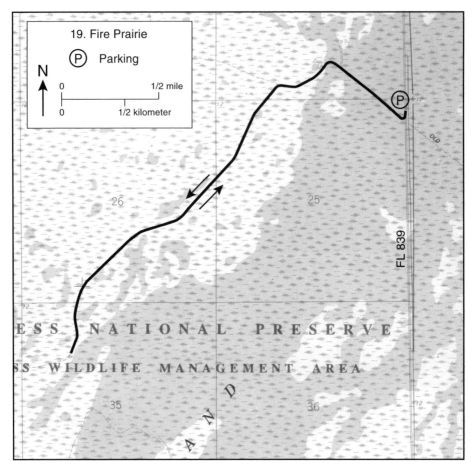

roads traverse portions of the preserve, but all risk inundation during the wet season. Visitors to the Big Cypress typically stop at the Oasis Ranger Station on the Tamiami Trail (US 41) for interpretive information.

Hikers have several options within the preserve. Intrepid backpackers take to the woolly beginning of the Florida National Scenic Trail at Loop Road, following the orange blazes north to Alligator Alley (I-75) to traverse the swamp. The three- to five-day trip is guaranteed to include some wading, even in the dry season. It's one of the most difficult hikes in the United States, and not to be undertaken without serious planning,

as it's easier than you'd think to get lost in this vast wilderness. Experienced activity leaders from the Florida Trail Association lead small groups through Big Cypress each spring; check with the Florida Trail Association for details.

For day hikers who want a taste of the Big Cypress without getting wet, there is a very short interpretive trail (the Tree Snail Hammock Nature Trail) off Loop Road, plus two longer trails that follow old oil exploration tramways. Both trailheads are located on Turner River Road. Although the Concho Billy Trail is less off the beaten path, it's presently open to off-road vehicles, making it a less-than-stellar wilderness experience for hikers. For peace and quiet in the midst of the wilderness, you'll want to focus on the Fire Prairie Trail.

Driving 14.7 miles west from Oasis Ranger Station on US 41, keep alert for the H. P. Williams Roadside Park. Turn right onto CR 839 (Turner River Road) at the park. Follow this scenic limestone road along the Turner River, which has been "tamed" into a long, broad canal paralleling the road. It's a great spot for bird-watching. After 6.9 miles, you pass the trailhead for the Concho Billy Trail. You reach the junction with CR 837 (Wagon Wheel Road) at 7.4 miles. Continue along CR 839 through the vast expanse of prairies and pine flatwoods until you reach the Fire Prairie Trail trailhead on the left at 14.6 miles.

To reach the trailhead from the west, use I-75 exit 80, Everglades City/Immokalee. Drive south 13.1 miles on FL 29 past Jerome to CR 837 (Wagon Wheel Road). Turn left. After 2.6 miles, you reach a T intersection. Turn left at the BEAR ISLAND CAMPGROUND sign. Continue along CR 837 for 5.1 miles—paying attention to the enormous numbers of birds roosting along the canal—until it ends at the next T intersection, at CR 837. Turn left and proceed north 7.1 miles to the Fire Prairie Trail trailhead.

Start your hike at the gate. Be sure to stop at the hiker register and sign in before setting off on this long green tunnel into the wilderness. Built as an access road for gas and oil exploration in the preserve, this hard-packed surface rarely floods, even in summer, making it an ideal path to access the prairie environment year-round for its parade of blooms. A cypress strand surrounds you, with tall pond cypresses thickly festooned with bromeliads. Wild pine glows red in a glimmer of sunlight.

Ferns dominate the understory, clinging to the disturbed land that is the trail: tall slender sword ferns, delicate limestone-loving long brake ferns, lacy hay-scented fern, and vine spike moss with feathery carrot-top-like foliage.

The green tunnel opens up, and the rough holey land of limestone karst surrounds you, with cypresses jutting out of the jagged rock. Purple aster cascades over a sea myrtle, while the slim glades lobelia dresses up the grassland with its deep purple blooms. The surrounding habitat shifts to a cabbage palm flatwoods studded with tall cabbage palm. Wax myrtle and wild coffee grow in the dry spots. Then another bower of trees canopies the trail and you enter a humid cypress swamp, where strangler figs tangle through the underbrush. Backlit by the sun, the reddish bark of a lone gumbo limbo tree glows. The cypress swamp is an interesting spot, dense in some places and sparser in others, with sawgrass growing around its edges and solution holes filled with aquatic plants. Every tree hosts hundreds of bromeliads.

At 0.4 mile, the trail opens up into a broad spot before it narrows down again. As you brush past the palm fronds, the trail curves to the left. Look down into the swamp. Although from a distance the water is brown, up close you can see clear down to the rough limestone base over which the water flows. As you emerge from the forest, the view opens up into a panorama of vast prairies, bounded only by the distant cloud formations. The surface underfoot changes from grass to a hard-packed limestone pavement. As the trail rises a little in elevation, it skirts stands of saw palmetto and sumac under sand live oaks on the edge of the prairie. The trail curves to the right, and you emerge onto the open prairie.

Fire Prairie Trail

Spider lily

This is a special place. You hear no rumble of trucks, no buzz of airplanes—just the calls of birds winging their way between islands of cypress. Watch for shadowy shapes in the distance, since both bears and Florida panthers roam this prairie. Alligator and deer trails cut through the tall cordgrass, with hoof prints and tail marks left behind in the goopy brown periphyton coating the prairie floor. These algal mats also creep onto the trail, so be cautious of any spots that look black and wet—they'll be slippery. Although the sweeping view is breathtaking, don't forget to look into the prairie as well, taking in its parade of grasses: tufted bluestems, tall cordgrass, pointy sedges, and purple lovegrass in wispy swirls. At 1.3 miles, notice a light spot out in the prairie on the right: a stand of sedges with white tips forming a colorful island. A shallow canal begins to parallel the trail, with duck potato blooming in profusion. Spider lilies peer out from under the rushes. A parade of pinkish purple island morning glories peeps out of the cordgrass.

Look down into the limestone bottom of the prairie, where chunks of rock lie under the marl-tinted water. Pinnacles of weathered limestone rise from the prairie floor, the exposed karst a continually changing landscape shaped by the flow of water through the prairie. Cypress snags look ghostly against the gray sky. After 1.8 miles, you see taller sedges lining the trail. Pickerelweed shows off its bright purple spikes. The trail curves to the left, past several cabbage palms and Brazilian peppers loaded with red berries. A coral-colored moth alights on the yellow bloom of a tall, thin cowpea. Tall lantana dangles bright metallic blue berries in the breeze.

After 2.2 miles, you reach another broad spot in the trail serving as a turnaround for vehicles. Continue straight, passing the shaggy clumps of cordgrass. Stretching off toward the distant hammock, the reeds in the swamp show an orange tinge, a harbinger of fall. Two cabbage palms flank the entrance to the trail's end at 2.6 miles. You reach a broad square island ringed with scattered cabbage palms, a spot where an oil derrick once pulled black gold from beneath this beautiful prairie. A charred spot on the limestone marks the site of an old campfire.

Turn around and continue back along the trail, past the spotted limestone boulders. Star-topped sedge grows in the middle of the footpath. A strangler fig happily sprouts from the base of a dead cabbage palm, reaching its long stems skyward. Tangles of love vine snake throughout the sedge, a bright orange wire against the deep greens and browns. A group of white ibises fly overhead, breaking apart and re-forming into smaller groups as a ray of sun illuminates the far strand of cypresses across the prairie. Clouds create virtual mountains rising beyond the prairie land-scape. You feel small in this domain.

After 4.4 miles, the trail curves back to the right, heading away from the prairie and into the cypress strands. Following the long green tunnel, you emerge at the trailhead after 5.2 miles. Be sure to mark the register on your way out and note any special plant or wildlife sightings.

If you're interested in a quiet place for camping, there are numerous primitive campgrounds (tent or RV camping; no water, no rest rooms) throughout the Big Cypress Preserve. One of the nicest, the secluded Bear Island Campground, lies about 7 miles north of the Fire Prairie Trail, north of I-75 but not accessible from the interstate. Continue north along Turner River Road until you see the sign for the campground on the right.

Highlands Hammock #1   *Clyde Butcher*

20

Paynes Creek Historic State Park

Total distance (circuit): 2.9 miles

Hiking time: 1 hour, 30 minutes

Habitats: Oak scrub, pine flatwoods, river bluff, hardwood hammock, floodplain forest

Maps: USGS 7½' Wauchula; park map

In the 1840s, South Florida was still a wild and rugged frontier, a place where few settlers dared to tread. The reason? The Seminoles. Driven out of their traditional lands by settlements farther north on the peninsula, they moved their villages to the remaining good lands north of the Everglades. After two wars with the U.S. government, fighting relocation to the West, the Seminoles remained ready to lash back at any attempt at incursion into their lands. By 1849, the government decided to build a trading post on the northern boundary of the Seminole Reservation, a creek that ran through what is now Bowling Green and emptied into the Peace River. By doing so, they hoped to head off potential conflicts between Seminoles seeking to trade goods and settlers in the newly founded towns along the Gulf Coast.

Several months after the trading post opened, on July 17, 1849, five Seminoles—one of whom was outlawed by his tribe—opened fire on the trading post. Captain George S. Payne, Dempsey Whiddon, and William McCullough took the bullets, and Payne and Whiddon died. Despite attempts by the tribes to appease the U.S. government, the incident sparked immediate conflict. Federal reinforcements were sent to Florida in anticipation of a third Seminole War to remove the Seminoles from Florida entirely. Part of the plan was to build a chain of forts across the state, every 10 miles, along the northern border of the Seminole Reservation. With ground broken

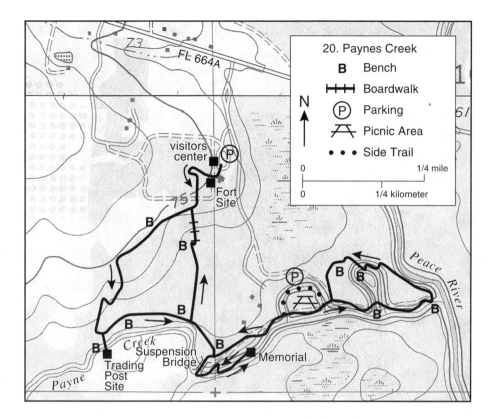

in October 1849, Fort Chokonikla was the first fort built, the nearby creek named for the captain killed at the trading post.

Paynes Creek Historic State Park sits just outside the small Hardee County town of Bowling Green. From FL 60 in Bartow, drive 19.2 miles south on US 17 to Bowling Green. Turn left onto Main Street and continue 0.3 mile to Lake Branch Road. Turn right. After 1.1 miles, you reach the park entrance on the right. Pay your Florida State Parks fee at the entrance station and pick up a park map, which shows the hiking trails. Make the first right on the entrance road to park your car in front of the visitors center. If the center is open, take the time to explore the exhibits for a better understanding of the Seminole Wars.

Off to the right, next to the visitors center, is the sign TO FORT CHOKONIKLA TRAIL. Follow the footpath to a larger sign marking the trailhead. The trail winds off to the right through oak scrub with thickets of young Chapman oaks. Notice the sprays of orange sand amid the sparkling white—the entrances to gopher tortoise burrows. You walk into a wide-open space where the scrub has been burned to regenerate. Continue straight past a T intersection to the open grassy ground that marks the fort site. A garrison of up to 223 men occupied the fort for barely a year, until July 1850. Sickness quickly thinned the ranks, malaria being prevalent in this region in those days. Excavations in this area have brought up artifacts allowing archaeologists to determine the sites of the original

The trail leading to the remains of Fort Chokonikla

blockhouses, built with timbers from the surrounding longleaf pine forest.

Turn around and return back to the T intersection. Turn right, following the trail as it transitions from scrub to pine flatwoods. It comes up to another T intersection with small wooden signs listing destinations: PICNIC AREA, MONUMENT, and TRADING POST. This is the beginning of the Historic Trail, which follows Paynes Creek. Turn right. A Gulf fritillary flutters past, showing off black and white dots on its deep orange wings, while a yellow sulfur flits between blooms of yellow star grass. When you pass an interpretive marker with a trail off to the right, continue straight. A sea of cinnamon ferns surrounds the trail as you pass a bench and make a hard left into a shady hardwood hammock of hickory, sweetgum, and water oak. A goldfoot fern emerges from the bent trunk of a large saw palmetto. The trail drops steadily downhill as it zigzags through the forest.

At the next T intersection, you see the sign TRADING POST SITE. Turn right. The ground is soft and squishy underfoot. This short spur trail leads to a bench overlooking Paynes Creek, a swift-flowing tannic creek with steep sand banks. Draping from the underside of a sand live oak, butterfly orchids dangle over the water. In the clearing directly across the creek sat the government trading post where Payne and Whidden died. Although their deaths did not immediately lead to war, they sparked the U.S. government to actions that eventually culminated in the final conflict with the Seminoles, the Third Seminole War, just six years later. With federal troops in place, the government waited for a reason to cross the boundary into the Seminole lands. It came in 1855, when a group of Seminoles attacked a military surveying party near Fort Myers. Reprisals were swift.

Federal troops chased the Seminoles into the Everglades, seizing the reservation lands; those who surrendered were deported to reservations in Oklahoma. Some of the Seminoles, hidden too deep in the Everglades for troops to find, never surrendered. Their descendants signed a peace treaty with U.S. government in 1936 and now occupy a handful of small reservations throughout South Florida.

Turn around and continue back to the junction; turn right. The trail quickly emerges along the creek and turns east to follow it, crossing a bridge over a side channel. Wild pine in bloom festoons a water oak. Passing a bench, you cross another bridge. Royal ferns rise up from the sandy channel below. Resurrection ferns coat the limbs of the oaks shading the trail. Spent, the orange blooms of trumpet vine rain down on the forest floor. At 0.8 mile, you reach a trail junction. Continue straight, following the MONUMENT sign. At the next junction, walk past the bench and turn right, up to a large suspension bridge over the creek, a relict of Civilian Conservation Corps construction in Florida State Parks during the 1930s. Below the bridge, the water races through a tight spot, burbling as if it's flowing over rocks. The turbid water bounces up against a curve and flows backward, swirling into a confusion of whirlpools and eddies. When you reach the far side of the bridge, turn left to follow the trail downstream. Deeply cut ravines flow into the creek. At 1.1 miles, the trail ends in a clearing ringed by large sand live oaks covered with epiphytes. Sunk into a newer concrete base, an original granite slab marks the grave site of Payne and Whidden.

Retrace your steps across the suspension bridge to the trail junction and turn right at the PICNIC AREA sign. Sparkleberry edges the broad open path as you pass a swampy oxbow lake and emerge at a kiosk and picnic area along Paynes Creek. A set of steps leads down into the water, inviting waders and anglers. Continue straight across the clearing to the PEACE RIVER TRAIL sign and follow this trail downstream, passing a pair of benches. The trail is a wide jeep road with short side spurs overlooking the creek. Partridge-pea flashes its small yellow blossoms, while flat-topped goldenrod sways in the breeze. At the T intersection, turn right. You pass another pair of benches, this one overlooking the creek, where a tall silk bay rises along the edge of the forest. An alligator jumps into the water with an enormous splash. Cypresses poke through the sand bluffs lining the creek.

After 1.8 miles, you reach the confluence of the Peace River and Paynes Creek. The creek steadily pours into the placid river, where a largemouth bass chases a school of smaller fish. An alligator drifts by, monitoring the shoreline for signs of prey. A bench lets you sit and survey the scene. The trail turns to the left to follow the Peace River upstream. Wild coffee peeks out from under the shadows cast by clumps of greenbrier. Off to the left lies an oxbow lake forming a broad marsh, covered in a carpet of mustard-yellow duckweed. Water

lettuce floats on its surface. A zebra swallowtail examines the rounded blooms of a buttonbush arched over the edge of the marsh. You walk past a pair of benches before coming to a T intersection at a NATURE TRAIL sign. Turn left along the corridor of water oaks and sweetgum, past a double-trunked slash pine. At the next intersection, you've completed the loop portion of the Peace River Trail. Turn right.

At the picnic area, several pavilions sit along the paved pathways leading off to the right, as well as rest rooms and a large playground. Continue your hike at the HISTORIC TRAIL sign, retracing your path to the junction. Turn right. At the next junction, turn right, following the FORT sign. This is the other half of the Historic Trail loop, winding through mixed hardwoods with scattered slash pines and an understory of tall saw palmetto. You pass a set of benches at the beginning of a long boardwalk through a floodplain forest, a low area where the pine flatwoods drain toward Paynes Creek. The trail rises back up away from the boardwalk into the flatwoods, coming to the end of the loop at 2.8 miles. Turn right, following the signs to continue back to the visitors center. At the T intersection, turn right. The trail ends at the visitors center after 2.9 miles.

21

Highlands Hammock State Park

Total distance (five circuits): 5.1 miles

Hiking time: 3 hours

Habitats: Bayhead, cypress slough, flag pond, floodplain forest, freshwater marsh, hardwood hammock, hydric hammock, pine flatwoods

Maps: USGS 7½' Crewsville; park map

Ancient. No other word can better describe the virgin hardwood hammock preserved by Highlands Hammock State Park, one of Florida's original state parks. Walking through the hammocks that make up the heart of this park, you step back into Florida before the Europeans, before the Seminoles, before the land-hungry settlers, enjoying the shade of trees thought to be up to 1,000 years old. Although the trails here are short, they allow visitors of all ages to enjoy this rare and humbling forest, a restorative to the soul.

Highlands Hammock State Park sits just off US 27 in Sebring. From US 27 north of downtown Sebring, turn west onto CR 634 (Hammock Drive). Follow it 2.8 miles, straight into the park entrance. When you stop at the ranger station to pay your Florida State Parks entrance fee, ask for a map of the hiking trails. Bikes can be rented at the ranger station as well, for those who want to enjoy a spin along the park roads. A full-service campground sits along the pine flatwoods on the eastern edge of the park. Although bikes are allowed on certain trails, they are not allowed on any trails with boardwalks. Nor are pets, which might make too tempting a treat for the alligators.

Continue straight down through the second set of gates to Hammock Drive, which runs one-way through the deep, dark virgin forests of this very special preserve. Margaret S. Roebling, the widow of famed Brooklyn Bridge engineer John A. Roebling, purchased this land to prevent

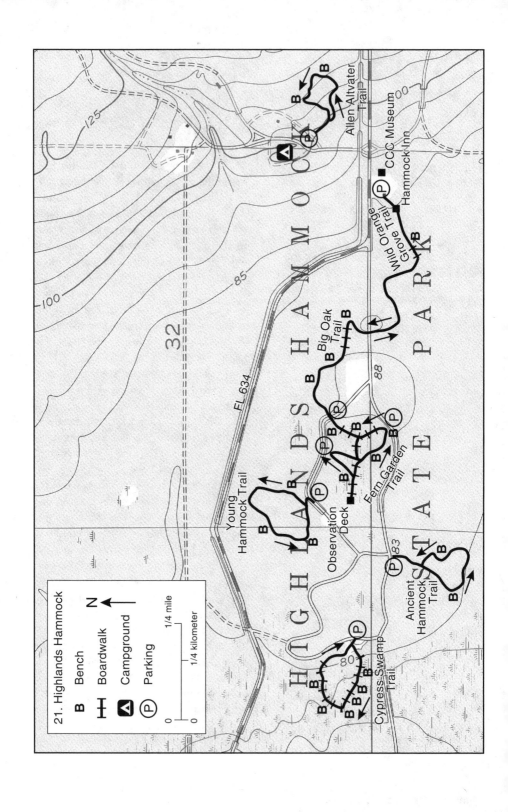

21. Highlands Hammock

B Bench
╫ Boardwalk
▲ Campground
Ⓟ Parking

N ◀

0 ——— 1/4 kilometer
0 ——— 1/4 mile

H I G H L A N D S   H A M M O C K   S T A T E   P A R K

Allen Altvater Trail

CCC Museum
Hammock Inn

Wild Orange Grove Trail

Big Oak Trail

FL 634

32

Young Hammock Trail

Observation Deck

Fern Garden Trail

Ancient Hammock Trail

Cypress Swamp Trail

125
100
85
88
83
80

its development as a farm. The park opened to the public in 1931. By 1935, Florida began its state park system, and Highlands Hammock was chosen to be one of the four original state parks (along with O'Leno, Myakka River, and Hillsborough River). The Civilian Conservation Corps (CCC) based its camp here so workers could construct the park roads, bridges, boardwalks, and trails.

Once you turn right onto Hammock Drive, keep alert for the first parking pulloff on the right at the HICKORY TRAIL sign. The Hickory Trail provides access to four other nature trails, enabling you to enjoy a 2.9-mile loop, the longest in the park.

HICKORY TRAIL, BIG OAK TRAIL, AND WILD ORANGE GROVE TRAIL

From the parking spot, head east on the trail in the direction of the HICKORY TRAIL TO BIG OAK TRAIL sign. You immediately enter the deep shade of an ancient hardwood hammock peppered with tall, regal cabbage palms. Massive live oaks spread their limbs to knit a tight canopy, providing niches for thousands of bromeliads and orchids large and small. Marlberry, sword fern, and wild coffee form the understory. Cold-tolerant needle palms rise out of damp spots. Velvety purple leaves twirl down from the sweetgum trees. You spy grapefruits dangling overhead. Numerous citrus trees have naturalized in this forest, thanks to the adjoining clearing along Hammock Drive where a pioneer family carved its mark on the Florida frontier in the 1800s.

The trail curves around the base of an ancient live oak, its trunk covered in sphagnum moss, its limbs swaddled in resurrection fern. As you round the oak to pass a bench, notice the cavity splitting the trunk apart—a hollow big enough for a tall person to step into. After 0.2 mile, you reach a T intersection at a bench. To the right lies the pioneer citrus grove. Turn left to begin the Big Oak Trail. Passing under hickory trees, citrus trees, and cabbage palms, you come up to a long, narrow boardwalk across the hydric hammock. A single rail helps you keep your balance as you cross just a few feet over the mucky black earth of this seasonally flooded hammock. The boardwalk ends at a bench, and the trail continues up to a fork. Keep to the right. In a few moments, you walk up to the base of the highlight of this trail—the gnarled and knobby Big Oak. Measured 4½ feet above the ground, the base of this ancient oak is more than 36 feet around; it's thought to be more than 1,000 years old. Although it is identified as a laurel oak, laurel oaks don't normally live more than a century. More likely, this is like the ancient Fairchild Oak at Bulow Creek State Park near Ormond Beach—a natural hybrid between a laurel oak and a live oak.

Turn right to pass the bench and follow the trail under a high canopy of hickory, laurel oak, and cabbage palm as you pass more grand old oaks, emerging at the park entrance road after 0.4 mile. Cross the road; veer right to start the Wild Orange Grove Trail. Wild citrus trees are dispersed throughout this dark hydric hammock, where you see nubby sugar hackberry trees and white mulberry trees. Wild hogs have dug up the deep, rich earth favored by needle palms. The trail curves to the left through the hammock. Streamers of shoelace fern dangle from cabbage palms. Duck under the laurel oaks leaning over the trail. Be cautious of poison ivy, which mimics nearby hickory leaves as it encircles a cabbage palm trunk. By 0.6 mile, the floodplain forest yields to a hardwood hammock dense with cinnamon and wood ferns. Sluggish tannic streams flow through the forest. As the trail gains a little elevation, slash pine flatwoods invade the hammock.

After 1 mile, you emerge behind a building at the end of the Wild Orange Grove Trail–the rustic Hammock Inn. This little concession stand is popular with hikers and campers because of its specialties of the house: wild orange ice cream and wild orange cream pie, both made with oranges from the hammocks. Take the time to stop and enjoy some, but do it early–the inn usually closes around 2 PM. Across the parking lot from the Hammock Inn is Florida's only Civilian Conservation Corps Museum. The museum preserves the memory of the thousands of men who worked in Florida's forests to carve trails and build bridges for public access and enjoyment of recreational lands. During the 1930s, the CCC put thousands of Floridians to work building infrastructure for public lands throughout the state. Nine of Florida's state parks and numerous county and city parks benefited from these efforts, and the CCC legacy of stone structures, boardwalks, and massive swinging bridges remains to this day.

Once you've enjoyed the diversions at the end of the trail, head back to the WILD ORANGE GROVE TRAIL trailhead sign and retrace your walk through the hammocks. On the way back, you'll notice strap ferns growing from the bases of various trees in the floodplain forest. A young raccoon sneaks through the shadows cast by the young cabbage palm fronds. After 1.5 miles, you cross the park entrance road and head back down the Big Oak Trail. When you get to the T intersection at the base of the Big Oak, turn right. As you walk along, notice the extraordinary size of the hickory, maple, and sweetgum trees.

This is an ancient forest, untouched by the lumberjack's saw. As the trail curves left around another large oak, take a closer look–the base of the oak is undercut by a massive cavity, large enough to serve as a bear's den. Mushrooms flourish in the dark humus. It doesn't take long before you complete the loop, reaching the junction at the boardwalk. Following the HICKORY TRAIL sign, turn right and walk back across the boardwalk. Take a moment to enjoy the silence, listening to the chirping of birds and the rain of hickory nuts. Passing under the grapefruit trees, you reach the next trail junction. Turn right. After 2 miles, you emerge at your parking spot.

FERN GARDEN TRAIL AND RICHARD LIEBER MEMORIAL TRAIL

Don't get into your car just yet–there's more to explore on this hike. Continue across the road to follow the Fern Garden Trail. Curving left past a bench, the trail continues through the dense hammock. Look up and notice the giant bromeliads perched well above the forest floor. The trail becomes a boardwalk through a wonderland of ferns as you walk up to a T intersection facing a flag pond. Turn right to start the loop. As the boardwalk ends, it drops you off on a narrow path flanked with sword fern. When you reach the bridge, cross it and turn left to continue on the Richard Lieber Memorial Trail, which follows a narrow ditch into a floodplain forest of cabbage palms, hickories, and elms. Once on the boardwalk, you're immersed in a primeval swamp surrounded by the stillness of the forest. Dark pools of water shimmer with tadpoles. Zigzagging through a dense thicket of hickory, the boardwalk reaches a junction at a bench. Continue straight. At 2.3 miles, the boardwalk ends at an observation platform. Sit and enjoy this peaceful place, where you

Sword ferns crowd the Fern Garden Trail.

can hear the leaves falling and the red-bellied woodpeckers knocking on snags.

Return along the boardwalk to the last trail junction, noticing the strangely knotted balls of roots sticking out of the swamp, mimicking cypress knees. At the junction, turn left. Squirrels chatter in the boughs of a live oak. The boardwalk ends, dropping you into a stand of tall cabbage palms and hickories. Past the bench, the forest floor disappears under a dense carpet of sword ferns. After 2.5 miles, you emerge at a trailhead behind a massive oak stump. Turn right to continue. Strap ferns radiate from the base of a water oak, while next to it a fallen branch is decorated in tufts of wild pine. Returning to the bridge, cross it and continue straight. At the next fork, check out your options before you make a choice. To the left, the trail crosses a wetland on stepping-stones. To the right, it sticks to the high ground to pass in front of a bench. An alligator and her offspring call this swamp home, so look over the water carefully if you decide to use the stepping-stones. The two sections of trail come back together, and you skirt a large swamp covered in water spangles before emerging at the Fern Garden Trail trailhead along Hammock Drive. Turn left to follow the boardwalk back around the loop. The swamp emanates an eerie green glow, with only the yellow blooms of primrose willow and the purple blossoms of pickerelweed adding contrast to the scene. You reach the end of the loop at 2.8 miles. Turn right. Follow the Hickory Trail back to your parking spot, emerging at the park road after 2.9 miles to complete this five-trail circuit.

YOUNG HAMMOCK TRAIL

Continuing your drive along Hammock Drive, pass the trailhead parking for the Richard Lieber Memorial Trail and continue around to the next trailhead, for the Young Hammock Trail, 1 mile into the park on the right. Start your hike by picking up an interpretive brochure from the kiosk. At the loop junction, stay right. Cabbage palm towers over the canopy of hickory, oak, and white mulberry. A dense mat of sword ferns and cinnamon ferns flourishes in the shade. The term *young* is relative here: This hammock is older than many in the state of Florida. It's a climax forest succeeding the surrounding pine flatwoods.

Passing a bench after 0.1 mile, the trail curves left under tall slash pines. Sweetgum leaves show off their fall colors. Damp spots encourage loblolly bay and sweetbay magnolia to thrive, coming together to form a new bayhead community. After 0.3 mile, the trail curves to the right and comes up to a bench. As the trail turns left, you see a catface on a slash pine, a reminder that the turpentine industry touched these woods before they were preserved. The forest becomes denser, crowded with the fronds of young cabbage palms. Wild oranges drop onto the trail, becoming a food source for raccoons and opossums. Crashing through the underbrush, several wild hogs break through the saw palmetto fronds as if crunching cardboard. After 0.6 mile, you complete the loop. Turn right to exit the trail, and drop your brochure in the box on the way out.

CYPRESS SWAMP TRAIL

Drive another 0.8 mile along Hammock Drive, passing both the amphitheater parking and a pulloff for bike trails before arriving at the parking area for the Cypress Swamp Trail. As evidenced by the size of the parking area, this is the most popular trail in the park. Follow the broad wheelchair-accessible boardwalk directly into the dark cypress swamp along Little Charlie Bowlegs Creek. You're immediately surrounded by the sensory experience of the cypress slough: midnight-black water flowing almost imperceptibly between the cypress knees, the stillness of the forest, the dank, sweet aroma of rotting leaves, the grunts of young alligators. Look out into the swamp and you see royal ferns and cinnamon ferns growing in clumps at the bases of the cypresses, and red maples dropping their leaves into the water. After 0.2 mile, the broad boardwalk ends. Now the hike becomes an adventure.

Continue out past the platform on the original narrow boardwalk with its low single rail. Take your time as you walk along these four linear planks just a couple of feet above the dark water of the creek, and don't jump the wrong way when an alligator startles you with a sudden slap of its tail. You reach a little observation platform with a bench. Sit down and look across the creek, and you might stare right into the eyes of a 'gator watching you.

The boardwalk curves to cross the creek, passing an observation platform with a bench where you can sit and look upstream. The sound of cicadas echoes through the forest, a low undercurrent like a crackling fire. A great blue skimmer hovers inches away from the red berries of a dahoon holly. The boardwalk creaks and groans as you continue through the swamp, passing another platform with a bench. Oyster mushrooms emerge from the base of a dead cypress. When the boardwalk ends, follow the path back through the hammock to complete the loop. Passing under a large wild grapefruit tree, the trail emerges from the forest. Cross the grassy area to return to the parking area, completing the 0.4-mile circuit.

ANCIENT HAMMOCK TRAIL

This is the last of the trails on Hammock Drive. At 2.2 miles along the road, park on the right and follow the footpath into the dark forest, a virgin hammock of incredibly old live oak and laurel oak. Some of the cabbage palms sport oddly fluted bases, like pottery. Sunlight barely filters through the thick canopy. After crossing the bridge, pause to read the PRAYER OF THE WOODS on a tree trunk on the left. At the T intersection, turn left, walking into the lush understory of needle palm and marlberry, where thick patches of sword fern thrive in the deep shade. Two pileated woodpeckers perform an unusual dance as they work their way around a cabbage palm trunk.

The trail sits high in the hammock, above a well-established old floodplain. Ancient oaks form the canopy, a true climax forest; numerous fallen trees attest to the age and size of these grand giants. The trail curves past the hulk of one fallen tree, now home to a riotous explosion of sword ferns. Even the wild citrus trees are huge. You pass a bench at 0.2 mile. The farther along you walk, the larger the trees become. A barred owl launches from a high branch, ruffling oak trees as it swoops beneath the canopy. A tall double-trunked oak rises from a sea of needle palms. You hear the constant *ker-plop* of hickory nuts falling to the forest floor.

As the trail curves to the right, it passes under an arch formed by an overleaning cabbage palm. Reaching a bench, the trail makes sharp right to skirt a fallen grand old oak. Another fallen and rotting oak provides a bed for strap ferns and sword ferns. The fiery blooms of coral bean stand out against the dark forest understory. Continue past another fallen oak, and you come back to the beginning of the loop at 0.5 mile. Cross the bridge, completing your hike at the parking area after 0.6 mile.

ALLEN ALTVATER TRAIL

Set apart from the other trails in the park, this trail is for the enjoyment of folks making use of the full-service campground. To find the trailhead, drive into the campground. Just past the dump station pullout, turn right at the 105–137 sign. Continue along the pavement to site 114, and park on the right side of the road. The trail starts across from site 115.

The trail starts out through a stretch of pine flatwoods recently thinned due to an infestation by the southern pine bark beetle. Younger pines remain, providing hope for the future of the forest. A dense thicket of saw palmetto makes up the understory. Scattered sand live oaks provide a middle canopy. A green anole vanishes under a saw palmetto frond as you approach the bridge. Cross the bridge and you're at the start of the trail loop. Turn right. Winged sumac and loblolly bay rise through the mass of saw palmetto. The purple blooms of a paintbush attract a zebra swallowtail.

As the trail gains a little elevation, the footpath becomes sandy underfoot. Curving left, you see a large number of bay trees on the right, forming a bayhead. Walking down a corridor defined by tall walls of gallberry, you reach a clearing with several benches at 0.3 mile. The trail curves left, and you start to see campers in the distance as you come back around the loop. Showing off its beautiful rusty autumn leaves, cinnamon fern stands out against the gallberry under the pines. Passing another bench, you see an eastern fence lizard. Curving away from the campground momentarily, the trail continues through a shoulder-high corridor of saw palmetto. After 0.5 mile, you complete the loop. Cross over the bridge and follow the footpath back out to the campground road, completing your 0.6-mile walk.

22

Lake June-in-Winter Scrub State Park

Total distance (two circuits): 3.6 miles

Hiking time: 2 hours, 15 minutes

Habitats: Bayhead, hardwood hammock, scrub

Maps: USGS 7½' Lake June-in-Winter; park map

Florida's desert: the scrub. Running down the central spine of the Florida peninsula from the rolling hills near Clermont to the marshes feeding Lake Okeechobee, the Lake Wales Ridge is Florida's definitive scrub habitat, dating back to the Miocene. These dune-capped islands standing above the sea defined ancient Florida, sheltering plant and animal species found nowhere else on earth. Today, they contain the highest concentration of endemic species in North America, many of which are in danger of extinction.

Since scrub environments are high and dry, the rolling hills of the Lake Wales Ridge were some of the first land to be turned to agricultural use. Ideal for citrus crops, easily developed, Florida's scrub continues to rapidly vanish as population explodes. Outside Lake Placid, Lake June-in-Winter Scrub State Park celebrates the scrub. It's a very young park, opened in 1999, but its mission is important: protecting more than 840 acres along Lake June-in-Winter, including a critical Florida scrub-jay habitat.

Although Lake Placid sits above the eastern shore of the lake, the park is off the beaten path. Heading north on US 27 from FL 70, drive north 6.5 miles to Lake Placid, continuing another 1.7 miles to the small BROWN PARK sign at CR 17/CR 621. Turn left. Southbound on US 27 from Sebring, the turnoff is 8.8 miles south of US 98. After 4 miles on CR 621, you see another park sign. Take the left fork. Another 0.3 mile later, turn left onto Daffodil Street in

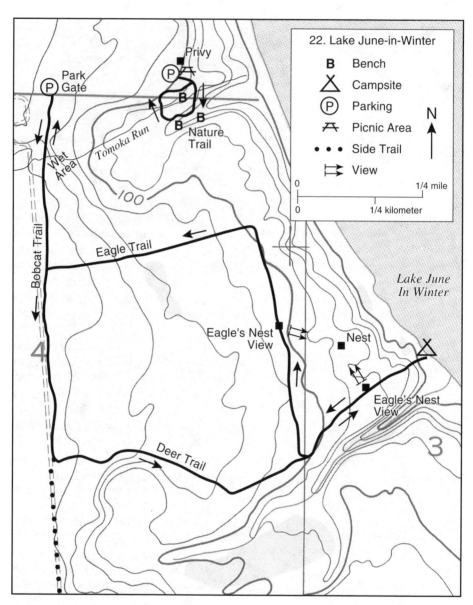

front of the gas station. Although the pavement ends after 1.4 miles, keep going. The park entrance is on the left after 2 miles. Pay your Florida State Parks entrance fee at the self-pay station, and pick up a trail map from the kiosk. Drive down the bumpy road to the parking area, which adjoins a composting toilet and a canopied picnic bench with view of the distant sparkling blue waters of Lake June-in-Winter.

TOMOKA RUN TRAIL

Walk down beyond the gate to the TOMOKA RUN TRAIL sign and turn right. This short nature trail enables you to explore a lush forest surrounding the burbling waters of Tomoka Run. Take the left fork, which descends from an oak scrub into a hardwood hammock, where a bayhead of loblolly bay and cinnamon fern soaks up the precious moisture. Sunlight dapples across the tea-colored flow of Tomoka Run as it bubbles over ledges on its rapid decent to the lake. Crossing a bridge, the trail rises up a steep hill toward the scrub, and turns to the right past a bench to follow the run. The splashing water echoes through the forest. Look for giant bromeliads in the trees. Crossing back over the run, the trail turns left and heads upstream through an oak hammock. Pause a moment to savor this leafy green grotto, where the ribbon of tannic orange water slices through the soft sand of the ridge. Making a sharp right, the trail continues uphill into an oak scrub under the slash pines. At the T intersection, turn right, walking under the Spanish-moss-draped scrub live oaks past a bench. Heading back downhill, you reach the end of the loop at 0.3 mile. Turn left to return to the parking lot.

BOBCAT, EAGLE, AND DEER TRAILS

Comprised of a series of blazed jeep roads, this 3.3-mile network of trails takes you out into the open scrub and to a group campsite along the shores of Lake June-in-Winter. Before setting out on the hike, remember that the scrub environment is a desert—hot, dry, and sandy. Take along plenty of water. There is no shade, so you'll want to wear a hat.

Trailhead access is at the park entrance, so you'll either want to walk up the park road (adding 0.4 mile to your hike) or drive back out to the entrance and park alongside the fence. Do not block the gates. Walk around the entrance gate along the fence line to a sign that says SOUTH BOUNDARY 1 MILE. A post with a bobcat paw provides your clue that the trail starts here. Turn left and follow the fence line along the edge of the citrus grove. Walking under a canopy of slash pines, you come up to flowing water across the trail—a wetland feeding Tomoka Run. Keep to the center hump of the jeep track to minimize the amount of water seeping into your shoes.

The rare beauty of the Lake Wales Ridge is in its diversity of plant life. Keep alert for the many scrub plants you see along the hike. Some are large and obvious, like the aromatic silk bay tree, the scrub hickory, and the pygmy fringe tree, which fills the air with its fragrant blossoms each spring. Some are small and precious, like scrub mint, pinweed, and the clusters of sand squares growing out of the blinding white sand. Watch along the edge of the trail for a tiny tree with thorny zigzagging branches: the scrub plum. Bearing pinkish flowers each February, it hangs with juicy green plums by May.

A six-lined racerunner dashes under a prickly pear cactus as you come up past a trail marker with a yellow blaze and a bobcat footprint. With yellow blooms atop silvery green leaves, golden aster waves in the breeze as you approach the junction with the Eagle Trail at 0.4 mile. You'll complete the loop at this junction. Continue straight, staying on the Bobcat Trail along the fence line. Fuzzy pink ball-shaped blooms of sensitive brier dangle from vines stretched across sand live oaks. As you pass a large silk bay tree, grab a leaf and crush it in your hand. It smells like menthol cough drops.

Veering left, the trail leaves the fence line to enter a stretch of mature scrubby flatwoods, with gallberry, saw palmetto, and sand live oak under the slash pine. A

The backpacker's campsite sits along Lake June-in-Winter.

yellow sulfur flits from bloom to bloom on a coastal plain palafox. Two red-bellied woodpeckers creep up the trunk of a slash pine, and you hear the fuss of a Florida scrub-jay in the distant oaks. Wispy wire-weed creates a taupe fog under the pines. On a bare patch of sand, you spy a beautiful and delicate garden of spike moss intermingled with deer moss and sand squares.

After 0.8 mile, you reach the junction with the Deer Trail. At the DEER TRAIL TO LAKE, 1 MILE sign, turn left to head down through the open scrub. Notice the deer scrape in the sand. The scrape marks a spot through which many deer pass, leaving messages of their presence to each other by rolling in the sand and urinating on the spot. As you meet up with a trail junction, keep to the left. Clumps of prickly pear show signs of being nibbled by gopher tortoises. The trail skirts an oak hammock draped in Spanish moss; the chirps of hundreds of birds rise from the shadows. As the trail turns, the miniature forest of the low scrub surrounds you. The broken and bleached bones of a cow are scattered throughout the underbrush. Listen carefully for the *shrweep* of the eastern towhee, and watch for the flash of blue of a Florida scrub-jay.

The trail passes a junction with the Eagle Trail at 1.3 miles. Continue straight, following the deer print marker with the yellow blaze. Past a signpost that says 3/4 MILE, you arrive at the EAGLES NEST OVER-LOOK sign. Turn and look off to the left at the tall slash pine. The nest is somewhat obscured from this direction, looking like a mound of Spanish moss. If the resident bald eagles are near it, you won't miss it. Eagles return to the nest every winter to mate and raise one or two fledglings to maturity.

Dropping down a sloping curve to the right, the trail ends at the Lake June-in-Winter group campsite, obviously set up for scouting groups with its outdoor movie screen, fire ring with benches, and picnic benches on the edge of the lake. Settle down on a bench and enjoy the view through the cypresses before heading back up the trail. Scan the ripples for the movement of alligators, and watch for herons and egrets picking through the shallows along the shoreline. The city of Lake Placid lies on the distant shore, with its giant tower and fancy waterfront homes. You've hiked 1.7 miles. After enjoying your break, head back up the Deer Trail. Pay attention to the flora on your return trip. You'll find diminutive scrub hickory along the trail's edge, and scrub beargrass growing out of the trail. This endangered species is a member of the agave family, bearing showy spikes of flowers each spring at the top of a tall stalk.

At the junction, turn right to follow the Eagle Trail into a forest of rusty lyonia. This wizened scrub tree is sometimes harvested before a controlled burn for use as the trunk of an artificial ficus. Sand pines provide scant swatches of shade. At the EAGLES NEST OVERLOOK sign, look to the right. This is a much better view of the aerie. Look at the slash pine in the distance, and you'll notice the 12-foot-tall jumble of branches and moss that makes up the massive nest. Lopsided Indiangrass shimmers in the sunlight. Look down and you'll see tiny clusters of sand squares and spike moss making up a miniature N-scale forest. Covered in delicate white flowers, the wispy shrub creeping across the trail is sandlace, another endemic plant of the Lake Wales Ridge.

After 2.5 miles, you reach a T intersection. Turn left to stay on the Eagle Trail; the trail to the right currently dead-ends.

Rising up through the sand pine scrub, you get a brief respite from the sun under a line of tall slash pines, where blazing star and wiregrass thrive under the pines. A Florida scrub-jay hops across the road as you climb farther up into high, dry rosemary-and-oak scrub. Look in the soft sand for dozens of footprints: deer, raccoon, opossum, and bobcat. Although the open scrub belongs to birds and lizards in the daytime, the foragers and their predators take to the trails after dark.

Returning to the fence line, you meet the Bobcat Trail after 2.9 miles. You've completed the loop. Turn right. Follow the fence down to the gate. Purple spiderworts emerge from a thicket of oaks. Walking back around the tangle of balsam apple vines, you finish your hike at the park entrance after 3.3 miles.

23

Platt Branch Mitigation Park

Total distance (circuit): 2.7 miles

Hiking time: 1 hour, 15 minutes

Habitats: Oak scrub, prairie, scrubby flatwoods

Maps: USGS 7½' Venus SW; park map

As you drive along the rolling hills south of Lake Placid on US 27, vistas of orange groves and cattle ranches stretch off to the horizon. Down here at its southern edge, the Lake Wales Ridge becomes a series of foothills dropping down to meet the level prairies of the Everglades. Thanks to centuries of settlement and development, you see very little of either environment. Drained dry by canals, the northern Everglades now hosts nearly half a million acres of sugar cane fields on its dark, rich soil. Hidden beneath the spread of citrus groves, cattle ranches, and development, the Lake Wales Ridge no longer supports its original habitat of a desertlike scrub. Situated along the northern edge of Fisheating Creek, Platt Branch Mitigation Park marks the southernmost extent of the Lake Wales Ridge, protecting more than 1,700 acres of scrub and scrubby flatwoods and the associated flora and fauna found in these rare habitats, including gopher tortoises, Florida scrub-jays, Sherman's fox squirrels, and four family groups of red-cockaded woodpeckers.

Platt Branch Mitigation Park lies south of Lake Placid and north of Palmdale off US 27. From FL 29 at Palmdale, head north 10.3 miles to CR 731. From FL 70 south of Lake Placid, drive 9.9 miles south to CR 731. Follow CR 731 west toward Venus for 1.2 miles. Immediately after you cross the railroad tracks, turn left on Detjens Dairy Road. Drive south 1.3 miles. Keep alert after you pass Placid Farms Drive, as it's the next turnoff on the right. A

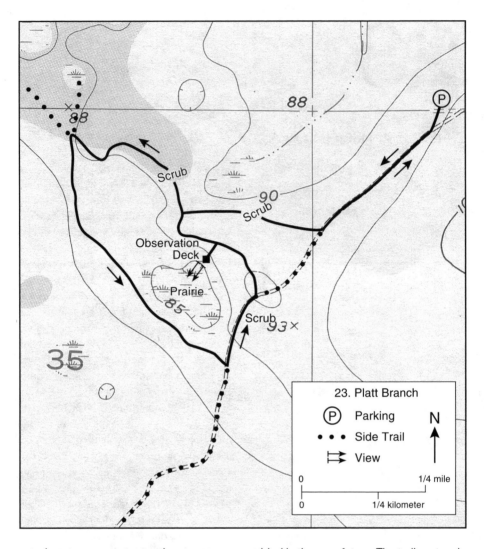

Scrub

88

88

Scrub

90

Scrub

Observation
Deck

Prairie

85

Scrub
93 ×

35

23. Platt Branch

Ⓟ Parking

N

• • • Side Trail

⇨ View

0   1/4 mile

0   1/4 kilometer

gated entrance protects the preserve; open the gate and close it behind you before driving down the one-lane jeep road for 0.8 mile to the kiosk marking the beginning of the trail system. Park next to the kiosk, and start your hike by walking through the open gate and continuing down the jeep road on foot.

According to the kiosk, 5 miles of trail are open year-round for hiking, and there are plans for a backpacker campsite to be added in the near future. The trail system is currently under development, however, so signage is sporadic. This hike follows the most obvious route through the preserve on jeep trails looping around a large flatwoods pond. Starting from the kiosk, follow the old jeep trail across the open ranchland, which is slowly reverting to its original scrub habitat. Flat-topped goldenrod peers out of the tall grasses, while wax myrtle and young slash pines move in from the edges. An osprey launches from the top of a tall snag, winging its way toward distant Fisheating Creek.

One of the few wild and scenic waterways left in the Lake Okeechobee region, and the only truly free-flowing water source emptying into Lake Okeechobee, Fisheating Creek rises out of rainfall spread across thousands of square miles on the fringe of the Lake Wales Ridge. Attracting swallow-tailed kites to nest, ancient cypresses define its winding path. Wood storks pick through the shallows. And canoeists have enjoyed its primeval nature for decades. But in 1989, the Lykes Brothers Corporation—which owns much of the land north of Lake Okeechobee, with vast cattle ranching and vegetable farming operations—posted NO TRESPASSING signs on the creek. Following the swift public outcry from locals who'd fished, swum, and canoed the creek all their lives, the state of Florida immediately sued to establish the right of the public to access the waterway, since all waterways in Florida belong to the state. The key point: Was it navigable? Although water levels rise and fall all over South Florida every season, it was proven that as far back as 1845, Fisheating Creek was considered a navigable waterway. And so the right to access remained in the hands of the people. Along with mitigation funds (fines paid for by developers to replace habitats that have been destroyed), funds from the Preservation 2000 land-conservation program allowed the state to buy up the land that now makes up Platt Branch Mitigation Park.

Where the jeep trail comes up to the corner of the fence line, you reach a junction of trails. Continue straight. In fall, fluffy puffs of white characterize the blossoms of the sea myrtles on the right. Off to the left,

saw palmetto blankets the understory of a scrubby area with young scrub oaks, mounds of blooming pennyroyal, and prickly pear cactus. The trail curves left under spreading slash pines. As it climbs a small rise, the habitat becomes scrubby. Thickets of reindeer lichen flourish on the bright sand. Look for splashes of orange, the sprays of freshly dug sand indicating the location of gopher tortoise burrows. A scrub plateau rises on the left, where the blinding white sand under the sand live oaks shows many animal tracks, including the distinctive marks of the gopher tortoise. Sandhill wireweed droops outside another burrow. This is certainly prime habitat for the gopher tortoise, a species considered a cornerstone in any Florida habitat because of other creatures' dependence on its burrow for survival. Each adult tortoise will dig as many as nine different burrows over its territory, up to 40 feet long and 10 feet deep. When the tortoise isn't at home, other species move in, forming a regular apartment complex. More than 360 different species of animals—including snakes, mice, opossums, quail, armadillo, burrowing owls, toads, and lizards—will take over the cool, damp hole while the tortoise is occupying one of its other burrows. Some will share the space simultaneously. When wildfire sweeps through the scrub, predators and prey take shelter in the burrows, miraculously leaving each other alone until the danger has passed.

At 0.6 mile, you pass a BURN HISTORY sign just before a junction of trails. Continue straight, following the trail as it rises higher up into the bright white sand of the scrub, where yellow buttons and woody pinweed add a splash of color. An eastern towhee perches in a young sand live oak, and you see the yellow flash of wings of a

Plants of the scrub habitat

palm warbler. A belted kingfisher perches high in a tangle of dead branches in the top of a pine snag. Past the interpretive marker, patches of Florida rosemary grow underneath the scrub oaks, which are just the right size for Florida scrub-jays. Walk quietly and you might see the blur of blue of a scrub-jay flying past: More than 20 individual jays live within the park.

Passing through a gap in a barbed-wire fence, the trail continues up into a rare and precious shady spot provided by a low canopy of sand live oaks, their branches festooned in ball moss and other small air plants. They rise out of a sea of saw palmetto sweeping off into the distance. Look up and you'll see golden orb spiders weaving their webs well above the trail. An enormous gopher tortoise slides headfirst into its burrow as you approach a T intersection in front of a couple of large sand live oaks at 1 mile. Turn left, making an immediate left at the subsequent junction of trails—until the trails are fully blazed, the idea of this hike is to keep making left turns until you come back around to the beginning of the loop.

With a grassy jeep road serving as a trail, you drop down into scrubby flatwoods under turkey oaks, through fields of waving bushybeard bluestem and wiry South Florida bluestem grass, with scattered slash pines that offer a minimum of shade. Clusters of primrose willow add a little color to the trail. A yellow sulfur lands on a tall blazing star. Emerging into an even more open environment, you enter a seemingly endless sea of palmetto prairie, the landscape faced by pioneers who came to this part of Florida in the mid-1800s to establish homesteads and raise cattle. The rolling hills north of Lake Okeechobee are still the largest cattle ranching region in the eastern United States, with more than 470,000 acres devoted to ranching.

Off in the distance you see a broad, wet prairie. The trail skirts its southern edge, and you can see an observation platform on the far side. As the trail curves to fit the edge of the wetland, notice the interesting contrast of the light green stalks of sawgrass peeping between the saw palmetto fronds where the two habitats meet. Rising up a little, the landscape becomes a scrub, with gopher tortoise burrows and mounds of pennyroyal. After 1.6 miles, you reach a T intersection on the far side of the wetland. Turn left and head into the thick of the scrub, with soft bright white sand all around you. Watch for scrub-jays in the young oak trees, and notice the small scrub palmettos, which look similar to but differ in character from saw palmettos. Saw palmettos have serrated edges on their stems. Each stem comes to an abrupt end where the frond starts. On the scrub palmetto, the stem is smooth and extends up into the frond, ending in a point—very similar to the frond of a cabbage palm. But scrub palmettos grow only in scrub habitats. Loose threads dangle from the scrub palmetto, and scrub-jays pluck these to use in lining their nests.

Tiny clumps of greenish yellow blossoms hug closely to the ground—wild bachelor's button. Gopher apple grows in large masses along the trail, and you can see the tracks of gopher tortoises that have been browsing through the plants. A scrub-jay runs across the road as you catch a glimpse of the expansive wetland, now off to the left. A black swallowtail flutters across a patch of spike moss, a strange little scrub moss that looks like clusters of slender green fingers pointing upward in groups. Crusty black lichen grows intermingled amid the spike moss and reindeer lichen. Curving sharply to the left past a gopher tortoise burrow, the trail passes through another gap in the barbed-wire fence, reaching a fork at 1.8 miles. Keep left.

You're walking through the old ranch-land, where mounds of sand from gopher tortoise burrows indicate a healthy tortoise population. The scrub habitat is moving in, slowly erasing the decades of human changes to the land. The trail curves left through a stand of young sand live oaks, then heads out into an open, dry scrubby flatwoods. Keep alert for a rough sand trail on the left that leads over to the observation platform on the wetland. The trail may not be well maintained, but it is passable. Once you reach the observation platform, you can sit on the bench and survey the scene, scanning for the activity of wading birds. A great blue heron works its way along the edge of a distant flag pond in the marsh, while a kingfisher skims down low across the open water. Along the wetland's edge, loblolly bay has taken hold. After you return along the side path to the main trail, turn left. You pass a few clumps of beargrass, the first seen along this hike. A spiky relative of the yucca plant, beargrass thrives in dry habitats. Early peoples in Florida used dried beargrass strips for basket weaving.

The jeep trail continues to curve to the right along the prairie before it comes to the junction of trails at the BURN HISTORY sign. After 2.1 miles, you've completed the loop. Turn right to exit the park, passing the fence line corner with its trail intersection at 2.4 miles. Continue straight, and the trail curves left to cross the long grassy expanse of former ranchland, ending up back at the trailhead kiosk after 2.7 miles.

Blowing Rocks   *Clyde Butcher*

24

Jack Island Preserve State Park

Total distance (circuit): 4.2 miles

Hiking time: 2 hours, 15 minutes

Habitats: Maritime hammock, mangrove forest

Maps: USGS 7½' Indrio, Fort Pierce; park map

A ribbon of salt water stretching 150 miles from Jupiter Inlet to Ponce Inlet, the Indian River Lagoon is one of Florida's many unique environments, and one of the largest lagoons in the world. More than 3,000 species live within its saline waters, including dolphins, sea turtles, and West Indian manatees. As an "Estuary of National Significance," the Indian River Lagoon merits constant monitoring. Ongoing projects work to improve water quality, to restore the seagrass beds, and to ensure the health of aquatic populations. Unfortunately, more than 75 percent of the lagoon's shores have been developed or modified, forever altering the natural interplay of terrestrial and aquatic ecosystems. Located just north of Fort Pierce, Jack Island Preserve State Park protects a sliver of the mangrove forests that are so important to the health of the lagoon. Sheltering nurseries of fish, crustaceans, shellfish, and shrimp, the mangrove forests filter the lagoon, contributing to the quality and clarity of the water.

To find Jack Island Preserve State Park, take either Florida Turnpike exit 152, Ft. Pierce/Vero Beach, or I-95 exit 129 (0.8 mile east of the turnpike). Follow FL 70 east into Fort Pierce. At 4.8 miles east of the turnpike, you reach US 1. Turn left. Drive north through downtown Fort Pierce for 3.2 miles to FL A1A (North Beach Causeway). Turn right. Cross the bridge and pass the entrance to Fort Pierce State Park. After 2.4 miles, you reach a traffic light. Turn left. Drive north 1.2 miles; the

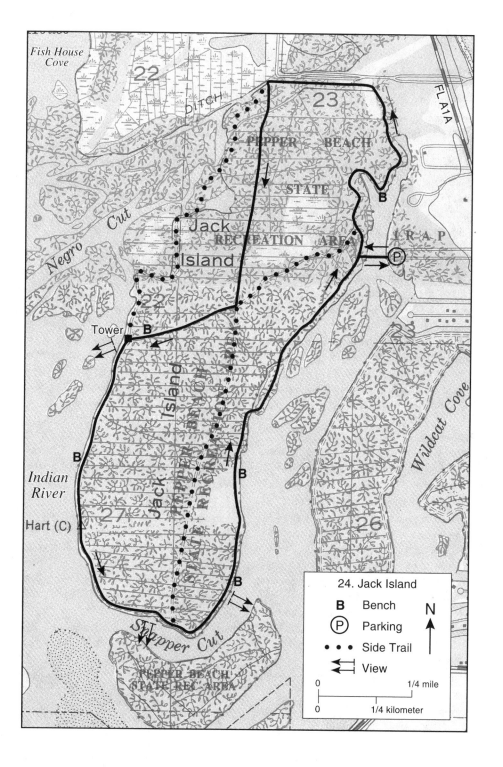

Fish House Cove

22

DITCH

PEPPER BEACH

23

FL A1A

STATE

Jack

RECREATION AREA

Island

I.R.A.P.

Negro

Cut

B

Tower

B

Jack Island

PEPPER BEACH STATE RECREATION

B

Wildcat Cove

Indian River

B

27

Hart (C)

26

B

Stuper Cut

PEPPER BEACH STATE REC. AREA

24. Jack Island

B   Bevich

N

P   Parking

• • • Side Trail

←↑ View

0   1/4 mile

0   1/4 kilometer

entrance is on the left. Parking is limited to a thin sliver of pavement between private residences. No fee is charged, and the park is open 8 AM–sunset. You'll want to enjoy this hike in the early morning, as the trails offer virtually no shade.

Start your hike by walking across the narrow bridge out to the Jack Island, where you may encounter people fishing for snook and redfish. The walkway provides a great view of the surrounding smaller mangrove islands set in the murky water of the inlet. As you approach, a green heron takes off from the railing. In summer, watch the water for the protruding gray snouts of West Indian manatees. At the end of the bridge, there's a kiosk with a trail map and interpretive brochures. Mangrove crabs scuttle out of your way as you walk between sea grapes and nickerbean to reach the trail junction in front of the kiosk. Although the hiking trails are limited to Jack Island, the preserve also encompasses neighboring King Island. This is an excellent destination for birding, especially in winter, when the resident population explodes with the arrival of migratory species.

A series of dikes leads around Jack Island, which was carved up into impoundments in the days of mosquito control. Turn right and head north, away from the kiosk. A marsh rabbit melts into the tangle of mangrove roots as you walk along the mangrove-lined canal, with the open waterway to the right. Buttonwoods and sea grapes abound along the lagoon inlet's shore. Along the canal, the pneumatophores of black mangroves march down into water the color of café au lait. You reach a trail intersection where a TOWER 1 MI sign points to the left. Continue straight to explore the north end of the island.

Sprigs of gumbo limbo sprout beneath a cabbage palm decorated with goldfoot fern. You breathe in the strong salt tang of Indian River Lagoon, and a great blue heron wings its way down the narrow channel. At high tide, the water almost sloshes onto the trail—notice how close the pneumatophores creep to the path. As you cross an outflow culvert, don't be surprised to see alligators or birds lurking on the outflow side, waiting for dazed fish. As you come around a curve to a bench at 0.4 mile, you start to see the large holes of giant land crabs. These burrows extend down to the water table. Sit still on the bench and you might see one of these terrestrial giants emerge: With an iridescent blue-green shell up to 5 inches across, it's a formidable sight. As you walk, out of the corner of your eye you constantly see the scuttling movement of crabs clearing the pathway. The trail turns a corner to the left to face a condo sticking up above the forest on the far side of the inlet. Rounding a bend past a stand of young Australian pines, the trail continues straight up the channel, giving you another good opportunity to watch for manatees. Perched on a black mangrove leaf, a pipevine swallowtail butterfly shows off its iridescent purple wings. Listen carefully and you can hear the croaks of tree frogs in the mangroves as you reach the north end of the island, and the trail turns left. Another outflow causes turbulence in the channel. A short boardwalk on the left crosses a mangrove-lined canal, affording a close look of the salt seeps on the bottoms of the red mangroves. While black and white mangroves excrete salt through their leaves, the red mangrove filters salt from its roots, passing mostly fresh water up into the leaf system.

As you continue down the dike under the shade of sea grapes, you catch a flash of white ibis wings in the tangle of mangrove jungle. Coming up to the cross-trail

The bridge to Jack Island

at 1.1 miles, you see a SALT MARSH RESTORATION PROJECT sign and instrumentation boxes. Turn left. This dike takes you through the heart of the mangrove forest, where narrow mosquito control canals line both sides of the trail and the mangroves crowd in closely. A little blue heron squawks as it rises from the water to perch in a high branch. Chunks of limestone make up the trail, containing glittering fossilized shells. Golden orb spiders weave their delicate webs well above head height, the strands glimmering in the sun. Hermit crabs build mud caves that look like little houses along the edge of the pickleweed beds. Look into the marsh, not down the trail, or you'll miss the intriguing details that surround you.

At 1.7 miles, you meet the central trail junction on the island. The cross-trail continues straight, and the intersecting trail is the one leading directly from the kiosk to the observation tower. Turn right to head down to the observation tower. In this mix of habitats, strangler figs grow between the mangroves. The salt tang increases. As you pass a bench, the trail continues along a broad canal. Watch for alligators drifting across the brackish water. Stands of sea oxeye line the dike. Coming to a T intersection at 2 miles, you reach the observation tower. Climb up. It offers a great view for birding—bring your binoculars! From the top, you can scan the adjoining islands in the Indian River Lagoon, where ospreys nest in the precarious snags of Australian pines. A sweep of condos defines the location of the Atlantic Ocean.

After you descend the tower, head south (a left at the T intersection) past the bench to walk along the Indian River Lagoon back to the bridge. You pass another boardwalk over the murky waters of the mangrove-lined channel. Crossing over culvert H, you can hear ospreys crying as they scan for fish. A bench invites you to take a moment's rest just beyond the culvert at 2.3 miles. Palm warblers flit between the trees. The dike curves to the left after crossing another culvert. Tiny fiddler crabs thread their way through mazes of pneumatophores to return to their holes. You catch glimpses of blue water through the tangle of roots on the right, and hear the sounds of mullet jumping. Like snowdrifts, puffs of sea myrtle blooms scatter across the trail. Emerging onto a sweeping view of a mangrove-lined inlet on the right, take the time to observe the ospreys as they plunge down to the lagoon to nab mullet and snook. Watch how they fish. Circling the skies at least 50 feet above the water, an osprey scans for prey, sometimes hovering in place to keep a close watch on its target. When ready, the osprey drops from the sky like a rock, hitting the water feetfirst. Its specially adapted toes allow it to grasp a squirming fish and hold on firmly as it lifts off.

At 2.9 miles, you meet the cross-trail coming in from the left. Continue straight to stay along the island's edge. The dike makes a sharp curve to the left and you're back along the interior waterway, a thin screen of mangroves dividing the trail from the tidal channel. Sea oxeye edges the grassy footpath. A belted kingfisher explodes from the mangroves and soars out over the open water. As you come up to a bench at 3.2 miles, you can look out across the channel and see how new mangrove islands form. Tides wash detritus across the roots of the young mangroves in the shallows, and as the mud sticks, the island grows. More mangroves take root, their seedpods borne on the tides, in an ever-expanding process that creates both land and the mangrove forest.

Several different types of crabs along this stretch of trail—blue, fiddler, hermit, and giant land crabs—live in harmony under the mangrove roots, retreating into their holes at the feel of vibrations from your footfalls. A bench tucked in the shade of a large sea grape affords a rare moment of respite from the sun. Crossing over culvert P, the trail veers left, and the vegetation becomes denser. Blue crabs with yellow stripes dive sidelong into their holes. Spanish bayonets grow under the white mangroves as the trail curves to the right, coming back to the stand of cabbage palms shading the kiosk at the beginning of the trail. After 4.2 miles, you've completed the loop. Turn right to walk back across the bridge to the parking area.

25

Hawks Bluff

Total distance (circuit): 1.1 miles

Hiking time: 45 minutes

Habitats: Cabbage palm flatwoods, coastal scrub, freshwater marsh, oak hammock, sand pine scrub

Maps: USGS 7½' Eden

Less than a mile from the Atlantic Ocean in places, a long, thin ribbon of freshwater savannas—open wetlands busy with the activity of thousands of birds—stretches 10 miles along Florida's southeast coast from Fort Pierce to Jensen Beach. Serving as a precious cache of fresh water, these wetlands filter both rainwater and runoff from the surrounding relict dunes and pine flatwoods, creating a unique biological community as they feed the estuaries of the St. Lucie Inlet. Encompassing more than 5,000 acres, Savannas Preserve State Park protects this unique natural resource. Given the sheer size of the savannas, access to the preserve comes from several widely distributed locations. Of these, Hawks Bluff, at Jensen Beach, provides the most pleasant hiking experience, a high and dry ramble along the eastern rim of the savannas.

To find Hawks Bluff from the north, use Florida Turnpike exit 142, Port St. Lucie. Follow Port St. Lucie Boulevard (SR 716) 4.1 miles east to US 1. Turn right and drive 2 miles south on US 1 to Jensen Beach Boulevard (SR 707A). From the south, use I-95 exit 101, Stuart. Take SR 76 east to US 1, and drive 4.1 miles north on US 1 to Jensen Beach Boulevard. As you drive up Jensen Beach Boulevard, you'll pass an entrance to Savannas Preserve State Park at 1.3 miles on the left, a picnic area with rest rooms. Continue another 0.9 mile to the traffic light at Savannah Road; turn left. Drive 1.2 miles to Hawks Bluff, at the gate on the left at the corner with Northeast

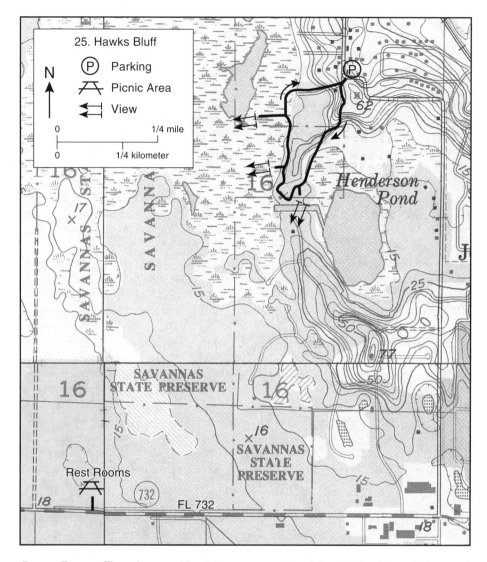

Dorsey Terrace. There is no parking lot, so turn your car around and park on the shoulder of the road along the state park. Do not block the gate. The park is open 8 AM–sunset, and leashed pets are permitted on the trail. Bicycles are not explicitly barred from the trail, but their tires could damage the soft scrub environment.

Start your hike by walking around the gate to follow the white blazes down this very steep hill, one of a ridge of relict sand dunes topping this high spot in the Atlantic Coastal Ridge. You immediately see a double blaze on a power pole. Turn left at the pole to follow the trail up the sandy bluff into the coastal scrub. The ivory and pale pink blooms of sandhill wireweed dangle like little bottlebrushes. Cardinal wild pine perches in the low branches of sand live oaks, while love vine throws a tangled web of orange and green across the taller trees. Bright yellow blossoms draw your eye to the sweet acacia, a member of the bean family. With its feathery leaves and sharply angled stems, you can see its relationship to tamarind and mimosa trees.

Leading up the steep dunes into the sand pines, the trail curves to the right and passes a wooden fence. Hog plums fill the hollows between the dunes, sporting juicy-looking brownish red ripe fruits. Since the scrub is rather open, keep an eye on where the footprints lead until you see the next blaze. The young sand pines look like wispy Christmas trees. Turning left, curving with the dunes, the trail comes up to a fence post with a double blaze. Turn right, passing a spindly sand live oak with giant wild pine and ball moss entwined in its limbs. Up on the crest of the ridge, spike moss runs rampant across the open sand. You reach a telephone pole with a double blaze. A broad path takes off to the right. Continue straight, past the telephone pole, to proceed down the dunes as the trail winds through a thick bed of gopher apple. Mourning doves strut beneath the sand pines. An eerie mass of thousands of slender green fingers, spike moss blankets the hillside. The trail curves to the right beneath stands of older sand pines, their cones virtually welded to their branches. Sand pine forests rely almost entirely on fire to regenerate, so the closed cones of a sand pine may become embedded and overgrown by bark rather than fall to the ground and sprout. When fire races through the sand pine forest, it quickly climbs the low dead branches. Like popcorn, the cones burst in the flames and release their seeds, ensuring the rebirth of the forest.

Notice the open pods and bright red seeds of the rosary peas, dangling from their woody vines. Although beautiful to behold, the seeds are deadly poisonous if eaten. Winding through the sand pine forest, the needle-strewn footpath is surrounded by spike moss. Sprouting from the thick pine duff, fallen bromeliads—particularly giant wild pine—grow like plantations of pineapples beneath the pines. The trail swings downhill to the left to skirt a fence built around an artifact that looks like a bumper from an old vehicle. Sporting silvery leaves, golden asters rise from clumps of deer moss and spike moss. Sand live oaks nearly suffocate under their load of thriving bromeliads. Slash pines and water oaks infiltrate the forest as you transition into pine flatwoods. A red-tailed hawk soars overhead, headed for the savannas.

After 0.4 mile, a double blaze prevents you from walking straight ahead into a lily-covered canal. Wander down to the end of the path anyway, which affords your first glimpse of the savannas, off to the right, beyond the residential area. Returning to the main trail, turn left at the T intersection. Scattered prickly pear cacti provide fodder for the gopher tortoises that reside here. The preserve also protects the highly endangered fragrant prickly apple cactus, a night-blooming species with fruits prized by birds and gopher tortoises. Limited to the sand pine scrub of the Atlantic Coastal Ridge along the Indian River Lagoon, this spindly species has almost been wiped out by development.

As the trail twists and winds through the forest, you catch occasional glimpses of the savannas through openings in the trees. At 0.5 mile, turn left and walk down a side trail to emerge along a bluff on the edge of the savannas. Surrounded by marsh ferns and the stumps of Australian pines, you look out over the marshes. An egret feeds in the shallows, which resonate with the chirps of

The Savannas

frogs. Restoration efforts have removed invasive species from the shoreline. Head back up to the main trail; turn left. Nourished by the humidity of the savannas, lush beds of bromeliads cover the trees and the ground all around the footpath under the pines. Turning left, you continue along a wall of saw palmetto. Winding uphill, then downhill, under the sand pines, the trail makes a sharp right through a sea of marsh ferns. Flanked by two cabbage palms decorated with shoelace fern, the trail emerges into a broad open grassy area along the savannas.

At 0.7 mile, a trail leads off to the left along a high and dry spit of land stretching out into the marshes. Turn left. The wind drives constant ripples across the deep blue water. Moorhens cruise close to shore, but decide to take flight as you approach. Catching a running start, they walk on water as they flap their wings, kicking up splashes as their feet leave the surface. An alligator drifts past, its eyes barely above water level. Overlooking the rapid current of the central slough through the savanna, you reach the end of the trail. In the distance, pine flatwoods line the western edge of the marshes. Seashore mallow towers almost overhead, waving its massive pink flowers in the breeze.

Follow the mowed area around the trees and return to the main trail. Turn left.

Woodlands phlox show off white and pink blooms under the shade of the slash pines as you continue along, your route confirmed by the next white blaze. Three mergansers sail overhead, looking for the perfect landing spot in the savannas. At 1 mile, you reach a trail junction. Turn left; white blazes lead you into a forest of cabbage palms and slash pines. Large bracken ferns grow beneath sand live oaks covered in a tinsel-like adornment of pine needles. Growing on the sunny side of a relict dune, numerous chandelier plants catch your attention with their fleshy reddish purple blooms dangling like bells from a tall, thin stalk. On the other side of the dune, numerous gopher tortoise burrows take advantage of the shape of the hill. The trail rises up into an oak hammock, where a strangler fig attempts to survive after its host plant—its means of support—has died. As the trail curves to the left, you see residences adjoining the preserve. Deep sand makes your footing difficult as you climb up toward the telephone pole, completing the loop. Walk back up the steep slope to the gate, finishing your hike after 1.1 miles.

26

Seabranch Preserve State Park

Total distance (circuit): 4.8 miles

Hiking time: 2 hours, 45 minutes

Habitats: Bayhead, oak scrub, rosemary scrub, sand pine scrub, scrubby flatwoods

Maps: USGS 7½' St. Lucie; park map

Not many people know about Seabranch Preserve State Park. It's one of Florida's newest state parks, encompassing nearly 1,000 acres along the Intracoastal Waterway south of Stuart. But it protects several critical habitats in an area overrun with coastal development. In addition to supporting populations of Florida scrub-jays and gopher tortoises across its many acres of diminutive scrub forest, Seabranch Preserve contains one of South Florida's rare bayhead communities. Also known as a baygall, this swampy habitat filled with loblolly bay and sweetbay magnolia filters runoff from the adjacent scrubby flatwoods as the water flows down toward the tidal marshes of the Indian River Lagoon.

To find Seabranch Preserve State Park, take I-95 exit 61, Stuart/Indiantown (FL 76). Follow Cove Road east for 4.5 miles, crossing US 1, until you reach CR A1A. Turn right and continue 1.5 miles south. Make a left into the small parking area across from the VFW. No fee is charged for the use of this park, where the local Tropical Trekkers Chapter of the Florida Trail Association built and maintains the hiking trail system. A composting privy sits near the shaded picnic tables.

Start your hike by walking over to the kiosk to pick up a brochure with a rough map of the hiking trail. A more detailed map is posted on the kiosk. A tiny sign on a post says TRAILHEAD 0.1 MILE AHEAD. Continue along an old jeep trail from the picnic area into the sand pine forest. The purple

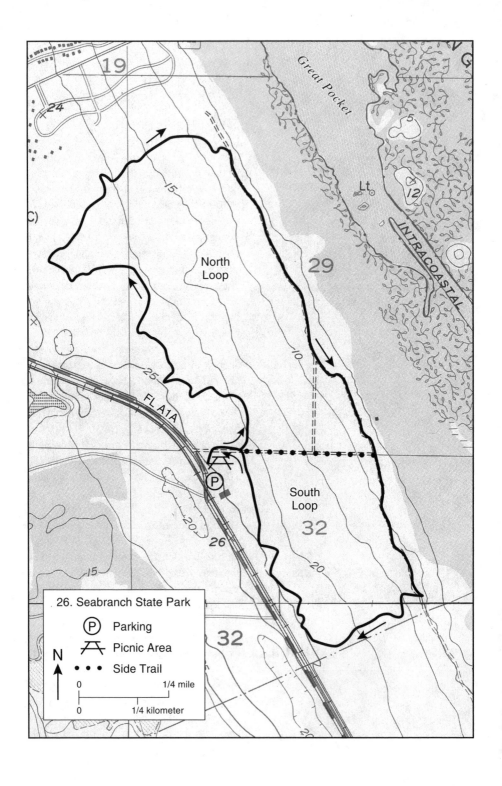

19

24

Great Pocket

V G

5

Lt

12

INTRACOASTAL

C)

15

North
Loop

29

10

25

FL A1A

South
Loop

32

20

26

15

20

20

26. Seabranch State Park

P Parking

N 🛆 Picnic Area

• • • Side Trail

0   1/4 mile
0   1/4 kilometer

32

blooms of spiderwort show up well against the pine duff. At the fork in the jeep trail, keep right. When you reach the T intersection with the jeep trail, turn right. You see little patches of pennyroyal under the pines, showing off their pinkish blooms. After 0.1 mile, you come to the main trail junction, with the signs NORTH LOOP 3.2 MILES and SOUTH LOOP 1.9. This jeep trail serves as the return to the parking area for both loops. Your hike follows the perimeter of the two loops back to this point. Turn left to follow the orange blazes into the sand pine forest.

The understory of the sand pine forest is very open, with clumps of Florida rosemary and saw palmetto. Keep alert for the orange blazes, since the footpath is indistinct through the pine duff. Passing a bed of gopher apple, the trail makes a hard left, then a sharp right. It meanders through a rosemary scrub, zigzagging between the giant clumps of rosemary across sand so white it looks like freshly fallen snow. At what seems to be a T intersection with a sandy corridor, the trail makes a sharp left into the open scrub. As you walk through the open scrub, be very careful about watching for the next blaze; some are painted on thin or low branches due to the diminutive nature of the trees. Love vine cascades over a sand live oak. The trail weaves in and out of open patches of sand between the rosemary and scrub oaks. Keep alert for that sudden blur of blue—a Florida scrub-jay glides past, alighting on a branch. Another scrub-jay hops around on the sand beneath the tree, looking for acorns. Endemic to Florida, these intriguing birds are members of the crow family, and as such are susceptible to the spread of West Nile virus across the state. Less than 10,000 scrub-jays are scattered across the state, living in small

family groups such as the one you just encountered. Preservation of scrub habitat is crucial to the survival of the species.

If you're not sure of where to find the next blaze, keep an eye on where the footprints define a path through the broad swaths of white sand. As you skirt another large patch of rosemary, watch for the constant movement of birds in the bushes—not just scrub-jays, but also cardinals, eastern towhees, and cedar waxwings. Notice the large numbers of bromeliads lodged in the branches of the sand live oaks, as well as copious amounts of ball moss. The small scrub palmettos provide scrub-jays with a source of nesting material. Like fireworks in miniature, the pinkish purple blooms of Feay's palafox are bursts of color swaying at the tops of tall stems. The wispy young sand pines look like Christmas trees awaiting decorations. Tall sandhill wireweed shows off its bottle-brushlike flowers.

As you follow the twisting, winding sand path, the trail heads back into a stand of oaks, attempting to keep to what little shade there is in the scrub forest. Heading through a profusion of scrub oaks, you pass under a towering slash pine. Keep watching for blazes along the narrow path. Saw palmettos sport a silvery sheen. Passing through a bald spot, the trail now heads toward some tall sand pines. You enter a small hammock created by the pines, crossing over the prone trunks of saw palmetto. Fluffy puffs of deer moss thrive under the oaks. A deep carpet of pine duff cushions your footfalls. Walking through the wall of tall sand pines, you enter a denser forest of older sand pines. After 1 mile, you reach an intersection with a jeep trail. Turn right. In moments, you're at another intersection. Follow the orange blazes to the left to reenter the forest. The trail wanders between

Shield lichen

Lilliputians—surrounded by tiny trees in every direction, you tower above the forest canopy.

At 2.2 miles, you reach a jeep trail. Turn right, following the jeep trail as it rises up into scrubby flatwoods. On the left is the bayhead—a wall of dense vegetation screening the scrub from the mangrove forests of the Indian River Lagoon, where loblolly bay and sweetbay magnolia crowd closely together. Covered in bright red berries, a dahoon holly is flanked by cabbage palms. Cinnamon ferns fill the understory. This shady portion of the trail can flood. A pileated woodpecker swoops past, headed for one of the many slash pines rising from the thicket of saw palmetto on the right. At 3.1 miles, you reach a jeep trail on the right, which heads into a corridor of saw palmetto. This is the return trail for the North Loop. Go straight to start walking the South Loop, continuing your hike along the perimeter of the trail system.

Rising up from the bayhead into scrubby flatwoods, the trail passes a tangle of love vine and greenbrier atop the gallberry. Two large gopher tortoises try to push their way into a single burrow, with neither one succeeding. Tiny light green bachelor's button grows along the edge of the footpath. The trail continues to gain elevation as it enters the sand pine scrub. You see a building in the distance, marking the south edge of the preserve. Keep alert for a double blaze on a tree on the left so you don't miss the turn that takes you off the jeep trail and back into the forest on the right, after 3.5 miles. Notice the bobcat tracks in the sand. At least one bobcat has been seen in the preserve during daylight hours. Nocturnal hunters, they can put a dent in the scrub-jay population.

Walking into another miniature forest, you look off to the taller sand pines in the

the trees before popping out into the white sand in front of a rosemary bush as it continues out into the open scrub. Half hidden by the pine duff, a Florida scrub lizard scurries into the shadows.

Duck under the low limbs of a sand live oak as the trail turns left and keeps curving along an artificially built-up ridge. At 1.4 miles, the trail makes a sharp horseshoe curve in on itself around a stand of silvery green saw palmetto, and then heads into the shade of tall sand pines. Oaks crowd closely into the footpath. Keep alert for the many twists and turns through this tight corridor as the trail pops in and out of stands of oaks and open scrub. At 1.8 miles, you cross a jeep trail and enter a stand of young sand live oaks. Emerging out into the scrub forest, you feel like Gulliver in the land of the distance. Here's where route finding gets a little tricky, thanks to controlled burns. The trail makes a sharp left at a fence post with a double blaze on it. Don't miss the turn. Look for the next blaze on the trees to the left as you scramble over deadfall. A scrub hickory grows next to one downed tree. The trail swings into the shade to the right, then turns sharply right into a forest of tall sand pines. Keep alert for the orange blazes as you twist and turn through the scrub, passing a scrub plum dense with fruit. With pine needles underfoot, you duck under the oaks and crunch the deer moss that's creeping back into the footpath.

At 3.7 miles, you cross a jeep road. Keep alert, as you must turn left and walk a little way down the jeep road to pick up the orange blazes again on the right, just around the far side of a huge rosemary bush. Passing under a slash pine, you emerge along a narrow path through rosemary scrub. After jogging left through an open spot, the trail turns to the right around a stand of silvery green saw palmetto, back into the shade of taller pines. You see cars passing by on the left, so you know you're getting close to the park boundary. After 4 miles, the trail emerges from the pines and faces the road. Turn right to follow the blazes back into the shady hammock, passing a huge gopher burrow on the left. When you emerge in the open area, look straight across and to

the left for the next blaze. Passing under a ghostly-looking oak with a large prickly pear cactus growing under it, the trail winds back around into the shade. You'll duck under more deadfall. Amid the reindeer lichen and deer moss in the pine duff, look for the delicate alien-looking earthstars, a type of puffball mushroom.

Reaching a clearing at 4.2 miles, the trail follows a double blaze to the left. Various members of the mint family grow in the open scrub. Keep alert for more double blazes as the trail continues to zigzag through stands of spiky silvery-leafed golden aster. Emerging at the edge of a burned area, the trail keeps to the edge, joining up with a jeep trail at 4.5 miles. Watch for a double blaze at the curve in the jeep trail: Don't follow the jeep trail past this point, but continue down the blazes along a cleared swath through the low scrub. You reenter the sand pine forest and encounter another family of scrub-jays hopping beneath the oaks while the trail makes a horseshoe curve to the left. As you enter a narrow corridor of vegetation, a giant bromeliad catches your attention, sitting on an oak that doesn't seem that it could support the weight. After 4.7 miles, you emerge at the beginning of the loop at 4.7 miles. Turn left. Keep alert—when you can see the road sign up ahead on CR A1A, take the jeep trail to the left into the forest. You emerge at the parking area after a 4.8-mile hike.

27

Jonathan Dickinson State Park

Total distance (two circuits, one round-trip): 17.5 miles

Hiking time: 8 hours, 30 minutes, or 2 days

Habitats: Cabbage palm flatwoods, cypress dome, hardwood hammock, freshwater marsh, mangrove swamp, oak hammock, palm hammock, pine flatwoods, prairie, rosemary scrub, sand pine scrub, scrubby flatwoods

Maps: USGS 7½' Gomez, Rood; park map; Florida Trail Association map SF-6

The Loxahatchee—"turtle river," in the Seminole language—is a dark black ribbon snaking between stands of cypresses, draining the northernmost extent of the Everglades into the Atlantic Ocean. Along its shores stand the densest of forests, shady hardwood hammocks of ancient oaks and cabbage palms, extensive flatwoods where slash pines brush the sky. In 1696, the native Jeaga who lived along its shores found a shipwrecked merchant and his family, survivors washed in from the sea. His name: Jonathan Dickinson. One of the earliest men to write about the wilds of South Florida, Dickinson survived brutish treatment at the hands of his captors, escaping up the coastline to St. Augustine to tell his tale.

Protecting more than 11,000 acres along the Loxahatchee River, Jonathan Dickinson State Park is a mecca for outdoor recreation on Florida's southeast coast. In addition to two popular campgrounds, visitors can enjoy horseback riding, mountain biking, paddling, picnicking, and ecotours up the river to the homestead of Trapper Nelson, a legendary figure in modern-day Loxahatchee history. Nelson established an encampment with cottages, picnic shelters, and a zoo, a popular getaway in the 1930s and 1940s. Fond of behaving and dressing like Tarzan, Nelson himself was the central attraction, a charismatic figure popular with the ladies. If the tides are right, the boat tour will drop you off at Trapper Nelson's, where a ranger leads an interesting interpretive walk around the encampment.

Atlantic Coast

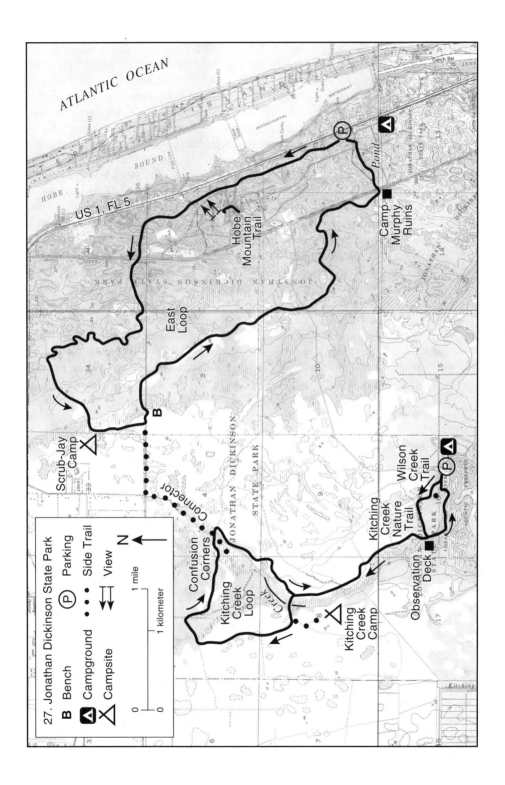

ATLANTIC OCEAN

SOUND

US 1, FL 5

HOBE

Hobe Mountain Trail

East Loop

B

Scrub-Jay Camp

Connector

Confusion Corners

Kitching Creek Loop

Creek

Kitching Creek Camp

Camp Murphy Ruins

Pond

Wilson Creek Trail

Kitching Creek Nature Trail

Observation Deck

JONATHAN DICKINSON STATE PARK

27. Jonathan Dickinson State Park

B   Bench
△   Campground
X   Campsite

Ⓟ   Parking
••• Side Trail
⇅   View

N

1 mile

1 kilometer

0
0

The real jewel of the park, however, is its hiking trail. Mapped out and constructed by members of the Palm Beach Pack and Paddle Club in the 1970s, it's been maintained by the Loxahatchee Chapter of the Florida Trail Association ever since their formation in the early 1980s, and is one of the most popular places in Southeast Florida for hiking. The trail system provides day hikers with two long loop hikes, and backpackers with the opportunity to plan a two- or three-day trek by putting the loops together via a connector trail—one of the best weekend backpacking experiences available in South Florida. This narrative describes the two loop hikes of 9.7 and 7.4 miles, respectively. If you don't plan to backpack the loops, consider a weekend stay at either the River Campground (popular with paddlers) or the Pine Grove Campground (nearest to the park entrance).

To find Jonathan Dickinson State Park, take Florida Turnpike exit 116, Jupiter/Okeechobee, SR 706 (Indiantown Road), or I-95 exit 87A, Jupiter/Okeechobee. Drive east 5 miles on SR 706, crossing the bridge over the Intracoastal Waterway before you turn left onto US 1. Continue north 5.1 miles to the park entrance, on the left.

DAY ONE: EAST LOOP TRAIL
(9.7 miles; 4 hours, 30 minutes)

Popular with backpackers, the East Loop Trail starts right next to the park entrance and traverses a 9.7-mile circuit, providing a backpacker's campsite at 4.9 miles and a connection to the Kitching Creek Loop. Using both loops, you can enjoy a 20-mile weekend of backpacking. Most hikers, however, prefer to day hike or overnight using either of the two loops without connecting them together.

When you enter the park and pay your Florida State Parks admission fee, ask for a trail map. If you intend to go backpacking, let the rangers know your plans: They can warn you about troublesome trail conditions (such as controlled burns and seasonal flooding) and the availability of water resources. Turn right and park at the park end of the large parking lot adjoining the ranger station. Start your hike at the FT sign. Beginning in a sand pine forest, the trail drops down into an open scrub. Saw palmetto glistens silver in the sun, just a scant mile from the sea. A young raccoon scurries for cover under a thicket of tiny sand live oaks. Love vine lays an orange net over Chapman oak. A zebra swallowtail butterfly alights on a bright coastal plain palafox. Deer moss creates a fuzzy carpet under the myrtle oaks as you descend into an open area, then rise back up again. This is the coastal scrub, one of Florida's most endangered habitats, a desert of ancient sand dunes topped with drought-tolerant plants. Open and sunny, it provides a physical challenge as you clamber up and down the sandy slopes. Crossing a broad firebreak, you rise up into an area that has recently been burned for habitat restoration, the tall pines around you reduced to charred husks. Paralleling US 1, you hear a constant buzz of cars. There are few blazes through this stretch, so keep to the well-beaten path, continuing in a straight line. Crossing a firebreak at 1 mile, you head straight down a hill, facing a cell phone tower. Florida rosemary clusters under the sand pines.

Passing by the foundation of an old building, you see some park housing on the left. A pinkish haze of muhlygrass waves in the breeze. At 1.4 miles, the trail crosses a paved road used by service vehicles. Look down and follow the blazes on the asphalt, which lead you back into a dense forest of sand pines. Near a rosemary thicket, you spy an old well. Scrub palmetto grows in the shade of rosemary where the trail starts curving to the left. You see snowlike balds of white sand covering the hilltops as you descend to the west, reaching the crumbling remains of old US 1 at 2.1 miles, the asphalt eroding back into the scrub. Turn right and follow the blazes along the pavement briefly. The next blaze on the left leads you back into the shade. Use caution when crossing the double set of railroad tracks. The trail continues slightly off to the right on the far side of the tracks, where it returns to the shade of tall sand pines. Watch for blazes closely as the trail zigzags through the forest, hopping on and off old jeep trails. As you follow a swath of low scrub between higher sand pines, listen for gopher tortoises rustling in the underbrush. Fragrant tarflower pokes out between the gallberry. A sawgrass prairie sweeps off to the left, beyond the scrub, as the trail narrows to a tight corridor along the ecotone. Passing a bench made of sawed logs, you plunge into a corridor of gallberry and blueberry topped by wax myrtle. Notice the Carolina willow rising above the scrub on the left, demarcating the edge of a willow marsh. Staying in the dry scrub, the trail skirts this hidden chain of wetlands. Look for a large gopher tortoise burrow on the left as you round a curve to the right in the semishade of young sand pines.

A southeastern five-lined skink scampers across the pine needles, flashing its electric blue tail, and a Florida scrub-jay fusses overhead as you follow the trail up into another stretch of oak scrub, where the diminutive oaks weave a dense canopy over silvery green saw palmettos. After 4.1 miles, you come to a fork where a jeep trail goes to the right; stay to the left, following the orange blazes. Slash pines provide a spot of shade. A jeep trail comes in from the right, and the trail turns left to join its course, still rounding the extensive willow marsh. Ducking into a tunnel of vegetation, you cross a series of bridges over drainages into the marsh. Wood ferns and sword ferns thrive in the perpetual dampness. Cross a concrete culvert over a waterway, and then a bridge over a slow-moving stream of dark water glistening with pennywort and water spangle. Passing a jeep trail coming in from the right, you continue over a bridge where a waterway pours out of a dark palm hammock. Just beyond, the trail rises up into open scrubby flatwoods, following a broad jeep trail. Tall purple blazing star waves in the breeze as you gain more elevation, rising into another open scrub.

At 4.7 miles, you reach a trail junction. The orange blazes lead you to the right. Crossing a stretch of open scrub, you see a cypress dome ahead. Keep alert, as the trail heads straight into cypresses, away from the jeep trail. Look for the orange blaze on the post ahead of you. Becoming a narrow corridor in a tangle of grapevine and gallberry, the trail makes a sharp left and crosses a long bridge along a broad marsh thick with pickerelweed and duck potato. When you reach the SCRUB JAY CAMPSITE sign, you've hiked 5 miles. Just off to the right, the small dry campsite has a fire ring and benches, but no shade or water. If you're staying overnight here, you'll want to set up camp and continue another 0.4 mile down the main trail to the pitcher pump.

Heading south from the campsite, you walk along the edge of a massive marsh. Pickerelweed comes up to the edge of the trail. As the trail curves along a vast wet

The East Loop Trail starts out in rolling hills covered in sand pine scrub.

prairie, water lilies float across the dark open water, displacing the mirrored images of clouds drifting across the blue sky. After 5.4 miles, you reach both the pitcher pump (nonpotable water; boil or treat before using) and the T intersection with the cross-trail that connects the East Loop to the Kitching Creek Loop. This is your decision point. If you are day hiking, do *not* turn right. Backpackers heading out to the Kitching Creek Campsite should turn to the right and follow the trail out to "Confusion Corners," described later in the narrative on the Kitching Creek Loop.

After you turn left at the T intersection to stay on the East Loop, the trail comes up to a ghostly cypress forest smothered under invasive climbing ferns, one of the scourges of the wilds of this park. Crossing a bridge into the wall of cypress, you continue over a series of bridges and culverts to walk through the cypress dome. Wire mesh makes the bridges less slippery to cross. Rising up into scrubby flatwoods, you come to a T intersection with a jeep trail. Turn right. The orange blazes lead you out into the bright white sand of the scrub, where patches of reindeer lichen show off their red tips beneath the rosemary. After 5.8 miles, you reach another T intersection. Turn right. A scrub-jay alights on the low branch of a slash pine as you walk through the forest of miniature oaks, spending more than a mile in the open scrub. Keep right at the fork, leaving the jeep trail to walk along the soft white ribbon of sand through the sand pines. At the next fork in the scrub, keep left. The footpath narrows; take care to watch for blazes. With tiny trees all around, you feel as if you're walking through a bonsai garden. After the trail makes a sudden sharp left, turning into scrubby flatwoods to skirt a depression marsh, it emerges at the main park road. You've hiked 7.4 miles.

Continue across the road to follow the blazes into the pine flatwoods, along an old jeep trail. A wall of young cypress rises to the right as the trail curves to the left. Although you see white blazes, follow the orange ones. The Camp Murphy mountain bike trail winds through this part of the forest, so you'll be crossing over and meeting up with the bike trail numerous times. At 7.7 miles, keep alert for a double blaze leading you to the left, back into the woods. You wander past another log bench before entering a tiny forest of sand pines. At the T intersection, the trail turns left. Curving to the right to leave the scrubby flatwoods, the trail enters a hammock of loblolly bays and red maples, where marsh ferns, royal ferns, and cinnamon ferns grow in the deep shade. Crossing a bridge, you rise back up into the scrub, winding past tall rosemary bushes. Decorated with flecks of fur, a deer scrape marks the spot where deer cross the trail.

Dropping down across a stream shaded by wax myrtle, you cross a bridge at 8.2 miles. Giant leather fern and swamp lily lend a primordial feel to the dark waterway. Rising back up into the sand pines, you can see blazes in the distance across the open understory, and you hear the soft hum of traffic on US 1. At the T intersection, the trail turns left. You emerge onto a jeep trail at 8.4 miles; turn right. Now paralleling the railroad tracks, you continue up the jeep trail, passing a large trap set for feral hogs. Burned for habitat restoration, this section of the scrub offers no shade—just charred tall pines under which the young plants are reemerging. At 8.7 miles, you reach a fork. Turn right, away from the railroad tracks and into the scrub. A crunchy layer of ash lines the footpath. Keep alert for the double blaze leading the trail off the beaten path and into the woods on the left. Zigzagging around deadfall, the footpath winds around a cypress dome and heads back toward the railroad tracks. Keep a sharp watch for blazes, as many of the blazed trees have fallen down. You encounter industrial waste: 50-gallon drums, old pipes, and broken toilets. You're now standing in the ruins of Camp Murphy. Built here in 1942 by the U.S. Army to take advantage of the high hills overlooking Hobe Sound—the better to watch for German submarines—Camp Murphy housed nearly 10,000 men, most working on the secret wonder of the era: radar. After the war, the federal government transferred the land to the state of Florida, and Jonathan Dickinson State Park opened in 1950. When you cross the old camp road, you can see several of the building foundations.

After 9 miles, you emerge in front of a crumbling ruin of a building topped with cattails. Turn left to follow the trail down to the railroad tracks. Walk around the gate and cross the tracks; keep alert for trains, because this is still a busy main line. On the other side, you encounter a patch of the old camp road, used by bikers. The East Loop Trail continues across the pavement, briefly following the asphalt path. Keep alert for a double blaze to the right. Two red-headed woodpeckers work their way up a tall pine snag. Watch the blazes, as the trail frantically zigzags through the forest. You emerge on the edge of a large pond, with the Pine Grove Campground on its far side. Lotuses ripple in the wind.

The trail turns left to follow the shoreline of the pond, where you catch a nice breeze. If water levels are high, you'll end up wading this mucky part of the trail through the tall sand cordgrass tufts (you can skip it by backtracking to the asphalt path to find the next orange blaze). Rising up to a post with double blazes at 9.4 mile,

the trail turns left up into the sand pines and rejoins the asphalt path at a T intersection. Turn right. After you cross the bike trail and pass by the back side of an FT sign, you emerge at the park entrance road after 9.5 miles. Walk straight up toward the ranger station, where that soda machine is looking mighty tempting. Keep to the left shoulder of the road, and turn left to return to the parking lot. You end your trek back at the trailhead after a strenuous but satisfying 9.7 miles of hiking.

HOBE MOUNTAIN TRAIL

As you drive down the main park road toward the Loxahatchee River (and the beautiful River Campground), turn right and follow Hobe Mountain Tower Road up to a small parking area. A 0.4-mile boardwalk trail over the relict dunes clambers up Hobe Mountain, which at 86 feet is highest natural hill in South Florida south of Lake Okeechobee. Take 10 minutes to scramble up through the sand pine scrub and survey the 360-degree view from the tower. To the west lies the forested watershed of the Loxahatchee River, encompassing nearly 200 square miles. Notice the ribbon of different-colored trees in the distance—cypresses tracing the banks of the river, standing out against a sea of slash pines. To the south, you can see towering condos along the beach in Jupiter and Juno Beach. To the east, that aquamarine ribbon of water is the Intracoastal Waterway, and the deep blue Atlantic Ocean stretches to the horizon just beyond the sliver of sand that makes up Jupiter Island.

DAY TWO: KITCHING CREEK LOOP (7.4 miles; 4 hours)

At the northern edge of the picnic area along the Loxahatchee River, the Kitching Creek Loop stretches off into the wilds of

Jonathan Dickinson State Park. Visitors have several hiking options here. Starting from the trailhead near the pavilion and rest rooms, you can follow any of four loops: the Wilson Creek Trail, a short loop near the picnic area; the Kitching Creek Nature Trail, a 1.3-mile walk out along the cypress-lined creek; the Kitching Creek Loop, 7.4 miles out into the hammocks and flatwoods along the creek; or the entire trail system, by using the connector trail over to the East Loop Trail.

Start your hike at the trailhead map at the parking area. When you reach the fork, keep right. You're walking into a vast pine flatwoods, the understory of saw palmetto vanishing off to the far horizon. An American kestrel perches in a tall slash pine, surveying the palmettos for signs of life—a rabbit, a mouse. The long slender stems of blazing star are afire with purple blossoms. Lopsided Indiangrass waves in the breeze, a delicate dance of yellow, black, and red. Sensitive brier clambers up and over the saw palmetto, covered in its tiny fuzzy purple ball blooms with deep red centers.

You cross the bridge over Wilson Creek after 0.3 mile. Immediately thereafter, the 0.5-mile Wilson Creek Trail turns to the left to follow the creek to make the shortest loop back to the parking area. Continue straight, ducking under the red bay covered in climbing fern. Purple morning glory blossoms peep out from the brush. When you reach the T intersection with a jeep trail, turn left. Walking along the corridor of saw palmetto, you hear the song of a palm warbler. At the NATURE TRAIL sign, you reach another T intersection. Turn right. This short spur trail ends at an observation platform on Kitching Creek at 0.7 mile, with benches overlooking beautiful view of the sluggish brackish creek. Giant cypresses reflect in the dark water,

while mangroves crowd the far shore. Ever since the draining of the northern Everglades and the creation of the Intracoastal Waterway, the Loxahatchee River has suffered from severe saltwater intrusion through Jupiter Inlet. Today, the tides reach miles upriver, and mangrove forests root where cypresses once lined the waterways.

As you leave the observation platform, turn left and cross the cable gate. This old jeep trail is part of a network of many old roads through the park, some of which are used for equestrian and biking trails. A gopher tortoise ambles past, blazing its own trail through the wiregrass. Paralleling the drainage of the creek, open cabbage palm flatwoods sweep into the distance on the right. The red-tipped post at 1.3 miles marks a horse trail coming in from the left. Keep alert for equestrians for the next mile, and step aside to let them pass. The trail points toward a line of sand live oaks outlining the edge of the creek drainage. Deer's tongue pokes up through the wiregrass as you come up to marker 5, the junction of the yellow and red horse trails. Continue straight, still heading toward that distant edge of the flatwoods.

At 2 miles, you see a silvery structure off to the left marked USGS, a water sampling station. Look past the station—your first orange blaze awaits. This is the lower end of the Kitching Creek Trail. Turn left and follow the blazes into the hardwood hammock down to the creek. Cross the creek on a narrow bridge covered with wire mesh. The trail makes a sharp left on the other side into a dense hammock, a tangled jungle of palm fronds and cypress knees, tall wild coffee, and goldfoot fern cascading from cabbage palm. This area will be flooded during the wet season—as will most of this loop trail from this point on. A steep drainage provides an outlet for rain to the creek; it can become a formidable obstacle if flooded. In the dry season, a bare trickle of water runs down inside it. The rooting of wild hogs makes it tough to follow the trail as it winds through the maze of tall saw palmetto. Little purple drumhead peers up between the gallberry; yellow-eye grass sports its bright yellow tops. The trail makes a hard left and crosses over a single-plank bridge through a cypress stand. The detached railing offers some support as you balance your way across.

You emerge from the pond cypresses to an open field of young pines. When you reach the T intersection, you've hiked 2.3 miles. To the left, the orange blazes lead 0.6 mile along this side of the creek to the primitive Kitching Creek Campsite, which has a pitcher pump benches and fire ring. It's a quiet, pleasant place to spend a night, but be prepared for mosquitoes. To continue on the day-hike loop, turn right. The trail follows a jeep road through the flatwoods, with scattered open patches of wet and dry prairie between the pines. The pink blossoms of pale meadow beauty poke out of the tall wiregrass. Look down at the footpath for the shimmering red forms of carnivorous sundew plants, sparkling like globs of strawberry jelly. A Carolina wren vanishes into a stand of young pond cypress edged with tall star rush. After pointing directly toward a communications tower, the trail curves to the right. During the wet season or after a heavy rain, this part of the trail will have deep puddles from the flatwoods draining into the low spots. At one place where water tends to stand, a telephone-pole bridge on the left provides a way to cross—but be careful! It's like walking across a slippery log, and easy to fall off.

The forest thickens; the saw palmetto becomes taller, more pines crowd together, and the understory transitions to cabbage palm flatwoods. After 3.2 miles, you come to a T intersection with another jeep trail. Turn right to follow the road into the cool shade of an oak hammock, where myrsine, coco plum, and wild coffee create a tropical understory. You reach a broad wooden bridge with short sides, built for park vehicles to drive across. It's a good place to stop and rest in the cool shade of the hammock, listening for splashes in water—otters! Slipping along the banks, they frolic as they chase fish through the shallows.

As you leave the bridge, you pass the back side of a NO HORSES symbol sign as you reenter the pine flatwoods. A jeep trail comes in from left. At the next junction at 3.4 miles, cross the jeep trail and enter the forest, following the orange blazes down a narrow footpath that winds through the wet flatwoods. At a double blaze, the trail turns sharply right and heads through a damp area. Keep watching for the next blaze, as the footpath is indistinct—it's easy to lose the trail here. Continuing through cabbage palm flatwoods, you come to a T intersection with a jeep trail at 3.6 miles. Turn left. After passing through a stretch of prairie with tall St.-Andrew's-cross and bushybeard bluestem grass, the trail curves to the right and drops down through a cypress dome. It's a place you're virtually guaranteed to get your shoes wet while pushing through the floating mats of vegetation to the next dry spot. Pickerelweed emerges alongside the footpath as you climb back up into the pine flatwoods.

Candy-striped green sugarcane plume-grass glistens in the sun as you approach "Confusion Corners," a five-way intersection of trails at 4.3 miles. A signpost with markers helps lessen the confusion. To your immediate left is the connector trail to the East Loop Trail, which you would use on a two-day backpacking trip as your return route if you started from the parking lot at the park entrance. To your immediate right is the red-blazed horse trail. The next right is your return trail back to the Kitching Creek Nature Trail. Follow the orange blazes to the slim footpath into the pine flatwoods, where the trail winds tightly through the silvery green and blue saw palmettos. Wiregrass forms a taupe fog between the palm fronds. At a double blaze, the trail makes a hard left. At the T intersection, turn right on the jeep trail. Keep alert for blazes as the trail then makes a hard right, leaving the beaten path to become a narrow footpath again as it skirts the edge of a cypress dome. Winding through the wiregrass under the pines, you approach the wall of cabbage palms and oaks that defines the shores of Kitching Creek.

After 5.3 miles, you emerge in front of the silver USGS box, completing the Kitching Creek Loop. Turn left and follow the broad jeep road, retracing your route south toward the Kitching Creek Nature Trail. You'll pass the yellow and red horse trail markers on the way; keep heading straight at each intersection. The tops of lopsided Indiangrass rise tall above the saw palmetto, creating a tawny haze. When you start to see grand tall cypresses and red mangroves off to the right, you return to the cable gate at 6.7 miles. Take a well-deserved rest on the bench on the observation deck, enjoying the view of Kitching Creek.

When you leave the observation deck this time, turn right. At the NATURE TRAIL sign, continue straight. The trail parallels Kitching Creek through the pine flatwoods. Perched on a tall snag beyond the creek, an osprey watches the water as mullet jump. Its mate sits in a nest towering over the mangrove forest. Bracken fern grows unusually tall, reaching up and over the saw palmetto clumps. Look for a bounty of blueberries in May. As the trail rises up into scrubby flatwoods, the footpath changes to soft sand. After 7.1 miles, you reach a junction as the Wilson Creek Trail comes in from the left. Continue straight, crossing a bridge over the creek, which is almost buried under masses of the invasive climbing ferns. As the trail curves left past a fence, a shortcut on the right leads directly to the picnic pavilion. Continue through the flatwoods. The trail makes sharp right, passing marker 23, before it drops down into another stretch of saw palmetto. At the junction, continue straight. Keep right at the fork. When you emerge at the parking lot after 7.4 miles, you've completed your hike.

28

Blowing Rocks Preserve

Total distance (circuit): 2.5 miles

Hiking time: 2 hours

Habitats: Coastal scrub, coastal strand, mangrove swamp, oak hammock

Maps: USGS 7½' Jupiter; park map

It's a scene unlike any other in Florida, a geologic wonder on the shoreline of Jupiter Island. Battered by waves, limestone cliffs define the edge of the beach, a steep drop down to the surf below. At low tide, the ocean pulls back to reveal a string of wave-worn sea caves, where thick beds of grass cling like hair to the damp rocks and crabs scuttle into crevices in the rock. At high tide, with an excitable surf, geysers of salt water spout from the holes in the caves, sending spectacular streams of spray up to 50 feet skyward. This is not a beach for swimming—there are too many rocks, and the undertow is severe. But this is a beach for exploring, a place to enjoy one of Florida's most unique geologic treasures.

From the Florida Turnpike, take exit 116, Jupiter/Okeechobee, SR 706 (Indiantown Road). From I-95, take exit 87A, Jupiter/Okeechobee. Drive east 5 miles, crossing the bridge over the Intracoastal Waterway before you turn left onto US 1. After 1.3 miles north on US 1, turn right at the JUPITER ISLAND sign onto CR 707 (Beach Road). Follow Beach Road over the bridge onto Jupiter Island. It swings north through Tequesta, passing Coral Cove, and reaches the boundary of Blowing Rocks Preserve after 2 miles. Watch for the small PARKING AREA sign on the right at 2.4 miles. The preserve is open 9 AM–5 PM daily, but the parking area closes at 4:30 PM. To access Blowing Rocks Beach, there is an admission charge of $3 per person ($1 for Nature Conservancy members), with children 12 and under free.

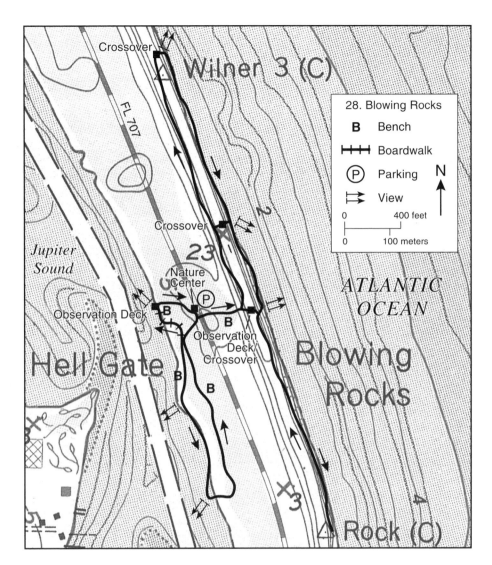

For an introduction to this 73-acre sanctuary, walk across Beach Road and up to the Hawley Environmental Center. Here, you'll find interpretive exhibits regarding the habitats protected by the preserve, as well as rest rooms and a small gift shop. When you exit the center, follow the porch around to the south side of the building. A set of stairs leads down to the Restoration Trail along the Indian River Lagoon. One of the world's longest lagoons, the Indian River Lagoon stretches 150 miles, from Ponce Inlet at New Smyrna to Jupiter Inlet, just 3 miles south of the preserve. More than 4,300 species live in this saltwater lagoon, including hundreds of dolphins, sea turtles, and manatees. The mangrove forests along the shoreline are crucial to the health of the lagoon.

Walking past identified plantings of Jamaican caper, pigeon plum, indigoberry, and other tropical hammock plants, you smell the distinctive skunk odor of white stopper on the salt breeze. A set of benches sits in the shade of a gumbo limbo tree. Passing a gnarled strangler fig, you emerge at the edge of the Indian River Lagoon. Across the lagoon, virtually every parcel of land is developed. But on this side, Blowing Rocks Preserve protects a mile of coastline, sheltering pristine beaches lined with mangroves and buttonwood. Up until 2001, exotic invasive plants covered this tract of land: Australian pine, Brazilian pepper, carrotwood, and latherleaf. Thanks to a concentrated effort by volunteers, more than 12 acres have been cleared—which meant the removal of more than 1,000 Australian pines. Additional acreage to the north of the environmental center will be returned to its natural state over the next few years. Although there isn't a lot of shade, and the natural coastal scrub will take a while to return, the Restoration Trail provides great views of the Indian River Lagoon.

At the next junction of two trails, keep to the right, following the edge of the lagoon. Saltmeadow cordgrass waves in the breeze beneath the tall sea grape, while samphire sprawls across open stretches of sand. A spur trail leads past blooms of painted leaf to a patio under a large strangler fig. At the next trail junction, continue straight. A black mangrove pushes its pneumatophores up through a sandy beach; these pencil-like protrusions help the plant to breathe, similar to a cypress knee. All three varieties of mangrove grow along this shoreline. To tell them apart, compare their shapes. Black mangroves are broad, and are always surrounded by their pneumatophores. Red mangroves have a distinct network of archlike prop roots. White mangroves look the most

treelike, and they have light green oval leaves—the other mangroves have dark green elliptical leaves.

Reaching a mangrove-lined beach, the trail turns sharply left. At the T intersection, turn left again to return through the regenerating coastal scrub. Wild balsam apple cascades over pigeon plum, its orange seedpods dangling like Christmas ornaments. Fragrant wildflower aromas fill the air as you approach a trail junction. Turn right. Mounds of moonflower and wild balsam apple vines cover the sea grape and saw palmetto. Christmas berry peeks out of the shade of a mahogany tree. Passing a bench at 0.5 mile, the trail completes its loop, reaching the incoming trail at a junction. Turn left and go straight across to walk along the lagoon back to the environmental center.

Walk along the front porch of the environmental center and down to the boardwalk. It weaves between buttonwoods and white mangroves, arriving at an observation platform on the lagoon. Sit down and take some time to study the water. You may see dolphins racing down the waterway, or loggerhead turtles surfacing for a breath of air. Watch for West Indian manatees swimming past.

When you turn around to leave the observation deck, take the left fork. This boardwalk ends at the environmental center parking lot, where a butterfly garden sits off to the left. Brick paths wind past benches in this small but fragrant garden. Continue back to the front of the environmental center and turn left, following the brick path back to Beach Road. Carefully cross the road and walk up the ramp to the kiosk for entry to Blowing Rocks Beach. After paying your entrance fee, continue down the Sea Grape Path toward the beach under a tight canopy of cabbage

A sea cave with a collapsed roof

palms, sea grapes, and gumbo limbo trees. The roar of the surf increases as you pass a shaded bench. Just beyond the service road, you emerge at an observation deck and dune crossover, reaching the beginning of the Dune Trail at 0.8 mile. Take a moment to climb up on the deck and survey the rocky shoreline, an outcropping of Anastasia limestone. Stretching beneath the sands from Anastasia Island at St. Augustine southward to Palm Beach, this ridge of limestone contains coquina, the compressed remnants of tiny seashells.

Turn north and follow the Dune Trail into a low tunnel of sea grapes. This path follows the route of the old coastal road, CR A1A, which eroded into the sea. Emerging out into the open, a bowl of silvery blue saw palmetto sits off to the left, and to the right you have a sweeping view of the beach. After a few more minutes under the sea grapes, you pop out at the next dune crossover, where a bench perches above the coastal strand. You've walked 1 mile. Continue along the Dune Trail. The sea grapes now form a hedge, providing little shade but screening your view of the sea.

Wild coffee grows in the shade of the sea grapes as you emerge at a dune fence along the dune line. Sea oats wave in the stiff salt breeze, while railroad vine spills over the dunes. The trail ducks back into the sea grape tunnel one last time before ending by dropping down over the dunes at 1.3 miles. Turn right to walk back to the south end of the preserve. Depending on the tide, you may want to walk as close to the water as possible in order to examine the wave-washed limestone formations. The sand tends to be soft and cinderlike, made up of a tiny particulate of crushed seashells, so it's not easy walking. Nevertheless, the views are worth it. The shifting

sands bury and uncover the limestone shelf along the shoreline, so you can never be sure where you'll first encounter it—most likely near the last dune crossover you passed on the Dune Trail. The farther south you walk, the more uncovered the rocks become, until they rise up to heights over your head. If you walk the beach at low tide, make a point of walking down below the rocks to enjoy one of Florida's most unusual landscapes—sea caves. The largest caves start about 0.2 mile south of the main dune crossover, or 2 miles into your hike. Carved out by the constant pounding of the high tide, some of these caves are big enough to pitch a tent inside. Wave-sculpted benches adorn the walls, and sea lice clamber up the pitted surfaces. Tidal pools contain mussels and grasses. With the constant erosion of the limestone shelf, cavern roofs do crumble—you'll skirt many massive fallen blocks of limestone as you walk along the shoreline. At high tide, water fills the caves, making it impossible to look at them from below. Take care not to linger along the caves if the tide is coming in. The famous spouting of Blowing Rocks occurs when a rough high tide hits the each cavern wall and pushes upward, emerging from chimneys in the tops of the caves to form natural waterspouts of surf.

When you reach the end of the caves, you've reached the southern end of the preserve. Climb up and around to the beach, taking care as you walk across jagged limestone emerging from the sand. Continue north along the beach to return to the dune crossover. As you walk, notice the unusual erosion of the surface rock—twisted stalactites, stalagmites, and columns in the weathered rock looking like a miniature version of an underground cave turned inside out. The reddish black hue to the rock comes from iron deposits in the limestone. From above, you can see the chimney holes at the tops of the larger caves. The eroded top of the limestone shelf looks as rugged as a lava flow. Markers on the high dunes indicate the location of sea turtle nests. Despite the jagged rocks, loggerheads make their way up to the coastal strand to lay their eggs. After 2.3 miles, you return to the dune crossover. Turn left and climb up and over the stairs to rejoin the Sea Grape Path. Continue down this shaded walkway to exit the beach, returning to the parking lot after your 2.5-mile walk.

29

Jupiter Ridge Natural Area

Total distance (circuit): 2.3 miles

Hiking time: 1 hour, 15 minutes

Habitats: Freshwater marsh, mangrove swamp, rosemary scrub, sand pine scrub, scrubby flatwoods

Maps: USGS 7½' Jupiter; park map

The scrub is Florida's desert, with bare spots of blinding white sand shimmering between islands of vegetation adapted to this nutrient-poor dry environment. As development ranged up and down South Florida's coastlines, scrub habitats vanished first—they made perfect building sites since they didn't have to be drained. The Jupiter Ridge Natural Area provides a rare look at mostly undisturbed Florida scrub. This site remained untouched until the 1930s, when dredging for the Intracoastal Waterway threw additional sand across the rolling hills, burying most of the freshwater marshes. In the 1980s, a developer planned a shopping center for the site. But public outcry led to Palm Beach County securing $23 million, including matching funds from the Preservation 2000 fund, to purchase the site. Protecting 271 acres, it is now the county's second largest remaining scrub habitat.

From the Florida Turnpike, take exit 116, Jupiter/Okeechobee, SR 706 (Indiantown Road). From I-95, take exit 87A, Jupiter/Okeechobee. Drive east 5 miles, crossing the bridge over the Intracoastal Waterway before you turn right onto US 1. Continue 1.4 miles south to the preserve entrance, on the right. A set of portable toilets provides the facilities for this park, which is open sunrise to sunset. Hiking is the only approved activity at the preserve.

Start your hike at the trailhead kiosk, where you can pick up a copy of the trail map and read about the various rare and endangered plants and animals protected

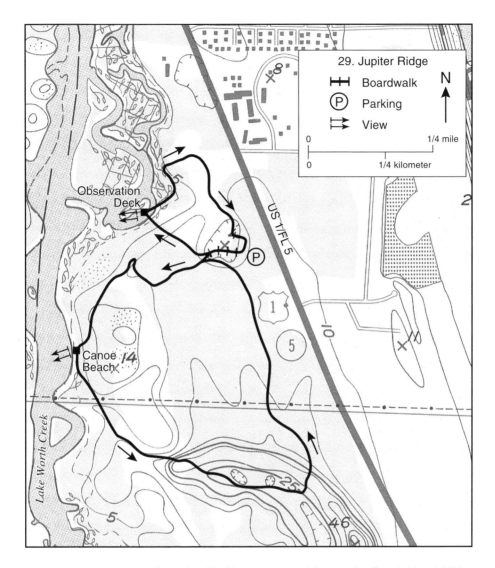

by the preserve, including the Florida scrub-jay. Populations of scrub-jays in Southeast Florida are thinly scattered across several coastal scrubs in this region. This hike provides a rare opportunity to walk through several scrub-jay family territories.

The trail system consists of the Little Blue Heron Nature Trail, a wheelchair-accessible sidewalk, and two attached nonpaved loops: the Scrub Lizard Hiking Trail, a 1.7-mile-long loop over rugged hills and through scrub-jay habitat, and the Pawpaw Hiking Trail, which leads 0.6 mile along a mangrove swamp and through open scrubby flatwoods under restoration. Your hike will make use of the entire trail system. Start off down the sidewalk past a large mound of coco plum bushes, thick with their dark brownish edible fruits.

Dropping downhill, the sidewalk reaches a boardwalk that crosses a small freshwater marsh. Dahoon holly outlines the edge of the marsh, its red berries bright against the deep green foliage. An osprey launches from a tall slash pine, cruising low over the water. Primrose willow and hottentot fern crowd the basin. When the boardwalk ends, you immediately rise up into the scrub, surrounded by small young sand pines. The sidewalk parallels a jeep trail on the left, reaching a fork at a yellow blaze marker. Turn left and step off the sidewalk to start your circuit of the Scrub Lizard Hiking Trail, following the broad sandy path up into the sand pine forest. The sand is so bright and white it looks like a soft fresh fall of snow beneath the pines. You see both reindeer lichen and deer moss growing on the pine duff beneath the understory of scrub oaks.

Listen for the shrill *shrweep* of the eastern towhee as you rise out of the shade and into the bright sun. Here, the pines are younger. Saw palmetto fronds show a silvery hue from their proximity to salt water, as they cluster into islands of vegetation surrounded by the bright white sand. The tall, slender, wispy white and pink blossoms of sandhill wireweed stand out against a backdrop of myrtle oak. The trail rises up past shoulder-high Florida rosemary growing out of a thick carpet of deer moss, and you enter a shady grove of older sand pine. Bits of broken tile attest to the preserve's former status as a construction dumping ground as you emerge along the banks of the Intracoastal Waterway. The trail swings left, passing a kiosk at 0.5 mile. Bromeliads grow thickly in the sand live oaks along the water's edge. You pass a small beach on the right, where kayakers can pull up and take a rest within the preserve. Look down at the ground cover on the left. Mingled in

with the deer moss and reindeer lichen are clusters of spike moss, with slender green fingerlings reaching for the sky. You hear a shrill catlike mewing from a bird high up in a slash pine—a Florida scrub-jay sentinel sounds the alarm for its family. Each family of scrub-jays ranges over a territory of up to 25 acres. The scrub-jay family includes a mated pair and up to several of their male offspring, who delay breeding for the sake of helping their parents raise the next generation. Curious and friendly, a scrub-jay may settle down close to you in the branches of a young oak tree.

A red-bellied woodpecker works its way up a pine snag as you reach a fork in the trail. Keep to the left, rising up away from the water. Passing a trail leading off to the left, stay on the broad jeep trail and cross under the power lines. Continue straight ahead into the scrub forest, following the yellow markers. Notice the egg-like fruits of the tallow wood tree, also known as the hog plum. These edible fruits have a mild, somewhat bland taste similar to the coco plum. The rustling in the underbrush, beneath the oaks, comes from scrub-jays as they hop around and dig, searching for acorns. Like a squirrel, a scrub-jay will make a cache of acorns, marking it with a leaf to find it again.

The trail turns to the left, away from a faint track, and upward into rolling relict dunes. Love vine spills across a Florida rosemary bush like thin green tinsel. The ground slopes away in all directions, the white sand looking like ski slopes as you continue to climb up and over the ancient dunes, winding through patches of rosemary scrub. At the fork, keep left. Crossing over a jeep trail at 0.9 mile, you continue toward the next yellow marker and descend through the scrub forest. Look closely at the sand live oaks on the left,

Ancient sand dunes in sand pine scrub

festooned with tiny bromeliads. The trail begins curving to the left as it works its way downhill back through the scrub toward the beginning of the loop. Standing atop tall stems, the pinkish white blooms of coastal plain palafox catch your eye. These daisylike flowers look almost naturally dried. Other plants add splashes of color to the white backdrop: bursts of greenish Curtiss' milkweed, an endemic scrub plant; pink and white bottlebrush blooms of sandhill wireweed; and the orange haze of the woody pinweed.

After walking through a dense thicket of young sand pines, you pass under the power line at 1.4 miles. The trail continues through the sand pine forest, where crispy old man's beard coats the dead lower limbs of scrub oaks and sand pines. The trail emerges within sight of the parking area before it turns to the left. In order to continue the figure-8 loop through the preserve, turn left to follow the yellow-blazed trail around the edge of the marsh. You reach the nature trail sidewalk at 1.7 miles. At the fork, keep to the right this time to stay on the pavement, walking through the islands of vegetation between the bright white sands. The silvery stems of golden aster support tiny yellow blossoms. Several prickly pear cacti grow near the base of marker 6. Descending the relict dune slope, the trail approaches its end at a covered observation deck on a sluggish tidal stream. White and red mangroves crowd the shores. Enjoy a few quiet moments on a bench, taking in the salt air and the sounds of ibises nosing through the mangroves in search of apple snails.

When you leave the observation deck, make an immediate left onto the red-blazed Pawpaw Hiking Trail, walking past the WETLAND RESTORATION PROJECT sign. A belted kingfisher flies overhead, a streak of bluish black against the clouded sky. The footpath keeps to the edge of the mangrove swamp, where you can see young mangroves sprouting in the shallows and watch blue crabs scuttling along the bottom of the silted waterway. The sand pine scrub comes up to the trail on the right, where an aromatic silk bay tree stands tall above wax myrtle and gallberry. The trail curves to the left to follow the mangrove-lined canal; you see the white blooms of loblolly bay on the far shore.

At 2 miles, the trail makes a sharp right turn away from the mangrove swamp and rises up into an open scrub, with no large trees to provide shade. At a T intersection with another jeep trail, turn right. Look for the endangered four-petal pawpaw, showing off its fragrant white blossoms in late spring. Endemic to just two South Florida counties, this member of the custard apple family grows in the driest of soils and can reach a height of 5 feet. It drops its yellow fruits in fall, providing gopher tortoises and raccoons with a tasty treat.

You see the roof of the trailhead kiosk ahead as you continue down the trail, which rises up from the white sand to become a grassy footpath along the edge of a stand of sand pines. As you approach the parking lot, the trail curves to the left and comes up to a large gate. Walk around the gate, and you're back to the parking lot, completing a 2.3-mile hike.

30

John D. MacArthur Beach State Park

Total distance (circuit): 3.5 miles

Hiking time: 2 hours

Habitats: Coastal strand, mangrove forest, limestone reef, tropical hardwood hammock

Maps: USGS 7½' Riviera; park map

Imagine the coast of Southeast Florida as it once was: a tangled jungle of tropical vines and Caribbean trees, alive with the screeches of birds and the constant movement of lizards. Now forming a tropical oasis in the midst of the playground of the rich, surrounded by the multimillion-dollar homes and condos of Singer Island, the 760-acre John D. MacArthur Beach State Park preserves an irreplaceable slice of tropical hardwood hammock and mangrove forests outside bustling Palm Beach. Walking through its hammocks and along its rocky reefs, you can appreciate MacArthur's grand gift to the people of Florida. When MacArthur died in 1978, he was one of the wealthiest men in America, the sole owner of the largest privately held insurance company in the nation. Along with his wife, Catherine, he established the MacArthur Foundation, which continues to provide huge grants and fellowships to people and projects that improve the human condition. It's fortunate that MacArthur listened to a university study regarding the biological significance of these tropical hammocks and mangrove forests, and donated the land for the enjoyment of future generations.

While the trails here are short, the beach walk is one of the most beautiful in South Florida. Besides exploring the trails, you can snorkel on the reef, kayak or canoe the inlets, or just swim around and enjoy a day on the beach. The park's nature center provides many interesting interpretive programs, including their popular night walks

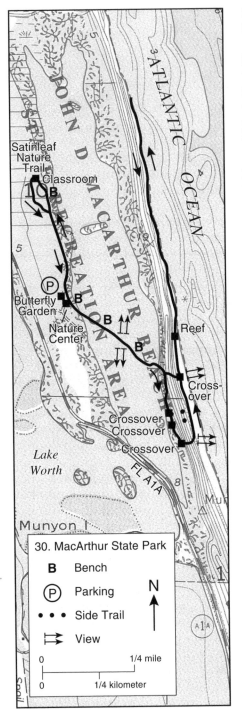

30. MacArthur State Park

B	Bench
Ⓟ	Parking
• • •	Side Trail
⇥	View

N

0	1/4 mile
0	1/4 kilometer

to watch sea turtles lay eggs along the beach.

To reach MacArthur Beach State Park from I-95, take exit 79A. From the Florida Turnpike, use exit 109, adding an additional 2.4 miles. Drive east on PGA Boulevard, which turns into FL A1A south after you cross US 1. After 3.9 miles, you enter the park boundary. Watch for the entrance road on the left at 4.7 miles. After you pay your Florida State Parks entry fee, continue down the entrance road, following the signs that say NATURE CENTER. On weekends, don't expect to be able to park close to the nature center—this is a very popular outdoor getaway.

A bark-chip trail runs along the edge of all the parking lots, connecting the Satinleaf Nature Trail with the nature center and boardwalk to the beach. Walk down to the end of the parking lot and turn right. The trail winds through the tropical hammock along the edge of the mangrove forest until it emerges at a shaded tram pickup point, which sits at the end of the boardwalk. Trams to the beach run 10 AM–4 PM, but you'll want to walk across the boardwalk yourself at least once to linger and enjoy the marine life and wading birds.

Before crossing the boardwalk, visit the nature center to acquaint yourself with the park. Turn right. At the base of the ramp is the brief Butterfly Garden Trail, which circles through a tropical forest in front of the nature center. Pick up a brochure to identify the plants as you take a few minutes to walk down the trail. Watch for zebra swallowtails alighting on the bright red and yellow tips of a firebush, and the lightly variegated leaves of red mahogany. Peeling gumbo limbo trees provide deep shade. Along with the brochure, interpretive markers help you identify the native plants of the tropical hardwood hammock.

A large Hispaniolan curly-tailed lizard vanishes under some leaf litter, distinctive with its massive curled tail. This non-native lizard is outcompeting native species such as the green anole and the six-lined racerunner. Wild coffee grows well above your head as you walk past a bench set under a strangler fig. The trail emerges back where it began. Turn right and walk up to the nature center; the rest rooms are to the left. Typically open 9 AM–5 PM, the center is closed on Tuesday but offers guided walks Wednesday through Sunday at 10 AM. Step in and explore the many exhibits, including a display of pottery found in a midden from the Jeaga people who once lived on this beach. Take a few minutes to watch the film on the park's fragile ecosystems before venturing back outdoors to the trail.

At the tram station, turn right and walk across the causeway, watching mullet jump in the shallows. At low tide, you'll see roseate spoonbills and white ibises feeding on the exposed mudflats at the far end of the boardwalk. Brown pelicans frolic, swooping down and catching fish, then retreating to shallow islands to strut their stuff. The broad boardwalk zigzags across the mangrove-lined lagoon, offering several spots where you can sit and watch the birds. Interpretive signs explain the bird and marine life around the lagoon. You'll see double-crested cormorants diving after long, sleek needlefish, and schools of finger mullet making the shallows shimmer as they swim en masse. A black-and-white eagle ray glides across the grassy bottom. Kayakers paddle past on a manatee-scouting expedition; they're headed out to the deeper channels of the Lake Worth Lagoon, on the other side of FL A1A.

Passing a canopied bench at 0.3 mile, the boardwalk rises to meet the mangrove forest. Just past the tram pickup point, you come up behind a building to the divergence of several boardwalks. Take the one to the right and follow the trail into the tropical hammock, down to the south end of the park. Where the boardwalk ends, there is a small container filled with brochures for a self-guided walking tour of the park's flora. Pick up one, as it will help you identify the native tropical plants in the forest. The trail marks the ecotone between the mangrove forest and a tropical hardwood hammock. You hear the scrabbling of raccoons in search of bird eggs, as fiddler crabs retreat into their muck-lined holes. Cruising over the mangroves, an osprey lets out its continual chirp as it scans for fish in the shallows.

Containing many of the trees and understory plants found in the hammocks of the Florida Keys, this sliver of tropical hammock provides a glimpse into what this coast of Florida used to look like—a jungle. Dangling juicy berries for birds to eat, wild coffee and white indigoberry flourish under the gumbo limbo and mahogany trees. Crush the leaf of a torchwood and you'll smell the distinctive aroma of oranges. A paradise tree spreads its broad sumaclike leaves. Fish poison vine grows in the shade of a strangler fig. Also known as coin vine or fishfuddle, these vines can create an impenetrable tangle in mangrove forests, and used to be used to catch fish. When immersed, the vines let off rotenone, a chemical that is harmless to humans but blocks the uptake of oxygen to fish gills, causing death. It's now illegal to stun or kill fish using this vine.

The trail jogs left and uphill, curving past a wild lime. From the shade of the tropical forest, you can look out and see border of blue that is the lagoon through the mangroves. A strangler fig has totally

Palm Beach at its most natural

wrapped around its host cabbage palm, preventing the palm's continued growth. Above you, a golden orb spider dangles over a Jamaican caper tree as you come up to a dune crossover boardwalk at 0.5 mile. Continue straight to stay in the shade of the forest, passing a Spanish stopper with its stinky flowers. White berries decorate a snowberry bush. The sound of the surf increases as the trail drops downhill to a bench set under the sea grapes; look in the leaf litter for the scurrying movement of mangrove crabs. Across the trail, you see the pneumatophores of the black mangroves and a tangled jungle of red mangrove prop roots. Notice the odd clicking sound? It's coming from oysters attached to the mangrove roots, as they close themselves up while the tide goes out.

At the next dune crossover, take a close look at the tree at marker 26—poisonwood, at the northern extent of its range. The sap of this member of the cashew family is 10 times as irritating as poison ivy; avoid getting any on your skin. As you continue along, the trail comes up to another bench. A red-bellied woodpecker works its way up a cabbage palm. You reach the final dune crossover at an old building (former rest rooms, now closed), where the trail ends. Climb up and over the crossover for your first glimpse of Palm Beach on Singer Island: shimmering blue-green water washing across the rocky reef. As you descend the stairs to the beach, notice the markers driven into the sand against the dune line, indicating sea turtle nests. This beach hosts an extraordinarily heavy concentration of nesting loggerheads in summer, with more than 800 nests spread along the park's shoreline.

The preserve ends just south of here where the condos rise from the dune's edge, so turn north to walk up the unspoiled beach within the state park boundary. The brownish seaweed lining the edge of the beach is sargassum, defining a sliver of habitat called the wrack line. Coconuts commonly wash up along this shore, as do the long green bean-shaped seedlings of red mangroves and the smooth rounded seedpods of the sea bean. Picking through the shells, seeds, and insects that flock to the sargassum are royal terns and laughing gulls.

Continue your walk past the two beach crossovers, where most of the sunbathers and swimmers congregate, to the start of the shoreline portion of the reef. As at Blowing Rocks Preserve (Hike 28), Anastasia limestone outcrops along this shoreline. Here, most of it is buried beneath the waves, heavily eroded into smooth, slippery expanses of pink and orange. Larger rocks break through the breakers offshore. This is a beautiful stretch of shoreline at low tide, with mats of sargassum caught in tidal pools lined with limpets. Willets and sandpipers pick through the shallows in search of their meals. Creating an almost surreal effect that brings the water alive, finger mullet shimmer inside the rolling waves as they break. Clouds hang like cotton puffs against the deep blue sky.

The unspoiled beach continues to the north. Don't be surprised if you startle a sunbather or two—they're not used to seeing hikers up here. The northern boundary of the protected beach ends where the next set of condos begin. Look offshore and you'll see an outcropping of limestone with waves breaking over it. The dunes form a tall wall, thickly covered in saw palmetto and sea grape. There is no sign to indicate the north end of the park, but when you're in line with the dark mahogany-colored limestone outcrop and you see a white post on the dunes marked 2A, you've walked 1.5 miles. Turn around and continue back down the beach. Notice the many seashells deposited by the waves, primarily prickly cockle, calico scallop, and the lustrous moon shells.

When you reach the first dune crossover, head up and over the dune on the ramps, past the concession stand and rest rooms, to descend back to the tram pickup point. You've hiked 2.5 miles. Continue across the boardwalk and take your time, watching for wading birds coming in at low tide for a meal. From the tram pickup point in front of the nature center, follow the bark-chip footpath back toward the parking lot—but don't stop there. Continue walking along the footpath along the mangrove forest, passing under large sea grapes and mahogany trees. Gray nickerbean cascades over the white mangroves as you cross another stretch of pavement, following the bark-chip footpath back into a tangle of strangler figs.

When you emerge onto pavement, continue across it, staying to the right. A playground sits off to the left. At 3 miles, you reach the start of the Satinleaf Nature Trail, a quarter-mile loop through another section of tropical hammock. Pick up an interpretive brochure at the kiosk. Wild coffee and silvery green saw palmetto dominate the understory, along with myrsine and red bay. At the loop trail junction, keep right.

You smell the stink of white stopper as you pass under a grove of gumbo limbo trees. A blolly sports bright red berries. Marsh ferns cluster under the shade of a cabbage palm as you come to a bench tucked under the low branches of a pigeon plum. The trail turns left into denser woods, where young trees compete with wild coffee for control of the understory. Winding past an outdoor classroom, you come up to a tall mastic tree at marker 12. With its distinctive lumpy trunk, the mastic is also known as the jungle plum. Although edible, its fruits are sticky sweet and can cause a burning sensation from their astringency, as well as stomach upset. Its decay-resistant wood is popularly used for boatbuilding in the Caribbean.

As the trail curves to the left, you enter a grove dominated by satinleaf. The leaves overhead have orange-brown fuzzy undersides, very striking with the sun shining down through the grove. A marlberry raises its white blossoms well overhead. You walk past a strangler fig with roots that look like bars on a jail cell, then through a grove of paradise trees before you return to the junction. Turn right to exit the trail, then left when you reach the kiosk. Continue across the parking lot to the PEDESTRIANS ONLY sign to follow the bark-chip path back to where your car is parked. When you complete your hike, you've walked 3.5 miles.

31

Gumbo Limbo Nature Center

Total distance (circuit): 1 mile

Hiking time: 1 hour

Habitats: Mangrove swamp, palm hammock, tropical maritime hammock

Maps: USGS 7½' Boca Raton; park map

Along the populous oceanfront of Boca Raton, the Gumbo Limbo Nature Center receives a steady stream of visitors every winter. They come for the wide variety of environmental activities offered, including sea turtle beach walks and Florida Master Naturalist training. They come to stare at the stingrays and snakes in the aquariums. And they come to get away, to touch nature by wandering through this 20-acre patch of ancient hardwood hammock, an island of beauty in the urban sprawl of the southeastern Florida coastline.

To find the Gumbo Limbo Nature Center, take I-95 exit 44, Palmetto Park Road. Follow Palmetto Park Road east through downtown Boca Raton and across the Intracoastal Waterway bridge. After 3.3 miles, the road ends at FL A1A (Ocean Boulevard). Turn left and drive 1.1 miles north to the entrance, on the left just beyond Red Reef Park. The center and its trails are open Monday through Saturday 9 AM–4 PM, Sunday noon–4 PM. Admission is free, but a $2 donation is suggested. If the parking lot is full, go south down FL A1A to Red Reef Park, since you can access the boardwalk trail from the north end of the Red Reef Park parking lot.

Before you take to the trails, explore the nature center, where you'll find numerous interpretive exhibits on the fish, reptiles, and mammals that live in and around the barrier island. Colorful fish of the saltwater reefs swim through their tanks in the gift shop, while stingrays glide through the larger

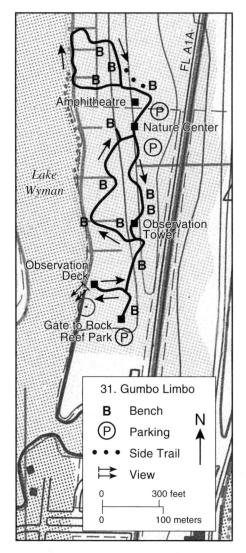

31. Gumbo Limbo

B   Bench

(P)   Parking

•••   Side Trail

⇨   View

N

0	300 feet
0	100 meters

intersection in the boardwalk, turn left. The boardwalk descends into a forest of gumbo limbo with deep red peeling trunks, strangler fig, cabbage palm, and other plants of the tropical maritime hammock, such as pigeon plum, marlberry, and inkwood. Nameplates along the boardwalk assist in plant identification as the boardwalk winds between the trees. The tight-knit canopy creates a dark forest. You pass a bench near a Spanish stopper, which displays its stinky white flowers in spring. The berries of these slender trees were once used as a remedy for diarrhea, hence the name *stopper*. Rounding a corner, you pass under a blolly, a tree that attracts songbirds with its bright red summer crop of fruits. The branches of this blolly point straight up rather than fanning out like normal tree branches.

At 0.1 mile, you reach the observation tower. It's a steep climb up to the top, but several broad platforms let you rest and look out over different canopy heights in the forest until you reach the top level, nearly 40 feet above the forest floor, looking down at the unbroken tree canopy. From here, you get an unobstructed view of the gleaming blue waters of the Intracoastal Waterway and the city of Boca Raton on the far shore. Turn to the east to see sun shimmering on the Atlantic Ocean.

When you return to the base of the tower, turn left to continue along the boardwalk. A brown anole scampers down the railing. After you pass a set of benches, the trail comes to a junction with a newer boardwalk off to the left, through a wooden gate. If the gate is open, turn left. Pay attention to the forest floor on the right as you walk—along the ecotone between the tropical hammock and the mangrove swamp are a series of oyster shell

open-air tanks outside. Knowledgeable naturalists provide interpretive information.

Exit the south end of the center, past the rest rooms, to start your walk on the Coastal Hammock Boardwalk. Notice the wooden blocks suspended from ropes on the left—representative chunks of wood from the various trees found in the hammock, such as mahogany, poisonwood, and pigeon plum. After you reach the T

Mangroves along the Spanish River

piles, middens left behind by the Tequesta. At least 3,000 years ago, these people roamed Southeast Florida, traveling in their canoes down the sloughs in a regular migration from the islands of the northern Everglades to the barrier islands of the Atlantic.

A bench sits in the shade of a blolly and a gumbo limbo as you approach a stand of cabbage palm on the edge of the mangrove forest. Delicately mending its web under a red bay, a golden orb spider gleams in a shaft of sunlight. On the right, a young strangler fig has woven itself like a basket around the base of a cabbage palm. Strangler figs grow from the top down. When bird droppings containing the seeds land in a tree, such as a cabbage palm, the seeds germinate and send dozens of tendril-like roots plummeting toward the ground. The roots eventually grab hold of the host tree. As both the tree and the fig grow, the dense net of roots can strangle the host's growth. If the host tree manages to survive the tight squeeze, it will eventually die out under the leafy shade of this member of the ficus family, which can grow up to 60 feet tall.

At the next trail junction, the boardwalk to the left leads to Red Reef Park. Walk down along it to the benches if you'd like to take a closer look at the mangrove-lined waterway. The water is surprisingly crystal clear; watch for fiddler crabs in the shallows. Yellow nickerbean spills over a tangle of small shrubs. Deep purple morning glories blossom along the edge of the waterway. After your exploration, return to the T intersection and turn left. Look down into the water and you see hundreds of red and white mangrove seedpods drifting through the shallows, seeking a place to take root. A mangrove snapper drifts by in the deep part of the channel. As you continue under the dangling prop roots of the red mangroves, keep alert for mangrove crabs. Decked out with beautiful mottled glossy black-and-white shells against a red body, these busy creatures sometimes drop down onto the boardwalk in search of a shortcut between the mangroves.

After 0.4 mile, the trail ends at an observation platform on the clear blue-green waters of the Intracoastal Waterway. Starting in the 1920s, the Army Corps of Engineers dredged channels and canals throughout South Florida, radically changing the natural water flow of the region. The saline stream you see before you today used to be the Spanish River, a seasonal freshwater drainage of the sloughs and swamps to the northeast into the Atlantic Ocean. The Tequesta followed its waters, as did the Spanish explorers who ranged through Florida in the 1500s—archaeological relics found nearby, such as a cannon and anchors, attest to their interest in this area. Once permanent outlets to the sea were dredged, the habitat shifted from a floodplain forest of cypress and pond apple to a mangrove swamp. In winter months, watch for West Indian manatees cruising the channel—they migrate southward from their North Florida domains to enjoy the warmer waters of the southern coasts.

As you walk through the mangroves, notice what a tangled thicket it is—tough for us to traverse, but easy for raccoons, opossums, and ibises to pick their way through in search of a meal. The sudden burst of monkeylike screeching comes from several raccoons in a hollow log, fighting with each other over today's catch. After you pass the side trail to Red Reef Park and walk back past the middens, the trail returns to its original junction with the main loop at 0.5 mile. The

TOWER and NATURE CENTER signs point to the right. Turn left to continue on your loop. The boardwalk quickly slopes down and into the mangrove forest, turning right when it reaches the edge of the water. Coconuts wash up along the shoreline. Notice the huge holes of the giant land crabs. These burrows can be as much as 4 feet long, pushing toward the water table. Each fall, the crabs scramble up and over the coastal hammock to the dunes—despite the obstacle of FL A1A—to mate and release their young.

Curving to the right, the trail rises away from the waterway and back up into the tropical hammock, passing under the shade of older Guiana plums and pigeon plums. A wild papaya grows in the deep shade of the forest. Brought here by the Spanish, papayas spread throughout the southern Florida peninsula in less than 200 years. Flashing its electric blue tail, a young southeastern five-lined skink climbs the trunk of a poisonwood tree. As you zigzag through a stand of cabbage palms, you can see the roof of the nature center beyond the trees. When you come to the T intersection, turn left, walking to the end of the boardwalk to see an unexpected resident of this hammock—pond apple. Pond apples flourish in the inland freshwater swamps and sloughs south of Lake Okeechobee, but are never normally seen on barrier islands. The presence of these trees indicates that this area was once a floodplain forest.

Turn around and return back along the boardwalk, passing the incoming trail as you head up to the back of the nature center to complete the Coastal Hammock Boardwalk. You've walked 0.6 mile.

Continue either through or in front of the nature center to access the rest of the trail system—the North Loop, which starts just north of the front entrance of the building, next to the parking lot. A sidewalk leads you back through a grove of strangler fig and cabbage palm into an outdoor auditorium. Turn right at the bench to follow a bark-chip path through a butterfly garden, where blooming salvia and periwinkle attract dozens of yellow sulfur butterflies. Turn right at the next bench, and right again when you reach the T intersection. Bees buzz from their nearby apiaries, where they cluster in dark masses against the white wood. Pass a trail on the right and continue straight into the grove of Australian pine, a thick carpet of pine needles providing a spongy footpath. Although it is an invasive species that drives out natural Florida habitats, the tall Australian pines seem majestic as they sway in the wind.

After 0.8 mile, the trail passes an outdoor classroom and reaches the Intracoastal Waterway. Two benches give you the opportunity to sit and relax along the water and watch the fish in the clear water. Checkered pufferfish dart in and out of the mangrove roots as they attempt to escape a cruising barracuda. When you leave the water's edge, continue north along the log-lined trail into the mangroves through a spot that can be a few inches under water during high tide. The trail loops back up into the dry hammock to a T intersection behind the classroom. Turn left and circle back around past a bench to the butterfly garden. Continue left at the next bench to exit the garden and return to the sidewalk. When you reach the nature center, you've completed a 1-mile walk.

32

Fern Forest Nature Center

Total distance (circuit): 2.2 miles

Hiking time: 1 hour, 30 minutes

Habitats: Cypress slough, freshwater marsh, tropical hardwood hammock, palm hammock, prairie

Maps: USGS 7½' North Fort Lauderdale; park map

There's something very special about bio-diversity in the midst of an urban area, which makes Fern Forest a jewel among Broward County parks. Hidden within its "designated urban wilderness area" of 243 acres are 91 species of birds, 49 species of butterflies, endangered indigo snakes and gopher tortoises, large mammals such as bobcats and foxes, and the park's namesake—34 different species of ferns. As you walk the quiet boardwalks and trails throughout the complex, you'll understand what a grave loss this part of Florida has suffered.

Driving southbound on the Florida Turnpike, take exit 67, Coconut Creek Parkway. Head straight out of the toll plaza and cross Coconut Creek Parkway to take a connector road 1 mile south to Atlantic Boulevard. Turn right at the light. Heading northbound on the Florida Turnpike, use exit 66 for FL 814 (Atlantic Boulevard). Follow FL 814 west to Lyons Road, keeping in the right-hand lane. Turn right just beyond the traffic light, at the FERN FOREST NATURE CENTER RAMP sign. The loop gets you southbound on Lyons Road. Just 0.3 mile after the traffic light, look for the entrance on the right. The park is open daily 8 AM–6 PM, and no pets or bicycles are allowed. Picnicking is permitted only near the parking area.

Your hike starts at the parking lot, from which a boardwalk leads up to shaded benches next to a kiosk with a map of the park. The trail crosses a wetlands canal, where giant leather fern reaches skyward

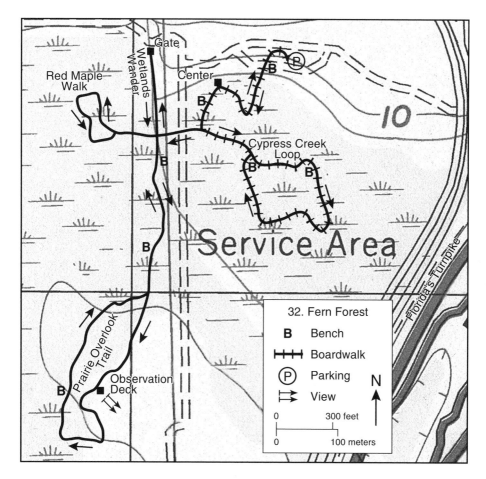

Red Maple Walk

Wetlands Wander

Gate

Center

Cypress Creek Loop

10

Service Area

Florida's Turnpike

Prairie Overlook Trail

Observation Deck

32. Fern Forest

B Bench

⊢⊢⊢ Boardwalk

Ⓟ Parking

⇨ View

N

| 0 | 300 feet |
| 0 | 100 meters |

from the banks, and silvery flashes of fish play hide-and-go-seek through the coontail. An iridescent green variable dancer dragonfly alights on a spatterdock. Rising upward, the boardwalk passes through a thicket of sea myrtle, wild tamarind, and pond apple. Laurel oak provides the high canopy, while wild coffee rises over your head.

Bees buzz around the blooms of marlberry as you approach the nature center, walking past an enormous cypress stump. A reminder of the ancient forest, it represents the awesome size of the cypresses that once lined Cypress Creek. Eroded

deep into the spongy marl limestone bedrock underlying this part of Florida, Cypress Creek once drained the Everglades toward the sea. But in 1906, Governor Napoleon Bonaparte Broward drew up plans to drain the creek to expose Everglades soil for farmland and development. By 1916, the creek dried up, replaced with the nearby C-14 Canal. The face of the land began to change. In the 1930s, the DuBois Land and Lumber Company began logging the giant cypresses. This tract of forest became dairy land, although its rocky sections were probably too difficult for the cattle to enter. A developer bought the land in 1965, but did not immediately try to build houses here. Fortunately, the people of Broward County voted to purchase the tract, and in 1979 Fern Forest was set aside as a preserve.

Inside the nature center, exhibits explain the habitats of Fern Forest and the creatures and plants that live within them. Borrow an interpretive guide from the desk before you head out to the trail. On the outside of the building, there are soda machines and rest rooms. A large classroom takes up the second floor, providing instructional space for nature programs and a meeting place for many local civic groups, including the local Happy Hoofers Chapter of the Florida Trail Association. Check the signboards for dates and times of meetings and activities.

Exiting the back door of the nature center, follow the boardwalk through the gate out into the forest. Mind the sign that says TRAILS CLOSE AT 5 PM, as the park gates close at 6 PM. Passing the benches and the *Fern Lore Guardian* sculpture, you walk under paradise trees, coco plums, and firebushes on your way to the T intersection. Signs direct you to the various trails. Turn left to start the Cypress Creek Trail. This boardwalk loop parallels the old channel of Cypress Creek, now hidden under a dense layer of ferns. Look closely into the forest as you walk and you'll see the deeply eroded rocky banks of the creek, undercut with small caves. Butterfly markers along the railing correspond to the interpretive guide for the trail.

Surrounded by marlberry, gum bumelia, and wild coffee, the trail drops down into the woods. Keep alert for the unusual ferns on the forest floor. In between the usual standbys like giant sword ferns, swamp ferns, and netted chains, you'll spy several spleenworts and southern wood ferns.

Jogging around a strangler fig, the trail continues through the tangled tropical thicket. Look for giant brake fern poking out from the limestone ledges, and strap fern cascading from the bases of tree trunks and the dark wood of rotting logs.

At 0.3 mile, you reach a trail junction that marks the beginning of the Cypress Creek Loop. Keep left, passing the bench. As you walk under the bald cypress, look ahead at the limbs of the marlberry, covered in balls of wild pine that look like tufts of grass. The trail drops lower, where giant leather ferns rise from marshy spots and wood ferns hide the rugged limestone creek bottom. Flaunting autumn shades of crimson, a red maple marks the edge of a wetland area where bald cypresses dominate. As you round a corner to the left, there is an umbrella tree in the understory and a garden of ferns clustered above and below a limestone ledge.

Several benches sit under the shade of a gumbo limbo where the trail turns right and crosses high over a cypress-shaded pond. Masses of purple-blooming pickerelweed poke out of the water. Pond apples reflect in the dark water. Royal ferns and cinnamon ferns emerge from mats of rotting vegetation, while dense beds of marsh ferns thrive in the damp soil edging the pond. On the still, dark water, water spangles and mosquito ferns float. Water spangles are ferns with small, round leaves that radiate from a base; mosquito ferns grow in strands. Scattered clumps of giant leather fern make the swamp feel primeval.

Rising back up into the hammock, the trail turns to the right. The skunklike odor of white stopper fills the air. The trail curves beneath towering gumbo limbo trees. Reaching a vantage point on the far side of the pond, the trail follows the other

Cypress Creek Trail

shore of Cypress Creek upstream. At 0.5 mile, stop for a moment on the bench-lined platform and take a close-up look at a cypress knee. Based on the height of the cypress knees rising from the old streambed, it's likely that Cypress Creek was at least 4½ feet deep. Hunters in search of egret, ibis, and roseate spoonbill plumes made their way up the creek in the late 1800s; these included Guy Bradley, who later became a notable figure in the Everglades as the first Audubon Society game warden in 1902, killed in the line of duty while attempt to prevent plume hunters from poaching vanishing species. Visitors from that period described Cypress Creek as a dark place under stately cypress trees draped in Spanish moss, where alligators frequented the banks.

Leaving the platform, the boardwalk continues up to a strangler fig with multiple taproots as thick as tree trunks, and then makes a sharp right. Look up into the tree for a rare whisk fern. This primitive member of the fern family sports no fronds. Winding under a satinleaf tree, the trail turns and descends to cross the floodplain of Cypress Creek. After 0.6 mile, you return to the beginning of the loop. Turn left.

At the trail intersection, the trail on the right leads back to the nature center. Continue straight as the boardwalk drops you off to cross a jeep road, then starts up again to cross a canal crowded with arrowroot and spatterdock. On the far side of the canal, you come to a junction with a trail map. To start your walk around this trail system, follow the PRAIRIE OVERLOOK TRAIL sign to the right. The broad path parallels the canal, passing a butterfly garden where yellow sulfurs and red admirals flit around the blooms. A bench overlooks the waterway; keep alert for alligators. The footpath of rough surface limestone leads to the beginning of the Prairie Overlook Trail at 0.8 mile. Turn right, following the narrow limestone- and root-studded path into the cool shade of the hammock, where tall slash pines rise from the shallow soil—a tiny remnant of the pine rocklands that once covered the coastline of Southeast Florida.

Keep left at the fork to start the loop section of the Prairie Overlook Trail. Paradise tree and indigoberry join marlberry and several varieties of wild coffee in the understory. Bracken ferns thrive in the pine straw. At 1 mile, a steeply sloped boardwalk rises up to an observation tower over a prairie, where young slash pines and other species appear to be filling in the vast open space. Not a natural prairie, this bald spot in the forest was cleared for cattle grazing. The subsequent change in habitat provided a home for gopher tortoises; this is now one of the few places in Broward County where these creatures can be found. Dropping back down to the forest, the boardwalk ends at a T intersection. Turn left at the PRAIRIE LOOP sign to take a short walk out to the edge of the prairie. Coontie, the only cycad in North America, grows in the deep shade. When you emerge from the forest, turn right onto the sand road, following the edge of the prairie. Look across the grassland for signs of deer feeding in the open meadows. Turn right at the PRAIRIE OVERLOOK TRAIL sign to reenter the forest.

As you walk under the shade of the cabbage palms, you pass another bench before the Prairie Overlook Trail comes in from the right. Continue straight. Cabbage palms show off their adornments of goldfoot and shoelace ferns. The trail rises up into a denser forest of older pines, cabbage palms, and laurel oaks. After you pass under a towering paradise tree, the footpath narrows; vegetation crowds in closely. The red berries and white blossoms of indigoberry add a touch of color to the pine-shaded hammock. After 1.4 miles, you reach the end of the loop at the TO NATURE CENTER sign. Continue straight.

When you emerge back onto the broad path under the power line, turn left and follow it up along the canal for the Wetlands Wander. Passing the trail junction, continue along the waterway, pausing at the various small overlooks to peer down into the wetland. Although it's a small, linear wetland, it attracts little blue herons, glossy ibises, and snowy egrets, which squawk and squabble if you draw too close. At 1.6 miles, the trail ends at a locked gate. Turn around and return to the trail junction.

If you don't mind getting muddy, wet, and perhaps a little bit lost, face the forest and follow the narrow track that is the Red Maple Walk. A slippery slab of limestone drops you down into the deep muck of the cypress slough. During the wet season, this trail will be entirely under water. At other times, it may be just muddy and slippery and full of puddles. Follow the red maple blazes into the dark forest through the cinnamon fern and lizard tail, keeping to the right as you wander through a maze of cypress knees to a sign that says BALD CYPRESS. Scattered along the trail are interpretive labels such as these to help you identify the plants. It is very easy to get lost in the open understory, so keep watching for the next red blaze. Curving to the right through dense lizard tail, the trail reaches a fork. To the right, a footpath vanishes into a deep thicket busy with ferns. Turn left. Skirting a small wetland with pickerelweed, you pick your way around scattered deep mud and puddles. The trail curves left, zigzagging through cypress knees, past a RED MAPLE sign. Rising up a little under the shade of laurel oaks, the footpath becomes drier. Making a sharp left, the trail becomes a recognizable swath through a broad bed of cinnamon ferns. When you see the BALD CYPRESS sign in front of you at 1.8 miles, turn right to follow the red blazes. Continuing along the edge of the marsh into a stand of crinium lily, the trail winds through slippery mud back to end the loop. Keep following the red blazes to the right tunnel your way back out of the forest, emerging at the trail junction. You've hiked 2 miles.

Continue straight across to follow the boardwalk over the canal and back to the nature center. After you cross the jeep road, make a left at the junction in the boardwalk. Walk around the nature center to exit back along the boardwalk to the parking lot, completing your 2.2-mile walk through Fern Forest.

33

Secret Woods Nature Center

Total distance (circuit): 1 mile

Hiking time: 30 minutes

Habitats: Floodplain forest, mangrove forest, oak hammock, tropical hardwood hammock

Maps: USGS 7½' Fort Lauderdale South; park map

From the buzz of nearby traffic, you'd never guess that the first nature center ever opened in Broward County lies hidden away in a stretch of woods just off the I-95/I-595 interchange. Tucked away along the South Fork of the New River, Secret Woods encompasses 56 acres of dark floodplain forest, a mixture of cypress strands and mangrove forest edged by tropical hardwood hammock. An island of calm amid the surrounding storm of rampant development and busy highways, this park has the distinction of being a "designated urban wilderness area" opened to the public in 1978.

To find Secret Woods from the Florida Turnpike, take exit 54, Fort Lauderdale, to go east on FL 84. Keep alert to the road signs on the spaghetti tangle of flyover ramps, since I-595 and US 441 share the same exit. The park entrance is just beyond Southwest 29th Avenue, on the left. Get in the left lane and look for the small brown sign that points you to a U-turn lane just beyond the next traffic light. Heading west, turn right into the park entrance. From I-595, take exit 9 to FL 84. From I-95, use exit 25. Follow FL 84 west over the bridge to the park entrance. The park is open 8 AM–6 PM, and no bicycles or pets are permitted.

Starting from the parking lot, walk down to the trailhead, where a map gives an overview of the park's trails and boardwalks. Follow the boardwalk into the forest, where satinleaf, coco plum, and marlberry shade an understory dense with cinnamon fern and sword fern. When you reach the nature center complex, stop in at the park office to pick up interpretive information. Wind between the exhibit hall—worth a look, if it's open—and the rest rooms to reach the TRAIL sign, which points you down a path to a pair of signs with trail maps. Turn right to start the Laurel Oak Trail. At the T intersection, turn left, following the thick bed of mulch that defines the footpath into the dark shade of the forest. Sunlight glints off the glossy leaves of marlberry and myrsine in the understory, while strangler fig and cabbage palm tower as high as the laurel oak canopy. The murky waters of the swamp lap at the bases of tall royal palms scattered throughout the forest, lifting their fronds well above the rest of the trees. A boardwalk traverses a permanent part of the swamp, where giant leather ferns rise out of the water and pond apples lean forward under the weight of their fruit. A member of the custard apple family, the pond apple sports a massive apple-shaped fruit that provides deer, raccoons, and other wildlife with an important food source—but it doesn't appeal to most humans, as it has a faint turpentine taste.

As the trail curves right past a bench, you notice numerous large holes in the soft sand beneath the duff of the forest floor. These holes stretch several feet deep to the water table, providing shelter to the giant land crab. At up to 6 inches across its shell, the giant land crab is Florida's largest terrestrial crab and can be found up to 3 miles from the ocean. They prefer saline environments such as the New River floodplain, digging their homes under the mangrove roots. Mostly vegetarian, subsisting on berries and young leaves, they will occasionally eat small insects. When giant land crabs are ready to

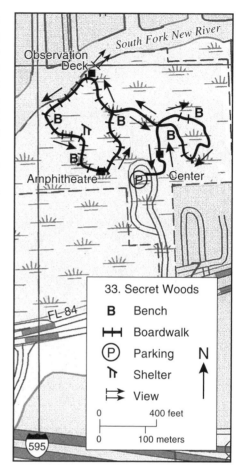

lay their eggs, they go on an expedition to the coastline—often fatal as they attempt to cross busy roads in Southeast Florida.

The trail continues past a cluster of benches sitting at the base of a massive strangler fig. Marlberry dominates the lower canopy. You cross another boardwalk over a murky section of swamp, where water flows in and out in rhythm with the tide beneath bald cypresses. The primeval bulk of a southern wood fern rises out of the forest floor. Surrounded by the dry orange powdery remains of orange poria, shelflike mossy maze polypore decorates a rotting log. A brown anole pauses

Ibises perched in mangroves

on a cabbage palm trunk run amok in a riot of color, carpeted with both mustard-colored lichen and tiny star-shaped green lichen. Circling the back of the nature center complex, the trail passes some benches before completing the loop at 0.3 mile. Keep left to walk back out to the trail junction.

When you emerge at the set of maps, turn right to start the New River Trail. Winding along under a low canopy of coco plums, the boardwalk parts a thicket of royal ferns, wood ferns, and sword ferns. Royal palms tower over the forest, while cabbage palms appear in various stages of youth, their full-sized fronds barely lifted off the forest floor by short trunks. Two types of wild coffee grow throughout the forest: *Psychotria nervosa,* with glossy green leaves, and *P. sulzneri,* with silvery blue-green leaves. Both bear bright clusters of white blooms in summer, and drip with shiny crimson to deep black coffee beans in fall. Roasted and ground, these beans create a passable brew. But in the hammocks, it's the birds that enjoy plucking these showy seeds from the tall bushes.

A large strangler fig winds its tendril-like roots down around the trunk of cabbage palm, enveloping it. Cabbage palms are often the hosts for strangler figs, whose seeds are dispersed by birds into the tops of other trees. Germinating as an epiphyte, the fig spends its formative years sending a network of taproots down the host tree until it, too, can pull nutrients from the ground. If the host is a hardwood, chances are that the strangler fig will strangle its growth. But in the case of cabbage palms, the fig doesn't affect the pliable trunk of the palm. Instead, the palm runs the risk of being enveloped in the dark shadow as the strangler fig grows to immense proportions.

At 0.4 mile, you reach a T intersection with a bench to the right. Turn right as the boardwalk leaves the tropical hammock to start out over the dark waters of the mangrove swamp, zigzagging among the trees. White and glossy ibises roost in the high branches of a white mangrove above an observation deck on the New River, a brackish channel affected by the tides. Development clusters along the far shore. The boardwalk continues along the river's edge, behind slim sandbars repopulated with native plants such as coco plum and sea grape. Red mangroves dangle prop roots that brush your head. A bench lets you sit and look out beyond a coconut palm planted along the river, where the trail makes a sharp left and leaves the water to head into a dense stand of giant leather fern. As the boardwalk winds back through the mangrove forest, keep alert for the scurrying of mangrove crabs on the limbs.

With a resounding *plop,* a leopard frog leaps into the water as you approach a covered shelter after 0.7 mile. When you come up to the T intersection, either route will take you back to the nature center. Turn right to follow the slightly longer path. The constant drone of traffic, an unfortunate by-product of civilization, lies over the forest like a deep fog. White mangroves grow tall in this part of the floodplain, rising as trees nearly 30 feet high. Passing through an outdoor amphitheater, you reach another trail junction. Continue straight. Leaving the mangroves for a tropical hammock under restoration, the boardwalk heads to a trail junction at 0.9 mile. Continue straight. When you reach the intersection with the bench, you've completed the loop portion of the New River Trail. Turn right. When you emerge at the junction of the two trails, continue straight to return to the nature center complex. Once you return to the parking lot, you've completed your 1-mile exploration of Secret Woods.

34

Greynolds Park

Total distance (one circuit, one round trip):
1.7 miles

Hiking time: 1 hour, 15 minutes

Habitats: Mangrove forest, tropical
hardwood hammock

Maps: USGS 7½' North Miami; park map

An island of wild in the middle of urban sprawl, Greynolds Park provides Miami residents with a back-to-nature escape along the Oleta River. One of the first public parks in Florida, it was built in 1933 with Civilian Conservation Corps labor and dedicated in 1936. In addition to its hiking and biking trails, it has a public golf course, opportunities for fishing, and loads of picnic pavilions. For the outdoors enthusiast, it's one of the best places in urban Dade County for bird-watching. This is an urban park, however, so use the same personal safety precautions that you would when walking around a major city.

From I-95, take exit 19, Miami Gardens Drive/North Miami Beach. Follow FL 860 (Miami Gardens Drive/Northeast 186th Street) east for 2.1 miles to Northeast 22nd Avenue. Turn right. From US 1 (Biscayne Boulevard), drive 0.6 mile west on FL 860. Turn left onto Northeast 22nd Avenue. The park entrance is immediately on the left.

Greynolds Park is open sunrise to sunset daily, with a $4-per-vehicle admission fee on weekends and holidays. As you drive in on the park road, follow the signs for the golf course. Continue past the golf course to the LAKESIDE TRAIL sign on the right. If you want a trail map, stop at the park office to request one. The park contains two nature trails—the Lakeside Nature Trail and the Oleta River Nature Trail—plus a long paved bike trail and numerous short trails connecting the picnic areas.

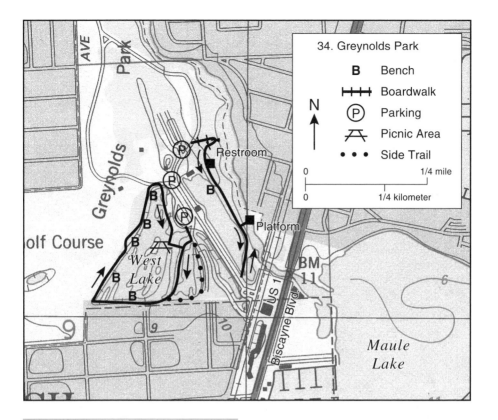

LAKESIDE NATURE TRAIL

To start your first hike, turn right into the next parking area, Paradise Park Circle, and drive to the south end of the circle. A stone bridge leads away from the parking lot and onto islands of limestone surrounded by mangrove swamps. Since this is an urban park, the sounds of the city intrude. But don't let that dismay you—what's preserved here is precious, an island of wildlife habitat in the heart of the city. Once pine rocklands topped with Dade County slash pine, it's now an artificial landscape created by rock mining in the 1890s, when a convict labor camp sat on this spot. But the intervening century allowed nature to regain a foothold, making this area lush and green. Long filled with water, the rock pits provide habitats for birds, turtles, and one of the less common

residents of North America, the American crocodile. Like its relative the American alligator, it can grow to 12 or more feet long—not a creature you want to tangle with. While the alligator has a rounded snout, the crocodile has a more elongated, pointed snout and a grayish tinge to its hide. An endangered species, it prefers to live in brackish water. Crocodiles have been sighted at this park—note the warning signs—so use caution as you hike. Do not approach a crocodile.

Cross the stone bridge, walking under the leafy shade of a strangler fig. Immediately, a wooden bridge leads to the right. Cross that bridge to begin your journey down the islands. No slash pines remain—just tall, old Australian pines, covering the bare limestone with a soft carpet of pine needles. Tamarind and sea grape grow

Boulders along the Lakeshore Trail

along the trail's edge. Red and white mangroves create a dense thicket along the water. At dawn and dusk, the mangroves come alive with thousands of roosting herons, egrets, and roseate spoonbills. Winter brings the colonial nesting birds inland to build their nests and raise their young on these islands, where they're protected from egg-stealing raccoons by the alligators and crocodiles that inhabit these waters. You see the white tail feathers from an egret, a reminder that the price paid for protection is the occasional loss of a member of the colony.

As you cross the next wooden bridge onto the next island, notice the gnarled and knobby base of the pine tree. Ebony spleenwort, a delicate limestone-loving fern, peeks out of a pile of limestone boulders. Watch for solution holes eroding the footpath beneath your feet. The air reeks with the odor of moldering muck. Watch the shallows as a Florida softshell turtle glides past. It's a weird-looking turtle, with alligatorlike protruding eyes, a tubular head, and a pointed snout. It's also a very different kind of turtle. To be able to remain submerged longer than the average turtle, the softshell has a leathery, blood-vessel-packed skin covering its almost pancake-flat shell, an adaptation that enables it to take in oxygen and expel carbon dioxide through the skin. Softshell turtles compete with the resident alligators when hunting fish, frogs, and small waterfowl.

Giant leather ferns grow along the water's edge. Plantings of crotons add color to a stand of thatch palms. At the T intersection, turn right. Shaded by strangler figs, the trail continues along the back of neighborhood yards along the mangrove-lined waterway. You hear the fussing of a little blue heron. Passing a bench, you see an anhinga emerge from the still water,

a gar in its beak. Firebush shows off its bright yellow-tipped red blooms where the trail reaches the edge of the golf course. Keep alert for an unmarked sharp turn to the right to continue along the water's edge. Older slash pines grow out on the golf course, while the lakeshore is a strip of tropical hammock, with pigeon plums and sea grapes providing shade. A zebra swallowtail flutters to a tamarind bloom. Where the limestone forms outcrops, you can see the impressions of fossilized seashells encased in the stone. Ladder brake fern grows along the shoreline. A heavy salt tang fills the air.

Sit down on a bench in the shade of a pigeon plum and look out at the mangrove islands. The long prop roots of red mangroves dangle toward the water. Covered in glossy white berries, a snowberry peeps out of the understory of wild coffee. The trail continues along a wall of stone, one of the former quarry walls, with a tangle of strangler fig roots draped down over it. Watch your step: The footpath narrows severely in places. Sunlight reflects off the opaque water, dappling on undersides of live oaks. A green anole scampers across the needle-covered footpath. The trail rises up to touch the golf course briefly, then drops back down under a stand of gumbo limbo trees. Look into the still shallows and you can see the spotted forms of checkered pufferfish gliding beneath the roots. Passing a large Australian pine, the trail jogs to the left to rise up to a triad of benches arranged around a memorial stone. You've hiked 0.5 mile. Dropping back down, the trail continues along the water. Turn left. Ladder brake ferns cascade off the exposed quarry wall, which has small caves in its mottled oolitic surface. Rising up past a bench next to a large pine, the trail seems to split in two—

two benches, or rock ledges, along the wall of the quarry. Take the upper one, as the lower one has a dangerously pitched slant toward the water. A strangler fig wraps around an Australian pine; you disappear into a forest of wild coffee. Movement on a mangrove branch catches your eye. No, it's not an optical illusion. It's an iguana, nearly 2 feet long. Descendants of local pets, iguanas have settled into these tiny wild spots in the urban jungle. Caught basking in the sun, the lizard decides to flee. Jumping into the water, the deep green iguana paddles over to a distant mangrove root, climbs up it, and spreads out to warm up once more.

Papyrus grows along the water's edge as you look down from the LAKESIDE NATURE TRAIL sign. You've reached the park entrance road. Continue along the grassy berm, passing a set of benches looking out over the mangroves. Across the road is an unusual stone tower capping the Mound. A 42-foot-tall artificial hill built to cover up the old rock mining equipment, the Mound was once the highest point in Dade County—now the landfills exceed its height. The small parking lot at its base also provides a place to access the Lakeside Nature Trail, but parking is extremely limited. When you reach the PARADISE CIRCLE sign, keep to the right along the side of road, walking under the paradise trees. There is no marked trail here. You loop back around along the grassy edge of the parking lot, next to the mangroves. At the big strangler fig, turn right to walk out to a picnic spot carved out of limestone, the stone walls and benches a great place to sit and watch for iguanas and crocodiles. When you leave the picnic area, turn right and walk along the mangroves back to the parking spaces by the stone bridge, completing this 0.8-mile loop.

OLETA RIVER NATURE TRAIL

Leave the end of Paradise Park Circle parking lot near the stone bridge and make a left at the stop sign. Drive past the Lagoon Picnic Shelter and turn right in front of the stone castle. Park your car just across from Fern Circle, near the boathouse.

To find the trailhead, walk across the parking lot toward the boathouse and turn right to follow the entrance road uphill, past a stand of wild coffee. The OLETA RIVER NATURE TRAIL sign is on the right; the trail takes off into the woods. Since you are just a few miles from the Atlantic Ocean, the Oleta River is affected by the tides. At high tide, a short stretch of the approach to the boardwalk may be under a few inches of water.

Walking along the boardwalk through the dense mangrove forest, you hear the fussing of herons and the calls of ospreys. Giant leather ferns and wild papayas rise out of the swamp. In this tidal jungle of mangroves, notice the small white spots on the bases of the red mangrove roots, near the waterline, as they exude salt. The boardwalk zigzags through the forest, ending at the base of a strangler fig. Continue forward on the trail as the fiddler crabs scatter out of your way. Curving to the right around a saw palmetto, the trail climbs the hill and emerges behind the rest rooms. Turn left. When you reach the paved trail, turn left. The boathouse sits off to the right. Since the paved trail provides the best views of the Oleta River, you'll be following it up to the south end of the park.

Keep alert for a well-worn footpath off to the left, which takes you on a brief excursion through the natural hammock along the edge of the mangrove forest. Turn right when you reach the wall of mangroves, and follow the edge of the swamp. Watch for the tiny holes and earth balls of fiddler crabs. The trail curves up and to the right along a waterway to return to the paved trail. Turn left to cross a bridge. A narrow screen of mangroves separates you from the lagoon on the right. At 0.3 mile, you reach a floating jetty over a deep spot in the river. Take a moment to enjoy the view. The Oleta River once drained the Everglades into the Atlantic Ocean, but the hydrologic changes wrought by canals and construction over the past century caused this saltwater intrusion upstream. Its waters now move sluggishly toward the Atlantic, beaten back by the tides. You see very different vegetation here than the Seminoles did in 1803, when the U.S. Army ran a trading post here on the military trail between Fort Dallas and Fort Lauderdale.

Returning to the paved path, turn left and walk across the covered bridge. On the left, you see the river flowing swiftly through a cut, a tiny reminder of the rocky rapids that this river and the former Miami River (now a canal) sported in the days before modern civilization. A yellow-crested night heron perches on a rock, waiting for a fish to jump as it rolls through the cut. After 0.4 mile, you reach a bridge that marks the end of this hike, near the back entrance to the park. Turn around and follow the paved trail back toward the boathouse. A green heron moves stealthily along a mangrove limb as it waits for the appropriate moment to spear a fish. You see a rapid movement of water in the shallows of the lagoon—perhaps a crocodile with today's catch. Like alligators, they feed not just on fish but also on unwary birds and raccoons that come to the water's edge.

When the trail swings left toward the boathouse, you can either return to the parking lot via the boathouse or follow the Oleta River Nature Trail back along the boardwalk through the mangroves. Arriving at the parking area, you've walked 0.9 mile.

V

The Everglades

Pay-hay-okee   *Clyde Butcher*

35

Corbett Wildlife Management Area

Total distance (one circuit, one round trip): 5.2 miles

Hiking time: 3 hours

Habitats: Cabbage palm flatwoods, cypress slough, freshwater marsh, hardwood hammock, prairie, pine flatwoods

Maps: USGS 7½' West of Delta; Florida Trail Association map SF-8

During the Second Seminole War, federal troops attempted to round up the Seminole tribes living in Florida, holding them to a document signed by a treacherous chief that gave him gold in exchange for his people moving to the "Indian Lands" of the American West. Escaping from the troops, a tribe of Seminoles made their way through the slough to a small hammock, where they set up camp. Drawing their ranks tightly so that the Seminoles could not hunt, the soldiers attempted to starve them out. But an old woman tricked the soldiers. By tending to the fire day and night, she allowed the rest of the tribe to slip away into the Everglades under cover of darkness. When smoke no longer rose from the hammock, the soldiers moved in. Alone, the old woman had died of starvation.

The Corbett Wildlife Management Area encompasses more than 60,000 acres of the northern Everglades, including the Hungryland Slough. Named for the siege and starvation of the Seminoles, Hungryland Slough is one of several sluggish cypress swamps that drain the Loxahatchee River basin into the upper Everglades. Two hiking trails enable visitors to experience the quiet and wild of this water-dependent region. Suitable for families, the 1.1-mile Hungryland Boardwalk and Trail leads hikers through the wet flatwoods and onto a boardwalk into the slough. The lengthy Florida Trail provides backpackers with several options for overnight or multiday backpacking trips.

Corbett lies at the northwestern edge of the suburban spread of Palm Beach

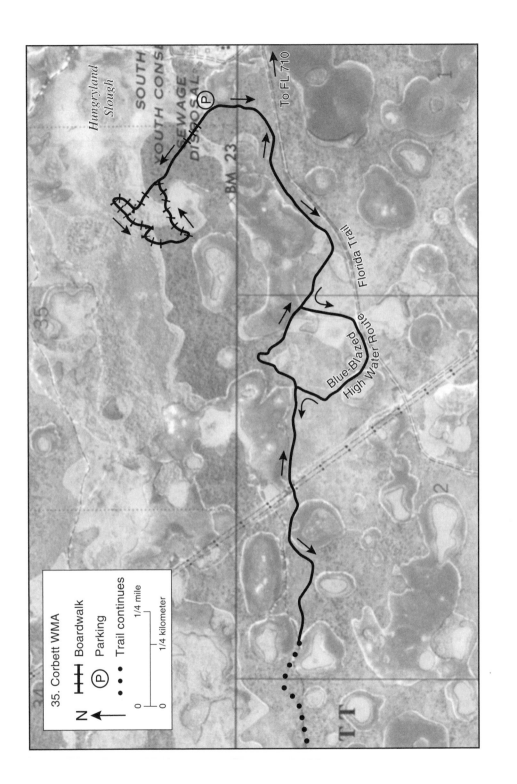

35. Corbett WMA

N

Boardwalk
Ⓟ Parking
Trail continues

0   1/4 kilometer   1/4 mile
0

Hungryland Slough

SOUTH

YOUTH CONS

SEWAGE

DISPOSAL

BM 23

To FL 710

Florida Trail

Blue-Blazed
High Water Route

County. From I-95, take exit 77. Follow Northlake Boulevard (CR 850) west for 12 miles to its end. From the Florida Turnpike exit 99, take FL 704 (Okeechobee Boulevard) west 1 mile to Jog Road. Turn right and drive north to FL 710 (Beeline Highway). Turn left and follow FL 710 for 1.2 miles to where it meets Northlake Boulevard. Turn left and drive 8.9 miles to the end of the road.

At the end of Northlake Boulevard, turn right onto Seminole-Pratt-Whitney Road. Almost immediately, you see the CORBETT WMA sign. Continue north as the road becomes hard-packed dirt; keep to the left at the fork. After 3 miles, you reach the sign that says EVERGLADES YOUTH CAMP. Turn left. Stop at the self-service pay station and drop off your entrance fee of $3 per person before continuing down the forest road for 0.5 mile. After you pass the lake, take the right fork to drive into the youth camp. Just before the gates, make a left at the HUNGRYLAND BOARDWALK sign and follow the one-lane jeep track down to where it ends in a clearing ringed by picnic tables. Park your car near the large sign. Both trailheads start at the edge of this clearing.

HUNGRYLAND BOARDWALK AND TRAIL

Walk over to the kiosk on the right and take a look at the map before starting down the Hungryland Trail. Coco plums tempt from the sides of the trail corridor as the footpath leads you into the pine flatwoods. Wax myrtle rises tall from the dense understory of silvery green saw palmetto. Scattered cabbage palms attest to the wetness of this flatwoods. Becoming a boardwalk, the trail crosses a wet prairie, where young pond cypresses grow along the edge of the ephemeral wetland. The boardwalk deposits you into a dense pine flatwoods with tall slash pines. Most of the pine forests at Corbett were logged out in the 1940s for timber, so this is a second-growth forest where cattle once roamed. A pileated woodpecker drums out a rhythmic tune from high atop a slash pine trunk. Bushy bluestem grass pokes up through the saw palmetto fronds, and a yellow sulfur flits between tickseed blossoms. Greenbrier cascades up and over young gallberry and wax myrtle. Occasional interpretive markers provide background on the flora and fauna.

You reach a pair of benches flanking an interpretive kiosk in a copse of tall slash pines, where their bright green needles graze the blue sky. Royal ferns peek out from a stand of saw palmettos as you come up to the beginning of the trail loop at 0.3 mile. Take the right fork. Coco plum crowds up to the footpath where tall torpedo grass lines the trail. The trail becomes a boardwalk into the dense cypress forest of Hungryland Slough. As you walk under the cypresses, look up—air plants festoon the branches and limbs of the cypresses. A tall pond apple dangles its large green fruits, the tree a remnant of the once great forest of pond apple that used to edge Lake Okeechobee.

Patches of alligator flag remind you that this part of the slough can get very wet. Marsh ferns grow out of its soggy bottom. Primordial giant leather ferns emerge from islands formed around the bases of cypresses. Palm warblers flit through the trees. The bane of Palm Beach County, an invasive climbing fern attempts to choke out growth in the cypresses. Some of the ferns have been killed off and hang in ugly blackened streamers from the treetops. At a pair of benches, the trail makes a hard left. Take a moment to sit and ponder the

Wet prairie

slough. The beauty of this place is the silence. You can't hear any road noise, or any other human activity: just the squawk of birds and the groan of trees as they move in the wind, a rare find in this part of Florida.

At least a dozen different types of ferns grow in this humid environment, among them veritable mounds of giant sword fern, and tall cinnamon ferns at the bases of cypresses. Stands of pond apple trees thrive beneath the cypress canopy. You come to a sharp bend, and the boardwalk turns left. A tangle of climbing aster and moonflower attracts zebra swallowtail butterflies. Zigzagging, the boardwalk reaches another set of benches at 0.5 mile. Dropping down into a hammock of water oak, live oak, and saw palmetto, the trail leaves the boardwalk behind. By the look of the boards lying around, this part of the trail can get mucky at times. Work your way down the rough path between the saw palmettos, the gouges in the earth the work of feral hogs. A coral snake disappears under a rotten log. This beautifully colored creature is a relative of the cobra, and one of Florida's venomous snakes. Its coloration is similar to that of the harmless scarlet kingsnake and scarlet snake. To distinguish among the species, look at the color bands: A coral snake's head is always black, with slim bands of yellow separating the thick bands of red and black. Unlike rattlesnakes and cottonmouths, the coral snake is not especially aggressive. Its toxic venom can only be injected when the snake chews on a soft part of the victim's skin.

The trail turns sharply left just beyond some benches at an interpretive marker. A barred owl swoops down from a live oak, perhaps in pursuit of the coral snake. You clamber up onto another stretch of boardwalk at 0.7 mile, following a fern-strewn strand of pond cypress on the edge of a broad prairie. Sawgrass pokes through the boards. The loop ends at 0.8 mile, at the PARKING LOT sign. Continue straight to exit to the parking area. When you reach the clearing, you've completed a 1.1-mile hike.

FLORIDA TRAIL

Built and maintained by the Florida Trail Association, a 14-mile-long linear trail connects Corbett with the adjoining Dupuis Wildlife Management Area. Corbett and Dupuis are two of the few places in South Florida where backpackers can stretch their legs. There are two campsites along the trail between the two preserves, allowing you round trips of 10 or 22 miles. With two cars, you can backpack a 27-mile linear route from the Corbett trailhead to the Dupuis trailhead.

Due to hunting regulations, however, the Dupuis WMA trails are closed to hikers during much of the prime hiking season. Corbett WMA remains open all year, but is a busy hunting area. Use common sense and check hunting dates beforehand; always wear a blaze-orange vest during a hunt. The trail is somewhat rugged for young children. Since the land is a mosaic of wet prairies, expect to wade along the way.

To complement your walk along the Hungryland Boardwalk, this hike provides a 4.1-mile day-hike exploration of the beauty of Corbett's prairies. Backpackers should obtain the official Florida Trail Association map to plan a lengthier trip into the wetlands. To start, walk over to the FT sign at the edge of the clearing in front of the parking area and sign in at the trail register. A narrow but well-defined footpath leads into the pine flatwoods through the saw palmetto. Look carefully into the grasses around you to notice the wildflowers: flat-topped goldenrod and hatpin, foxglove and rattlebox. Giant star rush draws your eyes to the footpath. And don't miss the terrestrial orchids that abound in this preserve. Look for the delicate pale grass-pink, and the bearded grass-pink. Glades lobelia sprouts everywhere, showing off purple flowers with a white mouth. No matter what time of year you visit, you'll always see blooms throughout the preserve, from delicate white violets to drumheads with purple tops. Leavenworth's tickseed, endemic to Florida and taller than regular tickseed, shows off bright yellow petals tightly packed around a black center. The Seminoles created an infusion from this wildflower to treat heat prostration.

As you skirt a large wet prairie on the right, a limestone road parallels on the left—the main road through the preserve. Seeping in from the wet prairie, puddles form in the footpath. The trail draws closer to the water's edge, and you see a flock of ibises in motion, skimming low across the prairie. After 0.5 mile, the trail crosses a faded swamp buggy track leading out into the water. Like airboats, swamp buggies were invented in the 1920s to penetrate the vast watery wilderness of the Everglades. With lightweight frames and massively oversized tires, they have no trouble penetrating the wetlands. Since there is no regulation in Corbett on where they can and can't go, expect to see swamp buggy tracks many times along this hike.

After jogging out toward the main road, the trail winds through an extensive understory of saw palmetto under the slash pines. Two red-bellied woodpeckers work their way up a pine trunk. Dropping down through a ditch, the trail rises back up into the pines and saw palmettos. Just past a deer stand, keep alert for a trail junction where both blue and orange blazes are painted on a slash pine. The main orange-blazed trail heads straight across the dark waters of the prairie. The "keep dry" blue-blazed trail turns to skirt the bulk of the water. Turn left and take the blue-blazed trail. You'll come back the other way on the return trek.

When you emerge at the preserve road, you've hiked 1 mile. Turn right. Just after you see a blue blaze on a tree next to the road, keep alert for a faded double blaze pointing out a right turn back on a narrow footpath into the prairie. You've missed the deepest part of the water, but this area is damp no matter the time of year. Foxglove and glades lobelia flourish here, nurtured by the wet marl soil of the Everglades. As you reach an open prairie, the trail curves to the left. Look across and to the left for the next blue blaze as you skirt the edge of the water, where the sudden shimmer of mosquitofish breaks up the mirrorlike reflection of sky and clouds on the surface. A thicket of sawgrass forms the heart of this prairie, and little green corkwood bushes surround the footpath. Staring off into the seemingly infinite distance, you enjoy a panorama of prairie and pines against the deep blue sky.

At 1.3 miles you reach a small diamond-shaped sign indicating the junction with the main orange-blazed trail. Turn left. The path across this next section of prairie is ill defined, broken up by swamp buggy trails. Keep watching for the next orange blaze as you slosh toward the power line in the distance. Tiny delicate carnivorous sundews grow on the drier spots, while *Sabatia grandiflora* sports a stunning five-petaled pink flower on its 3-foot-tall stem. An American kestrel soars over the pines, crying out *scree-scree*. Rising to slightly higher ground, the trail passes through a saw palmetto and gallberry thicket before dropping back into the water.

When you cross a swamp buggy trail with power-line poles on the left, continue straight toward the power lines, emerging on the sand road beneath them at 1.5 miles. Look for next orange blaze at a diagonal to the left. Wade through a watery drainage to pick up the trail as it enters the pine woods. The trail jogs right as it comes up to another vast expanse of wet prairie. Keep alert—the blazes twist and turn through this next section. Dahoon holly shows off its red berries. Watch for the next blaze as you cross the wet end of a prairie, where the trail works its way to a shelf along the edge of a stretch of pine flatwoods. A lone pond apple shows off its dangling fruits. You cross numerous swamp buggy trails that collect deep water in their tracks. The trail curves right and heads for drier ground, rising into the pine flatwoods. Climbing fern engulfs the trees in the hammock. A zebra longwing butterfly rests on a bright orange butterfly weed. Pine lilies peer out of the wiregrass. At the double blaze, the trail rises up and curves to the right, following a narrow footpath crowded by gallberry. Keep alert for the next blaze as you progress, since numerous game trails dovetail into the hiking trail through the dense thicket of saw palmetto and gallberry.

Crossing a swamp buggy trail, the trail swings sharply left. Keep to the cleared corridor. Flickers flutter back and forth between the pines. Sawgrass invades the footpath as you come up to the edge of a wet prairie on the right. The trail is following a ridge between two prairies, and the ridge continues to narrow until it comes to a point, forming a rocky peninsula. Your day hike ends at this peninsula, with the lovely sweeping expanse of wet prairie in front of you. Yellow bladderworts float through the shallows. An outcrop of marl defines the end of the peninsula. Islands of sand in the prairie contain tiny blooms of terrestrial bladderworts, tall yellow and small purple varieties, with bladders at the ends of their root systems to suck up microscopic creatures from the damp sand. You've hiked 2.1 miles. If you plan to camp out at Bowman Island, a tree island out in the midst of the swamp, you must wade across this prairie to the next blaze on a distant slash pine flanked by dahoon holly. Continue carefully along the blazed path for another 3 miles to the campsite, and be sure to carry a map and compass.

To complete your day hike, turn around and follow the orange blazes back along the peninsula, paying carefully attention to the route as you wind through the thickets of saw palmetto. After 2.4 miles you emerge on the edge of a prairie, skirting its slimmest point to wade across and follow the trail back to the power lines. A leopard frog makes a flying leap out of the water and into a saw palmetto frond. Following the edge of the wet prairie, the trail emerges at the power lines. Look for the diamond-shaped FLORIDA TRAIL sign, shot through with many bullets, to orient you with the trail's direction leaving the power lines. Follow the blazes back across the prairie.

At 2.9 miles, you reach the junction with the blue-blazed trail. Continue straight this time to cross the prairie—if you haven't gotten your feet wet by now, you will. The trail curves left to enter the pine woods. Tall slash pines yield to a head-height thicket of saw palmetto and gallberry. When you emerge from the woods, a deer stand is to the right. You reach the edge of prairie at 3.1 miles. Head out into the open and look for the orange blaze on the far side. Aim for it as you wade, pushing through the drifts of bladderwort tangling around your feet. A post with an orange blaze provides confirmation of your route in the middle of the prairie. Look straight ahead for the next blaze, high up on a slash pine on the far shore.

When you reach the shoreline, continue straight through the break in the saw palmetto. You immediately meet the junction with the blue blazed trail. Continue straight. Follow the hog-beaten track through the thicket. Be mindful of the poison ivy, half hidden in tall sand cordgrass. Paralleling the forest road again, the trail works its way along the prairie edge until it emerges back into the clearing at the trail register. You've completed a 4.1-mile hike. Be sure to sign out on the register before you leave.

36

Royal Palm Beach Pines Natural Area

Total distance (circuit): 3.6 miles

Hiking time: 2 hours

Habitats: Cabbage palm flatwoods, pine flatwoods, prairie

Maps: USGS 7½' Palm Beach Farms; park map

As more and more woodlands and farmland in the Royal Palm Beach area become gated and walled housing developments, natural space continues to vanish. Well hidden in a warren of newly sprouted neighborhoods, the Royal Palm Beach Pines Natural Area preserves nearly 770 acres of pine flatwoods and delicate prairies. Before development, this mosaic of habitats was an integral part of the northern Everglades. Soaking up rainfall during the wet season, it would gently overflow through shallow channels into the Loxahatchee Slough, which historically drained the northern Everglades to the Loxahatchee River and, eventually, the Atlantic Ocean. With access to the slough now broken, these delicate wetlands vanish under deep water in the wet season, only to reappear as the rains taper off. The adventuresome hiker will find this hike an interesting wade during the wet season, and a comfortable walk during the dry season.

Finding the preserve, however, is a trick. From Florida Turnpike exit 99, take FL 704 (Okeechobee Boulevard) west into Royal Palm Beach. Pay attention to the sudden drop in the speed limit from 50 to 35 miles per hour, as there's almost always a speed trap there. After 5.8 miles, you reach Royal Palm Beach Boulevard. Turn right and continue north 1.6 miles to Crestwood Boulevard. Make a left onto Crestwood, and drive 0.6 mile to the entrance of the Saratoga Pines subdivision, where you'll see a tiny brown directional sign for RPB PARK. Inside the subdivision, turn right onto Saratoga

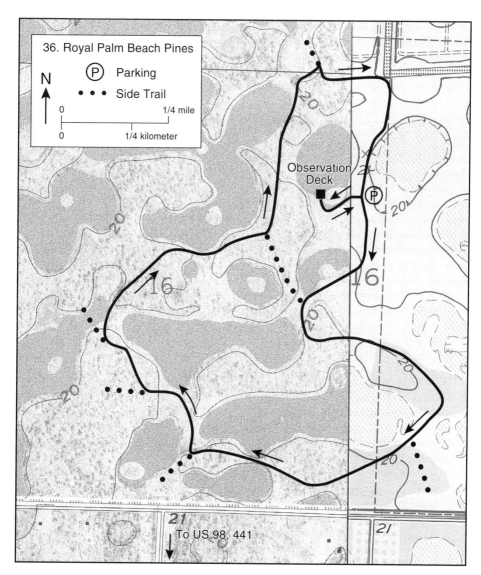

Observation Deck

To US 98, 441

Boulevard West, which makes a sharp curve to the right. After 0.7 mile, turn left onto Natures Way. This short street leads into the parking lot loop for the natural area. Open sunrise to sunset, the preserve provides two separate sets of trails—hiking and equestrian—and portable toilets near the trailhead. Take adequate water and a hat, since the trails have very little shade.

Start your hike from the trailhead kiosk by picking up a map (a necessity in this preserve; it's easy to get lost) and walking down the sidewalk leading into the wet pine flatwoods. Bog buttons and flat-topped goldenrod rise above the tall, dense carpet of grasses, and vivid red sprays of pine lilies attract your eye to the bases of the slash pines. This short wheelchair-accessible trail winds through the forest to reach a boardwalk out over the wet prairie. Blue jays chase each other around a wax myrtle. Marsh ferns wave in the breeze across the water. The trail ends at a canopied observation platform with a sweeping view of the wetlands. Crest raised, a colorful green heron stalks the shallows.

After some quiet contemplation at the marsh, turn around and walk back down the sidewalk to the kiosk. The hiking trails begin on the far side of the kiosk, to the right, and are blazed with red squares (for the Slash Pine Hiking Trail) and yellow circles (for the Pine Lily Hiking Trail). The two trails start out together from the kiosk down a corridor carved through the dense understory of saw palmetto and gallberry. Carolina wrens flit between the slash pines. At the T intersection with a jeep road, turn right. The trail system follows old jeep roads from this point on, so you can be assured of a broad footpath. With brilliant blue wings against a base of black, a white peacock butterfly rests on a saw palmetto frond. As the trail curves to the right, you see a plant that looks like star rush but is much too tall—a relative of star rush, the tall *Rhynchospora latifolia* displays crinkled white leaves atop a slender stem reaching 3 or 4 feet tall.

At 0.7 mile, the trails diverge at a fork. Keep to the left to follow the Slash Pine Hiking Trail, which forms the outer loop. Following the red blazes, you skirt another broad wet prairie, where clouds reflect in the open patches of still, dark water. An osprey flies across, searching for fish. A faint jeep trail comes in from the right as the trail curves left—watch for the red marker to guide you. Outlined with dew, tangled spiderwebs glisten in the early-morning sun. Notice the diversity of grasses that make up the understory of the flatwoods wherever it touches the prairies. Like a giant green candy cane, sugarcane plumegrass displays alternating stripes of white and light green. Wiry bluejoint panicum grows along the wet edges of the prairie, as well as other varieties of *Panicum*. Tufty-topped bushybeard bluestem grass prefers the shade of the pines.

The prairie grasses are a place to look into, not at, for their rich complexity. Within the grasslands, you'll see so much texture and color. Dozens of different wildflowers stretch their faces to the sunlight: the white bulbs of button snakeroot; the three-petaled blooms of yellow-eyed grass, floating atop their tall stalks; and St.-Andrew's-cross, a small shrub with four-petaled yellow blossoms. A glimmer of pink in the grass comes from the showy petals of pale meadow beauty, offset by slender yellow stamens. Pine lilies add brilliant splashes of color to the grassland as you continue along the trail. From November to August, look for the pale purple bell-shaped blooms of the pine hyacinth, a showy flower from a plant once used by the Seminoles to treat sunstroke.

A great pondhawk dragonfly rests on a dahoon holly, green wings fluttering against the red berries, as a covey of mourning doves rise up from the trail. The orchidlike blooms of duck potato bob at the tops of tall stems. The trail curves to the right into a stand of younger slash pines, the grassy carpet beneath them broken up by scattered clumps of silvery green saw palmetto. Barn swallows swoop overhead as you catch the retreating few feet of a darkly scaled snake vanishing into the grass—a black racer.

You reach a T intersection after 1.3 miles. The trail to the left leads to a

Wet prairie in Royal Palm Beach Pines Natural Area

neighborhood park. Turn right to continue on the Slash Pine Hiking Trail. A belted kingfisher skims the tops of the slash pines as you approach another open, wet prairie. Land managers are actively eradicating melaleuca from this preserve, as evidenced by the hundreds of slender peeling stumps rising from the wetland. The trail turns to the right, entering a corridor of saw palmettos under cabbage palm flatwoods. Goldfoot ferns dangle from the trunks of the cabbage palms. You emerge onto open prairie, where the trail divides two distinct wetlands. Mosquitofish shimmer in the open water as a great white heron flies overhead. During the wet season, this portion of the trail will definitely be under water. When you see the NO HIKERS symbol at 1.8 miles, make a right—this is one of several places in the preserve where it's easy to get lost. The red blazes lead you down a fading jeep trail, overgrown in places. Keep watching for the next blazed post as you skirt the edge of the open prairie. At the T intersection, turn left. Keep alert as you pass each blazed post. At the third marker, the trail leaves the jeep road by making a sharp right—and it's easy to miss. Red blazes lead you into an open area with scattered slash pines and clumps of silvery green saw palmettos.

After 2.2 miles, the Slash Pine Hiking Trail meets the orange-diamond-blazed horse trail at a T intersection. Turn right to continue around the loop, taking the right fork (the one with the NO HORSES symbol) at the next junction. Saw palmetto and wax myrtle crowd the understory of the pine flatwoods, where older, gnarled and twisted trees provide more shade, and tall hatpins poke their white bulbous tops out from among the grasses. More showy pine lilies catch your eye. As you walk down the

grassy footpath, several white-tailed deer race across, crashing into the underbrush. When you reach the T intersection at 2.7 miles, you meet up with the yellow-blazed Pine Lily Trail. Turn left to follow it along the outer edge of the preserve. Here, the wet prairie seeps close to the footpath, sparkling with its thousands of small wildflowers—miniature tickseed, pale meadow beauty, and star rush among them. Notice the delicate pinkish trumpet-shaped blooms that droop from the end of each stem of the small butterwort. Related to the floating bladderwort, this carnivorous plant traps and digests insects on its sticky leaves.

As the trail continues, it rounds the vast wet prairie that you originally visited along the wheelchair-accessible path. A flock of white ibises soars overhead, the black undersides of their wings showing. Bromeliads appear on the slash pine trunks and branches—particularly giant wild pine and cardinal wild pine, both showing off bright red and purple crested blooms in summer. As the trail turns to the right, you see in the distance power lines and the roofs of houses. The trail curves left to skirt a large wetland, which commonly overflows and inundates this section of the trail. Keep to the right to stay in the shallows. When you reach the T intersection at 3.1 miles, turn right—the yellow trail to the left leads to the park's northern entrance.

Entering the cabbage palm flatwoods again, the trail rises until it reaches permanently dry pine flatwoods on the southern fringe of the preserve. The denser pine forest provides shade as the trail curves sharply right to follow the park boundary, emerging along the edge of a large wetland. Lacy greenish yellow wormwood waves beneath the pines, and a pileated woodpecker rattles its beak against a tree trunk. You see the observation deck along the wetlands on the right as you approach the parking area. Walk around the gate to the parking area, completing your circuit hike of 3.6 miles.

37

Arthur M. Loxahatchee National Wildlife Refuge

Total distance (two circuits): 3.3 miles

Hiking time: 1 hour, 45 minutes

Habitats: Freshwater marsh, sawgrass prairie, cypress strand

Maps: USGS 7½' University Park; park map

It's the Everglades as interpreted by the hand of humankind. Here on the edge of Boyton Beach, where farmers coax copious quantities of vegetables and tropical fruits from the rich, dark soil that once lay under the river of grass, the Arthur M. Loxahatchee National Wildlife Refuge provides a buffer against further development into the relict Everglades, now sliced and diced into canals and impoundments that prevent flooding of nearby suburbia while providing vast marshlands for waterfowl to roam. This is an excellent site for bird-watching, where you'll see dozens of species and perhaps even thousands of birds on a single roam down the impoundments on the Marsh Trail. For a taste of the vanished cypress slough ecosystem of this region, you won't want to miss the short but beautiful Cypress Boardwalk behind the visitors center.

To get to the refuge, use Florida Turnpike exit 86, FL 804 (Boyton Beach Boulevard), and drive 1.9 miles west to US 441. Alternatively, use I-95 exit 57 to head west on FL 804. When you reach US 441, turn left and continue 2 miles south to the large brown NATIONAL WILDLIFE REFUGE sign at Lee Road. Turn right. The automatic gate remains open during the hours posted, typically between 6 AM and 8:30 PM. Stop at the self-pay fee station to drop off your park use fee ($5 per motorized vehicle, or $1 per pedestrian) and grab a park brochure with a map. Turn right at the VISITOR'S CENTER sign and park outside the center.

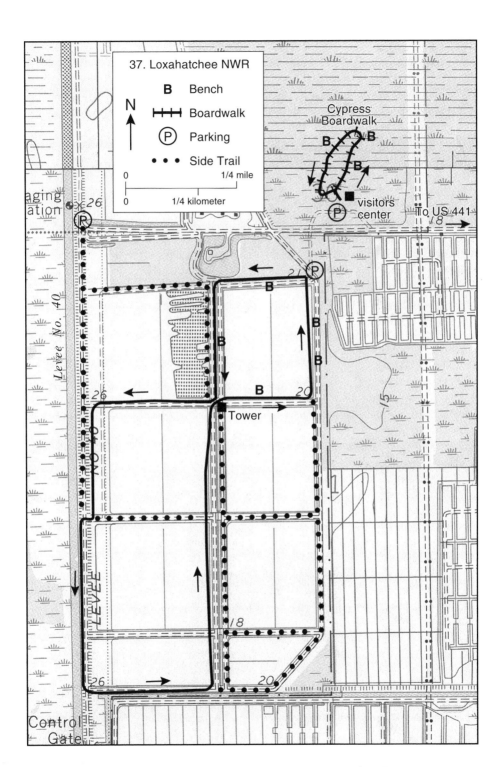

37. Loxahatchee NWR

B   Bench

Boardwalk

(P)   Parking

• • •   Side Trail

N

0   1/4 mile

0   1/4 kilometer

Cypress
Boardwalk

B   B

B

visitors
center

To US 441

aging
ation

26

Levee No. 40

26

40 N

26

Tower

LEVEE

18

20

20

18

21

Control
Gate

CYPRESS TRAIL

After you walk through the interpretive displays at the visitors center, head out the back door and down the boardwalk to start the Cypress Trail, a short loop through a picturesque cypress strand. If the visitors center is closed, go around the front and down the boardwalk to start your walk. With scattered guava, pond apple, and strangler fig, this jungle of pond cypress represents one of the many sloughs that used to naturally channel water from Lake Okeechobee to the Everglades. In 1928, a tidal surge created by a massive hurricane caused Lake Okeechobee to suddenly overflow toward the southeast, its traditional drainage route, spilling into the farming towns of Belle Glade and Pahokee. More than 1,800 people drowned, making it the second deadliest hurricane in U.S. history. To prevent a reoccurrence of the tragedy, the Army Corps of Engineers built a strong earthen dike around Lake Okeechobee, the third largest freshwater lake entirely within U.S. borders. The Corps of Engineers also built canals to channel existing sloughs and streams, drying out the land and changing the hydrology of the Everglades forever. With the steady flow of water removed, the rich mucky soil beneath the river of grass was exposed. Huge agricultural operations moved in, stripping away the original wetlands and planting thousands of acres of sugar cane. Loxahatchee National Wildlife Refuge protects more than 221 square miles of the original Everglades.

Keeping in mind the lack of railings on this boardwalk, look up and around you to marvel at the density of air plants in the cypress trees. You see occasional giant bromeliads. Ferns burst from the tiny islands created by the bases of the cypress trees, with giant sword fern and giant leather fern arching well overhead. Slender strap ferns climb up the sides of rotted trees. Reminiscent of the witch's apple proffered in *Snow White,* ugly green apples dangle from the pond apple trees, while red blanket lichen (also called baton rouge) marches up the bark of the cypresses. This is a beautiful and richly textured place, a complex ecosystem that has all but vanished from this part of Florida. Benches provide several spots for you to sit and contemplate the forest. Take your time and enjoy—but put on the insect repellent. The interpretive walk is over almost too soon, as you return to the parking area after 0.4 mile.

MARSH TRAIL AND IMPOUNDMENTS

Return to the park entrance road and turn right. Watch for the MARSH TRAIL sign, just before the bus parking. Make a left and drive down to the parking area in front of the large chickee. Start at the trailhead sign in front of you and pick up an interpretive guide. A labyrinth of levees slices through this 272-acre marsh, creating 10 separate impoundments known as Compartment C. In all, the refuge encompasses nearly 140,000 acres of marshland. In its interior, far from the levee trails, Florida panthers still roam, and tens of thousands of wading birds make their homes on tree islands, coming together in massive rookeries to raise their young.

Take in the broad view to the left, looking off to a distant observation tower across the purple blooms of pickerelweed. Look closely for white splotches on their stems, near the waterline: the eggs of the apple snail. Apple snails only thrive in clean freshwater marshes. The refuge actively manages these impoundments as habitat for migratory wading birds, native wading birds, and the endangered Everglades snail

Vast impoundments along the edge of the Everglades

kite, a rare raptor with an unusual appetite for apple snails, its primary food. Like the limpkin, the snail kite has a beak especially adapted for extracting these snails from their shells. Since its habitat of choice is the sawgrass prairie, the population of this small raptor has steadily diminished in proportion to the drainage of the Everglades marshes for agriculture and development. The invasive growth of water hyacinths across open water in the marshes also impedes the snail kite's ability to find its food. Less than 1,000 of these endangered birds still exist. About the size of a crow, males are a dark slate color, while females and young sport a brownish hue. Their distinctive curved beaks are their most dominant feature.

Two Gulf fritillary butterflies chase each other as you walk down the levee, arriving at a bench in the shade of a sea grape and a mahogany tree. Although it hails from the Caribbean, the mahogany also appears in dry tropical hammocks in South Florida. White herons poke their heads above the pickerelweed as you continue up to a T intersection with another levee. Turn left to continue along the edge of the C-7 impoundment. A canal parallels on the right, where a Florida softshell turtle lounges along the steeply sloped bank. Swamp lilies show off their delicate white blooms. A Louisiana heron picks through the shallows, striking suddenly to spear a small fish. Distinctive with its white belly, it's also called the tricolor heron and is slightly larger than a little blue heron. You hear squawking overhead as a flock of glossy ibises wings past. As you walk down the levee, a great blue heron stands next to a bench. On level ground, you can get a good look at just how large these birds are, standing nearly shoulder high to an adult. Although they range into the northeastern United States, the great blue heron is one of Florida's most common year-round resident waterfowl.

Red-winged blackbirds crowd the limbs of a dead tree as you approach the observation tower. A small alligator slides down the bank of the canal and into the water with a resounding splash. At 0.5 mile, you reach the observation tower. Climb up and enjoy the expansive view across the entire Compartment C complex. With binoculars, you may be able to see an Everglades snail kite searching for snails in the open waters of Impoundment C-8. Watch the willows, too. Snail kites roost in willows on tree islands and on the edges of marshes, making their nests close to the ground. The male snail kite builds the cuplike nest as part of the courtship ritual, and will attempt to attract a mate with gifts of food and sticks, showing off with aerial acrobatics. After the mating pair bonds, the female lays one to five eggs. Parents share the responsibility of incubating the eggs, which take up to a month to hatch, and of raising and feeding the young—until one of them decides to desert the nest, permanently ending the relationship and leaving the other to fledge the young.

The Marsh Trail continues to the left, but you'll enjoy better bird-watching by taking a longer route around Compartment C. Turn right and cross the bridge over the canal to the open area fringed by pond cypresses. Moonflower spills over the primrose willow. Continue straight up the levee between Impoundments C-3 and C-2. Listen to the constant chatter of the birds, hidden amid the cattails and spikerush. Yellow water lilies drift across a patch of open water. Passing a levee coming in from the left, you start to see scattered tree islands—primarily willows and giant leather ferns—that provide shelter and nesting spots for waterfowl. At the T intersection, turn left, heading toward the distant copse of trees.

Although Compartment C is chopped into a variety of wetland habitats by the levees, it still contains something truly special—a relict portion of the Everglades. Before the days of canals and levees, a sheet of water used to seep southward from Lake Okeechobee into this region during the rainy season, with the deepest water flowing through the cypress sloughs. Sawgrass lines the impoundment on the right as you parallel a taller levee, the C-40. Hikers and bikers can use the C-40 to access the Hillsboro Area of the refuge, located 12 miles south. It's a long, shadeless walk, however—better suited to mountain biking, since there are no camping facilities for hikers. Star rush grows in the trail as you come up to a T intersection at 1 mile. Turn right, passing the left-hand turnoff as you climb up the limestone embankment to the C-40 levee. From the top of this levee, you get a sweeping view of all the impoundments and of the paralleling canal. Turn left to head south along the C-40, following it to the end of Compartment C. Watch off to the left, as large numbers of both white and blue herons spend their time hunting for fish and frogs through this section of the marsh. When you reach the copse of trees—a tangle of melaleuca and Brazilian pepper—at 1.4 miles, turn left to drop down onto the levee following the C-30 canal.

As you sink back down to the level of the surrounding marsh, cattails tower over your head. Watch for alligators as they cruise through the broad, sluggish flow of the canal. Australian pines line the far levee. Tall maidencane grows in front of a stand of alligator flag. Coming to a junction with the central canal and its levees at 1.7 miles, turn left and stay on the west side of the canal. As you continue to parallel stretches of open water, watch for common moorhens. Although their plumage is dark, their red beaks stand out against the dark marsh water. When startled, they run across the surface of the water as they take flight.

Passing an overgrown levee coming in from the left, you continue along the canal. Casearweed pokes out of clusters of primrose willow. A little blue heron fusses as it rises up away from the canal, a streak of indigo against the blue sky. At 2.1 miles, you pass another levee to the left. The impoundment hides behind a screen of wax myrtle. Continue up to the cypress-lined clearing and turn right to cross the bridge. As you pass the observation tower, you once again join the interpretive Marsh Trail. Stop and admire the tawny chestnut brown bird with white spots: It's a limpkin, another protected species. Its diet consists mostly of the apple snail—so it competes with the snail kite for food—although it will also eat freshwater mussels, insects, small frogs, and crustaceans. Plumage hunters almost wiped out the species, but the limpkin has started to rebound in protected shallow wetland impoundments such as this refuge.

After you pass the shaded bench, watch for snail kites and anhinga in the pond cypresses on the islands in the impoundment to the right. Snail kites prefer to roost in willows, but can be seen in tall cypresses when willows are scarce. Anhinga sit in the trees to dry their wings. Also known as the snakebird or water turkey, the anhinga dives under water to chase its prey. Since it does not have oil glands to waterproof its feathers, the anhinga must stretch out its wings to the sun to dry.

At the T intersection, turn left. You've hiked 2.6 miles. Off to the right, the refuge borders private sugar cane fields—but the birds don't care. You'll see them on both sides of the levee. Flanked by coco plums, a bench overlooks a broad view across Impoundment C-7. Cabbage palms close in as you reach the end of the trail, passing a bench at marker 9 before you reach the MARSH TRAIL sign and the parking lot. Walk across the lot to return to your car, completing a 2.9-mile hike.

38

Tree Tops Park and Pine Island Ridge

Total distance (circuit): 3.1 miles

Hiking time: 2 hours

Habitats: Hardwood hammock, freshwater marsh

Maps: USGS 7½' Cooper City; park map

What changes the centuries have wrought. The view from the top of Pine Island in Davie is now a sea of housing developments stretching to the horizon, rather than the river of grass of the Everglades that Abiaka and his tribesmen traversed in the 1830s. Also known as Sam Jones, the inspirational medicine man left a legacy that endures to this day: the Seminole and Miccosukee tribes in Florida. Not content with the federal government's directive to remove all Native Americans to Oklahoma so Florida settlers could take over the land, Abiaka, a Miccosukee, kept the resistance alive with his "no surrender" attitude, leading his people first in ambushes during the Second Seminole War against the U.S. Army, and then into hiding deep into the Big Cypress and Everglades during the Third Seminole War. After the U.S. Army departed South Florida, Abiaka was the only remaining Seminole leader in the state, a pinnacle of strength around whom his people would gather. Pine Island was his home, a patch of pine rocklands jutting above the wet grasslands of the Everglades and topped with a village of at least 20 huts.

"Save the Everglades!" was the political platform on which Napoleon Bonaparte Broward was elected Florida's governor in 1905, but for him it had a very different meaning. Dredges and dynamite became the order of the day as he orchestrated plans to drain the vast prairies east of the Atlantic Coastal Ridge to create farmland. Dynamite blew apart the

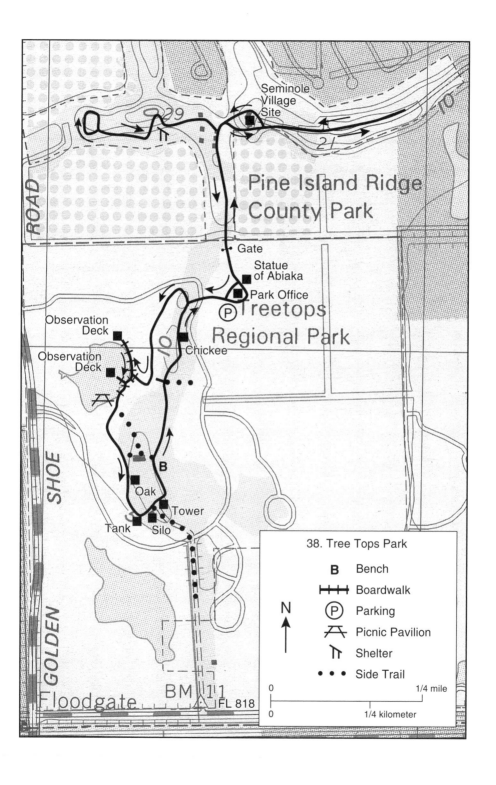

Seminole
Village
Site

Pine Island Ridge
County Park

ROAD

Gate

Statue
of Abiaka

Park Office

Treetops

Regional Park

Observation
Deck

Observation
Deck

Chickee

SHOE

B

Oak

Tower

Tank Silo

GOLDEN

BM 11

Floodgate   FL 818

38. Tree Tops Park

B   Bench

├┼┼┤   Boardwalk

Ⓟ   Parking

⩍   Picnic Pavilion

⋔   Shelter

• • •   Side Trail

N

| 0 | | 1/4 mile |
| 0 | | 1/4 kilometer |

fragile karst underpinnings of the Everglades, the limestone karst that soaked up water like a sponge; dredges created canals to divert the rainfall. Much of Palm Beach, Broward, and Dade Counties is now a wholly artificial landscape, the rivers and sloughs drained dry, the landscape laced with canals and piled with fill on which millions of homes are built.

To access Pine Island and its associated ridge, a trail system connects from the adjacent Tree Tops Park, a recreational facility with nature trails under spreading live oaks. From I-595, take exit 4, Nob Hill Road. Drive south on Nob Hill Road for 2.6 miles through Dania. Turn left into the park entrance. On weekends and holidays, you'll pay an entrance fee of $1 per person. Open 8 am–sunset, the park provides not just hiking trails but also paved trails for biking, an equestrian trail system, dozens of picnic pavilions, and a concession for canoe rental. Driving in on the entrance road, you pass a lake on the right with the canoe rental facilities and traverse a crosswalk with the sign NATURE TRAILS TO TREE TOPS TOWER. This is the south end of the trail system. Continue driving along the entrance road until you reach the large parking lot at the end of the road, in front of the park office.

Start your hike by walking over to the park office (rest rooms and soda machines are on the side of the building) to pick up a map and look at the interpretive displays regarding Abiaka and the Seminoles on Pine Island Ridge. Exiting from the back door, walk down the side stairs and turn left to follow the paved walkway. At the T intersection, turn left. The paved path loops around the back of the center under a canopy of spreading live oaks. You pass a bronze statue of Abiaka, and the sign TO PINE ISLAND RIDGE. A paradise tree rises out

of the understory of wild coffee, and a flock of noisy monk parakeets chatters in the treetops. Descended from birdcage escapees, these brilliant green birds range throughout urban areas in South Florida. Although they hail from South America, they found a natural niche in Florida's habitats—that abandoned by North America's only native parakeet, the Carolina parakeet, which was driven to extinction in the 1920s.

Crossing a horse trail and a bridge, you come to an open gate leading into Pine Island Ridge. The paved path continues uphill into this linear park; houses crowd the edges of the greenway strip as you plunge into the cool shade of ancient live oaks swaddled in resurrection ferns and epiphytes. Chunks of limestone remind you of what lies beneath your feet, the dense limestone bedrock of South Florida. At 0.4 mile, you reach a fork. Turn right, and make a right at the T intersection. Tall slash pines crown the hill. At the next T, keep right. After meandering out along the shadeless ridge, scattered pines and grass, the paved path ends, becoming a jeep track stretching out to a gate in the neighborhood. Turn around and return to the hill to explore. Blue jays and blackbirds poke through the grass looking for food. At the fork in the trail, keep right and climb up to the top of the hill where the Seminole village once stood, dating back to at least 1828. Surrounded by sawgrass prairies, three islands made up the settlement, a haven for refugees from the Second Seminole War.

Abiaka proved his military mettle against the U.S. Army in the Battle of Okeechobee, December 1837, by setting up "a brilliant defense" with the lake behind his people and swamps in front, the hammock in which they waited prepared for battle, trees notched for gun mounts, warriors posted in the tallest trees to scout the movements of the incoming troops. Although greatly outnumbered, the Seminoles felled 138 soldiers, killing 26, while 25 of their own people were counted as casualties. As a result, the U.S. Army both respected and feared what Abiaka would do next. On March 22, 1838, just a few months after respected Seminole leader Osceola died in prison, unjustly captured under a flag of truce, Lieutenant Colonel James Bankhead and Major William Lauderdale encountered the Pine Island settlement with their troops. While the Seminoles had taken defensive measures, the U.S. Army attempted to surround them on three sides, using rowboats in the deeper water and soldiers wading through the shallows. Outnumbered and outmaneuvered, Abiaka gathered up his people and vanished deeper into the Everglades, abandoning Pine Island. In later years, after the wars, Seminole refugees made their home on the high ridge, but the drainage of the Everglades around them forced them to move to uncontested ground.

When the pavement ends, cross the grass to the far side of the hill. A red admiral flits across a mat of *Rubiaceae,* the tiny purple flowers emerging from a dense mat. At the junction of trails, go straight, and keep to the right at the next fork, following the paved path as it flows around a large slash pine. Passing a couple of jeep trails, you arrive at a small pavilion. A hiking trail leads away from it to the right. Follow the bark-chip path into a thicket of wild coffee and beautyberry under the oaks. When the trail splits, keep left. Although this is disturbed land, the trail is an attempt to show you the natural undeveloped environment of Pine Island, where Abiaka and his family once lived. Gumbo limbo and

red bay tower overhead. Long-tailed skippers nose at a mangrove rubber vine, a relict of the Everglades habitat. The trail winds behind houses. Invasive air potato vines dangle like beaded curtains, creating a jungle feel. Masses of lantana show off their multicolored blooms. A staghorn fern drapes from its shieldlike attachment on a live oak.

At 1.3 miles, you reach a LOOP TRAIL sign. Turn left and continue down the narrow path. Large bromeliads grow from the crooks in the trunk of a red bay. A bed of sword fern thrives in the shade of a live oak. As you come up to a fence line, the trail turns to the right past a wild coontie—perhaps the descendant of one planted by the Seminoles for starch. Passing by a papaya tree, you finish the loop. Turn left to walk back down the trail, keeping right at the fork so you emerge at the shelter. Follow the paved path back to the trail junction, and keep to the right to follow it back to the gate at Tree Tops Park. You've hiked 1.7 miles.

When you return to the statue of Abiaka, turn right and go up the steps to circle the building; the trails continue on the other side of the park office. From the front entrance, follow the sidewalk up along the park road, crossing the road marked AUTHORIZED VEHICLES ONLY to reach the HIKING TRAIL sign. Turn right and enter the forest. At the T intersection, turn right. A footpath winds under the tall live oak and red bay, the understory of wild coffee and marlberry in dire danger of being smothered by air potato. Turn left at the T intersection, passing a bed of snake plants. At the next T intersection, turn right. The trees in front of you bend as if shaped by the wind, and the bright red blooms of firebush dance like little flames. This is an oak hammock with a tropical understory, although the masses of

The canopy view from the observation tower

air potato creating the green jungle canopy are *not* part of the natural environment.

The trail drops down to skirt a wetland area, and you hear the chirps of crickets and frogs. When you reach the paved trail, keep going—it leads to the start of the marsh boardwalk. The marsh is a shallow wetland reminiscent of the Everglades habitats that used to surround these rocky ridges. Ghostly swamp lilies rise from mats of purple pickerelweed, and duck potato waves in the breeze. Sawgrass and giant leather fern lend a primeval feel. Turn right at the T to walk down to the end of the boardwalk. Lance-leaved arrowhead surrounds a small tree island, while alligator flag grows from the deeper water. Yellow lotuses drift against the dark water, riffled by the wind, their stems moving as if manipulated from below. The boardwalk ends at an observation platform with benches, a great place to watch for alligators and wading birds.

Turn around and walk back up the boardwalk, passing your incoming route to get to another observation platform on the right, a good place to peer down into the water to see catfish, crappie, and sheepshead nosing around in the coontail. A cormorant perches in a nearby tree, eyeing the piscine bounty. Turn right as you leave the observation platform to continue along the boardwalk as it curves around, ending at the shoreline after 2.4 miles. Continue straight past the picnic pavilion. At the junction, keep going straight, but turn right at the following T intersection. You pass a trail coming in from the left as you walk through the hammock, well shaded by the dense live oak canopy. At the next trail junction, keep right. Pause to take a look at the fallen oak. A strangler fig emerges from its base. With its trunk lying on the ground but the tree very much alive, two branches of the oak have grown upward into trees.

Dropping downhill under tamarind trees, the trail curves left around a murky concrete tank. With the tropical trees and air potato all around, it's reminiscent of a jungle scene in India. But this is one of a handful of remnants of the dairy farm that occupied the property before it was preserved as a park. Coming up to a wall of strangler fig, the trail goes to the right around a large concrete silo. Walk around the front of the silo for a better look at the massive strangler fig tree, where the footpath meets the paved trail at 2.7 miles. The paved path to the right leads to the marina. Turn left and go up the ramp beneath the fig, entering a scene straight out of *Swiss Family Robinson* as you climb up the tall tower into the canopy. Although the tower isn't tall enough to let you look over the canopy, the view from within is beautiful: You can look over the butterfly orchids, wild pines, and resurrection ferns in the limbs of the ancient live oaks, feeling as if you're a part of the forest canopy. As you come down the staircase, notice the other crumbling ruins of the farm being eaten up by the "jungle" around you—a concrete slab and stairs vanishing under the waves of green.

At the bottom of the tower, take a right down the short set of stairs and turn right. At the T intersection with the paved trail, turn left. At the next T, turn right as the trail winds past a bench and through a grove of oaks swaddled in air potato. Where the paved trail loops back on itself, turn right to follow the footpath into the oak forest, brushing by indigoberry and wild coffee as you come up to another trail junction. To the right is a dense thicket. Turn left, walking past caladiums growing under the oaks. A yellow rat snake slips by, intent on following the scent of a mouse. Emerging at an open spot, you see the park road and pavilions to the right. At the trail intersection, continue straight; you meet up with the paved trail again at 2.9 miles. Make a quick right, then a left to get back on the natural footpath through the forest.

Draperies of air potatoes festoon the oak hammock as you duck under a trunk leaning well over the trail. Passing a chickee used for cultural education, you're reminded of the Seminole influence on this land. Pine Island and Tree Tops remain sacred sites for the Seminoles. As well as the importance of Abiaka and his home to their people's history, tucked away in these forests are the ancient burial mounds of their ancestors. Walk softly as you ponder how much the land has changed since the Seminoles lived here. When you emerge at the junction of trails right behind the HIKING TRAIL sign, turn right. At the parking lot, make a left to walk back to your car. You've completed a 3.1-mile hike.

39

Main Park Road Nature Trails

Total distance (five circuits): 2.7 miles

Hiking time: 1 hour, 45 minutes

Habitats: Sawgrass prairie, cypress strand, tropical hardwood hammock, pine rocklands, slough, mangrove forest, coastal prairie

Maps: USGS 7½' Royal Palm Hammock, Big Pine Key, Pa-Hay-Okee, West Lake, Flamingo; park map

Most visitors to Everglades National Park are on a day trip, looking to quickly sample what this vast mosaic of habitats has to offer. For those who don't have the time to get off the beaten path to enjoy the park's wilder trails, there are six excellent spots along the Main Park Road where you can access short interpretive nature trails. Scattered from Royal Palm Hammock to Flamingo, each offers a quick dip into the varied ecosystems of Everglades National Park, with excellent opportunities for wildlife-watching.

ROYAL PALM HAMMOCK

Known as Paradise Key in the 1890s, this mile-wide strand of royal palms in the midst of the Everglades was the first part of the region to be preserved for posterity. Henry Flagler owned the land; it was up to a fiercely dedicated conservationist, Mary Munroe, to convince him to part with the island. Construction plans for a highway to Flamingo were under way, a highway that would cross Paradise Key. Munroe asked, and J. E. Ingraham, one of Flagler's directors, agreed. Opening in 1916, Royal Palm State Park (predating the Florida State Parks system) encompassed the hammock, and provided a rustic lodge for its steady stream of visitors, attracting scientists, botanists, and birders to this lush forest topped with swaying royal palms. The Florida Federation of Woman's Clubs managed the park until 1947, when it became part of the new Everglades National Park.

Royal Palm Hammock contains two of the park's most popular nature trails: the

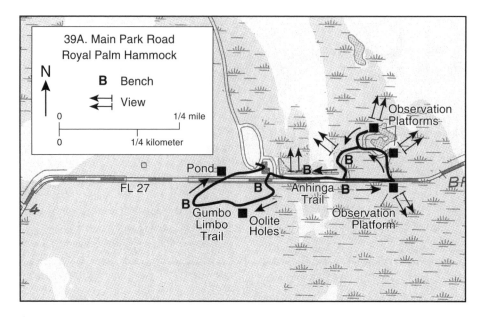

39A. Main Park Road
Royal Palm Hammock

N

B Bench

View

0   1/4 mile

0   1/4 kilometer

Observation
Platforms

Pond

FL 27

B

Gumbo
Limbo
Trail

Oolite
Holes

Anhinga
Trail

B

Observation
Platform

Anhinga Trail and the Gumbo Limbo Trail. From the park entrance, drive south 1.6 miles to the turnoff on the left for Royal Palm Hammock. Continue another 1.9 miles to the parking area. Walk up and check out the exhibit hall, then leave through the back entrance to walk along the walled waterfront of Taylor Slough. You'd almost swear you were at a zoo, since massive alligators lounge unnervingly close to the walkway, and the trees resonate with the gravelly clamor of cormorants. At the junction, turn left to start the Anhinga Trail. It's a paved trail—part of the original Ingraham Highway to Flamingo, circa 1916—leading out to a boardwalk that loops out over the dark waters of the slough. You'll be amazed at the sheer numbers of birds around you: cormorants hanging out on fence railings and in the trees, great white herons picking at the mud, little blue herons stalking the shallows, and anhinga drying their wings while roosting in the wizened pond apple trees. Like cars backed into driveways,

alligators lie at distinct intervals along the slough, their snouts touching the water. A cormorant swims defiantly close to a 'gator nestled in among the swamp lilies. Plenty of benches afford opportunities for visitors of all ages to stop and savor the plentitude of wildlife.

After 0.2 mile, you pass a boardwalk to the left—the return loop. Continue straight past the covered bench and interpretive signs. The open vista of sawgrass yields to tall rushes and water lilies; Florida cooters perch on tall lumps of silt. At the fork in the trail, keep right to walk down to an observation platform on Taylor Slough, a great viewing spot for watching alligators scramble up and over one another for a place in the sun. Cold-blooded creatures, they lie dormant in the mud when a winter chill arrives. But on a nice sunny day, they leave the water to warm up.

Turn around, walk back up the boardwalk, and turn right. As you cross the inky water of the slough, watch the alligators silently propel past. Cormorant droppings stain islands of pond apples, and a cormorant perches on the covered observation platform. At the next junction in the boardwalk, turn right to walk down to another platform, this one overlooking a stretch of open water where moorhens nose through the rushes. Returning back up the path to the T intersection, turn right. The boardwalk wraps around to face the visitors center, giving you a great view of the open slough. With most of the Everglades a shallow sheet of flowing water, the deeper sloughs attract a wider range of wildlife. A blue heron perches on the railing. When you reach the end of the boardwalk at the paved trail, turn right and walk back down along the waterway.

At 0.8 mile, you reach the trailhead for the Gumbo Limbo Trail. Turn left to walk into a lush tropical hammock crowded with towering gumbo limbo, mastic, and blolly trees. This short trail winds through the dense forest, where you can see the bases of the royal palms: stout and well rounded. Humidity fills the air; wild coffee and sword fern compete for the understory. Look carefully for white specks in the trees, and you may see a *Liguus*—a Florida tree snail. Living only in dense hammocks in South Florida, these colorful snails slide along the branches and trunks of smooth-barked tropical trees like Jamaican dogwood and poisonwood. An overlook gives you an up-close view of a water-filled solution hole (or oolite hole, named for the oolitic Miami limestone underlying the Everglades), where water spangles cover the dark surface. Walking beneath pigeon plum and paradise tree, satinleaf and poisonwood, you emerge at a short boardwalk across a broad solution hole, where cattails rise from standing water. After 1.2 miles, you emerge from the woods at the edge of the parking lot, completing the two trails.

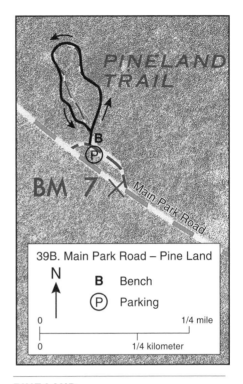

39B. Main Park Road – Pine Land

N

B   Bench

Ⓟ   Parking

0   1/4 mile

0   1/4 kilometer

PINE LAND

After you return to the Main Park Road, drive south 4.4 miles (past the Long Pine Key Campground) to the large PINE LAND sign. Turn right and leave your vehicle in the ample parking area. This 0.4-mile paved nature trail gives you an easy sample of the complex pine rocklands environment. Long Pine Key is one of only two places in Florida where a significant piece of this habitat remains.

Starting at the kiosk, take a right at the fork in the trail. The path curves through the woods past deep solution holes topped with a thicket of saw palmetto. Many of the spindly Dade County slash pines—a subspecies of the taller slash pines seen throughout Florida—were battered by Hurricane Andrew in 1992 but have since made a comeback. On this outcrop of the Atlantic Coastal Ridge, summer rains and

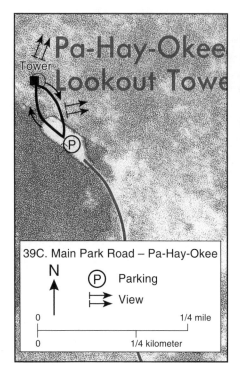

39C. Main Park Road – Pa-Hay-Okee

N

Ⓟ Parking

⊨➔ View

0   1/4 mile

0   1/4 kilometer

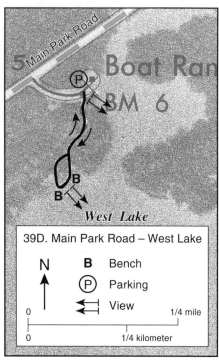

39D. Main Park Road – West Lake

N   B   Bench

        Ⓟ   Parking

        ⟵⊨ View

0   1/4 mile

0   1/4 kilometer

floods shape the soft Miami limestone into fascinating shapes: the landscape of karst. Boards help mark where deeply eroded solution holes stray a little too close to the footpath. You pass many solution holes, including a deep one the size of a small swimming pool, bounded by poisonwood. Tamarind and pigeon plum join poisonwood and wax myrtle in creating the middle canopy of the pine rocklands. Sumacs turn bright crimson in autumn. After 0.4 mile, you emerge at the kiosk; continue straight out to the parking lot.

For a more in-depth immersion into the pine rocklands habitat (and immersion may include getting your feet wet), plan to return to hike the wilderness trail through the Pinelands (Hike 41), which encircles this nature trail.

PA-HAY-OKEE OVERLOOK

As you drive south on the Main Park Road, notice the haunting forests of dwarf cypress sprinkled across the sawgrass prairies. Five miles south of Pine Land, there's a short boardwalk on the right side of the road at Rock Reef Pass that enables you to walk out into the cypresses.

Another 1.1 miles south of Rock Reef Pass, the turnoff for Pa-Hay-Okee Overlook is on the right. Drive 1.3 miles down the side road to the parking area. This is a particularly short walk, only 0.2 mile, but it gives you an excellent perspective on the river of grass. Walk up the broad boardwalk at the end of the parking lot, which sweeps upward into the treetops, headed for an observation tower. From the top, you can take in a broad view of the stands of cypresses marching out into the sawgrass prairie, an ethereal landscape of timeless textures. In the Seminole language, *pa-hay-okee* means "river of grass." And so it is—a shallow sheet of water almost 100 miles wide, moving ever so slowly toward the sea.

Walk down the steps from the observation tower, descending through coco plum and cypress, to the boardwalk along the sawgrass prairie. Your perspective shifts; you feel dwarfed by the landscape. Look straight down to see the rough limestone epikarst, a puzzle of pits and grooves beneath the water, coated in thick mats of periphyton, a living mass of algae, fungi, and bacteria. Continue along the boardwalk, enjoying the panorama, as it curves around and ends at the parking lot.

MAHOGANY HAMMOCK

Just 7 miles south of the Pa-Hay-Okee turnoff, this popular boardwalk trail through a mahogany hammock is now undergoing refurbishment.

WEST LAKE MANGROVE TRAIL

As you drive south from Mahogany Hammock, notice how habitat changes—the river of grass meets the sea as the freshwater marl prairies are supplanted by a tidal influx of salt water from Florida Bay, creating vast mudflats punctuated by mangrove islands. After 11 miles, you reach the turnoff for West Lake, on the left.

Paddlers enjoy the mangrove-lined tunnels surrounding this and the other brackish lakes around Flamingo, so a small building along the lake houses a canoe launch and rest rooms. The 0.4-mile nature trail starts at the parking area: the Mangrove Trail, a boardwalk through a dense tangle of mangrove forest. The roots of red mangroves dangle overhead, brushing your hair.

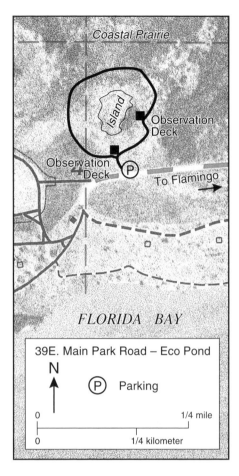

Despite devastation of this forest by two severe hurricanes over the past half century, the mangroves again thrive. It's a humid place. Notice the tremendous number of bromeliads climbing up the mangrove limbs, and the giant leather ferns rising from the brackish water. Half hidden by the shadows, a green heron picks its way down the crooked branch of a red mangrove.

When you reach the trail junction, turn left. The boardwalk emerges on the open waters of West Lake, where you can pause at one of the sets of benches and watch for birds in the mangroves. White

Ibises crowd the trees at Eco Pond.

ibises often pick through the shallows, and you might see a roseate spoonbill or two at low tide. As the trail rises back up into the mangrove forest, watch for mangrove crabs scuttling up their superhighways of mangrove stems. Returning to the beginning of the loop, you see giant bromeliads in the mangroves on the left. Continue down to the parking lot to complete the 0.4-mile loop.

ECO POND

The southernmost of the nature trails along the Main Park Road, Eco Pond is a favorite with visitors to the Flamingo Lodge and campground. Located 0.6 mile south of the lodge in Flamingo, this 0.5-mile loop trail circles a wetland created to naturally cleanse treated wastewater from the facilities in Flamingo.

Start your hike from the parking area, and walk up to the observation deck. Depending on the time of day, you'll see thousands of wading birds clustered in the island of buttonwoods in the middle of the lake—ibises, usually, jostling up against one another and fussing and squawking in an never-ending cacophony of bird talk. Roseate spoonbills wing overhead to distant islands, while white egrets pick through the cattails. Kingfishers swoop and dart over the water. Leaving the observation platform, turn left. A marsh rabbit pauses in midchew as you walk past the WILDLIFE OBSERVATION AREA sign. You hear the cackling laughter of a little blue heron. At the next observation platform, take a look down into the water, where an alligator is nestled up amid the coontail.

The trail curves to the left and you smell the sharp, sweet tang associated with the coastal prairie and its bountiful crop of pickleweed. Off in the distance, ibises cluster on snags and around water holes in the prairie. Near a bench, the autumn blooms of a sea myrtle drift like falling snow on the sea breeze. As the trail loops around, you enjoy great views of the open water, where moorhens squabble in the rushes. Coming back around to the main observation platform, you've walked 0.5 mile. Turn right to exit to the parking area.

40

Old Ingraham Highway

Total distance (round trip): 7.3 miles

Hiking time: 2 hours, 45 minutes

Habitats: Freshwater marsh, cypress dome, sawgrass prairie, tropical hardwood hammock

Maps: USGS 7½' Taylor Slough; park map

Opened in 1922 as the first motorway to Flamingo, the Old Ingraham Highway saw its share of Model Ts and other roadsters as intrepid motorists made their way down to the small fishing village on the edge of Florida Bay. After Everglades National Park was dedicated in 1947, the road continued to provide the park's visitors with access to Flamingo until a new highway opened in the 1960s. Created by a dredge floating on barges, much like the method used to push the Tamiami Trail across the Everglades, the Old Ingraham Highway was built on a pile of limestone dredged up out of the sawgrass prairie, which created the paralleling Homestead Canal. Parts of the old highway and the canal still stretch through the park, from a segment of the Anhinga Trail at Royal Palm Hammock (Hike 39) to the edge of Snake Bight (Hike 42). Off the beaten path, starting at Big Pine Key, you can walk the now eroding highway, one of the few long trails in Everglades National Park to expose you to broad vistas of the sawgrass prairies. It's also one of only two trails in the park with designated backcountry campsites. If you plan to backpack and set up camp, be sure to stop at any of the ranger stations beforehand for a backcountry permit. The Old Ingraham Highway has two designated campsite areas, the Ernest Coe Campsite (at 3.5 miles) and the Old Ingraham Campsite (at 11 miles). This hike describes a trip to the Ernest Coe Campsite. The trail is shared with bicyclists, but is usually broad enough (and desolate enough) to preclude conflicts.

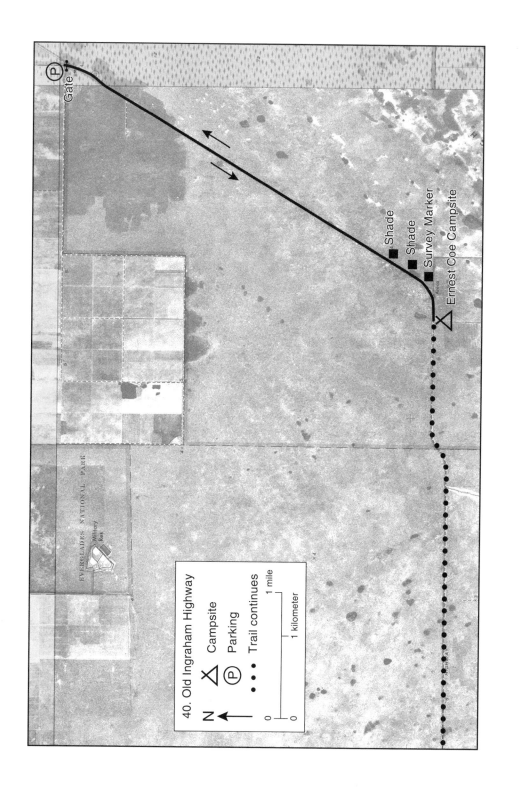

Gate

Shade

Shade

Survey Marker

Ernest Coe Campsite

EVERGLADES NATIONAL PARK

Military
Res

40. Old Ingraham Highway

N

△ Campsite

Ⓟ Parking

• • • Trail continues

0   1 kilometer
0   1 mile

To find the unmarked start of this trail, near the north end of the park, take the Main Park Road to the turnoff for Royal Palm Hammock. After 0.8 mile, turn right at the DANIEL BEARD RESEARCH CENTER sign. Drive another 0.5 mile to the HIDDEN LAKE ENVIRONMENTAL EDUCATION CENTER sign, and continue straight. The road surface becomes rough and eroded. Continue 1.5 miles to the gate that crosses the road, Gate 15, and park alongside the road. Do not block either gate. Your hike starts just beyond Gate 15.

There is little shade along the trail, so plan an early start and bring plenty of liquids. No matter the time of year, this trail is typically high and dry. Scrawny trees line both sides of the roadway, strays onto the disturbed land from tropical hardwood hammocks: a profusion of poisonwood, best identified by its droopy leaves and peeling black and orange bark; hog plum, with its distinctive oval leaves in both light and dark shades; and pigeon plum, with its spotted bark (easily mistaken for poisonwood) and dark fruits.

A coastal plain willow growing along the right edge of the trail indicates the dampness of the habitat as a segment of the old Homestead Canal begins to parallel the trail. In addition to providing road fill, the canal was built with the intent of channeling fresh water from Big Pine Key to Flamingo and Cape Sable, and creating a navigable waterway. With difficulty, the Audubon Society kept a section of it open for tour boats in 1949. But the very building of the canal, and the highway, disrupted the natural water flow across the river of grass and accelerated saltwater intrusion into the Everglades.

As you approach a trail junction at 0.6 mile, you catch your first glimpse of the sawgrass prairies off to the left, punctuated by dwarf cypress. Pale meadow beauty and yellow-tops show off their blooms along the edge of the trail. A grassy jeep track takes off to the right, pointed toward a now defunct missile base on Big Pine Key, manned during the Cuban missile crisis of 1962. Continue straight to stay on the trail. Hemmed in tightly by the thin strand of tropical hammock, the broad canal on the right serves as a water hole for alligators; watch for them sunning along its banks. Be mindful of the alligator crossings on the trail—places where the grass has been beaten down between the canal and the sawgrass prairie. Hog plum and poisonwood crowd out the views until you emerge onto the edge of the vast river of grass at 1 mile. Sawgrass recedes off to the horizon, unbroken except for tree islands. These scattered tropical hammocks, the only dry ground in the river of grass, provide refuges for wildlife.

At 1.7 miles, you pass a telemetry station. Look to the right and you'll notice broad views of the sawgrass prairie opening up into the distance beyond the canal, where pond cypresses cluster along the water's edge. A cormorant sits in a tall branch, drying its wings. The purple blooms of glades lobelia wave in the breeze. Sunlight glints off a treasure on the trail—a rounded apple snail shell, the color of white gold, left behind by an Everglades snail kite after its meal. Two great blue herons rise from the trees and fly away, casting massive shadows as they take off in different directions. You pause at a clump of panther scat deposited on the trail. The rarest mammal in Florida, the Florida panther is a subspecies of cougar. To help add genetic diversity to the dwindling Florida panther population, panthers from Texas have been introduced into the Everglades. Mating happens roughly and

Cypresses along the Ingraham Highway

quickly, and the female slinks off to bear her young alone. After 3 months of gestation, she delivers up to four spotted kittens, which stay with her for the first 18 months of their lives. While females stick to a territory of roughly 80 square miles, males are known to wander across up to 200 square miles. In case you're a little nervous about the idea of camping in panther habitat, don't worry—panthers are shy and go out of their way to avoid humans.

As you walk along, you enjoy an increasing number of scenic vistas of the sawgrass prairies between the screens of tropical trees. A charred poisonwood tree shows off its smooth orange inner bark. At 2.4 miles, the trail passes through a cypress dome. The tropical hammock crowds in closely thereafter, providing your first real stretch of shade along the hike. You emerge to walk along the river of grass. Decked out in bright red berries, a dahoon holly provides a stark counterpoint to the clusters of buttonwoods that begin to appear as the salinity of the Homestead Canal increases. After 3 miles, the forest closes in again, providing a shady corridor. Like a discarded necklace, the desiccated skeleton of a snake lies across the crumbling pavement, perhaps discarded by a bald eagle. The vegetation becomes denser on both sides, creating a shady spot at 3.2 miles. Beware of brushing against the poisonwoods and sharp sawgrass blades. Where marl washes across the trail, it turns gray when wet, creating a surface as slippery as an ice rink. Watch out for black slippery spots on the pavement, too, where periphyton attempts to retake the high ground. Coating the base of the sawgrass prairies, these living mats contain a mix of algae, bacteria, fungi, and invertebrates, and account for more than half of the vegetable matter in the Everglades.

After you pass a U.S. Geological Survey marker at 3.4 miles, the road starts curving to right, and the shoulder broadens. Pond cypresses reflect in the dark water of the canal. Look carefully at their bases and you might see an alligator nestled in among the roots. You pass a small data-collecting station on the left as trail curves farther to the right, continuing in the shade past an alligator crossing under a pond apple. When you emerge back into the sun, you can see the sawgrass prairie beyond the trees on the left. At 3.7 miles, you discover a broad open grassy space on the right that makes up the truly primitive (no water, no fire ring, no benches) Ernest Coe Campsite. Known as the Father of Everglades National Park, Coe founded the Tropical Everglades National Park Association in 1928, banding together like-minded South Florida conservationists to work for the establishment of a park. He lobbied, gave speeches, and dragged friends and media into the wilderness. By the time Coe died in 1951, his dream of seeing an Everglades National Park had come to fruition.

Although the campsite isn't much, it's a welcome spread of soft grass on which to pitch a tent. You can end your hike here, or continue backpacking along the highway to where it ends at the Old Ingraham Campsite, another 7 miles or so down the trail. On your way back up the road, savor the excellent views of the vast sawgrass prairie that is the Everglades. At 5.3 miles, a short boardwalk leads out into the sawgrass. It once ended at a data-collecting station, but now provides a platform for you to look off at the expanse. Passing the grassy road to the left at 6.8 miles, you return to Gate 15 after 7.3 miles of immersion in the Everglades.

41

Pinelands

Total distance (circuit): 5.9 miles

Hiking time: 2 hours, 30 minutes

Habitats: Pine rocklands, sawgrass prairie, freshwater marsh

Maps: USGS 7½' Big Pine Key; park map

Unnamed, unblazed, and wild, following an old jeep road, this extraordinary hike along the ecotone between two rare habitats—pine rocklands and sawgrass prairies—immerses you in one of the most intriguing parts of the Everglades: its rocky, pitted karst. Created by the steady erosion of the limestone bedrock, the barren karst is a jagged landscape of rough pinnacles, natural bridges, and solution holes. During the wet season, the trail vanishes under water. In the dry season, the solution holes provide havens for wildlife and host flourishing gardens of aquatic plants.

To find the trail, shown as the northernmost trail on the "Pineland Trails" map handed out at the visitors centers, drive along the Main Park Road south from Royal Palm Hammock. As you pass the Long Pine Key Campground (2.3 miles south of the Royal Palm Hammock turnoff), keep alert on the right for Gate G11, sitting slightly down from the shoulder of the road. The gate is 0.8 mile north of the Pine Lands parking area north entrance. Start your hike at the north end (Gate G11)—Gate G9 at the south end is more likely to get your boots wet, even in the dry season. With two cars, you can park at each gate and make this a 3.8-mile one-way hike. But with only one car, you'll need to use the park road as a connector. Leave your car at the Pine Lands nature trail parking area and start your hike by walking north for 0.8 mile along the left shoulder of the Main Park Road to access Gate G11. Keep alert for the turnoff on the left; the gate is

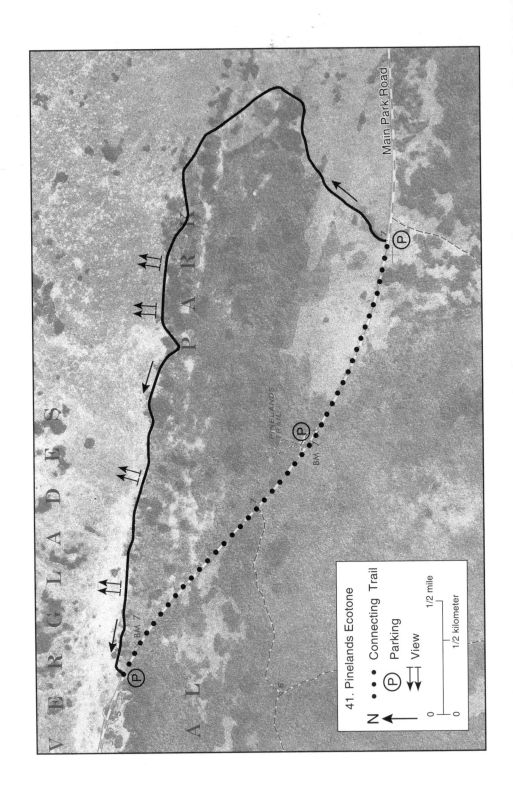

N

41. Pinelands Ecotone

• • • Connecting Trail

Ⓟ Parking

⇈ View

0 _____ 1/2 mile
0 _____ 1/2 kilometer

just a little way in from where the jeep trail leaves the park road.

As you walk into the pine rocklands, notice the skimpy slash pines rising against the blue sky. Hurricane Andrew trashed this forest more than a decade ago, but the wizened little trees fought back and reclaimed a foothold. Known as Dade County slash pine, a subspecies of southern slash pine, these trees—and this landscape—once ran along the Atlantic coastline throughout Dade and Broward Counties, defining the eastern edge of the Everglades. Now Florida's rarest natural community, extensive pine rocklands exist only here on Long Pine Key and on Big Pine Key (Hike 50) in the Florida Keys. Prized for their beautiful wood grain, Dade County pines vanished quickly beneath the logger's blade.

Despite the fact you're following an old road, the trail is rough and rugged—not recommended for young children—because of the loose limestone underfoot. Wear long pants and a long-sleeved shirt on this trail: The sharp stems of sawgrass intrude into the footpath, and clusters of poisonwood grow under the slash pines. Spiky long-stemmed pinnacles of stone define the edges of solution holes. Button snakeroot peeps out from beds of lovegrass. Corkwood rattles its orange berries in the breeze. Hog plums offer up a bounty of fruit, egglike in shape and color when underripe. Buttonwoods cling to the craggy forest floor. As the trail curves left, it weaves between small clumps of forest amid the plain of jagged rock, where winged sumac sports crimson fall colors and wax myrtle crowds the understory of each tiny hammock. A Florida petunia nods its purple head, while yellow bladderworts rise on slender stalks. You see glades lobelia, beard's-tongue, and tickseed,

hundreds of wildflowers creating splashes of color against the gray limestone.

Off to the right, a vast vista of the sawgrass prairie opens up as the forest on the left becomes a tangled wall of tamarind and poisonwood. Buttonwoods and poisonwoods crowd closely as the trail curves to the left around 1.6 miles. The footpath becomes even rockier underfoot. You're in the heart of the pine rocklands karst, surrounded by rough and jagged openings to solution holes below. Karst is an intriguing landscape where the rock acts like a sponge: It contains tiny networks of holes, cracks, crevices, and fissures. When the pine rocklands flood in the wet season, the water soaks right in and etches pathways through the stone, thanks to its corrosive load of carbon dioxide picked up from rotting plants and leaf litter. Mingling with the water, the carbon dioxide creates carbonic acid—the same acid found in soda pop. As the acidic water interacts with the limestone, it dissolves the bedrock, etching pathways through the karst as it flows down to the water table. When the pine rocklands dry out, the karst weakens, crumbling in places, creating rock pinnacles and solution holes.

Notice the dried bluish brown periphyton that covers all flat surfaces—the trail, the rocks, even bent blades of grass. In the wet season, this entire environment is part of the river of grass and would be several inches under water. Periphyton is the living web underlying the sawgrass prairie, containing a mix of algae, fungi, and bacteria, supporting the grazing of numerous microscopic invertebrates. The crusty appearance of dried periphyton comes from calcite crystals soaked up during the wet season from the karst. As you walk past a broad solution hole on the left, filled with

A solution hole along the sawgrass prairie

water, it looks like a garden full of succulents. Plants thrive around these almost permanent water sources, which trap receding floodwaters and cache the limited rainfall of the dry season. A yellow sulfur the color of lemons flits between the fruits of the hog plum, while a zebra swallowtail prospects for nectar in a swaying orange butterfly weed. Hairy trilsia peeps up from the edge of a solution hole. As you cross an open stretch of sawgrass prairie, you can see how the mats of periphyton plaster grass to the rocks during the dry season. At 2 miles, pause for a look at an extremely craggy solution hole on the right, filled with the fantastical forms of pinnacles and bridges in miniature. Another solution hole features duck potato growing in clusters from its watery base. Continuing through the pine rocklands, the trail is now entirely surrounded by craggy karst hiding under the sawgrass.

As you walk along the edge of a tropical hammock, surrounded by deep pits and grooves of solution holes, notice how the surface is so craggy that it looks like broken lava flows, the dried periphyton atop it mimicking a layer of ash. When you reach the open mudflat at 2.3 miles, keep to the left side to follow the trail. Numerous bathtub-sized solution holes filled with aquatic plants ring the trail. The trail curves left, rising up out of the rough karst into slightly higher ground topped by slash pines. You notice more scattered solution holes, but they are now more obvious as distinct geologic formations rather than dimples in a broken landscape.

Emerging along the sawgrass prairie, you walk the ecotone where the pine rocklands meet this vast sheet of marl topped by the river of grass. Sporting bright red berries, a dahoon holly stands guard over a coastal plain willow in a solution hole. In the distance, scattered stands of alligator flag in the sawgrass prairie indicate deeper spots where water will pool year-round. At 2.9 miles, the trail passes through a small hammock before returning to the edge of the prairie along the bare karst pinnacles. As the trail gets wet underfoot, watch your footing. When the periphyton gets damp, it's as slippery as black ice. The trail curves sharply left away from the prairie and heads back into the pine rocklands, passing through a heavy thicket of poisonwood and hog plum. Keep alert as to where you put your feet. There's the first of several small solution holes in the trail at 3.2 miles, just the right size for a misplaced step. Agaves grow beneath the poisonwoods. As the trail comes back out to the edge of the sawgrass, you pass a large water-filled solution hole at 3.3 miles, dense with aquatic vegetation. Delicate purple bubbles, the shells of apple snails are strewn across the trail, perhaps from the frenetic feeding of an Everglades snail kite. Tree snails live here, too—untouched by pesticides and other human intervention, *Liguus* colonies thrive on the tree islands in the sawgrass prairie. Watch the foliage for the glimmer of white that draws your attention to these delicate creatures.

You walk past a playground of karst surrounding a pond apple: rocks on top of rocks, some ash gray like lava flows, others shot through with holes. On the left, broad solution holes form small marshes. As the trail veers away from the prairie at 4 miles, water seeps into the periphyton on the footpath, creating a slippery mud that when crushed underfoot looks like swirls of turquoise paint: the mucuslike tendrils of blue-green algae that make up the majority of the periphyton mats.

Returning to the prairie's edge, the trail continues behind hammocks of buttonwood that shield your clear views of the river of grass. Passing another craggy garden, you see a broad depression out in the prairie, crowded with willows. Vegetation crowds close in at 4.3 miles as you drop down off a small hummock, walking through a low spot where the hydrated periphyton glows a bright greenish brown. Taking one last curve away from prairie, the trail ends at Gate G9. Walk around the gate and out to the entrance road. You've hiked 4.6 miles. To complete the full loop, turn left to carefully walk up the shoulder of the Main Park Road back to Pine Lands, completing your hike after 5.9 miles.

42

Snake Bight/Rowdy Bend Loop

Total distance (circuit): 7.6 miles

Hiking time: 4 hours

Habitats: Coastal prairie, mudflats, tropical hardwood hammock

Maps: USGS 7½' Flamingo; park map

Flamingos—they're not a common sight in the wild, especially not in the United States. We associate them with zoos, where they take on the hues of the food they're fed: creamy orange when stuffed with crabmeat, bright crimson with an ample supply of shrimp, pastel pink when they don't get enough seafood. Just 5.4 miles north of Flamingo, the settlement at the "end of the world" in Everglades National Park, the namesake of the original village can still sometimes be spotted along the mudflats of Snake Bight, a shallow bay inside of Florida Bay. To get there, though, you'll have to brave the Everglades' fiercest resident—the mosquito.

This hike combines two wild and interesting trails—Snake Bight and Rowdy Bend—along Florida Bay to create a 7.6-mile circuit, using the Main Park Road as a connector between trailheads. With two cars, you can shorten the hike to 4.9 miles. And if you're simply interested in walking out to Florida Bay to scan the shores for flamingos, you can shorten this to a 3.6-mile round trip. No matter the distance you plan to hike, no matter the time of year, bring mosquito gear! To maintain the natural rhythm of the wilderness, mosquito control is *not* practiced in Everglades National Park. Hiking out to Snake Bight, even in the dead of winter, you'll want to cover your arms and legs and carry a head net (available at the marina store in Flamingo) just in case: The mosquitoes are especially fierce along this trail, particularly after it rains.

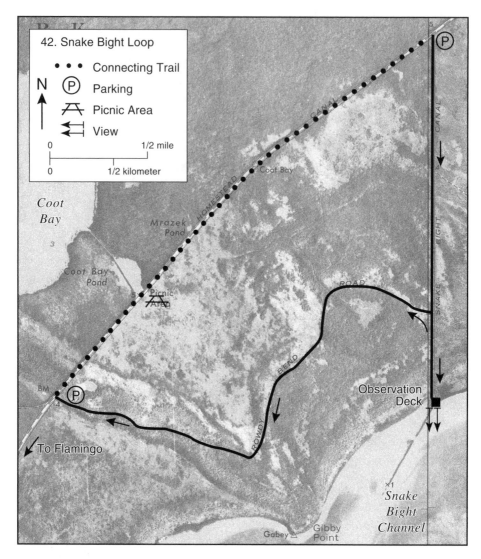

42. Snake Bight Loop

• • • Connecting Trail

N ⓟ Parking

🪑 Picnic Area

View

0 .... 1/2 mile

0 .... 1/2 kilometer

Coot Bay

Mrazek Pond

Coot Bay Pond

Picnic Area

Coot Bay

CANAL

HOMESTEAD

SNAKE BIGHT CANAL

ROAD

ROWDY BEND

Observation Deck

BM

To Flamingo

Snake Bight Channel

Gabey Gibby Point

From the visitors center in Flamingo, drive 5.4 miles north on the Main Park Road to the pulloff for Snake Bight, on the right. (If you're leaving a car at the Rowdy Bend trailhead, it's located 2.7 miles north of Flamingo on the right; park on the grass just after the ROWDY BEND ROAD sign.) Bicycles share both trails, so be cautious of bikers zipping past. Start your hike by entering the dark and junglelike green tunnel

paralleling the Snake Bight canal. This broad former road once led to the E. C. Knight Fish Company, a processing plant down at the end of the trail at Snake Bight. Despite this being an old road, the forest closes in so tightly you feel like you're on an adventure, walking beneath the peeling gumbo limbo trees. Purple morning glory blossoms dangle from vines strung across the black and red mangroves. Look at the base of a thick gumbo limbo: The bark wrinkles like elephant skin. Long spindly barbed-wire cactus sprawls across the leaf litter. A massive alligator vanishes in a brown swirl of bubbles as rain strikes the canal. Yellow nickerbean drapes its fragrant blooms over a West Indies mahogany. Looking up to watch a barred owl swoop low down the dark corridor, you spy butterfly orchids in the trees.

At 0.7 mile, you pass a land bridge on the left that leads to the old Crocodile Point trail system, no longer used by hikers. Although a backcountry permit will allow you to ramble, bushwhack, and camp anywhere you please inside Everglades National Park, rangers warn that the old cotton pickers' roads that once served as trails leading out to Crocodile Point now lead through thick forests of poisonous manchineel trees. If you're headed out for a bushwhack into any of the Everglades backcountry, have a chat with one of the Flamingo Visitor Center rangers beforehand about the terrain and plant life you'll expect to encounter in the area you plan to visit.

A coastal prairie eases in along the canal, with scattered buttonwoods and an understory of pickleweed, with that wonderful piquant salty tang that smells like nowhere else but Flamingo. Flesh-colored roots protrude from the base of a white mangrove trunk, its bark a dark mottled black. Black mangroves surround themselves with seas of pneumatophores. Christmas berry grows along the edge of the trail. Look up and you'll notice a proliferation of orchids in the canopy. After the rain, the mosquitoes grow thicker, virtual black clouds dogging your path. Get that head net on! After 1.4 miles, the Rowdy Bend Trail takes off to the right; there is no sign to mark the junction. Continue

straight. You cross a slippery mudslide, an alligator crossing from the canal to the waterhole on the right. Lignum vitae trees display their strangely crooked branches.

You emerge onto the coastal prairie after 1.7 miles, where thick salt hay carpets the trail, forming a soft blanket underfoot. A vast expanse of pickleweed stretches off to the right. The trail becomes marl, thick and gray and sticky when wet. Passing a bench as you walk through the former site of the fish-processing plant, you reach the boardwalk out to Florida Bay. The Snake Bight Trail ends at an observation platform with a sweeping view of the bay. Watch for the slim figures of flamingos on the mudflats. In the late 1800s, hundreds of flamingos used to wander these flats in the cooler months. But these days, perhaps 30 of the great pink birds arrive from the Yucatan Peninsula each December, scooping through the mudflats to feed. Bring strong binoculars, and consider yourself fortunate if you spot Florida's most unique migratory bird. The best time to look for them is high tide. Keep alert for movement in the water, as the endangered American crocodile also finds this habitat to its liking.

Leaving the observation platform, turn around and cross the saline creek back into the buttonwoods to return to the junction with the Rowdy Bend Trail. Sea lice scurry across the concrete-colored marl mud. A tiny purple bromeliad clings to a branch of a buttonwood. At 2.3 miles, you reach the junction with the Rowdy Bend Trail. It's not marked, so keep alert for the broad opening on the left that looks like a jeep road. Drop down into the buttonwoods and out into the coastal prairie, walking along a stand of sea oxeye with greenbrier and its red berries intertwined atop. The trail is very grassy, with lots of

Buttonwood snags in the coastal prairie

pickleweed beneath the buttonwood, interspersed with glasswort. Sweet acacia and limber caper grow in the understory. Look up into the limbs of the buttonwoods and you'll see air plants of all sizes clinging to their branches. In the early 1900s, buttonwood harvesting was one of the major income sources for residents of Flamingo. Charred into charcoal, the chopped wood was shipped to Key West to warm residents' homes.

The trail changes character at around 2.8 miles, leaving the coastal prairie for a corridor of dark tropical forest. Curving left, it passes a small swampy pond where bromeliads dangle from the buttonwood limbs. Narrowing to a very tight track—be especially cautious of bicycles here—the trail emerges along the edge of a vast open coastal prairie dotted with water holes. Prickly pear cactus towers out of

the pickleweed. Dipping in and out of the hammock, the footpath becomes cement-like marl underfoot at 3.4 miles, changing to a soft carpet of salt hay as you venture out into the open prairie. Ghostly gray in the dim light, the bleached bones of buttonwood snags gleam in the sun, silent sentinels of the passage of time. The trail becomes a deep rut through the prairie grass. You pass the remnants of an old faded sign at 3.8 miles, perhaps an old trail mileage marker in the buttonwood grove. The trail curves to the right. Prickly pear intermingles with barbed-wire cactus under the buttonwoods. A tangle of strangler fig emerges from a cabbage palm as the trail corridor narrows, entering the deep shade of tall, dark buttonwoods. As you round another bend, the ground boils with scurrying sea lice on the open marl. Continue down the tight corridor, walking under the cabbage palm, blolly, and mahogany. Roots make the walk rough going for a stretch.

Popping back out along the marl at 4.6 miles, you walk along the edge of more coastal prairie. Moonflower vines cascades from the buttonwoods, showing off massive white blossoms. After 4.8 miles, the hiking trail emerges on Rowdy Bend Road. Head straight. You reach the Main Park Road a few moments later, at 4.9 miles. If you're walking back to your car at the Snake Bight trailhead, turn right and head up along the grassy shoulder of the road. Mangrove forests crowd up to the edge of the berm. You'll pass Coot Bay Pond at 5.6 miles, where you can cross the road and stop to rest at one of the picnic tables while doing some bird-watching. A little farther north is Mrazek Pond, at 6 miles, with an interpretive marker on the east side of the road. By the time you reach the Snake Bight trailhead, you've completed a 7.6-mile hike.

43

Bear Lake Trail

*Total distance (round trip): 3.5 miles or
7 miles*

*Hiking time: 1 hour, 15 minutes, or
2 hours, 30 minutes*

*Habitats: Mangrove forest, tropical
hardwood hammock*

Maps: USGS 7½' Flamingo; park map

Sometimes a little serenity is all you need.
Hidden away at the end of the Bear Lake
Trail, a tiny beach on mangrove-lined Bear
Lake provides peace and quiet for the
hiker willing to plunge through a dark tropical forest in mosquito gear to seek it out.
From Flamingo in Everglades National
Park, follow the Main Park Road north for
0.5 mile to Bear Lake Road, on the left.
The road is frequently closed to traffic after
it rains, so you may find it necessary to
hike up the road to access the trailhead for
the Bear Lake Trail. Park on the shoulder,
and do not block the gate. Unless it's a
cool winter's day, be sure to dress for the
park's famous mosquito hordes. Carry a
mosquito head net, just in case.

Walking or driving along Bear Lake
Road, you parallel the Buttonwood Canal. A
small gap in the mangroves provides your
first look at this broad artificial waterway frequented by paddlers, anglers, and tour
boats. Dredging began in 1922. As the
dredge dug up rock, it piled it off to one side,
forming the roadbed for Bear Lake Road. By
1957, despite objections from ecologists
within the park, the canal stretched 3.2 miles
to link Florida Bay to Coot Bay. By enabling
the salt waters of Florida Bay to travel west
into the park, the canal modified Coot Bay's
environment, replacing fresh water with
brackish. The waterfowl—primarily ducks and
coots—that foraged in Coot Bay no longer
had a suitable habitat, and they left. Why,
then, build the canal? Starting at the
Flamingo marina, it's a crucial link in the
Wilderness Waterway, a maze of canoe

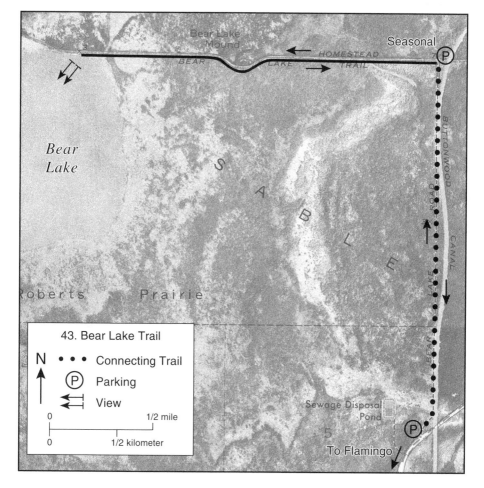

trails leading north from Flamingo toward Everglades City.

Tall gumbo limbo and mahogany trees remind you that you're walking along the edge of a tropical hardwood hammock. Like giant spiky lima beans, the seedpods of a gray nickerbean dangle from its meandering vines. Deep crimson flowers top a coral bean. On the left, the habitat quickly yields to a stretch of coastal prairie behind a screen of buttonwoods. A strong salt smell fills the air. Red mangroves arch their taproots out into the dark placid canal. After 0.5 mile, the road veers away from canal. Massive white mangroves form a dense canopy overhead, creating a long green tunnel through which the road continues.

Surrounded by the mangrove forest, the air becomes cool and damp. Gumbo limbo, strangler fig, and laurel oak grow close to the road's edge. The long vines of morning glory spill across the road, with its blossoms glowing vivid ultramarine. The dangling roots of red mangroves create virtual vines for swinging, reminiscent of a Tarzan movie. After 1.3 miles, the trail emerges from the shade to parallel the canal again. Watch for the gray bulk of an American crocodile cruising through the dark water—they've been sighted around the marina.

At 1.7 miles, you reach a T intersection; look for a sign with a canoe symbol. If the road is open to traffic, this is the parking area. Turn left to start the "official" Bear

It takes full mosquito gear to brave the wilds of the Everglades, except in the dead of winter.

Lake Trail, which begins just beyond the NO PARKING BEYOND THIS SIGN sign and leads you down a dark corridor under a dense canopy of tropical trees. Barbed-wire cactus snakes around the base of a tree-sized blolly. Bearing small red fruits, blolly is one of the first understory plants to establish itself in a tropical hardwood hammock environment. It often grows in dense thickets.

The canal on the right is the Bear Lake Canal, providing paddlers with access to Bear Lake. However, they must portage this section of trail from the Buttonwood Canal, putting in at a small dock. Go around the gate to continue down the trail, walking under the many gumbo limbos. Unlike the Buttonwood Canal, this canal looks muddied, the color of café au lait. Shared with bikes, the trail continues down a narrow corridor defined by the tropical vegetation. A mangrove forest lines both sides of the canal. Cardinal wild pine dangles its feathery scarlet blooms from a mastic. Looking somewhat like small snake plants, terrestrial *Spathoglottis* orchids peek from the leaf litter of the understory. A short thatch palm sits along the trail's edge.

By 2.3 miles, the mangrove forest crowds in on both sides. On the far side of the canal, the habitat yields to coastal prairie with clumps of buttonwood. A strangler fig snakes up a cabbage palm, wrapping it in a tight embrace. The trail rises up over knobby protruding roots and rocks, then drops back down and veers to the left along the spoil bank created by the digging of the canal. At 2.7 miles, the canal broadens. Take a moment to look at the water and study its movement. Although it looks like raindrops are falling in the water, it's not raining—you're watching the movement of water bugs. The trail veers right to parallel the canal, and

drops down to become a narrow track crowded by vegetation, edging ever closer to the water. You see the flutter of wings amid the interplay of shadow and light as ibises weave their way through the mangrove forest. The canal broadens, splitting into multiple channels. Walk through the dangling curtain of mangrove roots. A distinctly sulfuric smell fills the air, rising from the depths of the mangrove swamp. The pneumatophores of the black mangroves come right up into the footpath as you brush through more dangling vines. The footpath narrows. A ribbon of blue shows through the mangroves on the left as you approach the open waters of Bear Lake at 3.3 miles. Moments after crossing an alligator trail, you see a 'gator disappearing under the canal's surface, water swirling around the ridges on its head. A yellow-crested night heron perches on a nearby limb.

After 3.5 miles, the trail comes to an end on the shoreline of Bear Lake, at the little marl beach. Bear Lake is a broad expanse of tannic water—crystal clear at your feet, but a sea of brown beyond. Edged by mangroves, it's open and wild, a place where hundreds of white egrets perch in the trees and alligators swim swiftly across the sunlit waters. A flurry of splashing near your feet invites investigation. Is it a cormorant seizing a tasty needlefish? Or is it an alligator, thrashing its prey? Neither seems likely as the water calms and then, several minutes later, erupts again in the same peculiar rhythm. It's the peculiar breathing behavior of a school of walking catfish, *Clarias batrachus,* a non-native species that has cruised the canals and lakes of the Everglades since the mid-1970s. It's a Southeast Asian native, brought into Florida as an aquarium fish, and one of the stars of the 1960s roadside wildlife attractions that used to be found on every major Florida highway. With lungs rather than gills, the walking catfish must rise to the surface for air. But instead of coming up one at a time, as mullet do when airing their gills, the walking catfish wait for a group signal to rise to the surface, thrashing as they gulp air and head for the bottom.

Pull up a log and enjoy the serenity of this quiet spot—as much as the mosquitoes will allow—before making your way back along the linear trail. As you reach the lakeshore, keep alert on the right for a lignum vitae tree, its limbs crossing over each other in a distinct pattern that occurs only with this unusual species. Growing at the northernmost extent of its range, this West Indies tree is noted for its extremely slow growth and very dense hardwood—it will sink in water. With a name that means "tree of life," lignum vitae parts were once used to treat illnesses such as gout and syphilis. The largest stand of lignum vitae in the United States is on an island in nearby Florida Bay, Lignumvitae Key (Hike 47).

On the return trip, you especially appreciate the shady nature of this trail. Sunlight gleams through the peeling red bark of massive gumbo limbo trees. A zebra longwing butterfly floats from morning glory to morning glory, the ultraviolet purple of each blossom standing out sharply against the deep green of the forest. At 4.4 miles, the trail rises distinctly, following the spoil path along the canal. You reach the gate and canoe dock at 5.2 miles, emerging from the forest to Bear Lake Road.

If the road is open and you've parked here, you've completed a hike of 3.5 miles. If your car is out at the Main Park Road, however, turn right to walk back out along Bear Lake Road, completing a 7-mile hike.

44

Bayshore Loop

Total distance (circuit): 1.3 miles

Hiking time: 1 hour

Habitats: Coastal prairie, mangrove forest

Maps: USGS 7½' Flamingo; park map

Established in the 1890s, the fishing village of Flamingo sat along Florida Bay at the easternmost end of Cape Sable, where the coastal prairie yielded to hammocks of tropical trees. With no road to connect them to the mainland, the residents almost dubbed the place "End of the World," but settled on naming the village for the stately flocks of tropical birds that once roamed its shores. It was truly the frontier: House entryways featured smudge pots and palmetto fronds where you would stop and brush off the thick, clinging clouds of mosquitoes before you stepped inside. Notorious for a certain brand of lawlessness, this wild Florida frontier appealed to people who wanted to get away from it all. They grew sugar cane, coconuts, and pineapples, shot at wading birds to collect plumes, and cut buttonwood to burn down into charcoal for sale. In later years, they planted tomatoes and peppers, part of the vast vegetable farming industry spreading out of Florida City. But it was never much of a village—just a handful of homes with their homestead claims. In 1922, the Ingraham Highway connected Flamingo with Homestead, the first opportunity for residents to travel overland. And they did. Instead of growing, the population rapidly shrank. After waves from the "storm of the century" hurricane of 1935 salted the vegetable and cane fields, destroying the land for farming, the farmers moved away. And by 1947, the last residents of Flamingo called it quits, their lands taken as part of Everglades National Park.

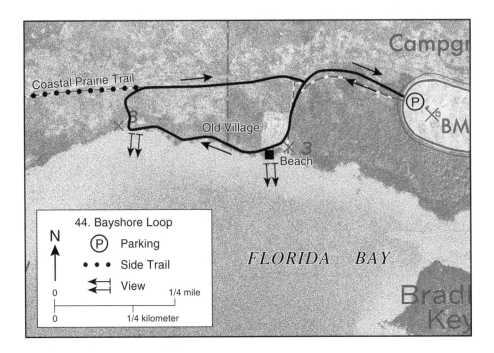

One remnant of those prepark times is the Coastal Prairie Trail, the longest hiking trail in Everglades National Park. It follows a cotton pickers' road. In 1932, Works Progress Administration crews fanned out across the Everglades looking to eradicate native wild cotton, a plant that grows to tree height. Since the wild cotton harbored pink boll worms, the U.S. government attempted to destroy all of Florida's native cotton to "protect" the cotton crops of the South. The Coastal Prairie Trail follows one of the old roads from Flamingo out to Cape Sable, providing a 14-mile round trip to a small marl beach called Clubhouse Beach, where backcountry camping is permitted (a permit is required from the visitors center). This trail also crosses vast shadeless open prairies filled with saline vegetation, however, and the powdery limestone marl footpath becomes a slippery, slimy goop after even a touch of rain.

Following a small portion of the Coastal Prairie Trail, you can enjoy a sample of the coastal prairie habitat *and* a beautiful walk along Florida Bay through part of old Flamingo by hiking the Bayshore Loop. Unlike most of the Flamingo-area trails, no bicycles are allowed on this route. To find the trailhead for the Coastal Prairie Trail, drive from the Flamingo Visitors Center south to the Flamingo Campground. Stop and tell the toll collector you're headed for the hiking trail. Where the campground road forks, keep to the right at the B-C loop junction, following the outer loop road around until you see the COASTAL PRAIRIE TRAIL sign on the right side of the road, in the shade. Park on the grass and start your hike by walking around the gate to access the trail. Scattered tannic pools reflect the shade of buttonwoods as you walk down the dark, shady corridor. Buttonwoods form a bower overhead, providing a canopy so low in places that you must duck under them. Like miniature mimosas, sweet acacias sport bright yellow blooms from amid their featherlike leaves. Vines twist tightly around towering bamboo, while moonflower spills out and over the understory into the trail.

After 0.2 mile, you reach a directional sign indicating the parting of the two trails. Turn left to follow the Bayshore Loop. Underfoot, the footpath is a bed of matted grass, heavily hemmed in by vegetation. The broad blooms of pink and white hibiscus nod in the breeze. As you duck and swerve through the brush, you see a glimmer of silver off to the left beyond the mangroves, catching the salt tang of Florida Bay as you come up to the mangrove forest on the water's edge. Looking like giant green beans, mangrove seedpods lie tangled up in the mats of sargassum washed up under the mangroves. Duck through the low limbs and look out over the shimmering water.

One of the unfortunate realities of shorelines in the Florida Keys is the debris washed up from careless boaters: a parade of flotsam and jetsam, everything from bumpers to buoys, fruit baskets, and shopping bags. At 0.4 mile, the trail emerges on a "beach" on Florida Bay—a broad opening between the mangroves with a hard-packed mat of sargassum above the marl. Hollow and crisp, the exoskeletons of giant horseshoe crabs rattle as the mild surf pushes them against mangrove roots. Since the trail sits on the high-tide line, you may get your feet wet. As you walk along, you're right behind the line of mangroves on the bay, so you can peek out here and there to see shorebirds roaming the mudflats. Watch for flashes of pink: Just 10 miles offshore is Sand Key, a rookery of

roseate spoonbills. One of Florida's most colorful birds, the roseate spoonbill sports bright pink plumage and a broad bill, which it uses as a sifter to scoop fish and insects from the mudflats.

You see a cluster of non-native palms growing along the water's edge, all coming out of a single base, perhaps planted in a front yard during Flamingo's heyday. Flamingo didn't get a lot of press until the death of Guy Bradley, the first Audubon Society game warden. In 1901, responding to pressure from the public, Florida outlawed plume hunting, one of the top ways to make money in the Everglades. Guy Bradley came to Flamingo soon thereafter with his wife and two children. His job: to stop the plume hunters from raiding the important Cuthbert Rookery at Cape Sable. After Bradley arrested a teenage hunter, the boy's father, Captain Walter Smith, murdered Bradley in 1905. With friends in the right places, Smith was never indicted. But the nationwide furor over Bradley's murder led to legislation that ended the plume trade in the United States. Buried at Cape Sable, near the rookery, Bradley is remembered with a monument in front of the visitors center in Flamingo.

Mimicking Spanish moss, clusters of sargassum drape from the tall standing roots of mangroves, drying as they sway in the salt breeze. A thicket of Christmas berry grows along the right side of the trail, sporting tiny lavender flowers in fall. Keep alert for a cistern hidden by the underbrush, one of the few remaining remnants of the fishing village—the wooden buildings and fishing piers of Flamingo rotted away long ago, returning to the earth. The trail curves right, the narrow footpath following the shoreline, rounding clumps of buttonwoods and

The coastal prairie, dominated by pickleweed

winding through masses of pickleweed. Also known as saltwort, this succulent plant prefers salt-rich soil and can be used as an herb to add salt to dishes.

At 0.7 mile, the trail curves away from the waterfront to head into the coastal prairie. A side spur leads off to the left out to one last view across Florida Bay. Continuing along the trail, you quickly reach a junction just beyond a stand of sea oxeye, where the landscape opens up to broad views of the prairie. Stay to the right. Within a few moments, you reach the well-worn footpath of the Coastal Prairie Trail. You've hiked 0.8 mile. Turn right to walk along the slippery, marly mud. Clusters of salt cordgrass grow between the sea oxeye and salt hay; glasswort shows off its red tips. Islands of buttonwood punctuate the prairie.

After 1.1 miles, the trail curves away from the prairie and into a stand of buttonwood to return to the junction, completing the loop. Turn left to head back to the trailhead. Emerging from the shady corridor of buttonwood, you complete your hike at the campground road after 1.3 miles.

VI

The Florida Keys

Key Largo Buttonwood   *Clyde Butcher*

45

Key Largo Hammocks Botanical State Park

Total distance (circuit): 1.1 miles

Hiking time: 45 minutes

Habitats: Tropical hardwood hammock

Maps: USGS 7½' Garden Cove; park map

It's the "Land of the Little Giants," according to *American Forests* magazine, keepers of the National Register of Big Trees, a statistical database ranking the sizes of America's trees. Fourteen national-champion trees lurk in the thickly wooded tropical hammocks of Key Largo Hammocks Botanical State Park–that's more national champions in one park than many states can claim. Yet they're tiny, and they're tropical. The smallest of the champions, a Florida crossopetalum (a member of the celastraceae, or staff-tree, family, like Christmas berry and boxwood) rises only 11 feet. Most of the champions are less than 30 feet tall, including the grand-champion cinnamon tree. And to think that this forest almost vanished under development! It's a success story in preservation of the natural habitats of the Keys.

Managed by nearby John Pennekamp Coral Reef State Park, the park covers nearly 3,000 acres along the north end of Key Largo, adjacent to Crocodile Lakes National Wildlife Refuge. As you drive north on US 1 through Key Largo, watch for the spot where FL 905 (Card Sound Road) turns to the right, 3.7 miles north of the entrance gate at John Pennekamp Coral Reef State Park. The trailhead parking area is on the right after 0.5 mile, in front of a large archway–a remnant of the Port Bougainvillea condominium complex, a monstrosity that all but paved over this precious hammock. Of 110 species of trees found in the Florida Keys, 40 of them can be seen along this trail. Plan your visit

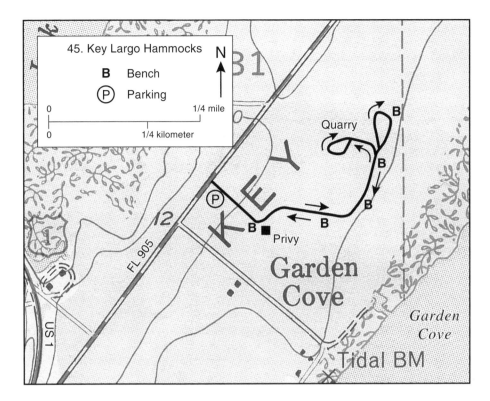

to enjoy the company of Ranger Joseph Nemec, who leads 35-minute guided walks through the preserve every Thursday and Sunday at 10 AM.

Park next to the archway and follow the pavement into the woods. It doesn't look like a trail at all—it's the old paved access road to Port Bougainvillea, and is open to bicycles. In his novel *Native Tongue,* Carl Hiaasen played off the attempted development of the hammock with a zany send-up. When the faux "Mediterranean coastal village" finally went belly-up in 1985, the state acquired the land and extended protection to 84 species of plants and animals living in this forest, the largest remaining tropical hammock in the United States.

Lignum vitae trees flank the front entrance. Listen for the rustle of palm fronds overhead, and look up: White-crowned pigeons nestle in the treetops. These threatened birds come for the copious amounts of poisonwood fruit in the hammock. Although poisonwood isn't something you want to lean up against—the toxicity of its sap is 10 times that of poison ivy—these mottled tropical trees bear fruits with a high amount of lipids, perfect for the nourishment of the pigeons. Interestingly, poisonwood is in the mango family, just like cashew trees, as is manchineel, the most dangerous tree in the United States. Although you won't brush into it if you stick to the trail, manchineel grows throughout Key Largo Hammocks, particularly in the backcountry. Its caustic sap burns through skin, and, according to those who have survived the experience, its tempting yellowish green fruits will tear up your insides as badly as a swig of drain cleaner. Yet it's a beautiful tree, easily mistaken for a slender ficus, providing a bounty for tropical wildlife adapted to its use.

As you walk along the ribbon of pavement, look into the forest, not at the trail. Identification tags help you pick out trees from the jumbled thicket. Keep alert for the scurry of rodents in the leaf litter. Both the endangered and endemic Key Largo wood rat and the tiny Key Largo cotton mouse make their homes in hollows at the bases of trees. Searching out these tasty morsels, indigo snakes slip through the underbrush. Pay attention to the smooth bark of the trees around you, where five different colorful varieties of the Florida tree snail, *Liguus,* slip along sucking up algae and lichens. Jamaican dogwood seems to be a favorite perch. Collected almost to extinction, these colorful snails are a species of special concern in South Florida—do not remove empty shells from the forest. The *Liguus* hunker down on a tree limb and seal themselves in during the dry season, in a process called estivation. When summer rains soak into their mucous seal, the snails detach, awakening from their hibernation to begin feeding.

The trail curves past a composting privy, and turns to the right past a picnic shelter. In the shadows of the hammock, an American kestrel perches in the low branches of a black ironwood. At 98 pounds per cubic foot, the black ironwood has the densest wood of any tree found in the United States. Tropical trees often have dense wood, perhaps as an adaptation against hurricane-force winds. In addition to black ironwood, the rarer red and white ironwoods also grow in the hammock. Pay attention to the plant identifications and notice the subtle differences among the various trees, which blend together to form a thick green screen on both sides of the old road. Not far off in the woods are the grand-champion roughleaf velvetseed and boxleaf stopper, at 17 feet and 19 feet, respectively. Of the all of the grand-champion trees in the hammock, few of them reach 30 feet in height—the 34-foot blolly being a notable exception.

As you walk past a bench to the start of a stone wall on the left, watch for a break in the wall. After 0.3 mile, turn left at the NATURE TRAIL sign and follow the narrow footpath into the cool deep shade of the forest. At night, apple cactus puts forth fragrant blooms, attracting pollinating moths. The leaves of torchwood trees give off a citrus oil odor when crushed. These delicate trees serve as a nursery for the eggs of one of the rarest butterflies in America, the Schaus' swallowtail. A subspecies of the giant swallowtail endemic to Key Largo, it spends most of its life in a pupal stage to survive the dry season, emerging to feed, mate, lay eggs, and die during the rainy season.

At the fork, keep left, walking past a number of small trees with interpretive markers. As the trail curves to the right, it comes out into an open, disturbed area on the edge of the forest, on the edge of a quarry created during the building of Port Bougainvillea. Walk down the short spur trail on the left for a sweeping view of the water. On the far side, wild cotton fills a human-made ravine. Considered the scourge of the agricultural industry in 1932, South Florida's wild cotton harbored pink boll worms, which the U.S. Department of Agriculture assumed would infect domestic cotton crops. Now, in an ironic touch, the species is protected and listed as one of Florida's most endangered. With showy creamy yellow flowers and fluffy cotton balls, it's a beautiful shrub.

Retrace your steps to the footpath and turn left. Make a right into the shady hammock at the four-way junction to complete the loop. When you emerge at the bench, turn left to parallel the wall back down to the pavement. Signs and fences warn you away from the crumbling ruins of the model condos of Port Bougainvillea, which the park hopes to raze at some point. But just as the jungles of India bury ancient temples, this tropical hammock works to erase the more recent hand of humankind. Although the remaining buildings of the old condo complex are closed to the public, they burst with life, with whisk ferns growing at the bases of supporting columns, and narrow-leaved figs breaking up through the concrete to mimic banyan trees.

When you reach the pavement, turn right. Turn right again at the T intersection. You've walked 0.8 mile. West Indian mahoganies form mushroomlike canopies overhead. It only takes a few moments to return to the NATURE TRAIL sign. Continue down the pavement, looking carefully at the parts of the forest that you haven't yet seen. Along with the mahoganies, gumbo limbo and poisonwood trees are the true giants, the high canopy of the hammock. But the thickets still guard their treasures: milkbark and red stopper, limber caper and saffron plum, a parade of tropical species like no other on this continent.

Continue past the picnic area, turning left to follow the road back out to the

White alamanda in bloom

parking lot to complete your 1.1-mile walk. If the stroll through the hammock has whetted your taste for more adventure, drive down to John Pennekamp Coral Reef State Park and request a day-use backcountry permit for a wander into the wilds of Key Largo Hammocks, down the old jeep trails that once served as access for far-flung parts of the Port Bougainvillea complex and a former missile silo complex from the Cuban missile crisis of 1962. No camping is permitted, so you must be out of the woods before dark. The backcountry includes vast salt flats along the edge of mangrove forests, as well as the dense thickets of tropical trees that make up Key Largo Hammocks. Take plenty of water, as water sources have high salinity. And don't forget a USGS map that shows the old roads, or use your GPS—with stands of manchineel and poisonwood in the hammock, you don't want to bushwhack your way back out to civilization.

46

Windley Key Fossil Reef Geological State Park

Total distance (circuit): 1.4 miles

Hiking time: 1 hour, 15 minutes

Habitats: Tropical hardwood hammock, mangrove forest

Maps: USGS 7½' Plantation Key; park map

One of only two Florida State Parks devoted to geology, the Windley Key Fossil Reef Geological State Park provides an up-close look at the ancient coral reefs that make up the Key Largo limestone formation that underlies the Upper Keys. Besides its significance as a geologic and historic site, the park protects more than 30 acres of tropical hammocks and mangrove forests once slated for condominium development. Fortunately, local residents petitioned the state to use the new Conservation and Recreation Lands fund to purchase the property. With help from public and private donations, the state bought this portion of Windley Key in 1985, saving it from development. The Alison Fahrer Education Center, which contains both the visitors center and a classroom complex, was named in honor of the lady who spearheaded the conservation effort.

Located 0.5 mile south of MM 85 on US 1 on Windley Key, the park entrance is on the right. The park is open 8 AM–5 PM, Thursday through Monday. After you park your car, walk up to the visitors center and pay your Florida State Parks entrance fee. Pick up a copy of the "Trail Guide," which provides an excellent geologic history of the Keys as well as detailed interpretive information linked to the markers found throughout the trail system. The center contains some interesting interpretive exhibits as well as rest rooms and a small store. Rock collectors take note: All plant life *and* rocks are protected throughout this park. If you

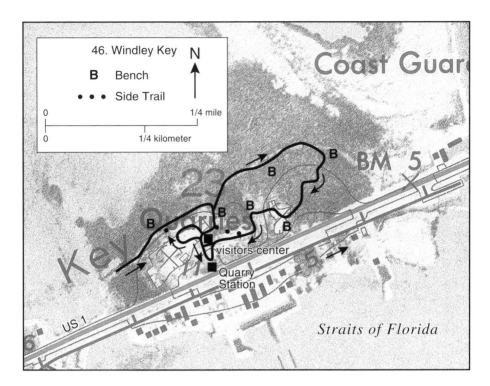

want to take home a piece of fossilized coral, buy one at the visitors center.

To orient yourself to the historical significance of this park, start your hike by walking down behind the visitors center into the Windley Quarry. The park contains three historic quarries: the Russell Quarry, the Flagler Quarry, and the Windley Quarry. In 1908, during the construction of the Overseas Railroad from Miami to Key West, Henry Flagler purchased this land and opened the Flagler Quarry to provide crushed limestone for the railbed. By 1912, the interest had shifted to decorative stone, since these slabs of fossilized coral reef polished up nicely. The Windley Quarry provided ornamental stone for numerous buildings throughout the state of Florida, including John Deering's Vizcaya estate and the Key West and Miami post offices.

Following the interpretive markers around the quarry, notice the fossil corals embedded in the quarry walls *and* beneath your feet: finger coral, with its tiny cups; star coral, with large cups; and brain coral, shaped (as you might expect) like a brain. Up on the east wall of the quarry is a cutter that was used to extract slabs of rock. Follow the markers across to the western wall. As you walk along the wall of the quarry, notice the particularly showy exposures of brain coral and star coral at marker 77. Eroded by rainwater, the natural formations of jagged solution holes provide a direct geologic counterpoint to the stone sliced like butter by the cutter. The blocks placed across the quarry floor near marker 84 were the ones quarried here when the operation ceased in the early 1960s. Follow the markers back around up to visitors center. An American kestrel dives down from the gumbo limbo trees, swooping low as it eyes a mouse.

Passing through the breezeway, follow the brick path down to the CUTTING CORAL sign, next to the channeling machine that cut the slabs. The trail system starts to the right. Step down into the shady tropical hardwood hammock to follow the mulch path beneath the trees. Notice that none of these trees grows particularly tall; their root systems have been stunted due to the difficulty of growing on a base of solid rock. One of the tallest members of the hammock is the gumbo limbo, also referred to as the tourist tree since it's always peeling.

After 0.3 mile, you reach a junction. Turn left to follow the combined Hammock and Sunset Trails. Take the next left to walk the Sunset Trail, a round-trip along the long ridge above the Windley Quarry. With the open understory, you see a lot of long, thin cacti—*Cereus pentagonus,* also known as the barbed-wire cactus. It blooms only at night, attracting large moths that pollinate the flowers. A relative of the sapodilla, the wild dilly, grows along the trail. Its sweet fruits are a favorite food for wildlife. Notice the scratch marks on the pigeon plum trunk? Raccoons love these tropical fruits so much that they go out of their way to climb the trees and pick the plums.

This is a narrow corridor where the vegetation crowds closely, forcing you to duck down occasionally. Trees grow out of cracks and crevices in the bare limestone, and you see the patterns of fossilized coral in the rocks along the sides of the trail. A strong salt aroma rises from the mangrove forest as you approach a fork in the trail. Keep right; the left fork heads down to the picnic benches inside the Windley Quarry. The trail drops down into a buttonwood grove, and you start to see salt-loving plants like sea oxeye, glasswort, and pickleweed as you enter the edge of the mangrove forest. The trail winds through the thicket of mangroves and plunges into a dark, shady corridor lined with tropical plants. Interpretive markers add to your understanding of the flora of this hardwood hammock. Key thatch palms, one of six palm species native to the Keys, grow along the edges of large limestone slabs.

The trail ends at a sign at 0.5 mile. Interestingly, this trail was meant to provide a sweeping view of Florida Bay, including a nearby island with a rookery of roseate spoonbills. But while building the trail and making plans for the observation tower, park officials discovered a stand of rare prickly cordgrass growing down in the clearing below, along the salt marsh. To protect the species, the trail ends here; future plans may place the observation tower at another spot along the trail. Turn around and retrace your route, keeping alert for the scuttling of fiddler crabs between the puddles of water around the pneumatophores of the black mangroves. At marker 65 you pass a limber caper tree with lacy, delicate-looking leaves, a relative of the Mediterranean trees that bear capers used in Italian cooking. Its large, showy flowers attract moths after dark.

At the T intersection, turn left. Tangled thickets of pigeon plum and gumbo limbo provide shade as the trail rises back above the mangrove forest and reaches the crest of the ridge. When you reach the junction with the Hammock Trail after 0.8 mile, turn left. Winding beneath gumbo limbo, pigeon plum, and Jamaican caper trees, the trail goes slightly downhill. You see little depressions in the rocky floor of the forest—solution holes, karst formations carved by the action of rainfall on this soluble limestone. Early settlers attempted to raise small crops in some of the larger solution holes in the Keys. Since some solution holes retain water, they were also used as cisterns. At marker 27, notice the tree with the extremely smooth bark. It's a milkbark, covered with small white lichens. Marlberry and wild coffee struggle to grow on this harsh rocky soil. Passing a large solution hole, you smell the skunky aroma of a white stopper as you come up to bench under a large mahogany tree. Sunlight makes peeling bark of a gumbo limbo glow. Sporting knobby grayish bark that looks like papier-mâché, a tall mastic tree rises over a grouping of pigeon plums. Curving left, the trail drops back down along a line of black mangroves and then rises up into more plum trees: This section of the forest is a regular tropical plum grove. Besides the mastic, also known as jungle plum, and the pigeon plum, you'll find hog plum, saffron plum, and darling plum in this forest. All are edible, but many of them are too astringent for most people's tastes—and the sticky-sweet jungle plum has a reputation for making your lips stick together. Where there is such a bounty of fruit, there is wildlife. Expect to see a raccoon or two skulking through the trees, and plenty of birds flitting through the forest, including the white-crowned pigeon.

The trail rounds a turn to the left, passing through a corridor of thatch palms. Following the twisting, winding footpath, you see a small stand of endangered prickly apple cactus both growing on the ground and draping from the trees. Long and thin like barbed-wire cactus, it also blooms at night, relying on moths for pollination. After 1 mile, you pass a bench. Notice the blown-over pigeon plum with its exposed root system. Trees in this rocky environment develop shallow spreading roots

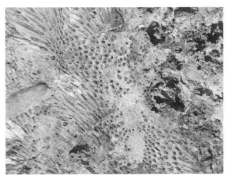

Exposed fossilized coral in the Flagler Quarry

rather than taproots, easy targets for high winds. Still, falling over didn't kill this tree—the roots simply started anchoring themselves back to the rocks. In addition to the roots, one of the most interesting aspects to this tropical hammock is the unusual bark found on most of the trees: naked, peeling, varnished, or mottled like leopard-skin. Pay attention to the rich textures found in the wood. One of the rarest trees in the Keys, the white ironwood, has a bark that evokes hammered bronze.

At marker 47, you pass a piece of railroad rail driven into the ground to anchor winches to move stone slabs. The trail reaches the edge of the Russell Quarry. Look straight down into the quarry at marker 48 for the remains of an old well used by homesteaders. Wild lime shades a bench at 1.2 miles, where the trail makes a sharp right following the edge of quarry before it drops down into it. Rising back out of the quarry into the shade of gumbo limbos, you reach a T intersection. The Hammock Trail turns left to return to the visitors center. Turn right to continue your circuit of the park along the Flagler Quarry Trail. The trail drops down into the Flagler Quarry, where the rocky walls have a pattern like corrugated aluminum. An island of rock left in the middle of the quarry provides an excellent place to examine the eroded exposures of various fossilized corals. Follow the markers along the quarry wall on the right to learn more about the various fossils and solution holes in the Key Largo limestone. Scattered picnic tables provide a grove for visitors.

Cross the central trail and follow the markers along the wall down to the old quarry station, passing a cluster of joewood with its fragrant white blossoms. In front of you are the ruins of the old Windley Key Depot on the Overseas Railroad—a foundation and some cradles for water tanks. Topped by a gumbo limbo, an excellent cross section of a solution hole is exposed in the corner of the quarry wall on the right. Turn left at the ruins and follow the markers back around to the picnic grove in the middle of the quarry. To exit the trail system, turn left. Walk up the ramp to the parking lot, completing your 1.4-mile exploration of this park. If you borrowed an interpretive guidebook, be sure to return it to the visitors center before you leave.

47

Lignumvitae Key Botanical State Park

Total distance (circuit): 1.3 miles

Hiking time: 1 hour

Habitats: Coastal berm, tropical hardwood hammock, mangrove forest, transition zone

Maps: USGS 7½' Upper Matacumbe Key

It's a funny-looking name, and hard to pronounce: lignum vitae (LIG-numb vie-TEE), "tree of life" in Latin. And it's a funny-looking tree, as well: the only one on earth whose branches crisscross each other at sharp angles. Growing on the edge of the tropical hammock near the transition zone, it's credited with amazing medicinal properties: Its bark, sap, and leaves are used to treat syphilis, arthritis, headaches, and gout.

Encompassing 280 acres of ancient tropical hammock, Lignumvitae Key Botanical State Park protects the largest stand of lignum vitae trees in the United States: There are more than 1,000 of these gnarled trees hidden in the dense forests of this island, making it a truly unique preserve. Blanketed by a robust West Indian tropical hardwood hammock, Lignumvitae Key is one of the nation's botanical wonders.

Because of the fragile nature of this ecosystem, hikers can access the trail system only twice daily, during ranger-led walks. Held at 10 AM and 2 PM daily, the walks are most popular in the cooler months, late November through early March, as no pesticides are applied to the forests of Lignumvitae Key. During all other months, you'll need a long-sleeved shirt and pants, copious amounts of insect repellent, and a head net to deal with the hungry mosquitoes that thrive in the island's solution holes. Only 25 people are permitted on each walk. The route of each hike varies according to visitor preferences. Although there are 3.5 miles of trail on the island, the typical hike covers 1.3

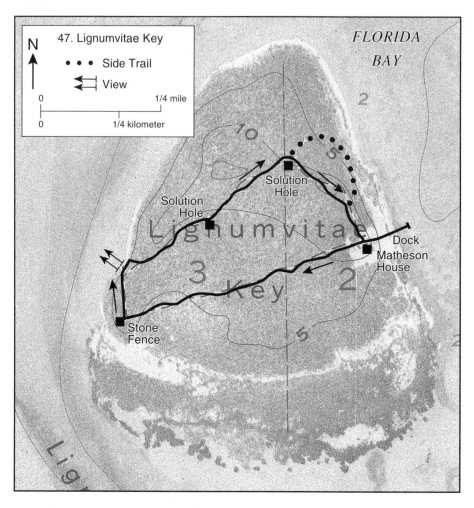

• • • Side Trail

View

0   1/4 mile

0   1/4 kilometer

N

FLORIDA
BAY

Lignumvitae
Key

Solution
Hole

Solution
Hole

Stone
Fence

Dock
Matheson
House

miles. This discussion follows the main 1.3-mile loop around the island.

Since this is an offshore park, you may take a private boat in to the dock, rent a sea kayak and launch from nearby Lower Matecumbe Key, or arrive at the ferryboat concession at Robbie's Marina, at the southern end of the bridge from Indian Key Fill, south of MM 78, 45 minutes before tour time. Advance reservations are recommended (305-664-9814) during winter months. The round-trip fare on the ferryboat costs $15, with an additional $1 tour fee collected at the state park. En route, watch for silver tarpon flashing through the shallows of Florida Bay. When you arrive at the dock and step off the boat, look down to see the waving tentacles of the Florida lobsters that hide out in the jumble of rocks below. Sergeant majors and other colorful reef fish scoot through the crystal-clear water, and you'll see an amberjack or two. Sometimes a nurse shark hides under the dock. Fishing is *not* permitted from the dock.

Walk up the dock to the park entrance gate, where a ranger will meet you and guide you up into the clearing. Built in 1919, the stone house dominating the hill is the Matheson House. Five acres around the house have been preserved since circa 1936, when W. R. Sweeting acted as island caretaker for the Mathesons—a wealthy Miami family that owned most of Key Biscayne. A windmill supplied the caretaker's power; a 12,000-gallon cistern provided fresh water from rainfall channeled off the roof of the house. In the 1950s and up until the island became a state park in the 1970s, Russ and Charlotte Niedhauk, former caretakers of Elliott Key, took care of Lignumvitae until it passed into state management.

Notice the cannons placed around the home—the first-ever use of decorative cannons in the United States. Since they had the money to burn, the Mathesons could afford to underwrite a 1938 dive on the HMS *Winchester,* a wrecked British man-of-war on Carriesfort Reef. Despite the early Keys economy's basis in shipwreck salvage, no one had ever bothered to go out to the *Winchester* because it didn't carry treasure or gold. The Mathesons' dive team came up with the cannons and other artifacts from 1695, when the ship went aground after its crew died of scurvy. These are the original cannons: Replicas have been made and sunk at the wreck.

Before you head out into the woods, the ranger-led tour starts inside the house. It's a small place for its time, but comfortable, and has a few unique touches. Made of coral rock, it's relatively impervious to fire, so the kitchen is inside the home: rare for those days, especially in Florida. The interior paneling is tongue-and-groove Dade County pine, the wizened slash pine subspecies that thrives in pine rocklands and is now found in only a few protected spots in South Florida. Period furnishings dress up the rooms. In the dining area, blocks of polished hardwoods introduce you to the many rare tropical trees found on this island. Both ironwood and lignum vitae are so heavy that small pieces sink in water. Weighing 80 pounds per cubic foot, lignum vitae is one of the strongest and densest woods on earth. Its resistance to rot and insects, as well as its beautiful grain, made it popular for shipbuilding and furniture making. But the slow growth of the tree guaranteed that demand would outstrip supply. It's now a protected species in the United States and in parts of the Caribbean.

When you exit the house, notice the huge osprey nest on the old lighthouse tower. The surrounding seas provide a copious bounty for the ospreys, which return every winter to raise their young. Walking through the open clearing, note that the soil to create this grassy strip was trucked in from off-island back when the house was built—the rocky substrate underlying the forest couldn't support the exotic tropical species that Matheson wanted to introduce, like banyan and sapodilla. Earlier settlers cleared much of the forests and planted coconut palms. Although the hammock you're entering is dark and tropical, only parts of it are more than a century old.

As the ranger guides you down the path, he or she will elaborate on everything from the ground cover to solution holes to the local fauna, which includes raccoons, opossums, mice, and rats. Introduced to keep the rodent population down, red rat snakes make their homes in the tops of the scattered coconut palms. Protected native species include the white-crowned pigeon, drawn here by the fruits of the many poisonwood trees, and numerous varieties of *Liguus,* the Florida tree snail. Some are endemic to this island. And then there are

The branches of the lignum vitae tree are like no other—they crisscross each other.

the mosquitoes. With water-filled solution holes throughout the forest, several different species breed throughout the wet season. Unlike most of the Keys, no pesticides are used here: Too many fragile symbiotic relationships rely on the insects of the tropical hammock. For instance, the blolly tree is also known as the antwood. It's relatively easy to identify, with its oval teardrop leaf and multiple branches sticking straight up. Personified by some as a tree with a sacrificial nature, the blolly will "recognize" that a branch is dying and drop the branch, ants and all. The bodies of the ants add a little food source to the base of the tree, and the tree maintains its overall integrity. Ants play a more important role in the survival of the lignum vitae tree, which is prone to a scale disease. Ants will actively attack the scale disease as a food source. There is also an insect

that taps sap out of the lignum vitae tree, and the ants will attempt to break into the waxy cocoon of the insect to consume it, too. Pesticides could tip the balance against the survival of this endangered tree, so visitors have to grin and bear the natural mosquito-filled environment while visiting the island.

Walking past a young grove of the Florida thatch palm, *Thrinax radiata,* notice how similar it is to the silver palm of the Lower Keys—but it lacks the silvery underside. Native to the Keys, these short palms are in the same family as the Key thatch palm, but the leaflets on each frond are divided almost all the way to the back. A *Liguus fasciatus graphicus* clings to the underside of a frond. With its viny growth habit, cat's claw sends shoots across the trail unless it has something else to attach to. Barbed-wire cactus thrives in the open understory. Despite its relatively rarity, you'll see a lot of black ironwood—like the lignum vitae, a wood nearly as dense as concrete. Incredibly tall old poisonwoods mingle with West Indies mahogany and mastic, climax trees for this forest. Look up in the branches of the mahoganies for clusters of orchids, including butterfly and clamshell orchids. Slender torchwood, lancewood, and crabwood grow in the deep shade of the giants. Much like torchwood, the crabwood has speckles on its leaves caused by a species of mite. The leaf comes to a point, like a cherry leaf.

Coconut palms rise around a solution hole filled with palm fronds as you come up to a small trail leading off to the right. At its end is a quarry inside a solution hole and a jumble of historic mining equipment, including a 1900s Caterpillar diesel steam plow and a rock crusher. This quarry supplied the building stone for the Matheson House. Back on the main trail, you continue through a grove of coconut palms, considered an invasive species on this island. Long before Europeans set foot on Lignumvitae Key, the Calusa had a settlement here—as attested to by burial mounds found in the forests. The Spanish came here in the 1500s, and it's thought they had a small settlement, as well. Settlers prior to the Mathesons' purchase of the island lived down at this end, tending their coconut palm plantations.

At 0.6 mile, you approach one of the most distinctive human-made features on the island: "the Great Wall of Lignumvitae." Similar in nature to what you'd see on a farm in New England, this stone fence has a distinctive Keys twist—it's made of coral rock, hand-laid, without mortar. No one knows exactly why it's here, but the fence goes on for nearly a mile and a half. One of the theories is that the early Spanish set-tlers built the fence. In southern Spain, low stone fences like these were used to corral sheep and tortoises. Since the bones and shells of Galapagos tortoises have been found on the island, perhaps the Spaniards farmed tortoises for meat. Or perhaps Mr. Matheson, with his fondness for unusual tropical species, brought Galapagos tortoises here to roam as pets. In any case, the stone corral would have kept them from ranging down to Florida Bay.

In the 1970s, the original caretaker's trail system was expanded to make a loop past this point. Turning right, you follow the stone fence until you come to a fork. Keep left and walk through the thatch palm grove for a fabulous view of Florida Bay. An ancient galled-up poisonwood stands sentinel over the small clearing. Flat slabs of limestone define the water's edge, where bay cedar—an aromatic relative of sea lavender, with a growth habit similar to a piñon pine—crowds the shoreline. Several specimens of agaves live along the shoreline, left here by botanist Henry Perrine as he experimented with tropical plantings in the Middle Keys in the 1830s. Shallow, clear waters stretch to the horizon. Just offshore is a coral reef where timid snorkelers can jump off their boats and swim around in a few feet of water to watch angelfish and sergeant majors darting between the corals.

Turn around and return to the junction at the T intersection. Depending on time of year and the density of mosquitoes along the trail thus far, your guide will either lead you back along the path to the right or, in winter, plunge into the dark forest on the left to complete the loop. Black, red, and white ironwoods grow in these woods, with tall mastic, gumbo limbo, poisonwood, and mahogany all around. Like plum trees, the lignum vitae trees are short and spreading, deeply shaded by the canopy above. Dangling over the trail, a lignum vitae displays its bonsailike growth habit and bizarre branching. The branches zigzag and crisscross each other, touching in places. Because of their shallow root systems, they frequently blow over—but, like the other trees of the hammock, they then dig in their roots and keep on growing. This part of the hammock hosts a tremendous number of lignum vitae trees. Watch for their weird branches and you'll notice them all over the place. One extremely gnarled tree turns in on itself almost completely.

Ducking under a pigeon plum leaning out over the footpath, you pass dozens of mastic trees—the sticky-sweet jungle plum, its distinctive smooth gray bark exfoliating. One of the mastics has a buttress root growing on the fallen trunk of a Jamaican dogwood—a trunk that's lain there in the forest for at least a century, according to hearsay, and never rotted. In the understory, notice the terrestrial *Spathoglottis* orchids, brought to the Keys by the propagation of avocados and mangoes from the Caribbean. Their delicate pink blooms add a touch of color to this dark forest.

After 1 mile, you reach a trail junction. Straight ahead is a 0.5-mile loop leading out into the transition zone between the tropical hammock and the mangrove forests along the island's shore. Occasionally, rangers lead hikers down that path, but more often than not it's flooded. The normal hike route makes a left in front of a deep and beautiful solution hole. The exposed limestone wall drops down into a watery pool, forming a gorgeous grotto. It's the perfect backdrop for the park's star feature. On the far side of the solution hole, notice the trees with their exposed root systems clinging to the rocky slope. Overshadowing the numerous strangler figs and the huge Jamaican dogwood is the U.S.-champion lignum vitae, gnarled and prehistoric. According to carbon-14 dating, this tree is more than 1,000 years old, and it's the largest lignum vitae in the United States. Mimicking a banyan tree, the adjoining Jamaican dogwood sports an unusual broad buttress root.

How can a tree be so old and yet so small? It's the nature of the Keys. With limestone bedrock scant inches under the forest floor, these tropical trees have very little medium to keep them alive. Despite the lushness of the forest, it's an incredibly harsh environment. Some trees, like the gumbo limbo, Jamaican dogwood, and poisonwood, adapt to the lack of water by losing their leaves if they become stressed by drought. The mast generated by fallen leaves acts like a sponge. It holds as much as 30 percent of the water needed for these trees to survive into the next rainy season. In the Caribbean, these trees grow much taller. But here in the Keys, they're giants among the native tropical trees of Florida.

The trail drops down a deep dip past a large spreading lignum vitae on the right. Barbed-wire cactus clusters around its base. Passing another remnant of the coral stone fence, you reach the incoming end of the transition zone trail, rising up through the buttonwoods. Your walk ends as you emerge in the clearing next to the Matheson House, completing a 1.3-mile circuit of one of Florida's most beautiful forests. Turn left and walk over to the path. Head down to the boat dock, catch your ride back off the island, and plan to come back sometime for another hike.

48

Long Key State Park

Total distance (two circuits): 1.4 miles

Hiking time: 1 hour

Habitats: Coastal berm, mangrove forest, transition zone, tropical hardwood hammock

Maps: USGS 7½' Long Key; park map

Botanical diversity runs rampant in the Florida Keys. Unfortunately, development has erased many of the strange and wonderful ecosystems that are unique to the Keys. But on Long Key, early development managed to save a patchwork of habitats for the public. First held by Spanish explorers, the island (then called Rattlesnake Key) became the property of Charles Howe, a resident of Indian Key, in 1827. A decade later, noted botanist Dr. Henry Perrine came to the Keys, experimenting with growing tropical plants. He and Howe planted mulberry trees on Long Key with the plan of starting a silk industry. But in 1840, a raiding party of Seminole Indians drove the settlers off Indian Key, killing Perrine. By 1884, the new owners of Long Key had planted it with more than 17,000 coconut palms. When Henry Flagler's Overseas Railroad came through, Flagler offered them a tidy sum to take over the plantation. Enchanted by the beautiful beach, Flagler wanted to build a fishing camp on the spot. By 1906, the Long Key Fishing Club consisted of a lodge, clubhouse, post office, and 14 guest cottages. At the time, sportfishing was the domain of the rich and famous. Novelist Zane Grey, one of the regulars at the club, fell in love with Long Key. It was here, outwitting tarpon and bonefish, that he wrote his novels *Wild Horse Mesa* and *Code of the West,* as well as numerous articles for the fledgling conservationist Izaak Walton League. In addition to Grey, many other famous men came here to fish, including William

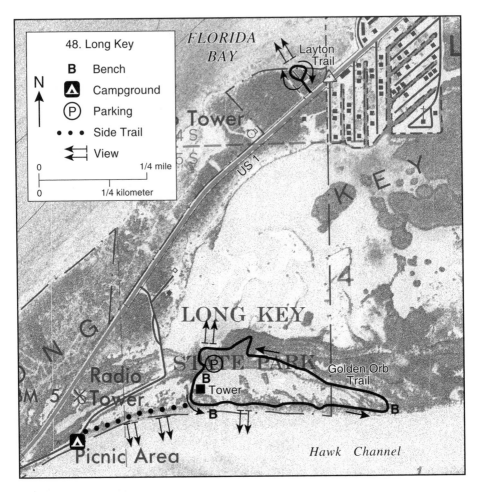

Randolph Hearst, Richard Mellon, Herbert Hoover, and Franklin Roosevelt.

When the Labor Day hurricane of 1935 struck, it destroyed the Overseas Railroad as it engulfed the nearby Matecumbe Keys in a 17-foot tidal wave, washing more than 500 people into the sea. Long Key was wiped clean of its human touch. But nature, left to its own devices, heals all. Later rebuilt, the fishing camp attracted a parade of celebrities in the 1950s and 1960s. The state of Florida began to acquire the land in 1961 and by 1969 had opened Long Key State Park, providing

visitors with one of the most popular and beautiful campgrounds in the Keys. Encompassing 965 acres, it protects an unusually diverse set of habitats for hikers and paddlers to enjoy.

The park is located just past the city of Layton on US 1, 0.5 mile south of MM 68, with its main entrance on the left. When you stop at the ranger station and pay your Florida State Parks entrance fee, ask for a park map. The park contains two hiking trails: the popular Golden Orb Trail and the much shorter Layton Trail. If you're camping at the park—highly recommended, as

The Florida Keys

campers enjoy oceanfront views—you'll access the Golden Orb Trail from the north edge of the campground, along the waterfront. Otherwise, as you drive in on the park entrance road, keep left at the fork (turning away from the campground), then right at the next fork. Park your car near the boardwalk and rest rooms.

GOLDEN ORB TRAIL

Your hike on the 1.2-mile Golden Orb Trail starts along this access boardwalk leading out to the ocean. From the parking lot, follow the boardwalk up and around the rest rooms to drop down into the mangrove forest. You come to a broad observation platform with benches, where the red mangroves dangle their tentaclelike roots into people's laps. The boardwalk crosses a tidal creek busy with marine life. You see the reflection of an ibis in the shallow water as it spreads its wings; a green heron works its way through the marly mud. Sticking out of the center of the channel, the seedpods of red mangroves will eventually establish a new island. A mangrove crab scuttles down the boardwalk as you approach the observation tower. Climb up for a bird's-eye view of the mangrove forest. Looking south, you can see the glistening blue-green waters of the Atlantic beyond the coconut palms. As you continue down the boardwalk, keep alert for the sign on the left that marks the beginning of the Golden Orb Trail. The boardwalk beyond the sign comes from a beautiful seaside connector trail to the campground, providing several picnic pavilions with an ocean view.

Step off the boardwalk and start down the narrow path through the mangrove forest, where you see the massive holes of giant land crabs under the prop roots. This is an interpretive trail, so take the time to look at the markers. Infused with the aroma of salt, the ocean air is bracing as you skirt the pneumatophores of black mangroves, walking past a bench and up and over a bridge above a deep mangrove-lined creek. Purple spiderworts bloom beneath the buttonwoods, and gray nickerbean cascades over a seven-year apple. Fussing under the mangroves, ibises let out squawks. A black racer moves swiftly across the footpath.

After 0.2 mile, you reach a side trail. Turn right. Crowded by sea oxeye, the trail leads to a mangrove-flanked beach on the Atlantic. The footprints of herons are like plaster casts embedded in the marl. Notice the lack of waves here—the sea is mirror calm. Living coral reefs shelter the Florida Keys; Tennessee Reef, out by the distant lighthouse, breaks up the surf well before it reaches this shore. Unfortunately, there is a lot of debris on the beach: the refuse of careless boaters, the bane of the Keys. Turn around and head back to the main trail; turn right.

With the removal of exotic plants—notice the stumps and snags of former Australian pines—morning glory and gray nickerbean now take over the understory, their vines draping over the smaller tropical plants. The trail curves to parallel the shore, winding its way along the coastal berm as it stays in the open to provide sweeping scenic views. Keys lily and painted leaf, a form of wild poinsettia, add color to the grass. Off to the left is the mangrove forest. A gray nickerbean dangles its giant green fuzzy seedpods, while a snowberry groans under the weight of its branches, heavily laden in white berries. You breathe in a confusing aroma of fragrant nickerbeans and salt. Watch for poisonwood trees along the edge of the trail. Entering the deep shade of a stand of sea

A mangrove anchors a new island in the still waters of the Atlantic off Long Key State Park.

grapes and buttonwoods, the trail curves left and drops down past at bench at 0.6 mile, crossing a small bridge through the mangrove forest.

As the trail rises up, you feel as if you've stepped into a desert. Welcome to the Keys version of Florida scrub: the transition zone. With salt-rich soil that appeals to a handful of plants, this habitat defines a boundary between mangrove forests and coastal berm. The bleached white forest floor and stunted shrubs remind you of scrub. Shade is at a premium. Bay cedar thrives here, resplendent in its tiny yellow blooms. Seven-year apple lifts its scrubby branches to the sky. Love vine cascades over a fish poison tree. Blolly grows in a shady patch. A *Liguus* tree snail inches its way along a buttonwood branch. Just off the well-worn footpath, notice how the soil is a surreal mix of chalky white sand peppered with chunks of embedded weathered coral. As it curves, the trail winds past a shadeless bench at 0.8 mile. Dozens of fiddler crabs scuttle out of the way: At high tide, you may encounter puddles across the trail. After crossing a short bridge over a mangrove swamp, the trail continues through the open plain. Salt hay edges the mangrove forest. Notice the peace and quiet here, as the trail is well distanced from US 1 across a broad inner lagoon. A steady cool breeze blows off the Atlantic. But as the trail turns, your illusion of wilderness is shattered by the view of a cell phone tower in the distance.

Ducking under the low boughs of mangroves and buttonwoods, you enter a hammock of sea grapes and Jamaican capers, with vegetation crowding closely into the footpath. The trail may be damp in places until it rises up into a tropical hardwood hammock. Barbed-wire cacti snake through the understory, where small century plants

The "soil" of the coastal berm is made up of dead coral.

poke out between the tall cacti. Peeling gumbo limbos lean over the trail, and you encounter both pigeon plum and poisonwood trees. Notice how similar their bark is, but how different the leaves are: Poisonwood leaves look like they're drooping from a lack of water. Despite its toxicity to humans, the fruit of the poisonwood is a favorite of the white-crowned pigeon and provides an important food source for many of the birds of the tropical hammock.

Dropping down to the edge of the mangrove forest, you can now see the inner lagoon on Long Key. The trail emerges at the park road. Cross over it to return to the parking lot, completing your 1.2-mile hike. If you are staying at the campground, return via the boardwalk to the beautiful seaside walk through the picnic grove, an enjoyable connector trail adding a round trip of 0.6 mile to your hike for a total of 1.8 miles.

LAYTON TRAIL

Leave the park's main entrance and drive north on US 1 for 0.6 mile, just past MM 68, to find the trailhead to the Layton Trail. It's marked with a small sign set back into the forest along the shoulder of the road. Park along the shoulder and follow the path into the woods to access this brief trek out to Florida Bay. You immediately plunge into the darkness of a tropical hardwood hammock, surrounded by thatch palms, gumbo limbo, pigeon plum, and poisonwood. Surface limestone appears in the footpath. At the trail junction, continue straight. Ducking between the dense thatch palms, you emerge along the limestone shores of Florida Bay. Take in the view of the blue-green water stretching off to the horizon. Fed by the Everglades' river of grass, this shallow body of water is profoundly affected by the massive humanmade changes to the hydrology of South Florida. As a buffer between the mangrove forests of the Everglades and Keys and the living coral reefs, the health of Florida Bay affects that of the coral reefs. Sad to say, the agricultural runoff filtering through the Everglades has increased the salinity of the bay, creating immense algal blooms and areas entirely devoid of sea grass or fish. Looking at this lovely expanse, you'd hardly believe it's under siege. But the fate of Florida Bay—and of the coral reefs of the Keys—rests heavily on the Everglades restoration plan.

Turn right and pick your way along the limestone shoreline, behind the buttonwoods. White crab pot markers bob in the wind as brown pelicans swoop down low across the water. The shoreline is covered in sargassum tangled with sponges, coral, and a shameful amount of garbage. Follow the trail under the nickerbeans and sea grapes through salt hay grass. Step carefully across the seaweed-covered rocks. Make your way across a squishy seaweed bed to an interpretive marker, where the trail turns sharply right and enters the forest. Push through the thatch palms and you're back in the dense tropical hammock. A solution hole sits off to the left, and barbed-wire cactus pokes up between the rocks. You quickly come back to the end of the loop. Turn left to exit. When you return to your car, you've completed this 0.2-mile stroll.

49

Bahia Honda State Park

Total distance (one circuit, one round trip): 1.1 miles

Hiking time: 45 minutes

Habitats: Coastal strand, salt flats, tropical hardwood hammock

Maps: USGS 7½' Big Pine Key; park map

Some beaches are *much* better than others. And in the Florida Keys, Bahia Honda State Park provides what visitors to Florida seek—the ultimate beach experience. *Condé Nast Traveler* magazine called this the "Best Beach in America," and with its coconut-palm-lined shores, it's easy to see why. Although the beach isn't very wide, it offers a strand of soft powdery white sand along sparkling turquoise waters, an entire 2.5 miles of pristine oceanfront.

But beachgoers who don't wander off into the woods miss out on what's so special about Bahia Honda State Park: It's a botanical paradise. Encompassing the entirety of Bahia Honda Key, the park protects the largest stand of silver palms in the United States, as well as more than 150 other species of native plants. For some species of Caribbean origin, this is the one of the few locations they are found in the United States.

The park entrance is on Bahia Honda Key at US 1 MM 37, on the Atlantic side. When you enter the park and stop at the ranger station to pay your entrance fee, ask for an interpretive guide to the Silver Palm Nature Trail. Along with the old Bahia Honda Bridge, it's one of two short walks available within this park. Hiking isn't a major draw here, but outdoor recreation certainly is. Three campgrounds with cool ocean breezes and great views draw visitors from around the world. Thanks to the dive shop in the park, you can rent a sea kayak, snorkeling gear, a fishing rod, a beach chair, or scuba gear for exploration

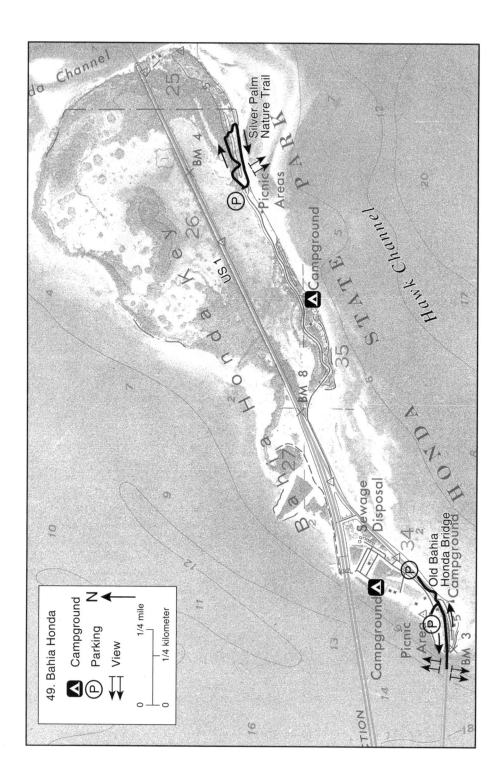

49. Bahia Honda

▲ Campground
Ⓟ Parking
⇵ View

N

0 — 1/4 mile
0 — 1/4 kilometer

da Channel

Silver Palm
Nature Trail

Picnic
Areas

BM 4

Honda Key 26

US1

P A R K

▲ Campground

S T A T E

35

BM 8

7

12

20

5

17

6

Hawk Channel

H O N D A

Sewage
Disposal

Old Bahia
Honda Bridge

Ⓟ

34

Campground

▲ Campground

Picnic
Area

Ⓟ

BM 3

Bahia

21

9

10

12

11

13

14

16

18

CTION

25

5

4

7

of the offshore reefs. And yes, you can walk the slender beaches–although you can't walk from one end of the park to the other unless you want to wade.

SILVER PALM NATURE TRAIL

At the T intersection just beyond the ranger station, turn left to drive north on the park road, passing the Sandspur Camping Area and a beach access parking lot. You reach the northern terminus of the park road in the second beach access lot, 1.3 miles north. The Silver Palm Nature Trail starts at the northern end of the parking lot, at the sign. From the trailhead, look off to the right and you'll see one of those classic Keys views of the placid aquamarine ocean stretching off into the distance beyond the coconut palms. Flanked by gumbo limbo and poisonwood, you start down the trail into the tropical hardwood hammock. An unusually diverse variety of tropical plants grows here. Besides the usual sea grape, Spanish stopper, Jamaica dogwood, thatch palm, caper tree, and pigeon plum, you'll find such oddities as Geiger tree, manchineel, and wild allamanda. Since Henry Perrine's explorations in the 1870s, botanists have visited Bahia Honda Key to study its unusual plants. Strong winds, migratory birds, and the flow of the nearby Gulf Stream are all credited with depositing the seeds of Caribbean species on these shores, where they thrive. If you bring a good field guide with you, you'll enjoy figuring out the various tropical oddities, from small-flowered lilythorn to wild dilly, blackbead, and salt marsh mallow. Notice the seven-year apple, a small, fragrant tree with waxy leaves. When its fruits mature, they shrivel and blacken. The aroma of white stopper intermingles with the salt breeze as you walk along the narrow path, passing the

holes of giant land crabs. Tall sea oxeye and bay cedar top the salt flats along the bay. Looking off to the left through the screen of mangroves, you see the inner cove. Mangrove crabs scurry up prop roots at your approach. In the early-morning hours, wading birds come to the salt flats to feed. You'll see white ibises and colorful pink roseate spoonbills, as well as great white herons stalking the flats. Limited primarily to the Keys and Everglades, the great white heron is a color morph of the much more common great blue heron.

Rounding a bend, you walk along a corridor of silver palms *(Coccothrinax argentata)*, the silvery undersides of their fronds shimmering in the sea breeze. Despite damage from Hurricane Georges in 1995, the grove continues to thrive. The silver palms around you represent the largest natural concentration of these rare native plants in the United States. Tucked in this little forest is the national-champion silver palm, topping out at 29 feet. Preferring soil with a high salt content, most silver palms grow no more than 20 feet tall. After losing their clusters of tiny white blossoms, silver palms bear small purple fruits in fall.

As the trail drops down into the coastal strand, you hear the increasing chatter of people on the beach. When you reach the dune crossover point at 0.1 mile, continue straight to keep walking along the coastal strand. A merlin soars overhead, scanning for beach mice. Cuban jacquemontia cascades over the dunes. The trail enters a corridor between two fences, put in to prevent people wandering off into the coastal strand and destroying this fragile habitat. Silver palms, slender and delicate, rise from the taller dunes. Passing through a forest of sea grapes, you continue between another set of fences, where more silver palms grow off to the left. Savanna sparrows scurry between the sea oats. Curving right, the trail heads out toward the water, ending on the beach after 0.3 mile. Turn right and walk up the beach. Notice the many drift seeds captured by tangles of sargassum. The Gulf Stream continues to strew its gifts across the shore, leaving tropical almonds, sea beans, and sea hearts on these bright white sands. When you reach the boardwalk, turn right and cross over the dunes. Returning back to the beginning of the trail, you've walked 0.6 mile.

OLD BAHIA HONDA BRIDGE

Get back in your car and head south on the park road. Just past the park entrance, make a left turn into the parking lot at the WINGS AND WAVES BUTTERFLY GARDEN sign. Walk through the small butterfly garden, which has several benches enabling visitors to sit down and watch the winged activity around them. Nearly 30 percent of all butterflies in the Florida Keys are brush-footed varieties, such as the painted lady, the red admiral, and the Cuban daggerwing. When you exit the far side of the garden, keep to the right to walk in front of the rest rooms, where outcrops of coral rock stud the footpath as you walk past shimmering silver buttonwoods. At the amphitheater, a trail leads down to the right to the dive shop, concession stand, and parking lot. Continue straight along the limestone path. Gulf fritillaries flutter between the sea grapes. You feel immersed in the Tropics, as coconut palm rises tall over the understory of gray nickerbean and pigeon plum. Continuing up the increasingly steeper grade, you catch a glimpse of US 1 off to the right: the bridge framed by coconut palms, sailboats moored in the harbor. The sweep of Atlantic beach fills the sky to the left. You're walking on the

old Overseas Highway, once the Overseas Railroad—Henry Flagler's dream wrought in steel. After spanning the state with his Florida East Coast Railroad in the early 1900s, Flagler proposed the "Key West Extension," bridging 153 miles of open seas to reach the port at Key West. Many thought he was crazy. But with thousands of workers laying girders, building support piers, and blasting out coral rock under water, it took Flagler's crews seven years to make the dream come true. On January 22, 1912, Flagler stepped out of his private railcar to the cheers of half the population of Key West, officially inaugurating the Overseas Railroad.

To get to Key West, the railroad had to span nearly a mile across the Bahia Honda Channel. This short trail leads you up to a restored remnant of the railroad bridge. This bridge was one of the most difficult to build along the Overseas Railroad. First, the crews encountered deep water in the channel—up to 35 feet, which is very deep for the Keys. Nine concrete arches support a framework of girders from which the railroad tracks were hung from the trusses. The railroad is below you. Walk up to the end of this bridge segment and look over to the next piece to see the framework. While it was still under construction in 1910, a vicious hurricane washed across the Lower Keys, displacing one of these massive bridge piers. But this was by far the sturdiest bridge built along the entire route—so much so that the Overseas Highway was built on top of the bridge in 1938, the upper deck used as the route for US 1 through the 1970s.

When you turn around and look back to where you walked from, you see the entire sweep of Bahia Honda Key, and beyond to the curve of the Seven Mile Bridge. It seemed ludicrous in the early 1900s to be

The view from the Old Bahia Honda bridge

spanning islands with massive bridges, but when the Overseas Railroad opened for business, the media stopped harping about "Flagler's Folly" and started calling the railroad "The Eighth Wonder of the World." And it remained so until 1935, when the "storm of the century" laid waste to the Keys. Packing winds of more than 200 miles per hour, the nameless category 5 hurricane razed the Matecumbe Keys. More than 600 people died when a wall of water toppled a rescue train into the sea. With its rails reduced to twisted wreckage through its middle stretch, the Overseas Railroad was no more.

As you walk back down the path, notice how the strongly fragrant blossoms of the gray nickerbeans attract zebra longwing butterflies and yellow sulfurs. Continue past the amphitheater and the rest rooms and back through the butterfly garden to complete your 0.5-mile walk.

50

National Key Deer Refuge

Total distance (one circuit, four round trips): 7.2 miles

Hiking time: 3 hours, 30 minutes

Habitats: Coastal berm, mangrove forest, pine rocklands, salt flats, tropical hardwood hammock

Maps: USGS 7½' Summerland Key, Big Pine Key, Saddlebunch Keys; park map

In the Lower Keys, several animal species have adapted to an environment shaped by winds and water, where a lack of fresh water and seasonal storms create especially harsh conditions, and plants from the Caribbean overlap the southernmost range of North American mammals. Endemic species such as the silver rice rat and the Lower Keys marsh rabbit eke out an existence in a land of surface limestone and salt marshes. But of all the creatures of the Lower Keys, the Key deer invites the closest study. It's the smallest deer in the world: so small you could hold a newborn fawn in your cupped hands. A full-grown buck stands no higher than your waist, rarely topping 100 pounds in weight. And it's only found in the Lower Keys. In 1957, the National Key Deer Refuge was established to protect the dwindling herd, which hit an all-time low of 50 individuals in 1947. By eliminating hunting and protecting the deer's habitat, the population grew to more than 400 by the 1970s. Now nearly 800 of these tiny deer roam the pine rocklands, tropical hammocks, and mangrove swamps of Big Pine Key and 30 adjacent islands.

When you drive south on US 1 to Big Pine Key, notice the fences flanking the road. Built by the Florida Department of Transportation, these recent additions (built in conjunction with culverts to allow the deer to pass under the road) are expected to lower deer mortality, which has been as high as 10 percent of the overall population each year. Use special caution when you

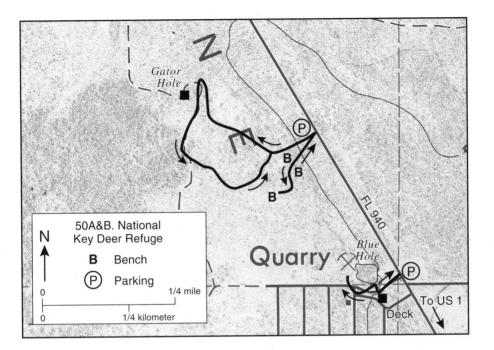

drive the roads in the Lower Keys, especially at dawn and dusk, as most of the deer mortality comes from automobiles.

After MM 31, turn west onto CR 940 and drive 0.2 mile to the shopping center hidden away in the trees to the right. The Florida Keys National Wildlife Refuge's visitors center sits across the parking lot from the Winn-Dixie. In addition to the National Key Deer Refuge, this office also manages the Great White Heron National Wildlife Refuge, Crocodile Lakes National Wildlife Refuge (on Key Largo, next to Hike 45), and Key West National Wildlife Refuge. Unlike many of the other units of the National Wildlife Refuge system, no hunting is allowed on these lands, which protect endangered species.

Pick up both the park brochure (including a map showing the nature trails on Big Pine Key) and the flyer "National Key Deer Refuge Hiking and Bicycling Trails," which explains how to find trails in the refuge on other Keys along US 1. All refuge lands are open daily from half an hour before sunrise to half an hour after sunset.

BLUE HOLE

Drive north on Key Deer Boulevard, crossing Watson Boulevard. After 3 miles, you reach the parking area for Blue Hole on the left. Follow the gravel trail that winds away from the parking lot into an area planted with native trees such as pigeon plum, gumbo limbo, and silver buttonwood. The gravel path meets up with the wheelchair-accessible sidewalk coming in from the handicapped parking area. Turn left and follow the sidewalk over to the observation platform overlooking Blue Hole.

On tropical islands with karst landscapes, a blue hole is a type of sinkhole where a lens of fresh water (supplied by rain during the wet season) floats atop a layer of salt water seeping in from the sea. Think of Big Pine Key as a giant sponge:

Fresh water soaks down 22 feet, with salt water lying below it. Early settlers dug shallow wells to trap this natural resource, but the population has long since outstripped the availability of fresh water on Big Pine Key. Desalinization of salt water to obtain fresh water in the Keys dates back to the 1860s. While Big Pine Key has the proper geology to create a blue hole, this particular Blue Hole is artificial, forming within a quarry where rock was mined for construction of the Overseas Highway. By exposing the freshwater lens in the karst, the Blue Hole is the primary source of fresh water for the wildlife of Big Pine Key.

Look down into the Blue Hole and you'll see a constant parade of aquatic life. Large Florida softshell turtles drift through the shallows. Bluegill, bass, and bream dart among coontails. Watch for the bobbing heads of Florida cooters and Florida mud turtles as they scoot across the limestone bottom. A massive giant oscar noses up to the platform piers. If you see an alligator, don't be surprised—a single bull alligator inhabits the lake at any given time.

Continuing along the trail, you pass a sign regarding poisonwood. Notice its distinctive mottled-brown-and-orange bark with black patches, and its leaves that look perpetually curled, as though the tree is suffering from drought. Poisonwood is a common component of the forests of the Keys, and should be treated with caution, especially if you're sensitive to poison ivy—its toxicity is 10 times that of poison ivy. You'll find poisonwood along *all* the trails in National Key Deer Refuge.

The trail curves along the rocky edge of Blue Hole, where ladder brake fern clings to the limestone outcrops. Because it tends to colonize disturbed areas in pine rocklands, poisonwood clusters along the trail's edge as you follow the old limestone path around the quarry. Watch the far side of Blue Hole for Key deer coming for a drink. This is one of the rare places in the Keys where the deer have access to copious amounts of fresh water. When you get to the Y junction and see a paved road on the left, keep to the right. The trail soon ends at an AREA CLOSED sign with a fence, blocking off the rest of the quarry road to enable deer to access Blue Hole without human disturbance. Turn around and retrace your steps, enjoying the numerous scenic views across the water. Lancewood dominates the understory with its sharply pointed leaves. A yellow sulfur alights on a bright orange butterfly weed. Continuing along the path past the observation deck, you end your 0.2-mile stroll at the parking lot.

WILDLIFE TRAILS

Drive north on Key Deer Boulevard another 0.2 mile to the WILDLIFE TRAILS sign, and turn left. This large parking area provides access to two hiking trails: the wheelchair-accessible Fred Manillo Trail and the rougher Jack Watson Wildlife Trail. Start by taking the trailhead to the left of the bicycle rack, the Fred Manillo Trail. To accommodate wheelchairs, the footpath is hard-packed emulsified gravel. Pick up a brochure at the kiosk for an overview of the trail and the ecosystems along it. You're in pine rocklands, here featuring saw palmetto and gnarled and stunted slash pines at the southernmost extent of their range. The tropical understory contains poisonwood, wax myrtle, scattered thatch palm, and occasional silver palm. Unlike the Keys to the north, the ancient reef rock under the Lower Keys is overlain with a layer of oolitic Miami limestone, like the bedrock of the Everglades. As a result, the exposed limestone dissolves into a rough karst landscape of pinnacles and solution holes where pine rocklands thrive. The solution holes trap rainfall, providing critical freshwater resources for the Key deer as well as creating cool, damp spots where ferns and orchids grow in miniature gardens. National Key Deer Refuge protects more than 80 percent of the remaining pine rocklands of the Florida Keys.

Feathery ladder brake fern casts shadows on the footpath as you brush through a crowded grove of silver palms. Giant bracken ferns grow in a clearing under the pines. Keep to the right as a deer trail forks left. The trail eventually rises up to a boardwalk surrounded by a freshwater wetland, a rocky sea of sawgrass in the midst of the pines. Poisonwood lines the edges. The colorful pink blooms of glades lobelia sway in the breeze. Looking down, you see the depressions in the limestone, which trap precious rainwater and create havens for wildlife. The trail ends here. Turn around and retrace your path to the parking lot, noticing the many small beaten paths through the forest created by the tiny Key deer. The Manillo Trail ends back at the parking lot after 0.3 mile.

Turn left to start hiking the Jack C. Watson Wildlife Trail. Responsible for the recovery of the Key deer population, Watson managed the refuge between 1954 and 1975. Surface limestone outcrops all around you as the trail curves left past a stand of poisonwood. At 0.4 mile, you come to the beginning of the loop. Turn right, following the arrow. Blackbead and cat's claw crowd the understory. This trail gives you a good immersion into the pine rocklands, a harsh-looking landscape with its trees stunted by limited water yet surrounded by watery wetlands in solution holes brimming with life. The slash pines here match the deer: much smaller than any you'll see on the Florida peninsula. Young poisonwood grows throughout the forest. You walk under a strangely shaped pine with all its needles on top like a giant's pincushion. Be careful of sawgrass intruding into trail as you pass a small but shiny silver palm. Be cautious of the poisonwood crowding in closely—avoid getting any sap on your skin. A blue-gray gnatcatcher perches in a wax myrtle. As the trail curves left at 0.6 mile, you see a sparkle of water through the underbrush: an alligator hole. You continue through another stretch of sawgrass, the trail rounding a wetland edged by landscape timbers. Look down and you'll see tiny mosquitofish shimmering in the shallows, responsible for the surprising lack of mosquitoes in this part of the refuge.

The trail rises, slightly elevated to prevent flooding, and you see deer trails broken through the underbrush. Notice the wonderful silence: no road noise, no airplanes, just the breeze rustling through the saw palmetto fronds. Buttonwoods grow out of a series of solution holes. At the AREA CLOSED sign, the trail curves left past a satinleaf tree and some thatch palms, and a cabbage palm rises out of a deep solution hole. Slathered in mud, a large snapping turtle crawls across the trail at a narrow mosquito control ditch, stymied since it can't fit through the culvert. When you reach the end of loop, continue straight, emerging at the parking lot after a 1.1-mile hike.

NO NAME KEY

Although the only trails on No Name Key are old roads built during the Cuban missile crisis and in more recent times, in anticipation of never-completed development, you'll enjoy hiking there because it's wild. Walk

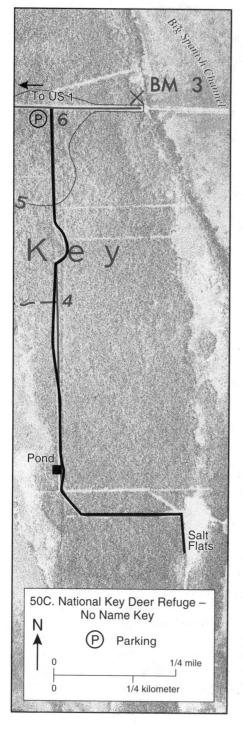

**50C. National Key Deer Refuge –
No Name Key**

N

Ⓟ Parking

| 0 | 1/4 mile |
| 0 | 1/4 kilometer |

softly and you will see deer. Walk attentively and you'll spot hundreds of *Liguus*, Florida's native tree snail family that comes in a variety of colors, shapes, and sizes. To find No Name Key, return down Key Deer Boulevard for 1.3 miles to Watson Boulevard, and turn left. After 0.7 mile, you reach a stop sign. Turn left, continuing on Watson as it crosses the bridge to No Name Key. After 2.6 miles, you come to the ROAD ENDS 1000 FEET sign across from Paradise Drive. Park on the right; do not block the gate.

Start your hike down the gated refuge road. Although it follows an old road, this is a rugged trek along an uneven rocky surface with only scattered amounts of shade. Oolitic limestone outcrops underfoot, surrounded by tropical hammock. The forest opens up briefly, and you catch a whiff of salt from a buttonwood marsh off to the right, with sea grapes growing on the edges of a salt flat. Watching several ibises pick their way across the marsh, you hear the rustling of the tiny Key deer in the underbrush. The deer are certainly here—you see thousands of hoof prints in the sand of the trail. Keep still for a while and a few may venture out into the open. Isolated on these islands by the rising of the seas more than 5,000 years ago, the Key deer is the smallest subspecies of the Virginia white-tailed deer. The deer are most active between September and December, during the breeding season, and again in April and May, when does prepare to bear their fawns. Browsing more than 160 different types of plants, the Key deer are well adapted to their unique environment.

Approaching a rusted gate at 0.4 mile, you pass another old road coming in from the right. To the left are mounds of dirt left from old construction. Look for the colorful purplish blue blooms of rockland ruellia growing atop long stems. Keep alert for flecks of white standing out against the dark bark of the trees. This is one of several hammocks in the Keys where you'll spot the Florida tree snail, with showy varieties like *Liguus fasciatus graphicus* growing up to 3 inches long. Native only to Cuba, Hispaniola, the Isle of Pines, and South Florida, these tree snails live in tropical hardwood hammocks and are most active during the wet season. Fifty-nine different color varieties have been identified, some of which are now extinct. The snails feed on microscopic lichens and algae growing on smooth-barked tropical trees, preferring to live on such species such as tamarind, Jamaican dogwood, pigeon plum, and poisonwood.

As you continue out into a shadeless area, you're surrounded by salt-loving buttonwoods and sea grapes, and you pass another construction mound on the left. The trail becomes very rocky underfoot. After 0.6 mile, you reach a set of ponds blocking your forward progress. Take the trail to the left, a road cut built through the drier hammock to skirt the wet area. Several raccoons melt into the underbrush. Cut directly into the smooth slabs of island bedrock, the trail bypass rejoins the main trail by jogging to the right. Look back across the ponds and you might see ibises or roseate spoonbills picking through the salty mud.

At 0.8 mile, you cross an intersection of old roads. Continue straight. The skunklike odor of white stopper grows stronger as you approach the edge of the tropical hammock and emerge onto open salt flats, a coastal berm environment surrounded by marly mud. Scattered mangroves recede to the horizon. Off to the left and straight ahead, the trail ends in the muck on the fringe of Florida Bay, a fine spot for bird-watching if the ground underfoot is solid enough to ap-

The showy Liguus fasciatus graphicus *variety of Florida tree snail grows up to 3 inches long.*

proach the water. Another old road turns to the right and continues a little farther until it becomes sticky wet marl at 1.1 miles, surrounded by red-tipped annual glasswort, beds of salt hay, and sea purslane. Buttonwoods break up the broad flats. After exploring the edge of the bay, turn around and follow the trail back into the tropical hammock, retracing your route to the gate where your car is parked. On your way back, notice the proliferation of snails—not just tree snails, but also several salt marsh species with less showy shells. They cling to grasses and rocks along the trail's edge.

A cool breeze sets in as you return to the shade of the tropical hammock. Continue around the pond bypass and back to the old rusted gate. Loaded with deep

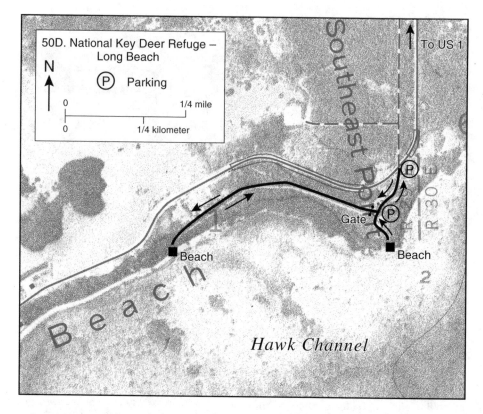

**50D. National Key Deer Refuge –
Long Beach**

N

℗ Parking

0   1/4 mile

0   1/4 kilometer

To US 1

Southeast Po

Gate

Beach

Beach

R 30 E

Hawk Channel

yellow fruits, a hog plum tempts. Its fruit has the texture and taste of a peach with a bitter tinge like lemon. As you circle the buttonwood marsh, you know you've almost completed the hike. Emerging at the yellow gate at Watson Boulevard, you've hiked 2.2 miles.

LONG BEACH TRAIL

The Long Beach Trail provides access to a rare sight on Big Pine Key: wilderness beaches. According to park rangers, it's also one of the best places on the refuge to find the mangrove cuckoo, an almost foot-long grayish brown bird with a buff-colored breast. This is truly a wilderness trail. Although it's only a 1.2-mile round trip, the trek follows an overgrown road from an open coastal prairie into a tropical

hammock thick with poisonwood trees.

To find the Long Beach Trail, return to US 1 and head north to Long Beach Road. It's the last right turn just before the bridge, at the end of the deer protection fencing. Drive 0.5 mile and park on the left side of the road, near the entrance to the rough gravel road. If you trust your car to take on rougher stuff, you can cut 0.2 mile off the hike by driving down the gravel road to the refuge gate, but parking there is very limited, too—do not block the gate, and avoid getting your tires into the sticky marl mud on the edges of the road.

Mangroves line the first section of trail—the prime place for spotting a mangrove cuckoo. During a trip to Key West in 1862, John James Audubon captured the beauty of this rare bird in one of his paintings. The reclusive cuckoos roost in mangrove forests along the salt flats, feeding exclusively on insects. As you come up to the gate, a sometimes sticky path leads off to the left. Continue straight. Beyond the gate, the trail leads into an open coastal prairie with lots of glasswort and pickleweed—the colloquial South Florida term for saltwort, a succulent plant with a pleasant salty brine taste. Its leaves were once used to cure constipation and rheumatism. Sea purslane spreads across the trail, showing off tiny white cloverlike blooms. Notice the rock in the footpath. Unlike the other side of Big Pine Key, where you're walking on oolitic Miami limestone, on this side of the island the bedrock is the typical Key Largo limestone, dense with fossilized coral.

After 0.2 mile, the trail narrows and vegetation closes in. If you're sensitive to poison ivy, don't venture any farther, as you will have to push poisonwood branches out of the way to continue down the footpath. The trail is lightly maintained. Beautiful rosemarylike clumps of bay cedar grow along the edges of the footpath. Buttonwoods form a low canopy, and you'll have to duck under them in places. Lancewood and cat's claw flourish in the understory. Notice the mounds of sand from giant land crab holes. Growing as large as 6 inches across its carapace, the giant land crab is the largest terrestrial crab in Florida. A vegetarian, it pokes through the saline underbrush in search of young leaves and berries.

Passing a mound of household debris, you catch a glimpse of brilliant blue water beyond the trees on the left. The refreshing salt aroma increases as you walk through an open area thick with salt hay, then reenter the tropical hammock. The fading pink flowers of a Jamaican caper tree catch your eye. The fragrant blossoms of seven-year apple add to the tropical atmosphere. When you emerge from the hammock at a NO TRESPASSING sign, turn left. A line of Keys lilies grows along the footpath. Walk down to the beautiful secluded beach, the trail's end at 0.6 mile. Settle down and take in the view of the glimmering milky turquoise waters of the Atlantic Ocean, calmed to stillness by the distant coral reefs.

It's hard to leave this lovely spot. The beach itself is too awash in deep drifts of rotting seaweed to attempt a beach walk back toward your starting point, so you'll want to retrace the footpath through the tropical hammocks and out to the coastal prairie. Watch for tree snails along the way. When you return to the gate, notice the glimmer of blue off in the distance, beyond the prairie. If the prairie is dry, walk across to the now obvious cut that leads out to the ocean. The beach itself isn't much, as it's buried under a thick mat of seaweed. But the beautiful view is worth the extra effort of crossing the prairie. After you leave the beach and return to the gate, turn right to walk back up to your car, completing a 1.2-mile hike.

LOWER SUGARLOAF KEY TRAIL

Of the three refuge trails located west of Big Pine Key, the one on Lower Sugarloaf Key is most suitable for hikers. It's a paved trail, but with a twist—the pavement belongs to the original Overseas Highway, and is in the process of breaking back down into chunks of limestone. As a result, the footpath is rather rugged in places. Consider this a backcountry trail—it's well off the beaten path—and treat it accordingly, especially if you think you might take on the entire 8-mile round trip available from this trailhead. Take plenty of water along, and let someone know where you're headed. This hike explores a shorter distance, the shady first 1.2 miles of the old highway route.

To find the trailhead, follow US 1 to Lower Sugarloaf Key. Drive south on Sugarloaf Boulevard, found near MM 17. Follow the road for 2.6 miles to a stop sign. Turn right onto CR 939-A and continue another 3.5 miles to where the road ends. Turn your car around and park on the side of the road. The trail starts down the road past the gate, your only clue to its existence the small brown WILDLIFE REFUGE sign. On first glance, it looks like a trail, not a road—where the asphalt has eroded away, the underlying layer of limestone remains. You start off on a thin sliver of land between two dense mangrove forests, where ibises roost in the trees. Watch for mangrove crabs scuttling along the limbs of overhanging trees, and ibises roosting in the deep shade. Enjoy the brisk aroma of salt as you walk between tamarind and sea oxeye. All three varieties of mangroves—red, black, and white—as well as buttonwoods are represented in this forest. Bay cedar thrives along the trail's edge, showing off delicate yellow blooms. A marsh rat dives off the footpath and disappears into the swamp. Curving to the left, the trail opens up a little after 0.2 mile, where you can take a short path on the left down to the edge of a mangrove swamp. Prior to the construction of this portion of the Overseas Highway in 1938, this artificial berm served as part of the route for Henry Flagler's Overseas Railroad, which began construction in 1906. Gaze off into the salt marsh and you'll see what looks like a set of railroad trucks (wheels attached to their frames) discarded, sinking into the ooze.

Continuing along the footpath, you catch glimpses of the mangrove swamp off to the left as you enter a long straight corridor tightly wrapped in vegetation. Expect to encounter some poisonwood. Carry a stick (but make sure it *isn't* a poisonwood branch) to gently push away the spiderwebs that block your path. Watch your step: A solution hole has opened up right down through the eroding asphalt. A raccoon with an unusually light-colored coat skulks in the upper branches of a buttonwood tree. This is a quiet, peaceful place, the backcountry of the Keys as approachable on foot, an ironic counterpoint to the busy railroad and highway that once traversed this corridor.

As the shade cover diminishes, you catch nice views of little mangrove islands growing amid the salt flats, especially along an opening on the left that provides an excellent panoramic view of the marsh. Stiff salt breezes whip across this tiny finger of land, keeping it mostly mosquito-free. Entering another shady hammock, you see cat's claw growing under the buttonwoods. Watch for tree snails on the pigeon plum, poisonwood, and Jamaican dogwood trees. The Jamaican dogwood is not a variety of dogwood, but gets its name from a small wedge called a "dog," used to keep planking attached to the keel of wooden boats. Like many of the trees of the tropical hammock, its dense wood, impervious and poisonous to insects, makes it an ideal building material.

In its green stage, a chameleon scampers up a mahogany tree. A flock of small brown house sparrows explodes out of the underbrush, heading for the opening where the trail emerges back into the sun. Salt hay grows along the edges of the footpath. Mangrove swamps stretch out in large expanses just beyond the buttonwoods flanking the trail. A colony of spindly white snails clings to the low grasses. After 1.1 miles, you enter a

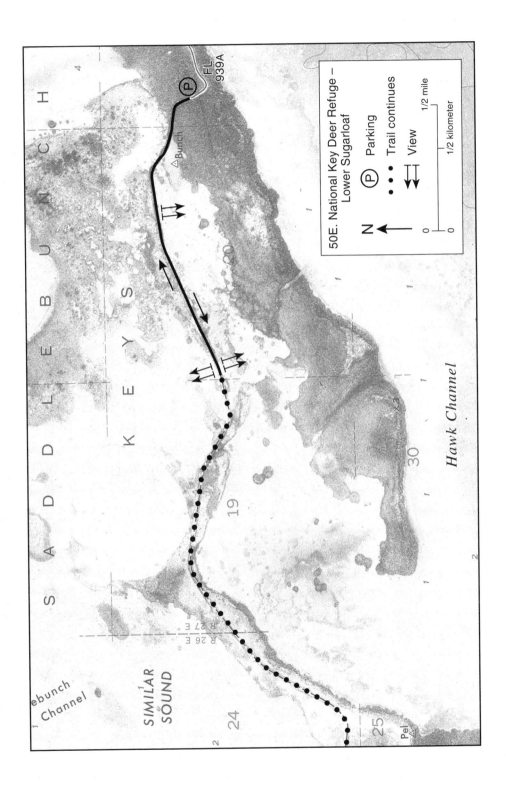

50E. National Key Deer Refuge –
Lower Sugarloaf

Ⓟ Parking

• • • Trail continues

↓↓ View

N

0 ────── 1/2 kilometer
0 ────── 1/2 mile

Hawk Channel

SIMILAR SOUND

ebunch
Channel

S A D D L E B U N C H

K E Y S

Bunch

FL 939A

bower of trees creating a tight canopy overhead, where you'll have to duck under the low-hanging limbs. Coming back out into the sun, you're surrounded by coastal prairie and mangrove swamps. This is an open place where the trail widens back to its original size, looking much like the road once traversed by tourists to Key West. Off in the distance on the right, well beyond the shimmering expanse of brackish water, you can see cars streaming past on US 1. Walk over to the water's edge and look down. It's like looking through a sheet of glass.

Although the trail continues nearly another 3 miles to the west end of Lower Sugarloaf Key, it's all in open sun, best saved for a rare cool winter's day or for exploration by bicycle—permitted, but not recommended due to the copious foliage you've encountered thus far. Turn around here to retrace your route along the mangrove forests, returning to your car after 2.4 miles.

Index